ALL · IN · ONE

aPHR™

Associate Professional in Human Resources Certification

EXAM GUIDE

ALL · IN · ONE

aPHR™
Associate Professional in Human Resources Certification
EXAM GUIDE

Dory Willer, SPHR, SHRM-SCP
William H. Truesdell, SPHR, SHRM-SCP
Willam D. Kelly, SPHR-CA, SHRM-SCP

New York   Chicago   San Francisco
Athens   London   Madrid   Mexico City
Milan   New Delhi   Singapore   Sydney   Toronto

Cataloging-in-Publication Data is on file with the Library of Congress

McGraw-Hill Education books are available at special quantity discounts to use as premiums and sales promotions, or for use in corporate training programs. To contact a representative, please visit the Contact Us pages at www.mhprofessional.com.

aPHR™ Associate Professional in Human Resources Certification All-in-One Exam Guide

1 2 3 4 5 6 7 8 9   LCR   21 20 19 18 17

ISBN: Book p/n 978-1-260-01946-9 and CD p/n 978-1-260-01947-6
of set 978-1-260-01948-3

MHID: Book p/n 1-260-01946-2 and CD p/n 1-260-01947-0
of set 978-1-260-01948-9

Sponsoring Editor Amy Stonebraker	**Technical Editor** William D. Kelly	**Production Supervisor** James Kussow
Editorial Supervisor Jody McKenzie	**Copy Editor** Kim Wimpsett	**Composition** Cenveo Publisher Services
Project Manager Anju Joshi, Cenveo® Publisher Services	**Proofreader** Lisa McCoy	**Illustration** Cenveo Publisher Services
Acquisitions Coordinator Claire Yee	**Indexer** Karin Arrigoni	**Art Director, Cover** Jeff Weeks

To all HR professionals who constantly strive to do better. This book is dedicated to all of the new human resource management professionals who are entering our field of special skills. We need new talent. Whether you are in HR for your entire career or on a rotational assignment, we welcome you and want you to know how important your role is going to be for your organization.

—The authors

I dedicate this book to my first HR boss, the late John Sharkey, who guided me to the career path of human resources, becoming my mentor and inspiring me to do well as an HR professional. He has left a great legacy for the profession.

—Dory Willer

My efforts are dedicated to the HR professionals who will find excitement and confidence in the process of gaining professional certification. Congratulations on your achievement.

—Bill Truesdell

I dedicate this book with love to my wife, Cheryl. Through days and nights, thick and thin, and months that have grown into years, you are always there—sometimes for support, sometimes for your knowledge and insights, sometimes to push, and sometimes just to be together. You are my rock. I love you!

—Bill Kelly

ABOUT THE AUTHORS

Dory Willer is a certified executive coach with more than 30 years of experience as a senior HR executive, keynote speaker, and strategic planning facilitator. She has broad and diverse experience working for blue-chip and Fortune 100 companies, leaving her last corporate position as a vice president of HR to open Beacon Quest Coaching based in the San Francisco Bay Area. Willer coaches senior and C-suite executives in leadership enhancement, performance improvement, and career renewal, helping her clients to thrive in life and careers. Additionally, she facilitates strategic planning sessions that stretch paradigms, align behaviors with goals, and hold groups accountable to produce results. She was among the first graduating classes from Stanford's Executive HR Certification Program (Graduate School of Business 1994). Willer achieved the designation of SPHR more than 25 years ago. She holds a B.S. degree in behavioral science from the University of San Francisco and several advanced certifications in executive coaching.

William H. Truesdell is president of The Management Advantage, Inc., a personnel management consulting firm. He spent more than 20 years in management with American Telephone and Telegraph in HR and operations. Truesdell is an expert on the subjects of personnel practices, employee handbooks, equal opportunity, and performance management programs. He is past president of the Northern California Employment Round Table and former HR course instructor at the University of California – Berkeley extension program. Truesdell holds the SPHR certification and a B.S. in business administration from California State University – Fresno.

William D. Kelly is the owner of Kelly HR, an HR consulting services firm specializing in providing generalist HR consulting services and support for small business enterprises. Bill's experience includes more than 40 years of professional-level HR responsibilities, including 22 years at Bechtel in San Francisco and, later, at Brown and Caldwell Environmental Engineers in Pleasant Hill, California. His credentials include experience in employee relations, state and federal legal compliance, staffing and recruitment, equal employment opportunity and affirmative action, compensation, benefits, training and development, health and safety, and government contract management. Bill also has 20 years of experience in HR consulting that includes providing HR services, support, and advice to a wide range of Northern California clients. He has 17 years of experience as an instructor for the University of California extension program teaching such courses as Management of Human Resources; Recruiting, Selection, and Placement; California Employment Law; and Professional HR Certification Preparation. Bill has taught the Professional PHR/SPHR Certification Preparation Course for more than 17 years, SHRM's recently introduced SHRM-CP and SHRM-SCP Certification

Preparation Course, and the California HR Certification Preparation Course for 8 years for the Society for Human Resource Management (SHRM) and the Northern California HR Association (NCHRA). He played a key role in the development of California's HR certification credential; he was also the project manager for the team of California HR professionals who developed SHRM's first California Learning System in support of California certification. Bill's professional leadership also includes roles on the board of directors and as national vice president for the Society for Human Resource Management (SHRM), the board of directors and president for the HR Certification Institute (HRCI), state director for the California State Council of SHRM, the board of directors and president for the Northern California HR Association (NCHRA), and commissioner and chair for the Marin County Personnel Commission. Bill received his B.S. in political science from Spring Hill College in Mobile, Alabama, and undertook post-graduate studies in organizational management at the College of William and Mary in Williamsburg, Virginia, and the University of Virginia in Richmond, Virginia. Prior to HR, Bill had a military career achieving the rank of major in the United States Army with tours of duty in the United States, Germany, Thailand, and Vietnam.

CONTENTS AT A GLANCE

CONTENTS

ACKNOWLEDGMENTS

First, we'd like to thank all the highly skilled staff at McGraw-Hill Education for their help and juggling timelines to get this book to print sooner rather than later. Thanks to our editor, Amy Stonebraker, for her endless patience and guidance on this project keeping us all on task and focused on the end result as we wove our way through many unforeseeable diversions of our time. She has been supportive and empathetic beyond belief. Thanks to executive editor Tim Green who kept his faith in us and our ability to create a product quickly so that the graduating class of 2017 can use our study guide to help them take and pass their aPHR certification exam.

Additionally, a special word of appreciation goes out to Christina Nishiyama, who unselfishly shared her personal HR experiences with you in Chapter 9, providing her insight about her own early career days as an HR professional. You will find them helpful in identifying how activities you will participate in relate to real-world impact. It is always helpful to know how what you are doing will influence the world of work in which you are part of. Thank you, Christina.

Last comes a note of acknowledgment from Dory to her coauthors, Bill Truesdell and Bill Kelly, whom she affectionately refers to as her HR Jedi Knights. When the new aPHR exam was created, we just knew in our hearts that we needed to make time in our schedules to write this aPHR exam study guide and present a realistic view of the roles and task responsibilities for aspiring early-career HR professionals. There are no better professionals than Bill and Bill to collaborate with on a short aggressive time frame as we were given to complete this project. This book truly is a loving legacy to our profession from us, and it was her ultimate pleasure coauthoring this work with those wonderful Jedi Knights.

INTRODUCTION

Allow us to be the first to congratulate you on making the decision to sit for the HR Certification Institute (HRCI) certification exam and to strive to obtain your Association Professional in Human Resources (aPHR) certification! Professional certifications are a mark of distinction that sets you apart in the profession and speaks volumes about your commitment to your career. More than 140,000 of your colleagues around the globe have obtained the HRCI certifications, including us.

Human resources is most likely part of our DNA makeup; we've lived it and breathed it for many decades. Our purpose is to share with you some strategies and experience that will assist you when you sit for the certification exam. It is our intention that this book will provide the knowledge and concepts you are expected to have mastered as an aPHR candidate. It is our pleasure to share those things with you. You also bring your own professional experience to the process. As you combine your experience with the information included in this book, you will be better able to answer the situational-based and competency-based questions about human resource situations that you will find on the exam.

We want you to be successful. It is our belief that the HRCI professional certifications are important because the certifications endorse your knowledge and expertise to employers and clients. Having a professional certification has become increasingly important. It may be a requirement of your next job assignment or the promotion you are pining for within your organization. You may decide that these certifications are necessary qualifications for future HR professionals that you may hire in your future. In any event, we wish you the best professional regards and success in passing your exam and earning the prestigious designation of aPHR.

HRCI Certification vs. SHRM Certification

At the time of this writing, there is a great deal of buzz from both the Society of Human Resource Management (SHRM) and the HRCI regarding the two accredited institutes certifying HR professionals. Both certifications have their merits and result in a professional level of recognized achievement in HR. HRCI will continue to confer its industry-recognized certifications for professional levels of achievement in the application of knowledge and competencies expected of HR professionals.

How to Use This Book

This book covers the entire aPHR Body of Knowledge (BOK) as it has been divided into functional topic areas of human resources. Our ordering of the functional areas is as follows:

1. U.S. laws and regulations

2. HR operations

3. Recruitment and selection

4. Compensation and benefits

5. Human resource development and retention

6. Employee relations

7. Health, safety, and security

8. Early human resource career-level tasks

Additionally, within each functional area, we have organized the presentation of topics to follow this same logic. As you progress through the material, we hope you will do so with a feeling of accomplishment at mastering the information presented and thereby increase your drive and motivation to continue.

The following is a brief overview of the organization of this book and how we feel this organization will benefit you.

Chapter 1: Human Resource Certification

In Chapter 1, we explain everything you need to know about aPHR exam and also discuss the different types of HRCI and SHRM certifications. Additionally, you'll find information about the process of registering for the exams, the actual exam experience, and what the style and format of questions are on the exams.

Chapter 2: U.S. Laws and Regulations

Chapter 2 provides a list of all the U.S. laws and regulations that you will need to know. We placed this information in a chapter rather than an appendix to emphasize the importance of reviewing these laws and regulations prior to diving into the functional areas. Understanding these laws should make it easier for you to grasp the reasoning behind the material that is presented in Chapters 3–8. You will find some questions on the certification exams that are directly related to these laws. While it is true that you don't have to be a lawyer to function as an HR professional, it is critical that you have a grasp on the essential requirements of each federal law so you can guide your internal organization clients toward legal compliance.

Chapter 3: HR Operations

This chapter lays out information about HR functions, the differences between HR generalists and specialists, organizational accountability, and organizational strategy.

It also covers organizational culture, confidentiality and privacy, business functions, HR policies and procedures, HR metrics (measuring HR performance), and reporting on HR results. You will discover how to determine a job's Fair Labor Standards Act (FLSA) classification (exempt/nonexempt) for overtime purposes and how to create job descriptions and decide where in the hierarchy of jobs they should fall.

Chapter 4: Recruitment and Selection

In this chapter you'll find information about how to identify recruiting sources, management of applicant databases, methods of recruiting, and alternative staffing practices. It also covers interviewing techniques and post-offer activities (medical exams, background checks).

Chapter 5: Compensation and Benefits

Compensation and benefits are topics held dear by every employee. This chapter includes how to determine base pay, incentives, differentials, and job evaluation programs. Employee benefits are always receiving attention in the news. Here you will find information about determining which benefit programs might be best for your organization and how to support them with enrollment and training efforts.

Chapter 6: Human Resource Development and Retention

In this chapter you'll find information about how to deliver and evaluate training programs, what career development programs mean to your organization, and how to support performance management practices, including methods of performance appraisal.

Chapter 7: Employee Relations

Employee relations includes information about methods for gaining employee feedback, establishing and implementing expectations for employee behavior, handling complaints and grievances, and progressive discipline approaches. If you ever wondered about employee relations programs, you will find what you need here. And, taking employees off the payroll is a key portion of HR responsibilities, along with supporting programs that result in workforce reduction and restructuring.

Chapter 8: Health, Safety, and Security

Many legal compliance issues are associated with health and safety programs. As a new HR professional, you will be involved in some or all of them. Risk management and processing safety reports are components that you will discover are critical to the success of HR programs.

Chapter 9: Early HR Career–Level Tasks

In this final chapter, you will find a series of 31 HR tasks that will occupy your time as a new HR professional. While the tasks will not appear on the aPHR exam, they all derive from the knowledge areas in preceding chapters and are extracted from the aPHR Exam Content Outline.

Additionally in Chapter 9 you will find some practical impact revelations from another HR professional, Christina Nishiyama, MBA, PHR, SHRM-CP. These special sections, titled *In the Trenches,* contain valuable insight and advice about several of the HR tasks from her perspective during the years early on in her HR career.

Exam Tips

Sprinkled throughout the book are "Exam Tips" designed to give you a bit of a head start over those who don't have the advantage of seeing them; they point out areas to pay attention to that will help you on the exam.

Questions and Answers

At the end of Chapters 2 through 8, you will find a set of review questions and answers to help you test your knowledge and comprehension. Practice, practice, practice—it will pay off on exam day.

Appendixes

We have also included four appendixes to supplement the information you need to know.

Appendix A

Appendix A is a list of acronyms. The HR field is notorious for abbreviations creating the jargon in HR language, and these abbreviations have flowed into the everyday business language of employers, employees, and the public at large. It is likely that you will see questions on the exams that include and reference these acronyms, so please familiarize yourself with this list.

Appendix B

In Appendix B, we have listed all the associated legal cases you should know and review prior to sitting for the exams. The cases are organized by functional area and include a brief synopsis of what each case addressed. A URL is provided so that you can review the case in more detail, and we recommend that you spend time reviewing these cases.

Appendix C

Here are resources you will find helpful if you choose to extend your study.

Appendix D

Appendix D provides information for the accompanying test engine that can generate full-length practice exams or customized quizzes by exam topic. The test engine includes 250 practice questions with answer explanations for each answer choice, both correct and incorrect. These practice questions should help you prepare yourself for the real McCoy when sitting for an actual aPHR HRCI exam.

Glossary

A glossary of terms has been created for your ease of reference. Using the glossary will help you review the key terms covered in this book and for the HR profession in general.

Index

In the very back of the book is an index that will guide you to the appropriate pages where a term is mentioned or discussed.

The Examination

The aPHR exam is not a simple true/false or memory-recall exam. You will be sitting for a 2-hour and 15-minute, 100-question multiple-choice (plus 25 pretest questions) exam that will test your knowledge of the HR profession. The knowledge-based questions will require you to know your facts. These questions test your knowledge of different HR laws. Sometimes you will be asked to identify an example chart or graph, so pay attention to the figures that are included in the chapters.

 EXAM TIP It usually takes roughly a year (or more) for the HRCI exam to reflect new laws, executive orders, and regulations. Don't be fooled, though. You may still see questions related to changes that have been recently introduced by the U.S. president or Congress. It is your responsibility to follow these updates and master the new requirements.

Preparing Is the Key

Preparing for any type of certification exam is not about memorizing information. The aPHR exam requires that new HR professionals are capable of understanding the laws and concepts in which HR management is based.

 EXAM TIP You may have already invested in an education for your career; investing in serious study time and preparation will pay off so that you can pass your exam.

For those with more limited experience or the minimal experience qualifications, we suggest you begin preparation and study six months prior to your exam date. For those with significantly more experience and time on the job as an HR professional, three months should be your yardstick. If you want to not study the material outlined in this book, your chances of passing the aPHR exam will likely be low even if you have been in an HR exempt position for a few months or years. We aren't saying that it can't be done, but your chances of passing the exams are much better if you study the information in this book and the questions in the accompanying test engine, as well as use the companion practice exam book, *aPHR Associate Professional in Human Resources Certification Practice Exam,* to prepare for the time when you will sit in that room with only a computer screen. Guessing strategies are not foolproof and not a good substitute for solid study habits in preparation for an exam. The best preparation strategy is one that is focused on committed preparation with study time spent in a productive manner.

Final Thoughts

2017 saw the beginning of a new administration in Washington, DC. There have already been some changes made with executive orders, and more have been promised for the future. How these changes affect your organization and HR is yet to be seen. Your responsibility as an HR professional is to monitor what is happening and guide your employer through the changing compliance requirements as laid out by the U.S. president or Congress. There will also be many related policy choices to be made. If you have a labor-management attorney, getting updates from that person would be helpful.

This book has been designed not only to assist you, the HRCI exam candidate, in studying for the aPHR exam, but also to serve as a reliable reference book to be placed on the shelf in your office. There is a lot for a human resource professional to remember. It is our hope that this book becomes a convenient resource that guides you when something pops up that you need a refresher on. At a minimum, we hope it gives you direction in your effort to improve your HR circumstance.

Finally, thank you for selecting this book. We sincerely hope your aPHR exam goes well and wish you the absolute best on exam day!

PART I

The Human Resource Profession

CHAPTER 1

Human Resource Certification

As you begin a career in human resources (HR), the skills and abilities that you as an HR professional will use to produce desired results require a mastery of sorts. Mastery of any profession will involve a continuous career-long commitment to learning, and that is a foundational truth within the HR profession. HR has been, and continues to be, an evolving component of an organization because its basic focus is on people. The constant changes and outside influences on an organization's workforce increase the demands on HR professionals. HR professionals today must master the art of staying two steps ahead while having one foot firmly planted in the present.

Professional Certifications

Certifications demonstrate what professionals do and why it matters. Credentialing as an HR professional demonstrates to your employer and colleagues that you are committed to a higher standard and ethic and dedicated to the HR profession. When you achieve your first HR credential, it signals your mastery of core knowledge in human resources, raising the confidence of an employer and your peers in your knowledge and abilities. Because the HR profession is constantly evolving, it is important for HR professionals to constantly update their HR competencies and knowledge. Achieving certification and recertification is a good method to do this.

A professional certification should not be confused with a certificate program. Professional certifications are based on work experience and education along with recertification requirements. Certificate programs do not require work experience or an educational component, and they do not require recertification. Competency-based certifications address a critical need in the global marketplace because employers expect more today from their internal experts, and the HR profession must be ready to meet those expectations.

HR Certification Organizations

As of 2015, there are two certifying organizations for HR professionals to receive their certifications from: the HR Certification Institute (HRCI) and the Society for Human Resource Management (SHRM), both of which are accredited. As of this writing, only HRCI offers a certification for first-level career HR professionals with the Associate Professional in Human Resources (aPHR) exam. Both organizations' certifications test knowledge that the profession requires as their baseline. While both HRCI and SHRM test knowledge, only the SHRM certifications for experienced HR professionals focus their test content on applying that knowledge and the importance of behavioral competency. Both organizations have their merits, which is why both certifications exist.

The HR Certification Institute (HRCI)

The HR Certification Institute (www.hrci.org) was established in 1976 as an internationally recognized certifying organization for the human resource profession. Its mission is to develop and deliver the highest-quality certification programs that validate mastery in the field of human resource management and contribute to the continued improvement of individual and organizational performance. Nearly 140,000 HR professionals in more than 100 countries are certified. Until 2015, HRCI was the only certifying organization for the HR profession.

HRCI exists to enhance the professionalism of the HR profession with its various certification processes. HRCI certifications demonstrate relevance, competence, experience, credibility, and dedication to human resources. The institute is a nonprofit $(501)(c)(3)$[1] separate organization, an Internal Revenue Service (IRS) designation, from the Society of Human Resource Management, which is a $(510)(c)(6)$[2] organization. HRCI was accredited by the National Commission for Certifying Agencies (NCCA) in 2008.

HRCI's Body of Knowledge (BoK) is a complete set of knowledge and responsibilities statements required to successfully understand and perform generalist HR-related duties associated with each of its credentials, which are Associate Professional in Human Resources™ (aPHR), Professional in Human Resources® (PHR), Senior Professional in Human Resources® (SPHR), Global Professional in Human Resources® (GPHR), Professional in Human Resources – California® (PHRca), Professional in Human Resources – International™ (PHRi), and Senior Professional in Human Resources – International™ (SPHRi). The BoK is periodically updated, typically every 5 to 7 years, to ensure it is consistent with and reflects current practices in the HR field. Our book, *PHR/SPHR Professional in Human Resources Certification All-in-One Exam Guide,*[3] provides in-depth preparation for the PHR and SPHR exams.

aPHR

HRCI's Associate Professional in Human Resources is the first-ever HR certification designed for professionals who are just beginning their HR career journey. It proves that a person has the knowledge of foundational human resources.

Eligibility Requirements   To sit for the aPHR exam, you must have the following:

- A high-school diploma or global equivalent. No experience is required since the aPHR credential is a knowledge-based credential.

PHR

The Professional in Human Resources certification demonstrates that a person has mastery of the technical and operational aspects of HR practices and U.S. laws and regulations. The professionally relevant credential is for the HR professional who focuses on program implementation, has a tactical/logistical orientation, is accountable to another HR professional within the organization, and has responsibilities that focus on the HR department rather than the whole organization.

Eligibility Requirements   To sit for the PHR exam, you must have one of the following:

- A minimum of 1 year of experience in a professional-level HR position and a master's degree or higher
- A minimum of 2 years of experience in a professional-level HR position and a bachelor's degree
- A minimum of 4 years of experience in a professional-level HR position and a high-school diploma

SPHR

The Senior Professional in Human Resources certification demonstrates that a person has mastered the strategic and policy-making aspects of HR management as practiced in the United States. The credential is designed for the HR professional who plans rather than implements HR policy, focuses on the "big picture," has ultimate accountability in the HR department, has breadth and depth of knowledge in all HR disciplines, understands the business beyond the HR function, and influences the overall organization.

Eligibility Requirements   To sit for the SPHR exam, you must have one of the following:

- A minimum of 4 years of experience in a professional-level HR position and a master's degree or higher
- A minimum of 5 years of experience in a professional-level HR position and a bachelor's degree
- A minimum of 7 years of experience in a professional-level HR position and a high-school diploma

GPHR

The Global Professional in Human Resources is a global, competency-based credential that is designed to validate the skills and knowledge of an HR professional who operates in a global marketplace. The credential demonstrates a mastery of cross-border HR responsibilities that include strategies of globalization, development of HR policies and initiatives that support organizational global growth and employer retention, and creation of organizational programs, processes, and tools that achieve worldwide business goals.

Eligibility Requirements   To sit for the GPHR exam, you must have one of the following:

- A minimum of 2 years of experience in a global professional-level HR position and a master's degree or higher
- A minimum of 3 years of experience in a professional-level HR position (at least 2 in global HR) and a bachelor's degree
- A minimum of 4 years of experience in a professional-level HR position (at least 2 in global HR) and a high-school diploma

Global HR experience is defined as having direct, cross-border HR responsibilities for two or more countries or regions.

PHRca

The Professional in Human Resources – California demonstrates that an HR professional has mastered the laws, regulations, and HR management practices unique to the state of California. The PHRca is for professionals who either practice in California or are responsible for human resources in California. You do not have to be located in California to earn a PHRca.

Eligibility Requirements   To sit for the PHRca exam, you must have one of the following:

- A minimum of 1 year of experience in a professional-level HR position and a master's degree or higher
- A minimum of 2 years of experience in a professional-level HR position and a bachelor's degree
- A minimum of 4 years of experience in a professional-level HR position and a high-school diploma

PHRi

The Professional in Human Resources – International is a global, competency-based credential that is designed to validate professional-level core HR knowledge and skills. The credential demonstrates a mastery of generally accepted technical and operational

HR principles. Independent of geographic region, the credential complements local HR practices. Through demonstrated knowledge, the credential enhances the credibility of HR professionals and the organizations they serve.

Eligibility Requirements To sit for the PHRi exam, you must have one of the following:

- A minimum of 1 year of experience in a professional-level HR position and a master's degree or global equivalent

- A minimum of 2 years of experience in a professional-level HR position and a bachelor's degree or global equivalent

- A minimum of 4 years of experience in a professional-level HR position and a high-school diploma or global equivalent

SPHRi

The Senior Professional in Human Resources – International is a global, competency-based credential that is designed to validate professional-level core HR knowledge and skills. This credential demonstrates a mastery of generally accepted HR principles in strategy, policy development, and service delivery. Independent of geographic region, this credential complements local HR practices. Through demonstrated knowledge, this credential enhances the credibility of HR professionals and the organizations they serve.

Eligibility Requirements To sit for the SPHRi exam, you must have one of the following:

- A minimum of 4 years of experience in a professional-level HR position and a master's degree or global equivalent

- A minimum of 5 years of experience in a professional-level HR position and a bachelor's degree or global equivalent

- A minimum of 7 years of experience in a professional-level HR position and a high-school diploma or global equivalent

Recertification

Recertification is the process of renewing one's certification. To maintain certification, a certification holder must be prepared to show that they are building their knowledge, growing as a professional, and increasing their experience. HRCI recertification is required every 3 years through demonstrated professional development (the preferred method) or retaking the exam.

Recertification can be earned in the following categories:

- Continuing education
- Instruction
- On-the-job experience

- Research/publishing
- Leadership
- Professional membership

Recertification requires much more than attending conferences and workshops. Most certified HR professionals earn their recertification credits through the activities they do daily for their organizations.

The Society for Human Resource Management (SHRM)

For more than 65 years, the Society for Human Resource Management (www.shrm .org) has served the human resource profession and HR professionals worldwide. Founded in 1948, SHRM is the world's largest HR membership organization devoted to human resource management. Representing more than 275,000 members in more than 160 countries, SHRM is the leading provider of resources to serve the needs of HR professionals and advance the professional practice of human resource management. SHRM has more than 575 affiliated chapters within the United States and subsidiary offices in China, India, and the United Arab Emirates.

SHRM began offering its own certifications in 2015, the SHRM Certified Professional™ (SHRM-CP) and the SHRM Senior Certified Professional™ (SHRM-SCP) certifications, which are associated with its defined Body of Competency and Knowledge (BoCK). Accreditation was received in late 2016.

SHRM-CP

The SHRM-Certified Professional exam is for HR professionals who implement policies and strategies, serve as a point of contact for staff and stakeholders, deliver HR services, and perform operational HR functions.

Eligibility Requirements The following are the SHRM-CP eligibility requirements to sit for the exam:

Less Than a Bachelor's Degree*	**HR-Related Program** Three years in HR role	**Non-HR Program** Four years in HR role
Bachelor's Degree	**HR-Related Degree** One year in HR role	**Non-HR Degree** Two years in HR role
Graduate Degree	**HR-Related Degree** Currently in HR role	**Non-HR Degree** One year in HR role

*Less than a bachelor's degree includes the following: working toward a bachelor's degree, associate's degree, some college, qualifying HR certificate program, high-school diploma, or general educational development (GED).

SHRM-SCP

The SHRM-Senior Certified Professional exam is for HR professionals who develop strategies, lead the HR function, foster influence in the community, analyze performance metrics, and align HR strategies to organizational goals.

Eligibility Requirements The following are the SHRM-SCP eligibility requirements to sit for the exam:

Less Than a Bachelor's Degree*	**HR-Related Program** Six years in HR role	**Non-HR Program** Seven years in HR role
Bachelor's Degree	**HR-Related Degree** Four years in HR role	**Non-HR Degree** Five years in HR role
Graduate Degree	**HR-Related Degree** Three years in HR role	**Non-HR Degree** Four years in HR role

*Less than a bachelor's degree includes the following: working toward a bachelor's degree, associate's degree, some college, qualifying HR certificate program, high-school diploma, or GED.

Recertification

Recertification is how you will continue to grow and adapt to meet the evolving needs of the profession. SHRM-CP or SHRM-SCP credential holders must do one of the following for recertification:

- Earn 60 professional development credits (PDCs) within a 3-year recertification period that ends on the last day of the credential holder's birth month
- Retake the certification exam at the end of the 3-year recertification period

Benefits of Certification

Earning an HR credential adds a level of recognition as an expert in the HR profession. This certification is a distinction that sets you apart in the profession, indicating you have a high level of knowledge and skills. It adds to your career value and to the organization you work in. Your HR certification could mean the difference between you and your competition. In fact, 96 percent of employers say that an HR-certified candidate applying for a job would have an advantage over a noncertified candidate. In addition, HR professionals who hold certifications tend to make more money than their peers who do not.[4] According to PayScale Human Capital, this pattern is true for all industries and metropolitan areas in the United States. HR certification is becoming an important means for employers to recognize HR expertise and for HR professionals to increase their value and worth.

Earning an HR credential can help you do the following:

- Boost your confidence
- Create recognition for you as an HR professional
- Master expert knowledge for the HR profession
- Protect your organization from risk by knowing regulatory compliance
- Stand out from other HR candidates in job searches and promotions

Job Title Classification	Certification Required	Certification Preferred	Total
HR Business Partner	70%	30%	100%
Associate HR Director	35%	30%	65%
Senior HR Manager	10%+	45%	55%
HR Director	10%	45%	55%
HR Manager	5%	40%	45%
Senior HR Generalist		55%	55%
Senior HR Business Partner		45%	45%
Employee Relations Manager		30%	30%
HR Generalist		15%	15%
Other		30%	30%

Table 1-1   HR Certification Specifications by Job Title

- Broaden your perspective in the HR field
- Keep up with HR innovations, developments, and legislative/law changes
- Demonstrate your commitment to the HR profession

Many organizations, including a number of Fortune 500 organizations, now require or prefer HR certification for their new HR hires or for internal promotions. A May 2014 study from Software Advice, Inc., called "What Employers Are Looking for in HR Positions"[5] reveals that employers will be increasingly demanding certification for their job candidates. Table 1-1 lists the HR certification preferences, broken down by job title, published by the study.

This survey suggests that certification is essential for any professional-level HR job candidate. If an individual wants to be considered for a senior-level HR position, then certification is nearly an absolute requirement. Those expectations will be further solidified as time goes on.

The aPHR Exam

The aPHR exam is a computer-based test (CBT) that is 2 hours and 15 minutes long. It includes 100 multiple-choice questions plus 25 pretest questions. The multiple-choice questions consist of a statement, known as a *stem,* and four choices. The choices consist of one correct or best choice that is the correct answer and incorrect or inferior choices knowns as *distractors.* The pretest questions are new nonscored questions that are included to develop a statistical history that serves as a basis for validating the question for future use as a scored question. Pretest questions are randomly placed throughout the test. New exams are produced annually.

The aPHR exam covers the identified Body of Knowledge for the level of HR experience an aPHR professional would require and the federal laws that are applicable to the employment relationship, which is covered in detail in Chapter 2. HRCI realizes that employment laws change constantly. As such, exam candidates are responsible for knowing the HR laws and regulations that are in effect as of the start of their exam period.

The Significance of the HR Body of Knowledge

The Associate Professional in Human Resources (aPHR™) exam was created using the aPHR™ Exam Content Outline, which details the Body of Knowledge needed by those performing early HR career roles. HR subject-matter experts created the outline through a rigorous practice analysis study, validated by HR professionals working in the field through an extensive survey instrument. It will be updated periodically to ensure it is consistent with current practices in the HR field.

The Body of Knowledge (BoK) is broken down in to six functional areas. These functional areas, with their respective exam weighting noted, are covered in the following sections.

Functional Area 1: HR Operations (38%)

Understanding the tactical and operational tasks related to workforce management and the HR function. Complying with the laws, regulations, and policies that affect the organization.

Knowledge of:

1. Organizational strategy and its connection to mission, vision, values, business goals, and objectives

2. Organizational culture (for example, traditions, unwritten procedures)

3. Legal and regulatory environment

4. Confidentiality and privacy rules that apply to employee records, company data, and individual data

5. Business functions (for example, accounting, finance, operations, sales and marketing)

6. HR policies and procedures (for example, ADA, EEO, progressive discipline)

7. HR metrics (for example, cost per hire, number of grievances)

8. Tools to compile data (for example, spreadsheets, statistical software)

9. Methods to collect data (for example, surveys, interviews, observation)

10. Reporting and presentation techniques (for example, histogram, bar chart)

11. Impact of technology on HR (for example, social media, monitoring software, biometrics)

12. Employee records management (for example, electronic/paper, retention, disposal)

13. Statutory reporting requirements (for example, OSHA, ERISA, ACA)

14. Purpose and function of a Human Resource Information System (HRIS)

15. Job classifications (for example, exempt, nonexempt, contractor)

16. Job analysis methods and job descriptions

17. Reporting structure (for example, matrix, flat)

18. Types of external providers of HR services (for example, recruitment firms, benefits brokers, staffing agencies)

19. Communication techniques (for example, written, oral, e-mail, passive, aggressive)

Functional Area 2: Recruitment and Selection (15%)

Understanding the hiring process, including regulatory requirements, sourcing of applicants, formal interview and selection process, and onboarding of a new hire.

Knowledge of:

1. Applicable laws and regulations related to recruitment and selection, such as nondiscrimination, accommodation, and work authorization (for example, Title VII, ADA, EEOC Uniform Guidelines on Employee Selection Procedures, Immigration Reform and Control Act)

2. Applicant databases

3. Recruitment sources (for example, employee referral, social networking/social media)

4. Recruitment methods (for example, advertising, job fairs)

5. Alternative staffing practices (for example, recruitment process outsourcing, job sharing, phased retirement)

6. Interviewing techniques (for example, behavioral, situational, panel)

7. Post-offer activities (for example, drug testing, background checks, medical exams)

Functional Area 3: Compensation and Benefits (14%)

Understanding concepts related to total rewards such as pay and benefit programs. Responding to employee questions and handling claims in compliance with applicable laws, regulations, and company policies.

Knowledge of:

1. Applicable laws and regulations related to compensation and benefits, such as monetary and nonmonetary entitlement, wage and hour, and privacy (for example, ERISA, COBRA, FLSA, USERRA, HIPAA, PPACA, tax treatment)

2. Pay structures and programs (for example, variable, merit, bonus, incentives, noncash compensation, pay scales/grades)

3. Total rewards statements

4. Benefit programs (for example, healthcare plans, flexible benefits, retirement plans, wellness programs)

5. Payroll processes (for example, pay schedule, leave and time-off allowances)

6. Uses for salary and benefits surveys

7. Claims processing requirements (for example, workers' compensation, disability benefits)

8. Work-life balance practices (for example, flexibility of hours, telecommuting, sabbatical)

Functional Area 4: Human Resource Development and Retention (12%)

Understanding the techniques and methods for delivering training programs and developing individual employees.

Knowledge of:

1. Applicable laws and regulations related to training and development activities (for example, Title VII, ADA, Title 17 [copyright law])

2. Training delivery format (for example, virtual, classroom, on-the-job)

3. Techniques to evaluate training programs (for example, participant surveys, pre- and post-testing, after action review)

4. Career development practices (for example, succession planning, dual career ladders)

5. Performance appraisal methods (for example, ranking, rating scales)

6. Performance management practices (for example, setting goals, benchmarking, feedback)

Functional Area 5: Employee Relations (16%)

Understanding the methods organizations use to monitor and address morale, performance, and retention. Balancing the operational needs of the organization with the well-being of the individual employee.

Knowledge of:

1. Applicable laws affecting employment in union and nonunion environments, such as laws regarding antidiscrimination policies, sexual harassment, labor relations, and privacy (for example, WARN Act, Title VII, NLRA)

2. Employee and employer rights and responsibilities (for example, employment-at-will, privacy, defamation, substance abuse)

3. Methods and processes for collecting employee feedback (for example, employee attitude surveys, focus groups, exit interviews)

4. Workplace behavior issues (for example, absenteeism, aggressive behavior, employee conflict, workplace harassment)

5. Methods for investigating complaints or grievances

6. Progressive discipline (for example, warnings, escalating corrective actions, termination)

7. Off-boarding or termination activities

8. Employee relations programs (for example, recognition, special events, diversity programs)

9. Workforce reduction and restructuring terminology (for example, downsizing, mergers, outplacement practices)

Functional Area 6: Health, Safety, and Security (5%)

Understanding the laws, regulations, and policies that promote a safe work environment. Using risk mitigation procedures to protect against workplace hazards.

Knowledge of:

1. Applicable laws and regulations related to workplace health, safety, security, and privacy (for example, OSHA, Drug-Free Workplace Act, ADA, HIPAA, Sarbanes-Oxley Act)

2. Risk mitigation in the workplace (for example, emergency evacuation procedures, health and safety, risk management, violence, emergencies)

3. Security risks in the workplace (for example, data, materials, or equipment theft; equipment damage or destruction; cyber-crimes; password usage

The Test Development Process

HRCI follows certification-industry best practices to create and update all of its exams. Practicing HR professionals are involved in every step of the exam development process, which is overseen by the testing organizations Pearson Vue and Prometric. The following are the steps taken to develop all of HRCI's exams:

1. HRCI exams are based on Exam Content Outlines developed for each exam, which are created by a small group of practicing HR professionals and then validated by a much larger group through a practice analysis study.

2. Certified HR professionals write the exam questions (also known as *items*), based on the Exam Content Outline.

3. The questions go to another group, the Item-Review Panel, which checks for accuracy and proper coding.

4. Approved questions are then "pretested" for reliability.

5. Multiple exam forms are created and reviewed by a panel of subject-matter experts.

6. A passing score for each exam is determined.

The Exam Experience

Applicants must meet both HR work experience and education requirements to qualify for each exam. Applicants should complete the application process early to increase the chance of getting their first choice for test date and location. As of this writing, the current exam fee is $325 plus a $75 nonrefundable application fee. Testing for the aPHR exam is year-round, subject only to space availability at a Prometric or Pearson Vue testing center of your choice.

The aPHR Registration Process[7]

HRCI describes the application process in steps.

1. Create an online account with HRCI.

2. Choose the exam that's right for you, in other words, aPHR, PHR, SPHR, and so on. We will presume that your background and qualifications indicate that the aPHR exam is right for you.

3. Build your own bundle. Decide whether you would like to purchase preparation materials through HRCI's "Build Your Own Bundle" option. We feel that this study guide would be sufficient for your studying efforts.

4. Affirm that all the information submitted on the application is complete and true and that you have read the HRCI Certification Handbook (available online through the HRCI web site at https://www.hrci.org/).

5. Submit the application with payment.

6. Schedule your exam date with Prometric or Pearson Vue and plan your preparation.

7. Take the exam. Make sure to bring an official, valid, government-issued identification with you to take the exam.

8. Receive your preliminary results at the testing center and an official score report 2 to 4 weeks after testing.

Preparing for the Exam

From our years of experience helping HR professionals to achieve their certifications, we have compiled a list of tips for exam takers. First let's begin with studying. The following tips will help you get the most benefit from your preparation efforts:

- Before studying, go for a brief walk to take in some air and clear your mind in preparation for the focused time to study. Put all your other thoughts and projects of the day on a back burner and give your mind a clean slate, setting the intention that this specific amount of time is for the exclusive attention of HRCI studying.

- Make sure your "do not disturb" sign is on your door if you are at home or in the office and that others clearly know that nothing is to disturb you for the next hour. Speaking of an hour, that's plenty of time to devote on a regular schedule to study. Most people find that 4 or 5 hours a week is sufficient for this type of material.

- Clear your study area. It should be void of anything that might distract you from studying. Keep the focus on your studying, and to add a little incentive, create a bit of visual incentive for yourself—such as a letter mock-up stating you have successfully passed your exam. Spoof a letter from HRCI, print it, put it in a nice picture frame, and place it in front of you every time you begin studying. What the mind can conceive, you can achieve!

- Select a time of day that is optimum for you to study. Are you best in the wee hours of the early morning with a cup of coffee prior to work, or perhaps you're more focused at the noon hour? Maybe you're a person whose rhythm kicks in just after dinner. Find that sweet hour and make the appointment on your calendar, listing it as "VIP-HRCI." *You* are the very important person, and this appointment will cause you to think twice before allowing another activity to muscle in on your time slot.

- The old adage that practice makes perfect is not quite right. Perfect practice makes perfect is a better way to state the intention. As you make your study time perfect and practice saying "no, thank you" to others and other things that interrupt your study time, you are practicing the perfect combination that will allow you to stay focused and produce the results you want.

- Two days prior to the exam, be sure to get a full night's sleep each night, which is typically 7 to 9 hours for most people. Studies prove that a REM state of sleeping is extremely helpful for brain function.

- Hydrate, hydrate, hydrate the day before and the day of the exam. Try to avoid massive amounts of caffeine (it will keep you awake and rob you of precious oxygen). Water is good for the body but even better for the brain, bringing oxygen via water, which helps your brain functions improve.

The following are some suggestions to keep in mind as you take your exam:

- Trust your gut, or your first impression. First impressions of the correct answer are many times the best choice. This should not be confused with guessing. This refers to topics you know that you know.

- Watch out for basing your answer on what your current organization's policy is. Keep focused on generally accepted HR practices as the correct answer.

- There will be no patterns, so don't even try to look for them. The psychometric exam process used for the HRCI exam prevents questions from falling into patterns.

- Only federal laws apply—don't mix your state laws with your federal laws.

- The most common weakness of HR test-takers is overanalyzing the options. Be thorough, but be reasonable in your analysis and selection of the options.

- When stumped, try to eliminate the obvious answers and then just focus on what remains.

- Read all four answers—it may be that you need to select the best answer and yet all answers are correct.

- Resist the urge to change your answers. This goes hand in hand with trusting your gut. If you are absolutely, positively sure that you have an incorrect answer, go ahead. But for the most part, resist the urge to change answers.

- Don't rush. Manage your time. You will have a little over a minute for each question. A clock is visible on your monitor screen counting down the amount of time left.

Exam Readiness

HRCI's aPHR Exam Content Outline is one of your most important documents leading to a successful exam experience. Each exam question has a specific corresponding functional knowledge area that is identified in the applicable Exam Content Outline. As such, this valuable information will enable you to use the Exam Content Outline as an exam readiness checklist that will indicate the knowledge topics you need to know and comprehend in order to pass this exam. The following is the exam weighting given to each functional area:

- HR Operations (38%)
- Recruitment and Selection (15%)
- Compensation and Benefits (14%)
- Human Resource Development and Retention (12%)
- Employee Relations (16%)
- Health, Safety, and Security (5%)

At the HRCI web site (https://www.hrci.org/docs/default-source/web-files/aphr-exam-sample-questions.pdf?sfvrsn=2) you'll find exam questions that are similar to the ones you will see on the aPHR exam. These are examples from each of the six functional areas covered on the exam. We encourage you to try these questions. Additionally, we recommend you use our practice exams to determine which functional areas you may need to study more.

Chapter Review

The number of HR professionals needed in the coming years to manage the human capital in organizations will continue to expand. The U.S. Bureau of Labor Statistics anticipates that the number of HR manager positions will grow 13 percent and will grow 8 percent for HR specialist positions by the year 2022.[8] In addition, employer selection systems will increasingly use certification as an employment-screening element. Whether you choose to obtain a certification from HRCI, SHRM, or both is not going to be as relevant as when you will achieve your credential. The value of certification is being recognized in all levels of the organization and throughout the HR profession. We're confident that beginning your professional career in human resources by adding the aPHR certification to your résumé will draw special attention to your achievement and to the commitment of growing your abilities in the profession.

Endnotes

1. To be tax exempt under section 501(c)(3) of the Internal Revenue Code, an organization must be organized and operated exclusively for exempt purposes set forth in section 501(c)(3), and none of its earnings may inure to any private shareholder or individual. In addition, it may not be an action organization; i.e., it may not attempt to influence legislation as a substantial part of its activities, and it may not participate in any campaign activity for or against political candidates. Organizations described in section 501(c)(3) are commonly referred to as charitable organizations. Organizations described in section 501(c)(3), other than testing for public safety organizations, are eligible to receive tax-deductible contributions in accordance with Code Section 170. IRS Code (https://www.irs.gov/charities-non-profits/charitable-organizations/exemption-requirements-section-501-c-3-organizations)

2. IRC 501(c)(6) provides for exemption of business leagues, chambers of commerce, real estate boards, boards of trade, and professional football leagues (whether or not administering a pension fund for football players), which are not organized for profit and no part of the net earnings of which ensures to the benefit of any private shareholder or individual. IRS Code (https://www.irs.gov/pub/irs-tege/eotopick03.pdf)

3. Dory Willer and William H. Truesdell, *PHR/SPHR Professional in Human Resources Certification All-in-One Exam Guide* (McGraw-Hill Education, 2015)

4. PayScale Human Capital research report, "The Market Value of PHR and SPHR Certifications," http://resources.payscale.com (search on title of report)

5. Erin Osterhaus, "What Employers Are Looking for in HR Positions" (*The New Talent Times,* May 27, 2014), http://new-talent-times.softwareadvice .com/what-employers-look-for-hr-jobs-0514/

6. https://prometric.com

7. https://hrci.org/aphr

8. Bureau of Labor Statistics, U.S. Department of Labor, *Occupational Outlook Handbook, 2014-2015 Edition,* Human Resources Managers, www.bls.gov/ooh/ management/human-resources-managers.htm

U.S. Laws and Regulations

 This chapter introduces the federal laws and legislation that all human resource (HR) professionals must know and understand. When you thoroughly read these laws and regulations, you will better understand the material in Part II of this book. Knowing these laws can sometimes make the difference in selecting the right answer on the Associate Professional in Human Resources (aPHR) exam. After studying this chapter and completing the practice questions, you should have an understanding of the relevance of these laws in the employment relationship. HR professionals in both small and large companies play an important role in dealing with day-to-day employment issues relating to recruiting, hiring, managing, and training employees. HR systems implementation must be guided by legal requirements.

Many times as you read this chapter, you will discover the phrase "engaged in interstate commerce." This is a term used by Congress to identify which employers will be subject to a law's requirements. Interstate commerce includes shipping a Maine lobster to a New Mexico restaurant for tonight's dinner, for example. Also included are selling products on Amazon or eBay (and similar Internet sites) to customers in states other than the one you are in and purchasing products or components from a supplier in a state other than the one you are in. As you can tell, it is a broad application that captures a great many small employers as well as large employers.

The following sections cover what you need to know concerning laws and regulations that govern employment.

When You Have ONE or More Employees

Employers sometimes forget that the moment they hire their first employee they become subject to a host of legal requirements. Here are 53 laws that will impact an employer with one or more employees on the payroll.

The Clayton Act (1914)

This legislation modified the Sherman Anti-Trust Act by prohibiting mergers and acquisitions that would lessen competition. It also prohibited a single person from being a director of two or more competing corporations. The act also restricts the use of injunctions against labor and legalized peaceful strikes, picketing, and boycotts.

For more information, see 15 U.S.C. Sec.12 at www.law.cornell.edu/uscode/text/15/12 or perform an Internet search for the law by name.

The Consumer Credit Protection Act (1968)

Congress expressed limits to the amount of wages that can be garnished or withheld in any one week by an employer to satisfy creditors. This law also prohibits employee dismissal because of garnishment for any one indebtedness.

For more information, see www.dol.gov/compliance/laws/comp-ccpa.htm or perform an Internet search for the law by name.

The Copeland "Anti-Kickback" Act (1934)

This act precludes a federal contractor or subcontractor from inducing an employee to give up any part of his or her wages to the employer for the benefit of having a job. For more information, see www.dol.gov/whd/regs/statutes/copeland.htm or perform an Internet search for the law by name.

The Copyright Act (1976)

The Copyright Act offers protection of "original works" for authors so others may not print, duplicate, distribute, or sell their work. In 1998, the Copyright Term Extension Act further extended copyright protection to the duration of the author's life plus 70 years for general copyrights and to 95 years for works made for hire and works copyrighted before 1978. If anyone in the organization writes technical instructions, policies and procedures, manuals, or even e-mail responses to customer inquiries, it would be a good idea to speak with your attorney and arrange some copyright agreements to clarify whether the employer or the employee who authored those documents will be designated the copyright owner. Written agreements can be helpful in clearing any possible misunderstandings. For more information, see www.copyright.gov/title17/92appa.pdf or perform an Internet search for the law by name.

The Davis-Bacon Act (1931)

This law requires contractors and subcontractors on certain federally funded or assisted construction projects worth more than $2,000 in the United States to pay wages and fringe benefits at least equal to those prevailing in the local area where the work is performed. This law applies only to laborers and mechanics. It also allows trainees and apprentices to be paid less than the predetermined rates under certain circumstances. For more information, see www.dol.gov/whd/regs/statutes/dbra.htm or perform an Internet search for the law by name.

The Dodd-Frank Wall Street Reform and Consumer Protection Act (2010)

This law offers a wide range of mandates affecting all federal financial regulatory agencies and almost every part of the nation's financial services industry. It includes a nonbinding vote for shareholders on executive compensation, golden parachutes, and return of executive compensation based on inaccurate financial statements. Also included are requirements to report chief executive officer (CEO) pay compared to the average employee compensation and provision of financial rewards for whistle-blowers. Watch your federal law resources for updates on regulations implementing changes to this law. For more information, see www.sec.gov/about/laws/wallstreetreform-cpa.pdf or perform an Internet search for the law by name.

The Economic Growth and Tax Relief Reconciliation Act (EGTRRA) (2001)

Here are modifications to the Internal Revenue Code that adjust pension vesting schedules, increasing retirement plan limits, permitting pretax catch-up contributions by participants older than 50 in certain plans (which are not tested for discrimination when made available to the entire workforce), and modifying distribution and rollover rules. For more information, see www.irs.gov/pub/irs-tege/epchd104.pdf or perform an Internet search for the law by name.

The Electronic Communications Privacy Act (ECPA) (1986)

This is a unique law composed of two pieces of legislation, the Wiretap Act and the Stored Communications Act. Combined, they provide rules for access, use, disclosure, interpretation, and privacy protections of electronic communications, and they provide the possibility of both civil and criminal penalties for violations. They prohibit interception of e-mails in transmission and access to e-mails in storage. The implications for HR have to do with recording employee conversations. Warnings such as "This call may be monitored or recorded for quality purposes" are intended to provide the notice required by this legislation. Having cameras in the workplace to record employee or visitor activities is also covered, and notices must be given to anyone subject to observation or recording. Recording without such a notice can be a violation of this act. If employers make observations of employee activities and/or record telephone and other conversations between employees and others and proper notice is given to employees, employees will have no expectation of privacy during the time they are in the workplace.

For more information, see www.justice.gov/jmd/ls/legislative_histories/pl99-508/pl99-508.html or perform an Internet search for the law by name.

The Employee Polygraph Protection Act (1988)

Before 1988, it was common for employers to use "lie detectors" as tools in investigations of inappropriate employee behavior. That changed when this act prohibited the use of lie detector tests for job applicants and employees of companies engaged in interstate commerce. Exceptions are made for certain situations, including law enforcement and national security. There is a federal poster requirement. Note: Many state laws also prohibit the use of lie detector tests. Be sure you understand state laws where you have work locations.

For more information, see www.dol.gov/compliance/laws/comp-eppa.htm or perform an Internet search for the law by name.

The Employee Retirement Income Security Act (ERISA) (1974)

This law doesn't require employers to establish pension plans but governs how those plans are managed once they have been established. It establishes uniform minimum standards to ensure that employee benefit plans are established and maintained in a fair and financially sound manner; protects employees covered by a pension plan from losses in benefits due to job changes, plant closings, bankruptcies, or mismanagement; and protects plan beneficiaries. It covers most employers engaged in interstate commerce. Public-sector employees and many churches are not subject to ERISA. Employers that offer retirement plans must also conform with the Internal Revenue Service (IRS) code in order to receive tax advantages. For more information, see www.dol.gov/compliance/laws/comp-erisa.htm or perform an Internet search for the law by name.

The Equal Pay Act (an Amendment to the FLSA) (1963)

Equal pay requirements apply to all employers. The act is an amendment to the Fair Labor Standards Act (FLSA) and is enforced by the Equal Employment Opportunity Commission (EEOC). It prohibits employers from discriminating on the basis of sex by paying wages to employees at a rate less than the rate paid to employees of the opposite sex for equal work on jobs requiring equal skill, effort, and responsibility and which are performed under similar working conditions. It does not address the concept of comparable worth. For more information, see www.eeoc.gov/laws/statutes/epa.cfm or perform an Internet search for the law by name.

The FAA Modernization and Reform Act (2012)

Congress took these actions in 2012 to amend the Railway Labor Act to change union certification election processes in the railroad and airline industries and impose greater oversight of the regulatory activities of the National Mediation Board (NMB). This law requires the Government Accountability Office (GAO) initially to evaluate the NMB's certification procedures and then audit the NMB's operations every 2 years. For more information, see www.faa.gov/regulations_policies/reauthorization/media/PLAW-112publ95[1].pdf or perform an Internet search for the law by name.

The Fair and Accurate Credit Transactions Act (FACT) (2003)

The financial privacy of employees and job applicants was enhanced in 2003 with these amendments to the Fair Credit Reporting Act, providing for certain requirements in third-party investigations of employee misconduct charges. Employers are released from obligations to disclose requirements and obtain employee consent if the investigation involves suspected misconduct, a violation of the law or regulations, or a violation of preexisting written employer policies. A written plan to prevent identity theft is required. For more information, see www.gpo.gov/fdsys/pkg/PLAW-108publ159/pdf/PLAW-108publ159.pdf or perform an Internet search for the law by name.

The Fair Credit Reporting Act (FCRA) (1970), as Amended in 2011

This was the first major legislation to regulate the collection, dissemination, and use of consumer information, including consumer credit information. It requires employers to notify any individual in writing if a credit report may be used in making an employment decision. Employers must also get a written authorization from the subject individual before asking a credit bureau for a credit report. The Fair Credit Reporting Act also protects the privacy of background investigation information and provides methods for ensuring that information is accurate. Employers who take adverse action against a job applicant or current employee based on information contained in the prospective or current employee's consumer report will have additional disclosures to make to that individual. For more information, see www.ftc.gov/os/statutes/031224fcra.pdf or perform an Internet search for the law by name.

The Fair Labor Standards Act (FLSA) (1938)

The FLSA is one of a handful of federal laws that establish the foundation for employee treatment. It is a major influence in how people are paid, in employment of young people, and in how records are to be kept on employment issues such as hours of work. The law introduced a maximum 44-hour 7-day workweek, established a national minimum wage, guaranteed "time-and-a-half" for overtime in certain jobs, and prohibited most employment of minors in "oppressive child labor," a term that is defined in the statue. It applies to employees engaged in interstate commerce or employed by an enterprise engaged in commerce or in the production of goods for commerce, unless the employer can claim an exemption from coverage. It is interesting to note that FLSA, rather than the Civil Rights Act of 1964, is the first federal law to require employers to maintain records on employee race and sex identification.

Provisions and Protections

Employers covered under the "enterprise" provisions of this law include public agencies; private employers whose annual gross sales exceed $500,000; those operating a hospital or a school for mentally or physically disabled or gifted children; and a preschool, an elementary or secondary school, or an institution of higher education (profit or non-profit). Individuals can still be covered even if they don't fit into one of the enterprises listed. If the employees' work regularly involves them in commerce between the states, they would be covered. These include employees who work in communications or transportation; regularly use the mail, telephone, or telegraph for interstate communication or keep records of interstate transactions; handle shipping and receiving goods moving in interstate commerce; regularly cross state lines in the course of employment; or work for independent employers who contract to do clerical, custodial, maintenance, or other work for firms engaged in interstate commerce or in the production of goods for interstate commerce. The FLSA establishes a federal minimum wage that has been raised from time to time since the law was originally passed. The FLSA prohibits shipment of goods in interstate commerce that were produced in violation of the minimum wage, overtime pay, child labor, or special minimum wage provisions of the law.

Recordkeeping Requirements

The FLSA proscribes methods for determining whether a job is exempt or nonexempt from the overtime pay requirements of the act. If a job is exempt from those requirements, incumbents can work as many hours of overtime as the job requires without being paid for their overtime. Exempt versus nonexempt status attaches to the job, not the incumbent. So, someone with an advanced degree who is working in a clerical job may be nonexempt because of the job requirements, not their personal qualifications. Employers are permitted to have a policy that calls for paying exempt employees when they work overtime. That is a voluntary provision of a benefit in excess of federal requirements. State laws may have additional requirements. People who work in nonexempt jobs must be paid overtime according to the rate computation methods provided for in the act. Usually, this is a requirement for overtime after 40 hours of regular time worked during a single workweek. The act also describes how a workweek is to be determined.

Each employer covered by the FLSA must keep records for each covered, nonexempt worker. Those records must include the following:

- Employee's full name and Social Security number.
- Address, including ZIP code.
- Birth date, if younger than 19.
- Sex.
- Occupation.
- Time and day of week when employee's workweek begins.
- Hours worked each day and total hours worked each workweek. (This includes a record of the time work began at the start of the day, when the employee left for a meal break, the time the employee returned to work from the meal break, and the time work ended for the day.)
- Basis on which employee's wages are paid (hourly, weekly, piecework).
- Regular hourly pay rate.
- Total daily or weekly straight-time earnings.
- Total overtime earnings for the workweek.
- All additions or deductions from the employee's wages.
- Total wages paid each pay period.
- Date of payment and the pay period covered by the payment.

There is no limit in the FLSA to the number of hours employees age 16 and older may work in any workweek. There is a provision for employers to retain all payroll records, collective bargaining agreements, sales, and purchase records for at least 3 years. Any time card, piecework record, wage rate tables, and work and time schedules should be retained for at least 2 years. A workplace poster is required to notify employees of the federal minimum wage.

The federal child labor provisions of the FLSA, also known as the child labor laws, were enacted to ensure that when young people work, the work is safe and does not jeopardize their health, well-being, or educational opportunities. These provisions also provide limited exemptions. Workers younger than 14 are restricted to jobs such as newspaper delivery to local customers; baby-sitting on a casual basis; acting in movies, TV, radio, or theater; and working as a home worker gathering evergreens and making evergreen wreaths. Under no circumstances, even if the business is family owned, may a person under 18 work in any of the 17 most hazardous jobs. See Figure 2-1 for a list of the 17 most hazardous jobs.

For workers aged 14 and 15, all work must be performed outside school hours, and these workers may not work

- More than 3 hours on a school day, including Friday.
- More than 18 hours per week when school is in session.
- More than 8 hours per day when school is not in session.

• Manufacturing or storing of explosives	• Using power-driven meat-processing machines, slaughtering, meat and poultry packing, processing or rendering
• Driving a motor vehicle or working as an outside helper on motor vehicles	• Using power-driven bakery machines
• Coal mining	• Using balers, compactors, and power-driven paper-products machines
• Forest fire fighting and forest fire prevention, timber tract, forestry service, and occupations in logging and sawmilling	• Manufacturing brick, tile, and related products
• Using power-driven woodworking machines	• Using power-driven circular saws, band saws, guillotine shears, chain saws, reciprocating saws, wood chippers, and abrasive cutting discs
• Exposure to radioactive substances and ionizing radiation	• Working in wrecking, demolition, and ship-breaking operations
• Using power-driven hoisting apparatuses	• Roofing and work performed on or about a roof
• Using power-driven metal-forming, punching, and shearing machines	• Trenching or excavating
• Mining, other than coal	

Source: "U.S. Department of Labor, eLaws Fair Labor Standards Act Advisor" on October 26, 2016, http://www.youthrules.gov/know-the-limits/hazards/index.htm

Figure 2-1 Seventeen most dangerous jobs that may not be performed by workers younger than 18

- More than 40 hours per week when school is not in session.
- Before 7 A.M. or after 7 P.M. on any day, except from June 1 through Labor Day, when nighttime work hours are extended to 9 P.M.
- A work permit from the school district is required.

Until employees reach the age of 18 it is necessary for them to obtain a work permit from their school district. For workers aged 16 through 17, there are no restrictions on the number of hours that can be worked per week. There continues to be a ban on working any job among the 17 most hazardous positions. All of these conditions must be met or the employer will be subject to penalties from the U.S. Department of Labor.

Overtime Computation

Overtime is required at a rate of 1.5 times the normal pay rate for all hours worked over 40 in a single workweek. An employer may designate that their workweek begins at a given day and hour and continues until that same day and hour 7 days later. Once selected, that same workweek definition must be maintained consistently until there is a legitimate business reason for making a change. That change must be clearly communicated in advance to all employees who will be affected by the change. No pay may be forfeit because the employer changes its workweek definition. Compensating time off is permitted under the FLSA if it is given at the same rates required for overtime pay.

Enforcement

Provisions of the FLSA are enforced by the U.S. Department of Labor's Wage and Hour Division. With offices around the country, this agency is able to interact with employees on complaints and follow up with employers by making an on-site visit if necessary. If violations are found during an investigation, the agency has the authority to make recommendations for changes that would bring the employer into compliance. Retaliation against any employee for filing a complaint under the FLSA, or in any other way availing himself or herself of the legal rights it offers, is subject to additional penalties. Willful violations may bring criminal prosecution and fines up to $10,000. Employers who are convicted a second time for willfully violating FLSA can find themselves in prison.

The Wage and Hour Division may, if it finds products produced during violations of the act, prevent an employer from shipping any of those goods. It may also "freeze" shipments of any product manufactured while overtime payment requirements were violated. A 2-year limit applies to recovery of back pay unless there was a willful violation, which triggers a 3-year liability. For more information, see www.dol.gov/whd/regs/statutes/FairLaborStandAct.pdf or perform an Internet search for the law by name.

The Foreign Corrupt Practices Act (FCPA) (1997)

The FCPA prohibits American companies from making bribery payments to foreign officials for the purpose of obtaining or keeping business. Training for employees who are involved with international negotiations should include a warning to avoid anything even looking like bribery payment to a foreign company or its employees. For more information, see www.justice.gov/criminal/fraud/fcpa/ or perform an Internet search for the law by name.

The Health Information Technology for Economic and Clinical Health (HITECH) Act (2009)

The HITECH Act requires that anyone with custody of personal health records send notification to affected individuals if their personal health records have been disclosed, or the employer believes they have been disclosed, to any unauthorized person. Enacted as part of the American Recovery and Reinvestment Act (ARRA), this law made several changes to the Health Insurance Portability and Accountability Act, including the establishment of a federal standard for security breach notifications that requires covered entities, in the event of a breach of any personal health information (PHI), to notify each individual whose PHI has been disclosed without authorization. For more information, see www .hhs.gov/ocr/privacy/hipaa/administrative/enforcementrule/hitechenforcementifr.html or perform an Internet search for the law by name.

The Health Insurance Portability and Accountability Act (HIPAA) (1996)

This law ensures that individuals who leave or lose their jobs can obtain health coverage even if they or someone in their family has a serious illness or injury or is pregnant. It also provides privacy requirements related to medical records for individuals as young as 12. It also limits exclusions for preexisting conditions and guarantees renewability of health coverage to employers and employees, allowing people to change jobs without the worry of loss of coverage. It also restricts the ability of employers to impose actively-at-work requirements as preconditions for health plan eligibility, as well as a number of other benefits. For more information, see www.hhs.gov/ocr/privacy or perform an Internet search for the law by name.

The Immigration and Nationality Act (INA) (1952)

The INA is the first law that pulled together all of the issues associated with immigration and is considered the foundation on which all following immigration laws have been built. It addresses employment eligibility and employment verification. It defines the conditions for the temporary and permanent employment of aliens in the United States.

The INA defines an *alien* as any person lacking citizenship or status as a national of the United States. The INA differentiates aliens as follows:

- Resident or nonresident
- Immigrant or nonimmigrant
- Documented and undocumented

The need to curtail illegal immigration led to the enactment of the Immigration Reform and Control Act (IRCA). For more information, see www.dol.gov/compliance/ laws/comp-ina.htm or perform an Internet search for the law by name.

The Immigration Reform and Control Act (IRCA) (1986)

This is the first law to require new employees to prove both their identity and their right to work in this country. Regulations implementing this law created the Form I-9,[1] which must be completed by each new employee and the employer. Form I-9 has been updated many times since 1986. Please be sure you are using the most current version of the form. There are document retention requirements. The law prohibits discrimination against job applicants on the basis of national origin or citizenship. It establishes penalties for employers who hire illegal aliens. For more information, see www.eeoc.gov/eeoc/history/35th/thelaw/irca.html or perform an Internet search for the law by name.

The IRS Intermediate Sanctions (2002)

Here we find guidelines for determining reasonable compensation for executives of non-profit organizations. It was enacted by the IRS and applied to nonprofit organizations that engage in the transactions that inure to the benefit of a disqualified person within the organization. These rules allow the IRS to impose penalties when it determines that top officials have received excessive compensation from their organizations. Intermediate sanctions may be imposed either in addition to or instead of revocation of the exempt state of the organization. For more information, see www.irs.gov/pub/irs-tege/eotopice03.pdf or perform an Internet search for the law by name.

The Labor-Management Relations Act (LMRA; Taft-Hartley Act) (1947)

Also called the Taft-Hartley Act, this is the first national legislation that placed controls on unions. It prohibits unfair labor practices by unions and outlaws closed shops, where union membership is required in order to get and keep a job. Employers may not form closed-shop agreements with unions. It requires both parties to bargain in good faith and covers nonmanagement employees in private industry who are not covered by the Railway Labor Act.

For more information, see 29 U.S.C. Sec.141 at www.casefilemethod.com/Statuters/LMRA.pdf or search the Internet for the law by name.

The Labor-Management Reporting and Disclosure Act (Landrum-Griffin Act) (1959)

Also called the Landrum-Griffin Act, this law outlines procedures for redressing internal union problems, protects the rights of union members from corrupt or discriminatory labor unions, and applies to all labor organizations. Specific requirements include the following:

- Unions must conduct secret elections, the results of which can be reviewed by the U.S. Department of Labor.
- A Bill of Rights guarantees union members certain rights, including free speech.

- Convicted felons and members of the Communist Party cannot hold office in unions.

- Annual financial reporting from unions to the Department of Labor is required.

- All union officials have a fiduciary responsibility in managing union assets and conducting the business of the union.

- Union power to place subordinate organizations in trusteeship is limited.

- Minimum standards for union disciplinary action against its members are provided.

For more information, see www.dol.gov/compliance/laws/comp-lmrda.htm or perform an Internet search for the law by name.

The Mine Safety and Health Act (1977)

Following a series of deadly mining disasters, the American people demanded that Congress take action to prevent similar events in the future. This law converted the existing Mine Enforcement Safety Administration (MESA) to the Mine Safety and Health Administration (MSHA). For the first time, it brought all coal, metal, and nonmetal mining operations under the same Department of Labor jurisdiction. Regulations and safety procedures for the coal mining industry were not altered, just carried into the new agency for oversight. For more information, see www.dol.gov/compliance/laws/comp-fmsha.htm or perform an Internet search for the law by name.

Provisions and Protections

This law requires the secretaries of Labor and Health, Education, and Welfare to create regulations governing the country's mines. All mines are covered if they are involved in commerce, which any active mining operation would be. Regulations that implement this law specify that employees must be provided with certain protective equipment while working in a mine. These devices relate to respiration and fire prevention, among other protections. Protecting against "black lung disease" is a key concern, even today, in the coal mining industry.

Recordkeeping Requirements

Employers engaged in mining operations must inspect their worksites and document the results, reflecting hazards and actions taken to reduce or eliminate the hazards. Employees are to be given access to information related to accident prevention, fatal accident statistics for the year, and instructions on specific hazards they will face while working in the mine. Requirements detail the content of written emergency response plans, emergency mapping, and rescue procedures. Individual employee exposure records must be maintained. Each mine operator is required to conduct surveys of mine exposures and hazards, a plan to deal with those problems, and a record of the results. This information must be made available to MSHA inspectors if they request it.

MSHA Standards

The agency enforces mine safety standards that involve ventilation, chemical exposure, noise, forklifts and other mining equipment, mine shoring, and more. Material Safety Data Sheets (MSDSs) must be available to employees in mining as they are in other industries overseen by the OSHA agency.

MSHA Enforcement

MSHA has a team of federal inspectors that conduct on-site audits of mining operations. MSHA has the authority to cite mine operators for violations of its regulations, and citations can carry a $1,000 per day penalty in some circumstances.[2]

The National Industrial Recovery Act (1933)

This was an attempt to help the country get out from the Great Depression. It proposed the creation of "Codes of Fair Competition" for each of several different industries. Essentially, every business would have to identify with and belong to a trade association. The association would then be required to create a Code of Fair Competition for the industry. Antitrust laws would be suspended in favor of the code. Of course, the code would have to be approved by the president of the United States, and the administration would issue federal licenses to every business in the country. If a business refused to participate in the code, its license could be suspended, and that would be the signal for that business to end all operations. There were financial penalties as well. This law didn't fare very well. It was declared unconstitutional by the U.S. Supreme Court in 1935 and was replaced by the National Labor Relations Act later that same year.

For more information, see www.ourdocuments.gov/doc.php?flash=true&doc=66 or perform an Internet search for the law by name.

The National Labor Relations Act (NLRA; Wagner Act) (1935)

This is the "granddaddy" of all labor relations laws in the United States. It initially provided that employees have a right to form unions and negotiate wage and hour issues with employers on behalf of the union membership. Specifically, the NLRA grants to employees the right to organize, join unions, and engage in collective bargaining and other "concerted activities." It also protects against unfair labor practices by employers.

Following on the heels of the National Industrial Recovery Act's failures, this law stepped into the void and addressed both union and employer obligations in labor relations issues. It established the National Labor Relations Board (NLRB), which would help define fair labor practices in the following decades. The NLRB has the power to accept and investigate complaints of unfair labor practices by either management or labor unions. It plays a judicial role within an administrative setting. This law is sometimes called the Wagner Act. The following are some key provisions:

- The right of workers to organize into unions for collective bargaining
- The requirement of employers to bargain in good faith when employees have voted in favor of a union to represent them

- Requirement that unions represent all members equally
- Covers nonmanagement employees in private industry who are not already covered by the Railway Labor Act

For more information, see www.nlrb.gov/national-labor-relations-act or perform an Internet search for the law by name.

The Needlestick Safety and Prevention Act (2000)

This law modifies the Occupational Safety and Health Act by introducing a new group of requirements in the medical community. Sharps, as they are called, are needles, puncture devices, knives, scalpels, and other tools that can harm either the person using them or someone else. The law and its regulations provides rules related to handling these devices, disposing of them, and encouraging invention of new devices that will reduce or eliminate the risk associated with injury due to sharps. Sharps injuries are to be recorded on the OSHA 300 log with "privacy case" listed and not the employee's name. Blood-borne pathogens and transmission of human blood-borne illnesses such as AIDS/HIV and hepatitis are key targets of this law. Reducing the amount of injury and subsequent illness due to puncture, stab, or cut wounds is a primary objective. There are communication requirements including employment poster content requirements.

For more information, see www.gpo.gov/fdsys/pkg/PLAW-106publ430/html/PLAW-106publ430.htm or perform an Internet search for the law by name.

The Norris-LaGuardia Act (1932)

Remember that this was still 3 years before the NLRA came to pass. When unions tried to use strikes and boycotts, employers would trot into court and ask for an injunction to prevent such activity. More often than not, they were successful, and judges provided the injunctions. Congress had been pressured by organized labor to restore their primary tools that could force employers to bargain issues unions saw as important. The following are key provisions of this law:

- It prohibited "yellow-dog" contracts. Those were agreements in which employees promised employers that they would not join unions. This new law declared such contracts to be unenforceable in any federal court.
- It prohibited federal courts from issuing injunctions of any kind against peaceful strikes, boycotts, or picketing when used by a union in connection with a labor dispute.
- It defined labor dispute to include any disagreement about working conditions.

For more information, see 29 U.S.C., Chapter 6, at http://uscode.house.gov/download/pls/29C6.txt or perform an Internet search for the law by name.

The Occupational Safety and Health Act (OSHA) (1970)

Signed into law by President Richard M. Nixon on December 29, 1970, the Occupational Safety and Health Act created an administrative agency within the U.S. Department of Labor called the Occupational Safety and Health Administration (OSHA). It also created the National Institute of Occupational Safety and Health (NIOSH), which resides inside the Centers for Disease Control (CDC).

Provisions and Protections

Regulations implementing this legislation have grown over time. They are complex and detailed. It is important that HR professionals understand the basics and how to obtain additional detailed information that applies to their particular employer circumstance. There are many standards that specify what employers must do to comply with their legal obligations. Overall, however, the law holds employers accountable for providing a safe and healthy working environment. The "General Duty Clause" in OSHA's regulations says employers shall furnish each employee with a place of employment free from recognized hazards that are likely to cause death or serious injury. It also holds employees responsible for abiding by all safety rules and regulations in the workplace. Some provisions require notices be posted in the workplace covering some of the OSHA requirements. Posters are available for download from the OSHA web site without charge. The law applies to all employers regardless of the employee population size.

Recordkeeping Requirements

OSHA regulations require that records be kept for many purposes. It is necessary to conduct and document inspections of the workplace, looking for safety and health hazards. It is necessary to document and make available to employees records about hazardous materials and how they must be properly handled. Employers with ten or more people on the payroll must summarize all injury and illness instances and post that summary in a conspicuous place within the workplace. That report must remain posted from February 1 to April 30 each year. Certain employers are exempt from some OSHA recordkeeping requirements. They generally are classified by industry Standard Industrial Classification (SIC) Code. A list is available on OSHA's web site at www.OSHA .gov. Any time there is a serious or fatal accident, a full incident report must be prepared by the employer and maintained in the safety file. These records must be maintained for a minimum of 5 years from the date of the incident. Known as a log of occupational injury or illness, it must include a record of each incident resulting in medical treatment (other than first aid), loss of consciousness, restriction of work or motion, or transfer or termination of employment. If you are in the medical industry, construction industry, or manufacturing industry, or if you use nuclear materials of any kind, there are other requirements you must meet. Key to compliance with OSHA rules is communication with employees. Training is often provided by employers to meet this hazard communication requirement. In summary, then, OSHA recordkeeping involves the following:

- Periodic safety inspections of the workplace
- Injury or illness incident reports

- Annual summary of incidents during the previous calendar year
- Injury and Illness Prevention Program (if required by rules governing your industry)
- Employee training on safety procedures and expectations
- Records of training participation
- Material Safety Data Sheets for each chemical used in the workplace (made available to all employees in a well-marked file or binder that can be accessed at any time during work hours)

Occupational Safety and Health Act Enforcement

OSHA inspections may include the following:

- **On-site visits that are conducted without advance notice** Inspectors can just walk into a place of employment and request that you permit an inspection. You don't have to agree unless the inspector has a search warrant. In the absence of the warrant, you can delay the inspection until your attorney is present.

- **On-site inspections or phone/fax investigations** Depending on the urgency of the hazard and agreement of the person filing the complaint, inspectors may telephone or fax inquiries to employers. The employer has 5 working days to respond with a detailed description of inspection findings, corrective action taken, and additional action planned.

- **Highly trained compliance officers** OSHA Training Institute provides training for OSHA's compliance officers, state compliance officers, state consultants, other federal agency personnel, and the private sector.

Inspection priorities include the following:

- **Imminent danger** Situations where death or serious injury are highly likely. Compliance officers will ask employers to correct the conditions immediately or remove employees from danger.

- **Fatalities and catastrophes** Incidents that involve a death or the hospitalization of three or more employees. Employers must report these incidents to OSHA within 8 hours.

- **Worker complaints** Allegations of workplace hazards or OSHA violations. Employees may request anonymity when they file complaints with OSHA.

- **Referrals** Other federal, state, or local agencies, individuals, organizations, or the media can make referrals to OSHA so the agency may consider making an inspection.

- **Follow-ups** Checks for abatement of violations cited during previous inspections are also conducted by OSHA personnel in certain circumstances.

- **Planned or programmed investigations**   OSHA can conduct inspections aimed at specific high-hazard industries or individual workplaces that have experienced high rates of injuries and illnesses. These are sometimes called *targeted investigations.*

Two Types of Standards

The law provides for two types of safety and health standards. The agency has therefore developed its regulations and standards in those two categories.

Normal Standards   If OSHA determines that a specific standard is needed, any of several advisory committees may be called upon to develop specific recommendations. There are two standing committees, and ad hoc committees may be appointed to examine special areas of concern to OSHA. All advisory committees, standing or ad hoc, must have members representing management, labor, and state agencies, as well as one or more designees of the Secretary of Health and Human Services (HHS). The occupational safety and health professions and the general public also may be represented.[3]

Emergency Temporary Standards   "Under certain limited conditions, OSHA is authorized to set emergency temporary standards that take effect immediately. First, OSHA must determine that workers are in grave danger due to exposure to toxic substances or agents determined to be toxic or physically harmful or to new hazards and that an emergency standard is needed to protect them. Then, OSHA publishes the emergency temporary standard in the *Federal Register,* where it also serves as a proposed permanent standard. It is then subject to the usual procedure for adopting a permanent standard except that a final ruling must be made within 6 months. The validity of an emergency temporary standard may be challenged in an appropriate U.S. Court of Appeals."[4] For more information, see www.dol.gov/compliance/guide/osha.htm or perform an Internet search for the law by name.

The Omnibus Budget Reconciliation Act (OBRA) (1993)

Signed into law by President Bill Clinton on August 10, 1993, this legislation reduces compensation limits in qualified retirement programs and triggers increased activity in nonqualified retirement programs. It also calls for termination of some plans. For more information, see www.gpo.gov/fdsys/pkg/BILLS-103hr2264enr/pdf/BILLS-103hr2264enr.pdf or perform an Internet search for the law by name.

The Pension Protection Act (PPA) (2006)

Focused solely on pensions, this law requires employers that have underfunded pension plans to pay a higher premium to the Pension Benefit Guarantee Corporation (PBGC). It also requires employers that terminate pension plans to provide additional funding to those plans. This legislation impacted nearly all aspects of retirement planning, including changes to rules about individual retirement accounts (IRAs). For more information, see www.dol.gov/ebsa/pensionreform.html or perform an Internet search for the law by name.

The Personal Responsibility and Work Opportunity Reconciliation Act (1996)

This law requires all states to establish and maintain a new hire reporting system designed to enhance enforcement of child support payments. It requires welfare recipients to begin working after 2 years of receiving benefits. States may exempt parents with children younger than 1 from the work requirements. Parents with children younger than 1 may use this exemption only once; they cannot use it again for subsequent children. These parents also are still subject to the 5-year time limit for cash assistance. HR professionals will need to establish and maintain reporting systems to meet these tracking requirements. For more information, see www.acf.hhs.gov/programs/css/resource/the-personal-responsibility-and-work-opportunity-reconcilliation-act or perform an Internet search for the law by name.

The Portal-to-Portal Act (1947)

By amending the FLSA, this law defines "hours worked" and establishes rules about payment of wages to employees who travel before and/or after their scheduled work shift. The act provides that minimum wages and overtime are not required for "traveling to and from the actual place of performance of the principal activity or activities which such employee is to perform" or for "activities which are preliminary to or postliminary to said principal activity or activities," unless there is a custom or contract to the contrary. For more information, see 29 U.S.C., Chapter 9, at http://uscode.house.gov/download/pls/29C9.txt or perform an Internet search for the law by name.

The Railway Labor Act (1926)

Originally, this law was created to allow railway employees to organize into labor unions. Over the years, it has been expanded in coverage to include airline employees. Covered employers are encouraged to use the Board of Mediation, which has since morphed into the National Mediation Board, a permanent independent agency. For more information, see www.nmb.gov/documents/rla.html or perform an Internet search for the law by name.

The Rehabilitation Act (1973), as Amended in 1980

This replaced the Vocational Rehabilitation Act and created support for states to create vocational rehabilitation programs. The term originally used in this legislation was *handicapped*. The law was later modified to replace that term with *disabled*.

Table 2-1 notes some of the most important sections of the Rehabilitation Act.

Section	Requirement
Section 501	Requires nondiscrimination and affirmative action in hiring disabled workers by federal agencies within the executive branch
Section 503	Requires nondiscrimination and affirmative action by federal contractors and subcontractors with contracts valued at $10,000 or more
Section 504	Requires employers subject to the law to provide reasonable accommodation for disabled individuals who can perform the major job duties with or without accommodation

Table 2-1 Key Employment Provisions of the Rehabilitation Act of 1973

For more information see https://www.disability.gov/rehabilitation-act-1973/ or perform an Internet search for the law by name.

The Retirement Equity Act (REA) (1984)

Signed into law by President Ronald Reagan on August 23, 1984, the REA provides certain legal protections for spousal beneficiaries of qualified retirement programs. It prohibits changes to retirement plan elections, spousal beneficiary designations, or in-service withdrawals without the consent of a spouse. Changing withdrawal options does not require spousal consent. It permits plan administrators to presume spousal survivors annuity and reduce primary pension amounts accordingly. Specific written waivers are required to avoid spousal annuity. For more information, see www.law.cornell.edu/uscode/text/29/1055 or perform an Internet search for the law by name.

The Revenue Act (1978)

This law added two important sections to the Internal Revenue Tax Code relevant to employee benefits: Section 125, Cafeteria Benefit Plans, and Section 401(k), originally a pretax savings program for private-sector employees known as Individual Retirement Accounts (IRAs), subsequently expanded to a second plan opportunity known as "Roth IRA" that permitted funding with after-tax savings. For more information, see www.irs.gov/pub/irs-utl/irpac-br_530_relief_-_appendix_natrm_paper_09032009.pdf or perform an Internet search for the law by name.

The Sarbanes-Oxley Act (SOX) (2002)

In response to many corrupt practices in the financial industry and the economic disasters they created, Congress passed the Sarbanes-Oxley Act to address the need for oversight and disclosure of information by publicly traded companies.

Provisions and Protections

This law brought some strict oversight to corporate governance and financial reporting for publicly held companies. It holds corporate officers accountable for proper record-keeping and reporting of financial information, including internal control systems to assure those systems are working properly. There are also requirements for reporting any unexpected changes in financial condition, including potential new liabilities such as lawsuits. Those lawsuits can involve things such as employee complaints of illegal employment discrimination.

It requires administrators of defined contribution plans to provide notice of covered blackout periods and provides whistle-blower protection for employees.

This law protects anyone who reports wrongdoing to a supervisor, appointed company officials who handle these matters, a federal regulatory or law enforcement agency, or a member or committee of Congress. It even extends to claims that prove to be false as long as the employee reasonably believed the conduct is a violation of Security Exchange Commission (SEC) rules or a federal law involving fraud against shareholders.

On March 4, 2014, the U.S. Supreme Court issued its opinion in the case of *Lawson v. FMR LLC.* (No. 12–3).[5] The 6–3 decision held that all contractors and subcontractors of publicly held companies are subject to the Sarbanes-Oxley Act, even if they are not publicly held. The takeaway from this ruling is that nearly everyone is now subject to the whistle-blower provisions of the Sarbanes-Oxley Act. As Justice Sotomayor suggested in her dissenting opinion:

> For example, public companies often hire "independent contractors," of whom there are more than 10 million, and contract workers, of whom there are more than 11 million. And, they employ outside lawyers, accountants, and auditors as well. While not every person who works for a public company in these nonemployee capacities may be positioned to threaten or harass employees of the public company, many are.

> Under [the majority opinion] a babysitter can bring a … retaliation suit against his employer if his employer is a checkout clerk for the local PetSmart (a public company) but not if she is a checkout clerk for the local Petco (a private company). Likewise the day laborer who works for a construction business can avail himself of [this ruling] if her company has been hired to remodel the local Dick's Sporting Goods store (a public company), but not if it is remodeling a nearby Sports Authority (a private company).

Recordkeeping Requirements

Internal control systems are required to assure that public disclosure of financial information is done as required. The registered accounting firm responsible for reviewing the company's financial reports must attest to the proper implementation of internal control systems and procedures for financial reporting.

SOX Enforcement

Enforcement of the law is done by private-firm audits overseen by the Public Company Accounting Oversight Board (PCAOB). The PCAOB is a nonprofit corporation created by the act to oversee accounting professionals who provide independent audit reports for publicly traded companies. It essentially audits the auditors.

Companies and corporate officers in violation of the act can find themselves subject to fines and/or up to 20 years imprisonment for altering, destroying, mutilating, concealing, or falsifying records, documents, or tangible objects with the intent to obstruct, impede, or influence a legal investigation. For more information, see http://taft.law.uc.edu/CCL/SOact/soact.pdf or perform an Internet search for the law by name.

The Securities and Exchange Act (1934)

When companies "go public" by issuing common stock for trade, it is done on the "primary market." This law provides for governance in the "secondary market," which is all trading after the initial public offering. It also created the Securities and Exchange Commission, which has oversight authority for the trading of stocks in this country. It extends the "disclosure" doctrine of investor protection to securities listed and registered for public trading on any of the U.S. exchanges. For more information, see www.law.cornell.edu/wex/securities_exchange_act_of_1934 or perform an Internet search for the law by name.

The Service Contract Act (1965)

Applying to federal contractors (and subcontractors) offering goods and services to the government, this law calls for payment of prevailing wages and benefit requirements to all employees providing service under the agreement. All contractors and subcontractors, other than construction services, with contract values in excess of $2,500 are covered. Safety and health standards also apply to such contracts.

The compensation requirements of this law are enforced by the Wage and Hour Division in the U.S. Department of Labor (DOL). The SCA safety and health requirements are enforced by the Occupational Safety and Health Administration, also an agency within DOL. For more information, see 41 U.S.C. 351 at www.dol.gov/oasam/regs/statutes/351.htm or perform an Internet search for the law by name.

The Sherman Anti-Trust Act (1890)

If you travel back in time to the latter part of the nineteenth century, you will find that big business dominated the landscape. There were Standard Oil, Morgan Bank, U.S. Steel, and a handful of railroads. They were huge by comparison with other similar enterprises at the time. And people were concerned that they were monopolizing the marketplace and holding prices high just because they could. John Sherman, a Republican senator from Ohio, was chairman of the Senate Finance Committee. He suggested that the country needed some protections against monopolies and cartels. Thus, this law was created and subsequently used by federal prosecutors to break up the Standard Oil Company into smaller units. Over the years, case law has developed that concludes that attempting to restrict competition, or fix prices, can be seen as a violation of this law. Restraint of trade is also prohibited. For more information, see 15 U.S.C. Secs. 1–7 at www.law.cornell.edu/uscode/text/15/1 or perform an Internet search for the law by name.

The Small Business Job Protection Act (1996)

This law increased federal minimum wage levels and provided some tax incentives to small business owners to protect jobs and increase take-home pay. It also amended the Portal-to-Portal Act for employees who use employer-owned vehicles. It created the SIMPLE 401(k) retirement plan to make pension plans easier for small businesses. Other tax incentives created by this law include the following:

- Employee education incentive—allowed small business owners to exclude up to $5,250 from an employee's taxable income for educational assistance provided by the employer

- Increased the maximum amount of capital expense allowed for a small business to $7,000 per year

- Replaced the Targeted Jobs Tax Credit with the Work Opportunity Tax Credit

- Provided a tax credit to individuals who adopted a child (up to $5,000 per child) and a tax credit of up to $6,000 for adoption of a child with special needs

For more information, see www.ssa.gov/legislation/legis_bulletin_082096.html or perform an Internet search for the law by name.

The Social Security Act (1935)

The Social Security program began in 1935 in the heart of the Great Depression. It was initially designed to help senior citizens when that group was suffering a poverty rate of 50 percent. It currently includes social welfare and social insurance programs that can help support disabled workers who are no longer able to earn their wages.

The Social Security program is supported through payroll taxes with contributions from both the employee and the employer. Those payroll tax rates are set by the Federal Insurance Contributions Act (FICA) and have been adjusted many times over the years. There are many programs currently under the control of the Social Security Act and its amendments. These include the following:

- Federal old-age benefits (retirement)

- Survivors benefits (spouse benefits, dependent children, and widow/widower benefits)

- Disability insurance for workers no longer able to work

- Temporary Assistance for Needy Families

- Medicare Health Insurance for Aged and Disabled

- Medicaid Grants to States for Medical Assistance Programs

- Supplemental Security Income (SSI)

- State Children's Health Insurance Program (SCHIP)

- Patient Protection and Affordable Care Act

There is currently a separate payroll deduction for Medicare Health Insurance, which is also funded by both the employee and employer. And the Patient Protection and Affordable Care Act is rolling out over the next few years and offers the opportunity to provide medical insurance coverage to a greater number of people.

A personal Social Security number is used as a tax identification number for federal income tax, including bank records, and to prove work authorization in this country. Social Security numbers can be used in completing Form I-9, which must be completed for every new employee on the payroll. Also required for the I-9 is proof of identity. For more information, see www.ssa.gov/history/35act.html or perform an Internet search for the law by name.

The Tax Reform Act (1986)

This law made extensive changes to the Internal Revenue Service tax code, including a reduction in tax brackets and all tax rates for individuals. Payroll withholdings were affected, many passive losses and tax shelters were eliminated, and changes were made to the alternative minimum tax computation. This is the law that required all dependent children to have Social Security numbers. That provision reduced the number of fraudulent dependent children claimed on income tax returns by 7 million in its first year. For HR professionals, answers to employee questions about the number of exemptions to claim on their Form W-4 are greatly influenced by this requirement for dependent Social Security numbers. For more information, see http://archive.org/stream/summaryofhr-3838t1486unit/summaryofhr3838t1486unit_djvu.txt or perform an Internet search for the law by name.

The Taxpayer Relief Act (1997)

Congress wanted to give taxpayers a couple of ways to lower their tax payments during retirement, so the Taxpayer Relief Act was passed to create new savings programs called Roth IRAs and Education IRAs. Many individuals were able to achieve a better tax position through these tools. For more information, see www.gpo.gov/fdsys/pkg/BILLS-105hr2014enr/pdf/BILLS-105hr2014enr.pdf or perform an Internet search for the law by name.

The Trademark Act (1946)

This is the legislation that created federal protections for trademarks and service marks. Officially it was called the Lanham (Trademark) Act, and it set forth the requirements for registering a trademark or service mark to obtain those legal protections. HR people may well have a role to play in training employees in how to properly handle organizational trademarks and the policies that govern those uses. For more information, see www.uspto.gov/trademarks/law/tmlaw.pdf or perform an Internet search for the law by name.

The Unemployment Compensation Amendments (UCA) (1992)

This law established 20 percent as the amount to be withheld from payment of employee savings accounts when leaving an employer and not placing the funds (rolling over) into another tax-approved IRA or 401(k). For more information, see www.socialsecurity.gov/policy/docs/ssb/v56n1/v56n1p87.pdf or perform an Internet search for the law by name.

The Uniformed Services Employment and Reemployment Rights Act (USERRA) (1994)

USERRA provides instructions for handling employees who are in the reserves and receive orders to report for active duty. The law protects the employment, reemployment, and retention rights of anyone who voluntarily or involuntarily serves or has served in the uniformed services. It requires that employers continue paying for the employee's benefits to the extent they paid for those benefits before the call to duty. It also requires that employers continue giving credit for length of service as though the military service was equivalent to company service. There are specific detailed parameters for how long an employee may wait to engage the employer in return-to-work conversations after being released from active military duty.

This law and its provisions cover all eight U.S. military services and other uniformed services. They are

- Army
- Navy
- Air Force
- Marines
- Public Health Service Commissioned Corps
- National Oceanic and Atmospheric Administration Commissioned Corps
- Coast Guard
- National Guard groups that have been called into active duty

For more information, see www.dol.gov/compliance/laws/comp-userra.htm or perform an Internet search for the law by name.

The Vietnam Era Veterans Readjustment Assistance Act (1974), as Amended by the Jobs for Veterans Act (JVA)

Current covered veterans include the following:

- Disabled veterans
- Veterans who served on active duty in the U.S. military during a war or campaign or expedition for which a campaign badge was awarded

- Veterans who, while serving on active duty in the Armed Forces, participated in a U.S. military operation for which an Armed Forces service medal was awarded pursuant to Executive Order 12985

- Recently separated veterans (veterans within 36 months from discharge or release from active duty)

These requirements apply to all federal contractors with a contract valued at $25,000 or more, regardless of the number of total employees.

This veteran support legislation requires all employers subject to the law to post their job openings with their local state employment service. These are the three exceptions to that requirement:

- Jobs that will last 3 days or less

- Jobs that will be filled by an internal candidate

- Jobs that are senior executive positions

Affirmative action outreach and recruiting of veterans are required for federal contractors meeting the contract value threshold. For more information, see www.dol.gov/compliance/laws/comp-vevraa.htm or perform an Internet search for the law by name.

The Wagner-Peyser Act (1933), as Amended by the Workforce Investment Act (WIA) (1988)

The Wagner-Peyser Act created a nationwide system of employment offices known as Employment Service Offices. They were run by the U.S. Department of Labor's Employment and Training Administration (ETA). These offices provided job seekers with assistance in their job search, assistance in searching jobs for unemployment insurance recipients, and recruitment services for employers.

The Workforce Investment Act created the "One Stop" centers within Employment Service Offices. The federal government contracts with states to run the Employment Service Offices and One Stop centers. Funds are allocated to states based on a complicated formula. For more information, see www.doleta.gov/programs/w-pact_amended98 .cfm or perform an Internet search for the law by name.

The Walsh-Healey Act (Public Contracts Act) (1936)

President Franklin Roosevelt signed this into law during the Great Depression. It was designed to assure the government paid a fair wage to manufacturers and suppliers of goods for federal government contracts in excess of $10,000 each. The provisions of the law included the following:

- Overtime pay requirements for work done over 8 hours in a day or 40 hours in a week.

- A minimum wage equal to the prevailing wage.

- Prohibition on employing anyone under 16 years of age or a current convict.
- The Defense Authorization Act (1968) later excluded federal contractors from overtime payments in excess of 8 hours in a day.

For more information, see www.dol.gov/compliance/laws/comp-pca.htm or perform an Internet search for the law by name.

The Work Opportunity Tax Credit (WOTC) (1996)

This law provides federal income tax credits to employers who hire from certain targeted groups of job seekers who face employment barriers. The amount of tax credit is adjusted from time to time and currently stands at $9,600 per employee.

Targeted groups include the following:

- Qualified recipients of Temporary Assistance to Needy Families (TANF).
- Qualified veterans receiving food stamps (referred to as Supplemental Nutrition Assistance Program [SNAP] today) or qualified veterans with a service-connected disability who
  - Have a hiring date that is not more than 1 year after having been discharged or released from active duty, or
  - Have aggregate periods of unemployment during the 1-year period ending on the hiring date that equals or exceeds 6 months
- WOTC also includes family members of a veteran who received food stamps (SNAP) for at least a 3-month period during the 15-month period ending on the hiring date or a disabled veteran entitled to compensation for a service-related disability hired within a year of discharge or unemployed for a period totaling at least 6 months of the year ending on the hiring date.
- Ex-felons hired no later than 1 year after conviction or release from prison.
- Designated Community Resident—an individual who is between the ages of 18 and 40 on the hiring date and who resides in an Empowerment Zone, Renewal Community, or Rural Renewal County.
- Vocational rehabilitation referrals, including Ticket Holders with an individual work plan developed and implemented by an Employment Network.
- Qualified summer youth ages 16 through 17 who reside in an Empowerment Zone, Enterprise Community, or Renewal Community.
- Qualified SNAP recipients between the ages of 18 and 40 on the hiring date.
- Qualified recipients of Supplemental Security Income (SSI).
- Long-term family assistance recipients.

These categories change from time to time.

In addition to these specific federal laws, there are laws dealing with payroll that HR professionals need to understand. While it is true that accounting people normally handle the payroll function in an employer's organization, occasionally HR professionals get involved and have to work with accounting people to explain deductions and provide input about open enrollment for healthcare benefit programs, among other things. Those things can include garnishments, wage liens, savings programs, benefit premium contributions, and income tax, FICA, and Medicare withholdings. For more information, see www.gao.gov/new.items/d01329.pdf or perform an Internet search for the law by name.

The Labor Management Reporting and Disclosure Act (1959)

Finally, this law provides for the reporting and disclosure of certain financial transactions and administrative practices of labor organizations and employers to prevent abuses in the administration of trusteeships by labor organizations and to provide standards with respect to the election of officers of labor organizations. It created a Bill of Rights for members of labor organizations (29 U.S.C. 401–402; 411–415; 431–441; 461–466; 481–484; 501–505).

For more information, see www.dol.gov/olms/regs/statutes/lmrda-act.htm or perform an Internet search for the law by name.

Whistle-Blowing

It is important to highlight the issue of whistle-blowing. Protections against retaliation are embedded in various laws we cover in this chapter; laws with those provisions and protections include the Civil Rights Acts, OSHA, MSHA, the Sarbanes-Oxley Act, ADA, and more.

Whistle-blower laws usually apply to public-sector employees and employees of organizations contracting with the federal government or state governments. They are designed to protect individuals who publicly disclose information about corrupt practices or illegal activities within their employer's organization. Often, such events occur when someone is mishandling money, contracts, or other assets. Construction projects not being built to specifications can result in whistle-blowing by governmental employees. Employees of financial services companies (banks, credit unions, stock brokerages, and investment firms) have been in the headlines during recent years. They uncovered and disclosed misbehavior among people in their companies and were protected under whistle-blower provisions of various laws. Whistle-blowers are protected from disciplinary action, termination, or other penalty. For more information, see www.osc.gov/documents/pubs/post_wb.htm or perform an Internet search for the law by name.

For FIFTEEN or More Employees

Once employers have added 15 or more employees to their payroll, it becomes necessary to comply with an additional 11 major federal laws.

The Americans with Disabilities Act (ADA) (1990), as Amended by the Americans with Disabilities Act Amendments Act (ADAAA) (2008)

Prior to this legislation, the only employees who were protected against employment discrimination were the ones working for the federal, state, or local government and federal government contractors. They were captured by the Rehabilitation Act. As a matter of fact, it was the Rehabilitation Act that was used as a model for developing the ADA. Five years after the Rehabilitation Act, the Developmental Disabilities Act of 1978 spoke specifically to people with developmental disabilities. It provided for federally funded state programs to assist people in that category of the population. The ADA had been first proposed in 1988, and it was backed by thousands of individuals around the country who had been fighting for rights of their family members, friends, and co-workers. They thought it was only appropriate for those people to have equal access to community services, jobs, training, and promotions. It was signed into law by President George H. W. Bush on July 26, 1990. It became fully effective for all employers with 15 or more workers on July 26, 1992.

Provisions and Protections

Title I—Employment—applies to employers with 15 or more workers on the payroll. Those employers may not discriminate against a physically or mentally disabled individual in recruitment, hiring, promotions, training, pay, social activities, and other privileges of employment. Qualified individuals with a disability are to be treated as other job applicants and employees are treated. If a job accommodation is required for a qualified individual to perform the assigned job, employers are required to provide that accommodation or recommend an alternative that would be equally effective. The interactive process between employers and employees should result in an accommodation or explanation about why making the accommodation would provide an undue hardship on the employer. Title I is enforced by the Equal Employment Opportunity Commission. Part of the interactive discussion about accommodation requests involves the employer investigating other accommodations that may be equally effective yet lower in cost or other resource requirements. Employers are not obligated to accept the employee's request without alteration.

U.S. Supreme Court Interpretation of the ADA

There were several U.S. Supreme Court cases that interpreted the ADA very narrowly. They limited the number of people who could qualify as disabled under the Court's interpretation of Congress's initial intent. Reacting to those cases, Congress enacted the ADA Amendment Act in September 2008. It became effective on January 1, 2009.

ADA Amendments Act of 2008

Following the U.S. Supreme Court decisions in *Sutton v. United Airlines*[6] and in *Toyota Motor Manufacturing, Kentucky, Inc., v. William,*[7] Congress felt that the Court had been too restrictive in its interpretation of who qualifies as disabled. It was the intent of Congress to be broader in that definition. Consequently, Congress passed the ADA Amendments Act to capture a wider range of people in the disabled classification. A disability is now defined as "an impairment that substantially limits one or more major life activities, having a record of such an impairment, or being regarded as having such an impairment." Although the words remain the same as the original definition, the Amendments Act went further. It said, when determining whether someone is disabled, there may be no consideration of *mitigating circumstances*. In the past, we used to say people who had a disability under control were not disabled. An employee with a prosthetic limb did everything a whole-bodied person could do. An employee with migraines that disappeared with medication wasn't considered disabled. Under the old law, epilepsy and diabetes were not considered disabilities if they were controlled with medication. Now, because the law prohibits a consideration of either medication or prosthesis, they are considered disabilities. You can see that a great many more people are captured within the definition of disabled as a result of these more recent changes. The only specifically excluded condition is the one involving eye glasses and contact lenses. Congress specifically said having a corrected vision problem if eye glasses or contact lenses are worn may not constitute a disability under the law.

An individual can be officially disabled but quite able to do his or her job without an accommodation of any sort. Having more people defined as disabled doesn't necessarily mean there will be more people asking for job accommodations. For more information, see www.eeoc.gov/laws/statutes/adaaa.cfm or perform an Internet search for the law by name.

"Substantially Limits"

Employers are required to consider as disabled anyone with a condition that "substantially limits," but does not "significantly restrict," a major life activity. Even though the limitation might be reduced or eliminated with medication or other alleviation, the treatment may not be considered when determining the limitations. So, people who use shoe inserts to correct a back problem or who take prescription sleeping pills may now be classified as disabled. The same might be said of people who are allergic to peanuts or bee stings. Yet there may be no need for any of them to request a job accommodation.

"Major Life Activities"

Caring for oneself, seeing, hearing, touching, eating, sleeping, walking, standing, sitting, reaching, lifting, bending, speaking, breathing, learning, reading, concentrating, thinking, communicating, interacting with others, and working all are considered "major life activities." Also included are major bodily functions such as normal cell growth, reproduction, immune system, blood circulation, and the like. Some conditions are specifically designated as disabilities by the EEOC. They include diabetes, cancer, human immunodeficiency virus and acquired immunodeficiency syndrome (HIV/AIDS), multiple sclerosis (MS), cerebral palsy (CP), and cystic fibrosis (CF) because they interfere with one or more of our major life activities.

"Essential Job Function"

An essential job function is defined as "a portion of a job assignment that cannot be removed from the job without significantly changing the nature of the job." An essential function is highly specialized, and the incumbent has been hired because he or she has special qualifications, skills, or abilities to perform that function, among others.

"Job Accommodation"

Someone with a disability doesn't necessarily need a job accommodation. Remember that we select people and place them in jobs if they are qualified for the performance of the essential functions, with or without a job accommodation. Someone with diabetes may have the disease under control with medication and proper diet. No accommodation would be required. However, if it were essential that the employee had food intake at certain times of the day, there could be a legitimate request for accommodating that need. The employer might be asked to consistently permit the employee to have meal breaks at specific times each day.

Job accommodations are situationally dependent. First, there must be a disability and an ability to do the essential functions of the job. Next, there must be a request for accommodation from the employee. If there is no request for accommodation, no action is required by the employer. It is perfectly acceptable for an employer to request supporting documentation from medical experts identifying the disability. There might even be recommendations for specific accommodations, including those requested by the employee.

Once an accommodation is requested, the employer is obliged to enter into an interactive discussion with the employee. For example, an employee might ask for something specific, perhaps a new piece of equipment (a special ergonomic chair) that will eliminate the impact of disability on their job performance. The employer must consider that specific request. Employers are obligated to search for alternatives that could satisfy the accommodation request only when the specific request cannot be reasonably accommodated. This is the point where the Job Accommodation Network (JAN)[8] can become a resource. It can often provide help for even questionable and unusual situations.

The employer must consider if making that accommodation would be an "undue hardship" considering all it would involve. You should note that most job accommodations carry a very low cost. Often they cost nothing. The larger an employer's payroll headcount, the more difficult it is to fully justify using "undue hardship" as a reason for not agreeing to provide an accommodation. Very large corporations or governments have vast resources, and the cost of one job accommodation, even if it does cost some large dollar amount, won't likely cause an undue hardship on that employer.

Recordkeeping Requirements

There is nothing in the Americans with Disabilities Act of 1990, or its amendments, that requires employers to create job descriptions. However, smart employers are doing that in order to identify physical and mental requirements of each job. Job descriptions also make it easy to identify essential job functions that any qualified individual would have to perform, with or without job accommodation. It is easier to administer job accommodation request procedures and to defend against false claims of discrimination when an employer has job descriptions that clearly list all of the job's requirements. It also makes screening job applicants easier because it shows them in writing what the job will entail. Then, recruiters may ask, "Is there anything in this list of essential job functions that you can't do with or without a job accommodation?"

If a job requires an incumbent to drive a delivery truck, driving would be an essential function of that job. A disability that prevented the incumbent from driving the delivery truck would likely block that employee from working—unless an accommodation could be found that would permit the incumbent to drive in spite of the disability.

People are sometimes confused about temporary suspension of duty being a permanent job accommodation. If that temporary suspension means the incumbent no longer is responsible for performing an essential job function, the job could not be performed as it was designed by the employer. It is not necessary for an employer to redesign job content to make a job accommodation. It is possible for such voluntary efforts to be made on behalf of an employee the organization wants to retain. Those situations are not job accommodations, however. They are job reassignments.

EEOC procedures prohibit employers from inviting job applicants to identify their disability status prior to receiving a job offer. Federal regulations related to affirmative action requirements for disabled workers[1] require contractors to invite job applicants to identify their status as disabled and then provide the same invitation to identify themselves as disabled once they have been hired. Federal contractors are also required to conduct a general survey of the entire employee population every 5 years (at a minimum) with an invitation to self-identify as disabled. At any time, employees are permitted to identify themselves as disabled to their employer.

An annual review of job description content is required under the EEOC guidelines. It is important to maintain accurate listings of essential job functions and physical and mental job requirements. An annual review will help assure that you always have current information in your job descriptions.

ADA Enforcement

The EEOC enforces Title I of the ADA. That agency will accept complaints of illegal discrimination based on mental or physical disability. Once an employee has established that he or she is disabled and claims that he or she has been prohibited some employment benefit because of the disability (hiring, promotion, access to training, or inappropriate termination), there is a *prima facie* case (meaning it is true on its surface). Then the EEOC notifies the employer of the complaint and asks for the employer's response. This process can work back and forth from employer response to employee response for several cycles. Ultimately, the agency will determine that the case has cause (is a valid claim of discrimination), the case has no cause (the claim cannot be substantiated), or the case should be closed for administrative purposes (the employee asks for the case to be closed, or time for an investigation has expired). Each of those three outcomes is followed by a "Right to Sue" letter, allowing the employee to get an attorney and file a lawsuit in federal court seeking remedies under the law.[9]

Once a complaint (called a *charge of illegal discrimination*) is filed with the EEOC, employers are instructed to cease talking about that issue directly with their employee. All conversation about the complaint must be directed through the EEOC. Unfortunately, that complicates the communication process, and it provides a strong incentive for employers to resolve complaints internally before they reach the formal external complaint stage. Working directly with an employee on the subject of accommodation, or any other personnel issue, is preferable to working through an agent such as the EEOC. For more information, see www.ada.gov/ or perform an Internet search for the law by name.

The Civil Rights Act (Title VII) (1964)

Although this was not the first federal civil rights act in the country,[10] it came to us through a great deal of controversy. It was signed into law by President Lyndon Johnson on July 2, 1964. Following the assassination of President John F. Kennedy the previous November, President Johnson took it upon himself to carry the civil rights banner and urge Congress to pass the law.

For more information, see www.eeoc.gov/laws/statutes/titlevii.cfm or perform an Internet search for the law by name.

Employment Protections

Title VII of the act speaks to employment discrimination and cites five protected classes of people. Before the final days when Congress was discussing the issues, there were only four protected classes listed: Race, Color, Religion, and National Origin. There was a great deal of opposition in the Senate from Southern states. They decided that they would strategically add another protected category to the list. They thought that if "sex" was added to the list, the bill would surely fail because no one would vote for having women protected in the workplace. Well, it passed…with all five protected categories in place. From that time forward, when making employment decisions, it has been illegal to take into account any employee's membership in any of the protected classifications.

Penalties for Violations

Penalties can be assessed by a federal court. Protocol requires a complaint be filed with the Equal Employment Opportunity Commission, the administrative agency tasked with the duty to investigate claims of illegal employment discrimination. Regardless of the outcome of that administrative review, a "Right to Sue" letter is given to the complaining employee so the case can move forward to federal court if that is what the employee wants to do next.

Penalties that can be assessed if an employer is found to have illegally discriminated include the following:

- **Actual damages**   Costs for medical bills, travel to medical appointments, equipment loss reimbursement, lost wages (back pay), lost promotional increase, lost future earnings (front pay). The limitation is usually 2 years into the past and unlimited number of years into the future.

- **Compensatory damages**   Dollars to reimburse the victim for "pain and suffering" caused by this illegal discrimination.
- **Punitive damages**   Dollars assessed by the court to "punish" the employer for treatment of the employee that was egregious in its nature. This is usually thought of as "making an example" of one case so as to send a message to other employers that doing such things to an employee or job applicant will be severely punished.

The Civil Rights Act (1991)

This act modified the 1964 Civil Rights Act in several ways:

- It provided for employees to receive a jury trial if they wanted. Up to this point, judges always heard cases and decided them from the bench.
- It established requirements for any employer defense.
- It placed a limitation on punitive damage awards by using a sliding scale depending on the size of the employer organization (payroll headcount):
  - For employers with 15 to 100 employees, damages are capped at $50,000.
  - For employers with 100 to 200 employees, damages are capped at $100,000.
  - For employers with 201 to 500 employees, damages are capped at $200,000.
  - For employers with more than 500 employees, damages are capped at $300,000.

For more information, see www.eeoc.gov/eeoc/history/35th/1990s/civilrights.html or perform an Internet search for the law by name.

The Drug-Free Workplace Act (1998)

This legislation requires some employers to maintain a drug-free workplace. Employee compliance must be assured by subject employers.

Provisions and Protections

This law applies to federal contractors and all organizations receiving grants from the federal government. If you are covered, you are required to assure that all the employees working on the contract or grant are in compliance with its drug-free requirements. Covered employers are required to have a drug-free policy that applies to its employees. To determine that an employer is in compliance with the requirements, drug testing is usually performed on employees and applicants who have received a job offer. Random drug testing is also used in some organizations to assure employees subject to the law or policy are continuing to comply with the requirements. Any federal contractor under the jurisdiction of the Office of Federal Contract Compliance Programs (OFCCP) in the Department of Labor must comply with this legislation.

Employee notification about the policy must include information about the consequences of failing a drug test. Whenever an employee has been convicted of a criminal drug violation in the workplace, the employer must notify the contracting or granting agency within 10 days.

Recordkeeping Requirements

Covered employers are required to publish a written policy statement that clearly covers all employees or just those employees who are associated with the federal contract or grant. Each covered employee must be given a copy of the policy statement, and it is a good idea, although it is not required, to have employees sign for receipt of that policy statement. The statement must contain a list of prohibited substances. At a minimum it must cite controlled substances.[11]

Some employers choose to include in the policy prohibition of alcohol and prescription drug misuse, although that is not a requirement. Subject employers must also establish a drug-free awareness training program to make employees aware of the dangers of drug abuse in the workplace; the policy of maintaining a drug-free workplace; any available drug counseling, rehabilitation, and employee assistance programs; and the penalties that may be imposed on employees for drug abuse violations. Records should be maintained showing each employee who received the training and the date it occurred.

Drug-Free Workplace Act Enforcement

Federal contractors under the jurisdiction of the OFCCP will find that the agency requires proof of compliance when it conducts a general compliance evaluation of affirmative action plans. Any employee who fails a drug test must be referred to a treatment program or given appropriate disciplinary action. Care should be given to treating similar cases in the same way. It is fairly easy to be challenged under Title VII for unequal treatment based on one of the Title VII protected groups.

Each federal agency responsible for contracting or providing grants is also responsible for enforcing the Drug-Free Workplace Act requirements. These responsibilities are spelled out in the Federal Acquisition Regulation (FAR). Failing to maintain a drug-free workplace can result in the following[12]:

- Suspension of payments for contract or grant activities
- Suspension or cancellation of grant or contract
- Up to 5 years' prohibition for any further contracts or grants

For more information, see www.dol.gov/elaws/asp/drugfree/require.htm or perform an Internet search for the law by name.

The Equal Employment Opportunity Act (EEOA) (1972)

The EEOA amended the Civil Rights Act of 1964 by redefining some terms. It also required a new employment poster for all subject work locations explaining that "EEO is the Law."

For more information, see www.eeoc.gov/eeoc/history/35th/thelaw/eeo_1972.html or do an Internet search for the name of the law.

The Genetic Information Nondiscrimination Act (GINA) (2008)

In general terms, GINA prohibits employers from using genetic information to make employment decisions. This legislation was brought about by insurance companies using genetic information to determine who would likely have expensive diseases in the future. That information allowed decisions to exclude them from hiring or enrollment in medical insurance programs. With the implementation of this law, those considerations are no longer legal.

For more information, see www.eeoc.gov/laws/statutes/gina.cfm or perform an Internet search for the law by name.

Guidelines on Discrimination Because of Sex (1980)

The Equal Employment Opportunity Commission (EEOC) published these guidelines to help employers understand what constituted unwanted behavior and harassment. They were issued long before the U.S. Supreme Court considered the leading cases on sexual harassment. This is about the only thing at the time that employers were able to turn to for help in managing the problem of sexual harassment in the workplace.

The Lilly Ledbetter Fair Pay Act (2009)

This was the first piece of legislation signed by President Barack Obama after he was inaugurated the 44th president of the United States. It was passed in reaction to the U.S. Supreme Court decision in *Ledbetter v. Goodyear Tire & Rubber Co., Inc.*, 550 U.S. 618 (2007).

This law amends the Civil Rights Act of 1964 and states that the clock will begin running anew each time an illegal act of discrimination is experienced by an employee. In Lilly Ledbetter's situation, her pay was less than that for men doing the same job. The old law didn't permit her to succeed in her complaint of discrimination because she failed to file 20 years earlier on the first occasion of her receiving a paycheck for less than her male counterparts. Under the new law, the 180-day statute of limitations for filing an equal-pay lawsuit regarding pay discrimination resets with each new paycheck affected by that discriminatory action. For more information, see www.eeoc.gov/laws/statutes/epa_ledbetter.cfm or perform an Internet search for the law by name.

The Pregnancy Discrimination Act (1978)

This law modified (amended) the Civil Rights Act of 1964. It defined pregnancy as protected within the definition of "sex" for the purpose of coverage under the Civil Rights Act. It also specifically said that no employer shall illegally discriminate against an employee because of pregnancy. It defines pregnancy as a temporary disability and requires accommodation on the job if it is necessary. It guarantees the employee rights to return to work to the same or similar job with the same pay following her pregnancy disability. For more information, see www.eeoc.gov/laws/types/pregnancy.cfm or perform an Internet search for the law by name.

The Uniform Guidelines on Employee Selection Procedures (1978)

This set of regulations is often overlooked by employers and HR professionals alike. Details can be found in 41 C.F.R. 60-3. For covered employers with 15 or more people on the payroll, this set of requirements is essential in preventing claims of discrimination.

There are two types of illegal employment discrimination: adverse or disparate treatment and adverse or disparate impact. The latter almost always results from seemingly neutral policies having a statistically adverse impact on a specific group of people. To avoid illegal discrimination, the guidelines require that all steps in a hiring decision be validated for the job being filled. Validity of a selection device can be determined through a validity study or by applying a job analysis to demonstrate the specific relationship between the selection device and the job requirements. Selection devices include things such as a written test, an oral test, an interview, a requirement to write something for consideration, and a physical ability test.

Employers can get into trouble when they use selection tools that have not been validated for their specific applications. For example, buying a clerical test battery of written tests and using it to make selection decisions for administrative assistants as well as general office clerks may not be supportable. Only a validity analysis will tell for sure. What specific validation studies have been done for the test battery by the publisher? Any publisher should be able to provide you with a copy of the validation study showing how the test is supposed to be used and the specific skills, knowledge, or abilities that are analyzed when using it. If you can't prove the test measures things required by your job content, don't use the test. According to the Uniform Guidelines, "While publishers of selection procedures have a professional obligation to provide evidence of validity which meets generally accepted professional standards, users are cautioned that they are responsible for compliance with these guidelines."[13] That means the employer, not the test publisher, is liable for the results. For more information, see www.eeoc.gov/policy/docs/factemployment_procedures.html or perform an Internet search for the law by name.

For TWENTY or More Employees

The next threshold for employers occurs when they reach a headcount of 20 employees. At that point another four major federal laws begin their influence on the organization.

The Age Discrimination in Employment Act (ADEA) (1967), as Amended in 1978, 1986

When this law was first passed, it specified the protected age range of 40 to 70. Anyone younger than 40 or older than 70 was not covered for age discrimination in the workplace. Amendments were made a few years later that removed the upper limit. Today, the law bans employment discrimination based on age if the employee is 40 years old or older. Remedies under this law are the same as under the Civil Rights Act. They include reinstatement, back pay, front pay, and payment for benefits in arrears. Some exceptions to the "unlimited" upper age exist. One example is the rule that airline pilots may not fly commercial airplanes after the age of 65.[14] For more information, see www.eeoc.gov/laws/statutes/adea.cfm or perform an Internet search for the law by name.

The American Recovery and Reinvestment Act (ARRA) (2009)

The thrust of this legislation was to create government infrastructure projects such as highways, buildings, dams, and such. It was an attempt to find ways to re-employ many of the workers who had become unemployed since the great recession began in 2007. There was a provision that provided partial payment of COBRA (see the Consolidated Omnibus Budget Reconciliation Act, covered next) premiums for people who still had not found permanent job placement. It applied to individuals who experienced involuntary terminations prior to May 31, 2010.

ARRA also modified HIPAA privacy rules. It applies HIPAA's security and privacy requirements to business associates. Business associates are defined under ARRA as individuals or organizations that transmit protected medical data, store that data, process that data, or in any other way have contact with that private medical information. All parties are responsible for proper handling and compliance with the HIPAA rules. For more information, see www.irs.gov/uac/The-American-Recovery-and-Reinvestment-Act-of-2009-Information-Center or perform an Internet search for the law by name.

The Consolidated Omnibus Budget Reconciliation Act (COBRA) (1986)

This law requires employers with group health insurance programs to offer terminating employees the opportunity to continue their health plan coverage after they are no longer on the payroll or no longer qualify for benefits coverage because of a change in employment status, i.e., reduction in hours. The cost must be at group rates, and the employer can add a small administrative service charge. It turns out that many employers turn these programs over to vendors who administer the COBRA benefits for former employees. They send out billing statements and provide collection services. Two percent is the maximum administrative overhead fee that can be added. The total cost of COBRA premiums and administrative fees is paid by employees participating in COBRA. The duration of coverage is dependent on some variables, so it may be different from one person to another. For more information, see www.dol.gov/dol/topic/health-plans/cobra.htm or perform an Internet search for the law by name.

The Older Workers Benefit Protection Act (OWBPA) (1990)

In the 1980s, it was common for employers, particularly large employers, to implement staff reduction programs as a means of addressing expenses. Often those programs were targeted at more senior workers because, generally speaking, their compensation was greater than that of new employees. Reducing one senior worker could save more money than the reduction of a more recently hired worker. Congress took action to prevent such treatment based on age when it passed this law.

The key purposes of the Older Workers Benefit Protection Act (OWBPA) are to prohibit an employer from the following:

- Using an employee's age as the basis for discrimination in benefits
- Targeting older workers during staff reductions or downsizing
- Requiring older workers to waive their rights without the opportunity for review with their legal advisor

For more information, see www.eeoc.gov/eeoc/history/35th/thelaw/owbpa.html or perform an Internet search for the law by name.

For FIFTY to ONE HUNDRED or More Employees

Once the employee headcount reaches these higher levels, additional legal obligations become effective for employers. Some of them apply only if the employer is subject to affirmative action requirements as a federal contractor.

Executive Order 11246: Affirmative Action (1965)

This is the presidential order that created what we now know as employment-based affirmative action. In 1965, President Lyndon B. Johnson was past the days when he approved the Civil Rights Act, and he was in the process of examining how it was being implemented around the country by employers. He concluded that the law was pretty much being ignored. He needed something to stimulate implementation of the employment provisions in the Civil Rights Act, Title VII. His staff suggested they require affirmative action programs from federal contractors. A new program was born. President Johnson said that if a company wanted to receive revenue by contracting with the federal government, it would have to implement equal employment opportunity and establish outreach programs for minorities and women. At the time, minorities and women were being excluded from candidate selection pools. If they couldn't get into the selection pools, there was no way for them to be selected.

So, affirmative action programs were created. Outreach and recruiting were the main parts of these programs. Analysis of the incumbent workforce, the available pool of qualified job candidates, and the training of managers involved in the employment selection process all contributed to a slow movement toward full equality for minorities and women.

The Office of Federal Contract Compliance Programs (OFCCP) is the law enforcement agency that currently has responsibility for enforcing the executive order along with other laws. Federal contractors must meet several conditions in return for the contracting privilege. One is the requirement to abide by a set of rules known as the Federal Acquisition Regulation (FAR). In addition, there is affirmative action for the disabled and veterans. Any business that doesn't want to abide by these requirements can make the business decision to abandon federal revenues and contracts. If you want the contracts, you also have to agree to the affirmative action requirements.[15] For more information, see www.dol.gov/ofccp/regs/statutes/eo11246.htm or perform an Internet search for the executive order by name.

The Family and Medical Leave Act (FMLA) (1993), Expanded 2008, 2010

In general, the Family and Medical Leave Act sets in place new benefits for some employees in the country. If their employer has 50 or more people on the payroll, then they are required to permit FMLA leave of absence for their workers. FMLA provides for leaves lasting up to 12 weeks in a 12-month period, and it is unpaid unless the employer has a policy to pay for the leave time. The 12-month period begins on the first day of leave. A new leave availability will occur 12 months from the date the first leave began. During the leave, it is an obligation of the employer to continue paying any benefit plan premiums that the employer would have paid if the employee had remained on the job. If there is a portion of the premium for health insurance that is normally paid by the employee, that obligation for co-payment continues during the employee's leave time. The 12 weeks leave may be taken in increments of 1 day or less.

To qualify, employees must have more than 1 year of service. The leave is authorized to cover childbirth or adoption; to care for a seriously ill child, spouse, or parent; or in case of the employee's own serious illness. The employee is guaranteed return to work on the same job, at the same pay, under the same conditions as prior to the leave of absence.

There are provisions for "Military Caregiver Leave" lasting up to 26 weeks of unpaid leave of absence for employees with family members needing care due to a military duty–related injury or illness. The 26-week limit renews every 12 months. The law provides for "National Guard and Military Reserve Family Leave." Employees who are family members of National Guard or Military Reservists who are called to active duty may take FMLA leave to assist with preparing financial and legal arrangements and other family issues associated with rapid deployment or post-deployment activities. An employer may agree to any nonlisted condition as a qualifier for FMLA leave as well.

FMLA provides for "Light Duty Assignments." It clarifies that "light duty" work does not count against an employee's FMLA leave entitlement. It also provides that an employee's right to job restoration is held in abeyance during the light duty period. An employee voluntarily doing light duty work is not on FMLA leave.

There is an employment poster requirement. The notice must be posted at each work location where employees can see it without trouble. A "Medical Certification Process" is part of the new provisions. DOL regulations have specified who may contact the employee's medical advisor for information, written or otherwise, and specifically prohibits the employee's supervisor from making contact with the employee's medical advisor.

Specific prohibitions are made against illegal discrimination for an employee taking advantage of the benefits offered under this law. These provisions are enforced by the EEOC. For more information, see www.dol.gov/whd/fmla/ or perform an Internet search for the law by name.

The Mental Health Parity Act (MHPA) (1996)

This legislation requires health insurance issuers and group health plans to adopt the same annual and lifetime dollar limits for mental health benefits as for other medical benefits. For more information, see www.dol.gov/ebsa/mentalhealthparity/ or perform an Internet search for the law by name.

The Mental Health Parity and Addiction Equity Act (MHPAEA) (2008)

This is an amendment of the Mental Health Parity Act of 1996. It requires that plans that offer both medical/surgical benefits and mental health and/or substance abuse treatment benefits provide parity between both types of benefits. All financial requirements (for example, deductibles, copayments, coinsurance, out-of-pocket expenses, and annual limits) and treatment requirements (for example, frequency of treatment, number of visits, and days of coverage) must be the same for treatment of both mental and physical medical problems. For more information, see www.dol.gov/ebsa/newsroom/fsmhpaea .html or perform an Internet search for the law by name.

The National Defense Authorization Act (2008)

This is the origin of benefit provisions under FMLA for leaves of absence due to military reasons. Qualifying events include notice of deployment, return from deployment, and treatment for an injury sustained while on deployment. The provision is for up to 26 weeks, which can be taken in increments of a day or less if, for example, treatment is required for a service-related injury. For more information, see www.dol.gov/whd/fmla/ NDAA_fmla.htm or perform an Internet search for the law by name.

The Patient Protection and Affordable Care Act (PPACA) (2010)

Signed into law by President Barack Obama on March 23, 2010, this law is commonly referred to as the Affordable Care Act. It has created health insurance trading centers in each state where employees and those who are unemployed can shop for health insurance coverage. These trading centers are the American Health Benefit Exchanges and Small Business Health Options Program (SHOP). Individuals and business owners of organizations with fewer than 100 workers can purchase insurance through these exchanges.

It applies to all employers with 50 or more full-time workers on the payroll. Employers with fewer than 50 full-time workers are exempt from coverage under the law. Effective January 1, 2014, covered employers must either provide minimum health insurance coverage to their full-time employees or face a fine of $2,000 per employee, excluding the first 30 from the assessment. Employers with fewer than 25 employees will receive a tax credit if they provide health insurance to their workers. In 2014, that credit will amount to 50 percent of the employer's contribution to the employee's healthcare program, if the employer pays at least that amount for insurance costs. A full credit is available for employers with fewer than 10 workers earning an average annual wage of less than $25,000. The credit will last for 2 years. For more information, see www.dol .gov/ebsa/healthreform/ or perform an Internet search for the law by name.

Executive Order 13706: Paid Sick Leave for Federal Contractors (2015)

Federal contractors are directed to provide up to 56 hours of paid sick leave annually. The leave is accrued at the rate of an hour for every 30 hours worked. It may be carried over from year to year. For more information, see https://www.gpo.gov/fdsys/pkg/FR-2015-09-10/pdf/2015-22998.pdf or perform an Internet search for the executive order by number.

For ONE HUNDRED or More Employees

The final major threshold for employers is reached when the payroll reaches 100 employees. At that time employers become subject to the WARN Act and are required to submit annual reports to the government summarizing their race and sex demographics.

The Worker Adjustment and Retraining Notification (WARN) Act (1988)

This was the first attempt by Congress to involve local communities early in the private sector's downsizing process. It also prevented employers from just shutting the door and walking away without any worker benefits. It applies to all employers with 100 or more full-time workers at a single facility. The law specifies a qualifying employer to be one that has 100 or more employees who in the aggregate work at least 4,000 hours per week (exclusive of hours of overtime).

Definitions

The term *plant closing* refers to the permanent or temporary shutdown of a single site of employment, or one or more facilities or operating units within a single site of employment, if the shutdown results in an employment loss at the single site of employment during any 30-day period for 50 or more employees excluding any part-time employees.

The term *mass layoff* refers to a reduction in force that is not the result of a plant closing and results in an employment loss at the single site of employment during any 30-day period for at least 500 employees to be laid off from a workforce of 500 or more *or* when at least 33 percent of the workforce (excluding any part-time employees) are going to be removed from the payroll in a layoff where there are a total of 50 to 499 workers before the layoff.

Required Actions

The law requires 60 days' advance notice to employees of plant closing or mass layoffs. Any employment loss of 50 or more people, excluding part-time workers, is considered a trigger event to activate the requirements. Notification of public officials in the surrounding community in addition to notification of employees are requirements.

The local community leaders must be informed and invited to participate in the process of finding new jobs for laid-off workers. There is a provision that says an employer can pay 60 days' separation allowance if it gives no notice to workers who will be terminated.

Exemptions to Notice Requirement

Notice is not required, regardless of the size of layoff, if the layoff, downsizing, or terminations result from the completion of a contract or project that employees understood would constitute their term of employment. It is not uncommon for workers to be hired in a "term" classification that designates them as employees for the life of a project. If they understand that from the beginning of their employment, their termination would not trigger the WARN Act.

WARN is not triggered in the following cases:

- In the event of strikes or lockouts that are not intended to evade the requirements of this law.
- In the event the layoff will be for less than 6 months.
- If state and local governments are downsizing. They are exempt from the notice requirement.
- In the event that fewer than 50 people will be laid off or terminated from a single site.
- If 50 to 499 workers lose their jobs and that number is less than 33 percent of the active workforce at the single site.

For more information, see www.dol.gov/compliance/laws/comp-warn.htm or perform an Internet search for the law by name.

For Federal Government Employees

The federal government is subject to some of the same laws as the private-sector employers. Yet, there are additional obligations that government employers have. Some of those obligations stem from the United States Constitution. Others come from the following laws.

The Civil Service Reform Act (1978)

This legislation eliminated the U.S. Civil Service Commission and created three new agencies to take its place:

- **The Office of Personnel Management (OPM)** This is the executive branch's human resource department. It handles all HR issues for agencies reporting to the U.S. president.
- **The Merit Systems Protection Board (MSPB)** This part of the law prohibits consideration of marital status, political activity, or political affiliation in dealing with federal civilian employees. It also created the Office of Special Counsel, which accepts employee complaints and investigates and resolves them.

- **The Federal Labor Relations Authority (FLRA)**   This is the agency that enforces federal civilian employee rights to form unions and bargain with their agencies. It establishes standards of behavior for union officers, and these standards are enforced by the Office of Labor-Management Standards in the U.S. Department of Labor.

For more information, see www.eeoc.gov/eeoc/history/35th/thelaw/civil_service_reform-1978.html or perform an Internet search for the law by name.

The Congressional Accountability Act (1995)

Until this law was implemented, the legislative branch of the government was exempt from nearly all employment-related requirements that applied to other federal agencies and private employers. This law requires Congress and its affiliated agencies to abide by 12 specific laws that already applied to other employers, in and out of government.

- Americans with Disabilities Act of 1990
- Age Discrimination in Employment Act of 1967
- Employee Polygraph Protection Act of 1988
- Federal Service Labor-Management Relations Statute
- Rehabilitation Act of 1973
- Civil Rights Act of 1964 (Title VII)
- Fair Labor Standards Act of 1938
- Family and Medical Leave Act of 1993
- Occupational Safety and Health Act of 1970
- Veterans Employment Opportunities Act of 1998
- Worker Adjustment and Retraining Notification Act of 1989
- Occupational Safety and Health Act of 1970

For more information, see www.compliance.gov/publications/caa-overview/ or perform an Internet search for the law by name.

The False Claims Act (1863)

During the Civil War, people were selling defective food and arms to the Union military. This law, sometimes referred to as the Lincoln Law, prohibits such dishonest transactions. It prohibits making and using false records to get those claims paid. It also prohibits selling the government goods that are known to be defective. For HR professionals today, it is wise to train all employees about the need to avoid creating records that are inaccurate or, even worse, fictitious. Doing things that are illegal, just because the boss says you should, will still be illegal. Employees need to understand that concept.

For more information, see www.justice.gov/civil/docs_forms/C-FRAUDS_FCA_Primer.pdf or perform an Internet search for the law by name.

The Homeland Security Act (2002)

This cabinet-level organization (Department of Homeland Security) was created by Congress and President George W. Bush to consolidate security efforts related to protecting U.S. geography. Immigration and Customs Enforcement (ICE) is part of this department. The E-Verify system resides here. Used by federal contractors as part of their affirmative action obligations and other private employers on a voluntary basis, the system is intended to assist in rapid verification of Social Security numbers (SSNs) and confirm that the individual attached to the SSN has a valid right to work in this country. For more information, see https://www.dhs.gov/homeland-security-act-2002 or perform an Internet search for the law by name.

The Privacy Act (1974)

This law provides that governmental agencies must make known to the public their data collection and storage activities and must provide copies of pertinent records to the individual citizen when requested—with some specific exemptions. Those exemptions include law enforcement, congressional investigations, census use, "archival purposes," and other administrative purposes. In all, there are 12 statutory exemptions from disclosure requirements. If employees are concerned about employers using their Social Security numbers in records sent to the government, this act ensures privacy. Although such private information is required by the government, the government is prohibited from releasing it to third parties without proper authorization or court order. For more information, see www.justice.gov/opcl/privstat.htm or perform an Internet search for the law by name.

The USA PATRIOT Act (2001)

The Uniting and Strengthening America by Providing Appropriate Tools Required to Intercept and Obstruct Terrorism (USA PATRIOT) Act was passed immediately following the September 11, 2001, terrorist attacks in New York City and at the Pentagon in Virginia. It gives the government authority to intercept wire, oral, and electronic communications relating to terrorism, computer fraud, and abuse offenses. It also provides the authorization for collecting agencies to share the information they collect in the interest of law enforcement. This law can have an impact on private-sector employers in the communications industry. It can also have an impact on any employer when the government asks for support to identify and track "lone wolves" suspected of terrorism without being affiliated with known terrorist organizations. HR professionals may find themselves involved in handling the collection and release of personal, confidential information about one or more employees. When legal documents such as subpoenas and court orders are involved, it is always a good idea to have the organization's attorney review them before taking any other action. For more information, see www.justice.gov/archive/ll/highlights.htm or perform an Internet search for the law by name.

Whistle-Blower Laws

Many conditions will activate protection for federal employees when they "blow the whistle" on their federal employer. A comprehensive report was prepared by the U.S. Merit Systems Protection Board in 2010 that explains these protections. For more information, see http://www.mspb.gov/netsearch/viewdocs.aspx?docnumber=557972&version=559604 or do an Internet search for the report.

Employment Visas for Foreign Nationals

Under some circumstances, it is possible for people from other countries to come work in the United States. There are several classifications of workers that can be used depending on the type of work to be done and the level of responsibilities.

E Nonimmigrant Visas

There are two types of E Nonimmigrant Visas, E-1 Treaty Traders and E-2 Treaty Investors. For more information on E Nonimmigrant Visas, see www.uscis.gov/portal/site/uscis.

E-1 Treaty Traders

The individual must be a citizen of the treaty country; there must be substantial trade; the trade must be principally with the treaty country; the individual must have executive, supervisory, or essential skills; and the individual must intend to depart the United States when the trading is completed.

E-2 Treaty Investors

The individual must be a citizen of the treaty country and be invested personally in the enterprise. The business must be a bona fide enterprise and not marginal, and the investment must be substantial. E-2 employees must have executive, supervisory, or essential skills, and E-2 investors must direct and develop the enterprise. The E-2 investor must depart the United States when the investment is concluded.

H Visas

These are visas available to employers and employees for specialized talent or educational requirements.

H1-B Special Occupations and Fashion Models

These visas require a bachelor's or higher degree or its equivalent. The job must be so complex that it can be performed only by a person with the degree. The employer normally requires a degree or its equivalent for this job. Fashion models also fall into this category.

H1-C Registered Nurse Working in a Health Professional Shortage Area

This requires a full and unrestricted nursing license in the country where your nursing education was obtained. Or, you must have received your nursing education and license in the United States. It also requires that you have appropriate authorization from the U.S. State Board of Nursing to practice within the United States. H1-C requires that you have passed the examination given by the Commission on Graduates for Foreign Nursing Schools (CGFNS) or have a full and unrestricted license to practice as a registered nurse in the state where you will work.

H-2A Temporary Agricultural Workers

The employer must be able to demonstrate that there are not sufficient U.S. workers who are able, willing, qualified, and available to do the temporary seasonal work. The employer must also show that the employment of H-2A workers will not adversely affect the wages and working conditions of similarly employed U.S. workers.

H-2B Temporary NonAgricultural Workers

The employer must show that there are not enough U.S. workers who are able, willing, qualified, and available to do the temporary work and that the employment of H-2B workers will not adversely affect the wages and working conditions of similarly employed U.S. workers. The employer must also show that the need for the prospective worker's services is temporary, regardless of whether the underlying job can be described as temporary.

H-3 Nonimmigrant Trainee

To qualify, employees must be trainees receiving training in any field of endeavor, other than graduate medical education, that is not available in their home country. Or, they must be a Special Education Exchange Visitor who will participate in a special education training program focused on the education of children with physical, mental, or emotional disabilities.

L-1 Intracompany Transferee

This allows a qualifying organization to move an employee from another qualifying country into the United States for a temporary assignment either that is managerial in nature or that requires specialized knowledge.

L1-A Managers and Executives

These are intracompany transferees coming to the United States to work in a managerial or executive capacity. The maximum stay in the United States allowed under this visa is 7 years.

Specialized Knowledge

This is someone with specialized knowledge of the employer's product, service, research, equipment, techniques, management, or other interests and its application in international markets, or an advanced level of knowledge or expertise in the organization's processes and procedures. An L1-B visa holder may stay in the United States for only 5 years.

O-1 Alien of Extraordinary Ability in Arts, Science, Education, Business, Athletics

These people have a level of expertise indicating that they are among the small percentage who have risen to the top of their field of endeavor. Alternatively, they represent extraordinary achievement in motion-picture and television productions, or they have extraordinary ability and distinction in the arts.

P Visa Categories

There are seven variations of athletics-based or art-based visas:

- P1-A Individual Athletes or Athletic Teams
- P1-B Entertainment Groups
- P1-S Essential Support needed for P1-A or P1-B
- P2 Artist or Entertainer Under a Reciprocal Exchange Program
- P2-S Essential Support for P2
- P3 Artist or Entertainer Under a Culturally Unique Program
- P3-S Essential Support for P3

EB Employment-Based Visas

There are five levels of employment-based visas. They are prioritized so that once the first-level immigrant applicants are processed, the next level of priority will be considered. That will continue until the maximum allotment of visas is reached. In recent years, about 140,000 employment-based visas were permitted each year.

EB-1 Alien of Extraordinary Ability

The employer must demonstrate that the alien has extraordinary ability in the sciences, arts, education, business, or athletics, which has been demonstrated by sustained national or international acclaim and whose achievements have been recognized in the field through extensive documentation. It must also be shown that the work to be done in the United States will continue in the individual's area of extraordinary ability. It shall also be shown how the alien's entry into this country will benefit the United States; 28.6 percent of the total employment-based visas are allocated to this category.

EB-2 Alien of Extraordinary Ability

This is a classification that applies to any job that requires advanced degrees and persons of exceptional ability; 28.6 percent of the employment-based visas are allocated to this category.

EB-3 Skilled Workers

This category applies to professionals and even unskilled workers who are sponsored by employers in the United States; 28.6 percent of the employment-based visas are allocated to this category.

EB-4 Certain Special Immigrants

Included here are some broadcasters, ministers of religion, employees or former employees of the United States government, Iraqi or Afghan interpreters and translators, and other similar workers; 7.1 percent of the employment-based visas are allocated to this category.

EB-5 Immigrant Investors

These are people who will create new commercial enterprises in the United States that will provide job creation; 7.1 percent of the employment-based visas are allocated to this category.

Chapter Review

While this chapter is not meant to be a comprehensive statement of each law, studying and learning these laws will help you understand the basics as you perform your professional human resource responsibilities. As you read through the other chapters in this book, it's important to remember that one or more of these laws will be the underlying basis for the HR Certification Institute's (HRCI's) subject matter. Additionally, while using this chapter as a reference guide in your day-to-day application as an HR professional, please also consult the statutes and regulations themselves via the URLs we have provided or perform an Internet search for the topic by name. A thorough understanding of the various laws and regulations that impact the employment relationship will enhance your ability to protect your organization in matters involving employment and employee relations.

Questions

The following are all questions about U.S. laws and regulations concerning employee management.

1. John, a new employee, has just arrived at the orientation program where everyone completes their payroll forms and signs up for healthcare benefits. He brings his W-4 form to you and says he isn't subject to payroll withholding because he pays his taxes directly each quarter. What is your response?

   A. "That's okay. We won't process a W-4 form for you. We will give you a Form 1099."

   B. "I'll check with the accounting department to find out whether you can do that."

   C. "Unfortunately, all employees are subject to payroll tax withholding."

   D. "If you can show me a W-10 form you have submitted to the IRS, we can block your paycheck withholding."

2. The Wagner-Peyser Act protects employees who are:

   A. Unemployed

   B. Injured on the job

   C. Unable to work because of pregnancy

   D. Have two or more jobs

3. Mary has had a bad encounter with her supervisor, Henry. That evening after getting home from work, she pulls out her computer and sends a blistering blog post to her Facebook page. She names her company and her supervisor. She calls him unfair, pigheaded, and without principles. What can the company do about her posting?

   A. The company can demand that she remove the offensive post. If she doesn't, the company can file legal action against her.

   B. The company can demand that Facebook remove the offensive post. If it doesn't, the company can file legal action against Facebook.

   C. The company is protected against such employee comments by the Fair and Decent Treatment Act and can take disciplinary action against Mary.

   D. The company is prohibited from any action against Mary because she is engaging in a protected concerted activity.

4. Pete is sensitive about the security of his personal identity information since his credit card has been stolen twice in the past year. He is trying to clear up his credit rating because of the problems with the stolen cards. Now, he has approached the HR manager at his organization and requested that his Social

Security number be removed from all of the company records. He thinks that a mistake could cause him more grief if the Social Security number were to be obtained by thieves. As the HR professional, what should you do?

    A. The company can and should delete the Social Security number from its records to protect Pete.

    B. There is a need for the company to keep the Social Security number for tax reporting.

    C. There is a need for the company to keep the Social Security number for census reporting.

    D. The company has no need for the Social Security number but should keep it regardless.

5. Pat is talking with her colleagues about illegal discrimination at work. Someone mentions that the company is going to be sending out a request for updated race and sex information. Pat says that isn't legal. The company isn't supposed to track any of that information.

    A. Pat has not understood the FLSA requirements that employers keep race and sex data on employees.

    B. The EEOC has issued guidelines that agree with Pat's belief that it is illegal to maintain that information in company records.

    C. Only federal contractors are required to maintain the race and sex identification for employees.

    D. It is only the public-sector employees who are exempt from providing their race and sex identification to employers.

6. The Tractor and Belt Company (TBC) handles conveyor belt installations for many small firms. Each of the customer projects begins on a day that is most convenient for the customer. Sometimes, that's Monday; sometimes it's Thursday or some other day. The HR manager says that the company will adjust its workweek to begin when the customer's project starts. That way, each installation team has a separate workweek, and those workweeks can shift several times a month. What is your advice about this strategy?

    A. The HR manager is simply taking advantage of the FLSA's provisions for flexible workweeks that support small business. No change is required.

    B. Once the workweek has been designated to begin on a certain day of the week, it should not be changed by the HR manager.

    C. It depends on state laws and regulations whether the workweek begins on any specific day of the week.

    D. The FLSA says a workweek should always begin on Sunday.

7. Sandy is 15 years old and a sophomore at Central High School. She gets a job at the local hamburger drive-in. Her boss says he needs her to work the following schedule during the Spring Break week: 4 hours at lunch time every day, 9 hours on Saturday, and 6 hours on Sunday. Is that schedule acceptable for Sandy given that she has a work permit from the school?

    A. Because it is a school vacation week, there are no restrictions on the hours that Sandy can work.

    B. Only state laws impact what hours Sandy can work because it happens during a vacation week.

    C. Federal law says Sandy cannot work more than 8 hours a day when it is a vacation week.

    D. Because Sandy won't be working more than 40 hours for the week, there is no problem.

8. Gary is a junior at Southpark High School. He is 17 years old. The school needs some help in its warehouse during the summer, and Gary needs a job so he can save money for college. His boss is the facilities manager. Gary is assigned to work 9 hours every day during the week because one of the other employees is on disability leave. And because the other employee was the forklift driver, Gary has been given training in how to drive that equipment around the warehouse and loading dock. He likes that duty because he has been driving a car for only a few months. The forklift is cool. Is there any difficulty with the facilities manager's requirements of Gary?

    A. Everything the facilities manager has required Gary to do is permissible under federal laws.

    B. Since there is no restriction to the number of hours Gary can work, everything should be okay.

    C. Whatever the facilities manager wants Gary to do is okay because it's only a summer job.

    D. Even though Gary can work unlimited hours, he cannot be assigned to drive the forklift.

9. Hank puts in the following hours at work: Sunday, 0; Monday, 8; Tuesday, 8; Wednesday, 9; Thursday, 8; Friday, 8; Saturday, 7. His boss says he will give Hank compensating time off for every hour of overtime Hank works. How many compensating hours off should Hank receive for this work time according to federal requirements?

    A. One day of compensating time off.

    B. 1.5 days of compensating time off.

    C. 7 hours of compensating time off.

    D. Compensating time off is not permitted under the FLSA.

10. The Tractor and Belt Company (TBC) doesn't have an HR manager. HR is handled by the payroll clerk. When a new employee is assigned to the production department as an assembler, the payroll clerk raises a question. Should the new person be paid the same as all the other employees, all women, in the department, or is it okay to pay her more because she made more at her former job?

    A. There are no restrictions on the amount a new employee can be paid. It is market driven.

    B. The Fair and Decent Treatment Act requires all people doing the same work be paid the same amount.

    C. There is no restriction on the amount paid because all the incumbents are women.

    D. Once a valid market survey has been done, it can be used to determine starting pay for new people.

11. Finding a life insurance company to provide benefits to its workforce has been difficult for Joan, the HR manager. She decides to recommend that her company offer a self-insured plan. What controls might Joan have to consider in her planning?

    A. There are no federal restrictions on a company providing its own life insurance plan to employees.

    B. The Employee Retirement Income Security Act regulates welfare benefit plans, including life insurance.

    C. The Life Insurance Benefit Plans Act has control over what Joan is able to do with her idea.

    D. Only state laws will have an influence on Joan's development of a self-insured benefit plan.

12. Simone has just been hired and is asked to complete a Form I-9. She offers her driver's license as proof of her identity. What else is required for her to complete the document?

    A. She may offer any document authorized on the Form I-9 instructions as proof of her authorization to work in this country.

    B. She must have a Social Security number to submit on the form.

    C. Simone has a U.S. passport but is told that she can't use it for her Form I-9.

    D. As long as Simone offers to get a Social Security number in the next 30 days, she can submit her Form I-9.

13. Steve is the HR director for a crane operations company. He just got a phone call from one of his field supervisors with tragic news. One of their units has collapsed, and their operator is in the hospital with serious injuries. What should Steve do with that information?

   A. Steve should immediately call the hospital to be sure all the insurance information is on file for their employee.

   B. He should notify the Occupational Safety and Health Administration about the accident and the injuries.

   C. He should notify the Crane Safety Institute of America to be sure they are able to add this accident to its database.

   D. Steve should call the crane operator's spouse to let her know about the tragedy.

14. Every year Donna has to attend training on the use of the company vehicles she drives. She thinks this is a silly waste of time. Donna knows how to drive, and she knows the company vehicles. Why should she attend training every year?

   A. There is no federal requirement for Donna to take yearly training.

   B. OSHA requires training be done only once for vehicle operation.

   C. Only state safety provisions govern how frequently training must be done in Donna's situation.

   D. Safety programs must be developed that provide for refresher training on all equipment operating procedures.

15. Jerry just arrived at work and found a sink hole in the parking lot. He is early enough that other people have not yet begun arriving for work. Because the hole is about 10 feet across at the moment, what should Jerry be doing about the problem?

   A. If Jerry is a management employee, he should take charge of the situation and begin the process of alerting others to the danger posed by the sink hole.

   B. If Jerry is a nonmanagement employee, he should give his boss a call and leave a voice mail message, if necessary, about the sink hole.

   C. If the sink hole poses an immediate danger of death or serious injury, Jerry should call 911 and report it. He should barricade the perimeter of the sink hole with tape or something else to prevent people from falling in.

   D. Jerry should first test the edges of the sink hole to see whether it could grow in size. Then he should barricade the perimeter of the sink hole so no one will fall in.

16. Theresa attended a seminar recently that pointed out the need to post a yearly summary of injury and illness cases. Her boss doesn't want to do that, saying he doesn't want to publicize the problems the organization has had. Theresa should tell him:

    A. Posting requirements call for display of the report in a prominent location if there are 10 or more people on the payroll.

    B. Posting requirements can be met by putting a report on the back of the closet door in the employee lounge.

    C. Posting requirements can be met by making the report available in a binder in the HR manager's office.

    D. Posting requirements are optional, but good employers are using the report as a "best practice" in safety programs.

17. An employer routinely works with hazardous chemicals, trucking them for delivery to various customer locations. After each load, the truck must be cleaned before being loaded with a different chemical. Cleaning has to be done by someone inside the tanker using special absorbent materials. What else should be considered?

    A. Personal protective equipment should be provided by the employer, including breathing apparatus and hazmat suits.

    B. Standard coveralls and boot covers should be provided for employees to use if they want.

    C. Workers should never be sent into a tanker truck for any reason.

    D. Breathing equipment is absolutely a requirement if someone will be in the tanker truck for longer than 30 minutes.

18. Shelly has worked for the same dentist for more than 10 years. In all that time, there has been no mention of any special requirements for handling syringes. She arranges the doctor's equipment trays every day and cleans them up after they have been used. She just tosses the used equipment into the autoclave or into the trash if it won't be used again. If you were advising Shelly about the practices used in her dental office, what would you say?

    A. Needles should be broken off before they are thrown into the trash can.

    B. Sharps should be triple wrapped in a stiff paper to protect from sticking someone handling the trash.

    C. Any possible harm can be prevented if used syringes are placed into an approved sharps container.

    D. Putting used syringes into any solid container that is wrapped in red paper is sufficient to meet requirements.

19. The price of gold is climbing, and folks at the Golden Nugget Mine are planning to reopen their operation. They know that safety is an important consideration. But what about federal regulations for gold mines? Are there such things?

   A. There are only OSHA regulations in general. All of those rules still apply.

   B. There are MSHA regulations to be considered, but because they are not in the coal mining business, the Golden Nugget Mine won't have to worry about them.

   C. MSHA rules apply to all mining operations in the United States. The Golden Nugget Mine will have to study those rules and get ready for inspections by the government.

   D. MSHA can tell the mine what to do, but it has no authority to conduct inspections because the Golden Nugget is not a coal mine.

20. Olivia suspects her payroll clerk of embezzlement. She has inspected the records for the past 3 months, and the pattern is clear. But to be sure it is the payroll clerk and not the accounts payable clerk, Olivia wants to confront her and demand she take a lie detector test.

   A. Good going, Olivia. You caught her. Sure enough, demanding that she take a lie detector test is a good way to confirm your suspicions.

   B. While lie detector tests can be used for some employees, accounting employees are exempt. You can't test her.

   C. Lie detector tests are not permitted for any use by any employer. You can't test her.

   D. Lie detector tests can be required only in limited circumstances, and this isn't one of them. You can't test her.

21. For the past 6 years, Sam's company has been a federal contractor working on equipment for the Department of Defense. The company has additional contract opportunities coming up, and Sam isn't sure if there will be an extra burden related to disabled workers because they are subject to both the Americans with Disabilities Act and the Rehabilitation Act.

   A. Sam should rest easy. The ADA and the Rehabilitation Act are identical in their content and requirements.

   B. Sam's company has already met its recruiting obligations and now only has to worry about meeting ADA requirements.

   C. Handling job accommodation requests is a requirement of the ADA but not the Rehabilitation Act. Things should be easier.

   D. Whatever Sam thinks, the ADA and Rehabilitation Act requirements have applied to his company for 6 years already. Adding more contracts won't change his current obligations.

22. Arthur has applied for a job with the AB Trucking Company. He is told he must take and pass a urine drug test. If he fails the test and any subsequent random drug test after he is hired, he will be dismissed from the company. Arthur reacts loudly and says, "That's an invasion of my privacy! I won't do it." What happens now?

A. Arthur can call his lawyer and have the drug test waived since he doesn't want to take it.

B. Arthur can discontinue his participation in the AB Transit Company's employment process.

C. Arthur can take the test now and still refuse to participate in random tests later.

D. Arthur can have his friend take the test for him.

23. Cynthia works for a large multistate manufacturing company and approaches her boss one morning and tells him that her husband has just received orders from the Coast Guard to report for deployment to the Middle East. They have a week to get everything ready for his departure. She wants to know if she can have excused time off during the coming week. If you were her boss, what would you tell her?

A. She can have the time off, but it will be logged as unpaid and charged as FMLA leave.

B. She can take the time off, but it will be unexcused because she didn't give more than a week's notice.

C. If she wants the time off, she will have to use her paid vacation time for the week.

D. Jennifer has already requested the week off for vacation, but only one person can be off at any one time or the unit won't be able to function. Cynthia's request is denied with regrets.

24. Robert works for a congressional representative and suffers a disabling injury in an automobile accident. Robert cannot work more than 3 hours per day according to his doctor. Weeks later, when he returns to work, he asks for a job accommodation and is told that it can't be done. When he presses the point, his supervisor says the reason is:

A. Congressional staff people aren't covered by the ADA, so they don't have to even discuss his request.

B. The request he has made would exempt him from several of his job's key responsibilities.

C. The request he has made would set a precedent that other representatives' offices would have to follow.

D. Because congressional staff members have to meet the public every day, they can't have people seeing disabled workers in the office. It doesn't look good.

25. Jimmy has been told he can get healthcare coverage from his company because of the new Affordable Care Act. His company employs only ten people, but Jimmy is excited that he will finally get some insurance. He hasn't been feeling very good lately.

    A. Jimmy might have to wait until he can arrange for insurance through one of the exchanges.

    B. Jimmy should get an enrollment form from his boss because all employees will be covered by the new requirement that employers provide healthcare coverage to workers.

    C. Jimmy is out of luck. The new law only covers employers with 50 or more people, and there is no way Jimmy will be getting health insurance under the new law.

    D. Jimmy's boss just ran out of forms, but he will get some more from HR and then have Jimmy sign up for his coverage.

Answers

1. **C.** If the new worker is classified as an employee, on the payroll, the IRS demands that income tax, Social Security tax, and Medicare tax be withheld. People are not allowed to opt out because they want to file their own tax payments each quarter.

2. **A.** The Wagner-Peyser Act of 1933 provides for federal unemployment insurance and sets guidelines for state unemployment insurance programs.

3. **D.** Mary is protected by the National Labor Relations Act (NLRA) of 1935. The National Labor Relations Board has taken the position that almost all postings on the Internet, whether complaining about supervisors or employers or making charges that employees are treated unfairly, are protected concerted activities under the act.

4. **B.** Both the FLSA and the IRS regulations require employers to obtain and report Social Security numbers from all employees. A Social Security number is required for completion of the Form I-9 to prove authorization to work in this country. The company may not remove it from its records, regardless of how concerned Pete may be.

5. **A.** Race and sex data is specifically required by the FLSA. For employers with 15 or more people on the payroll that are engaged in interstate commerce, EEOC regulations also require maintenance of those data records.

6. **B.** The FLSA requires employers to designate a day as the beginning of the workweek. To change that designation, there should be a significant business reason. Moving the workweek to begin based on projects is not acceptable. FLSA requires consistency because of the need to pay overtime for hours in excess of 40 in a workweek. Constantly moving a workweek could deprive employees of earned overtime.

7. **C.** The FLSA prohibits people aged 14 and 15 from working more than 8 hours in a day even when school is not in session.

8. **D.** Driving a "power-driven hoisting apparatus" is one of the 17 most dangerous jobs that may not be performed by workers younger than 18. At Gary's age, the FLSA has no restriction on the hours he may work in a week.

9. **B.** The FLSA requires all hours of work in excess of 40 in a week be paid overtime at the rate of 1.5 times the normal hourly pay rate. Compensating time off, in lieu of overtime pay, must be given at the rate of 1.5 hours for every overtime hour. So, a day of overtime (8 hours) should be compensated for with 1.5 days of compensating time off.

10. **C.** The Equal Pay Act requires men and women doing the same work to be paid the same rate. If there are no men in the job, only women, there is no Equal Pay Act issue. If all the incumbents are women, there is no employment discrimination based on sex because there is only one sex represented. So, with those conditions, there is no barrier to paying the new employee more based on her previous job's compensation.

11. **B.** ERISA specifically regulates welfare benefit plans such as health insurance and life insurance. That is in addition to regulation of pension and retirement plans offered by employers. It makes no difference who underwrites the life insurance—the employer or a vendor. ERISA will still provide requirements.

12. **A.** The deadline for completing a Form I-9 is 3 days after hire. Any documents listed on the form are acceptable. The employer may not designate certain documents as requirements. A Social Security number is one way to demonstrate authorization to work in this country. A valid U.S. passport is also a way to demonstrate both identity and work authorization.

13. **B.** The company has 8 hours after the accident to file its report of serious injury with OSHA. We don't know how long ago the accident happened, but it was long enough that the operator is now in the hospital. Steve should gather all the information needed for the report and get it called in to the OSHA office.

14. **D.** Injury and Illness Prevention Programs are required by OSHA. Part of the identification and remediation of workplace hazards is employee training. Even if employees have been trained on equipment operation, periodic refresher programs can help overcome bad habits that might have developed. Refresher programs conducted on a yearly basis represent a reasonable interval for Donna's situation.

15. **C.** It doesn't matter if Jerry is a manager or not. All employees should be trained to react to imminent dangers by taking immediate action to prevent anyone from serious injury. And walking up to the edge to see if it is going to collapse is just nuts.

16. **A.** If she must, Theresa should show her boss the requirement in OSHA regulations. A prominent display location excludes places such as the back of a closet door or inside a binder somewhere in the manager's office.

17. **A.** Working inside an enclosed space with dangerous fumes calls for hazmat equipment and adequate breathing equipment. OSHA regulations specify the personal protective equipment (PPE) necessary in this and other working conditions.

18. **C.** The Needlestick Safety and Prevention Act requires all sharps be disposed of in approved sharps containers. It also requires posting of warnings and information about blood-borne pathogens.

19. **C.** The Mine Safety and Health Administration has jurisdiction over all mining operations, not just coal mines. It handles safety complaints and conducts inspections of both above-ground and underground mining operations. All mine operators are required to conduct their internal safety inspections and maintain records of those inspections.

20. **D.** Except for law enforcement, security officers, and people who handle controlled substances, lie detectors are no longer permitted in the workplace. They were commonly used prior to 1988's Employee Polygraph Protection Act.

21. **D.** Sam's company will not incur any additional obligations for disabled workers if they seek additional government contracts. They have been obligated under both laws for 6 years.

22. **B.** Arthur has to decide whether he wants to continue seeking employment with the AB Transit Company. If so, he must participate in their drug testing program. If he wants to avoid testing, he must drop out of the job application process and seek employment elsewhere.

23. **A.** Under the FMLA, Cynthia is entitled to unpaid leave of absence as a spouse of a covered military service worker. It will be logged as unpaid time off, unless she wants to use some of her accrued paid time off. It will also be logged in her record as FMLA leave.

24. **B.** Even the congressional offices are subject to the ADA's requirement to consider and discuss requests for job accommodation. Job accommodations must be made to make it easier for an employee to perform one of the job's essential functions. If he can't do that, even with an accommodation, he is not eligible for assignment to that job. If there is no other job available, the employer can't return him to work until his status changes.

25. **A.** Employers are required to provide health insurance coverage, or pay a penalty in lieu of that insurance, only if they have 50 or more full-time workers. With only 10 employees, Jimmy's employer is not obligated to provide health insurance coverage. Jimmy may purchase it for himself through one of the exchanges set up for that purpose.

Endnotes

1. "Instructions for Employment Eligibility Verification," U.S. Department of Homeland Security, U.S. Citizenship and Immigration Services, accessed June 20, 2016, www.uscis.gov/files/form/i-9.pdf

2. "Federal Mine Safety & Health Act of 1977, Public Law 91-173, as amended by Public Law 95-164," U.S. Department of Labor, Mine Safety and Health Administration, accessed June 20, 2016, www.msha.gov/regs/act/acttc.htm

3. "OSH Act, OSHA Standards, Inspections, Citations and Penalties," U.S. Department of Labor, Occupational Safety and Health Administration, accessed June 20, 2016, www.osha.gov and search for *Inspections, Citations, and Proposed Penalties*

4. Ibid

5. *Lawson v. FMR LLC,* U.S. No. 12-3, retrieved from http://www.supremecourt.gov/opinions/13pdf/12-3_4f57.pdf on June 20, 2016

6. *Sutton v. United Air Lines, Inc.,* 527 U.S. 471 (1999)

7. *Toyota Motor Manufacturing, Kentucky, Inc. v. Williams*, 534 U.S. 184 (2002)

8. The Job Accommodation Network, 800-526-7234 or www.askjan.org (accessed on June 20, 2016) is a free resource for employers. It is a service provided by the U.S. Department of Labor's Office of Disability Employment Policy (ODEP). JAN has been providing services for more than 25 years.

9. "Disability Discrimination," U.S. Equal Employment Opportunity Commission, accessed on June 20, 2016, https://www.eeoc.gov/laws/types/disability.cfm

10. The first was the Civil Rights Act of 1866, which protected the right to enter into contracts regardless of race.

11. A list of controlled substances can be found in Schedules I through V of Section 202 of the Controlled Substances Act (21 U.S.C. 812) and as further defined in Regulation 21 C.F.R. 1308.11–1308.15.

12. "eLaws – Drug-Free Workplace Advisor," U.S. Department of Labor, accessed June 20, 2016, http://webapps.dol.gov/elaws/asp/drugfree/screenr.htm

13. 41 C.F.R. 60-3.7

14. Fair Treatment of Experienced Pilots Act (December 13, 2007), Public Law 110-135

15. 41 C.F.R. 60

PART II

aPHR Body of Knowledge Functional Areas

HR Operations

This functional area, HR Operations, counts toward 38 percent of the Associate Professional in Human Resources (aPHR) exam. Technically, human resource (HR) operations refer to services provided by an HR department to the organization's operations. It covers a wide range of services including administrative services, recruitment, employee relations, legal compliance, policy development, compensation and benefits, training and development, and safety. These are not all of the possibilities. There may be more or less depending on each organization's functional values. Smaller organizations may assign someone to be responsible for shared functions. Larger organizations typically have HR responsibilities organized by functions. Added to this is the role of the HR generalist and the HR specialist. The HR generalist is responsible for the day-to-day management of HR operations, which means they manage the administration of the organization's policies, procedures, and programs.

The last 50 years have seen considerable changes in the delivery of HR services. HR has developed from its early role of a group of industrial relations specialists negotiating terms and conditions of work to today's business partners working with line management to add value to the company. HR now performs two distinct functions: transformational HR, that is, delivering strategy and change, and transactional HR, dealing with a wide range of administrative and operational tasks in support of the organization.

The Body of Knowledge statements outlined by HR Certification Institute (HRCI) for the HR Operations functional area by those performing early HR career roles are as follows:

Knowledge of

- **01** Organizational strategy and its connection to mission, vision, values, business goals, and objectives
- **02** Organizational culture (for example, traditions, unwritten procedures)
- **03** Legal and regulatory environment
- **04** Confidentiality and privacy rules that apply to employee records, company data, and individual data

- **05** Business functions (for example, accounting, finance, operations, sales and marketing)
- **06** HR policies and procedures (for example, ADA, EEO, progressive discipline)
- **07** HR metrics (for example, cost per hire, number of grievances)
- **08** Tools to compile data (for example, spreadsheets, statistical software)
- **09** Methods to collect data (for example, surveys, interviews, observation)
- **10** Reporting and presentation techniques (for example, histogram, bar chart)
- **11** Impact of technology on HR (for example, social media, monitoring software, biometrics)
- **12** Employee records management (for example, electronic/paper, retention, disposal)
- **13** Statutory reporting requirements (for example, OSHA, ERISA, ACA)
- **14** Purpose and function of human resource information systems (HRISs)
- **15** Job classifications (for example, exempt, nonexempt, contractor)
- **16** Job analysis methods and job descriptions
- **17** Reporting structure (for example, matrix, flat)
- **18** Types of external providers of HR services (for example, recruitment firms, benefits brokers, staffing agencies)
- **19** Communication techniques (e.g., written, oral, e-mail, passive, aggressive)

Laws and Regulations

Three major legal compliance domains impact all levels of organizational management:

- Equal opportunity
- Affirmative action
- Sexual harassment

HR professionals provide services throughout the organization that are regulated by one or more of these laws. Managers depend on HR support to be in compliance with a multitude of federal, state, and local laws; rules; and regulations, and this is just the beginning. This would be a good time to review all the laws listed in Chapter 2 for the following:

- Coverage
- Application
- Compliance

Any of these laws may appear on your certification exam as a multiple-choice question. If you have reviewed these laws thoroughly, you will be prepared for them.

HR Functions

Some of the functions of an HR department are personnel sourcing, hiring, training, skill development, benefits administration, and compliance with applicable national, regional, and local laws. In short, HR is responsible for attracting, training, and maintaining the safety of the employees of the company. The following is a more detailed list of HR functions, with a brief description of each:

- *Hiring* is sometimes used interchangeably with *staffing,* which does an injustice to the broad scope of activities involved in staffing. Hiring might be thought more specifically as screening the best job candidates, but especially making a formal job offer to the best candidate.

- **Staffing and employment** Staffing includes a broad scope of activities, including the following:

  - Before a new employee is hired to do a job, the job should be clearly designed or defined. A job is a collection of tasks and responsibilities that an employee is responsible for conducting. Jobs have titles.

  - Jobs are usually designed by conducting a job analysis, which includes examining the tasks and sequences of tasks necessary to perform the job.

  - A task is a typically defined as a unit of work, that is, a set of activities needed to produce some result, e.g., vacuuming a carpet, writing a memo, sorting the mail, and so on. Complex positions in the organization may include a large number of tasks, which are sometimes referred to as *functions.*

  - Note that a role is the set of responsibilities or expected results associated with a job. A job usually includes several roles.

  - The job analysis also looks at the areas of knowledge, skills, and abilities (the competencies) needed by the job. Typically, competencies are general descriptions of the abilities needed to perform a role in the organization. Ideally, competencies are even described in terms such that they can be measured.

  - Job descriptions are often used to describe a job and include lists of the general tasks, functions, and/or responsibilities of a position, whereas competencies list the abilities needed to conduct those tasks, functions, and/or responsibilities. Typically, descriptions also specify to whom the position reports, qualifications needed by the person in the job, and salary range for the position.

  - Staffing is often a subset of the activities in human resource management.

- **Employment** Employment is an agreement between an employer and an employee that the employee will provide certain services on the job. The work will occur in the employer's designated workplace. The work is designed to accomplish the employer organization's goals and mission. In return, the employee receives compensation.

- **Co-employment** This refers to circumstances in which a worker has simultaneous employment relationships with two or more employers for one work situation. This typically comes into question with contingent workers as the staffing provider and on-site company both assume different portions of the responsibility for an individual's employment situation.

Co-employment is something that employers cannot afford to get wrong. Here are some things to consider to help avoid co-employment pitfalls:

- *Establish clear boundaries.* In a co-employment situation, for the staffing provider to be positioned as the primary employer responsible for the worker, there must be clearly outlined roles for each party. All employer responsibilities such as recruiting, pay negotiation, insurance coverage, HR issues, onboarding, and termination must be handled solely by the staffing provider, with the on-site company taking responsibility only for direction and supervision of day-to-day responsibilities. When either party goes beyond their role, it becomes unclear which party is the primary employer and will make determining employment more challenging. Employers must also be sure that contingent workers are identified differently in their organizations to further illustrate their role versus permanent staff at the organization; issuing separate ID badges, having their e-mail addresses look different, and so on further differentiates the two parties and their place within the organization.

- *Create a clear and differentiated benefits plan.* As organizations put together policies around their benefit offerings, it is important to be as detailed as possible, outlining exactly which type of employees are eligible for benefits. Clearly detail whether or not contingent, contract, and independent workers fall within the plan's remit. This sort of clarity can help you avoid questions and litigation in the future. In addition, another effective strategy is having contingent workers sign a waiver that they will not claim access to benefits from their assignment company at any point.

- *Stay current.* Knowing the latest in labor laws and government regulations can be a challenge. It is critical to select a staffing provider that can offer expertise and guidance around co-employment and other labor laws that can affect your business, both positively and negatively, to help mitigate risk.

 EXAM TIP Staffing, usually called *employment*, involves three activities: human resource planning, recruitment, and selection.

Employee Relations

This is the body of work concerned with maintaining employer-employee relationships that contribute to satisfactory productivity, motivation, and morale. Employee relations offers consultation, facilitation, and resolution strategies for workplace issues. Employee relations assists in communications between employees and supervisors, corrective action and planning, disciplinary actions, and explanation and clarification of policies and procedures.

Records Management

This refers to a set of activities required for systematically controlling the creation, distribution, use, maintenance, and disposition of recorded information maintained as evidence of business activities and transactions. The key word in this definition is *evidence*.

Compensation and Benefits

Simply, this is the monetary value you give to your employees in return for their services. In the book *Human Resource Management*, Gary Dessler defines compensation as follows: "Employee compensation refers to all forms of pay going to employees and arising from their employment." An example of good pay management is the implementation of wage guidelines that avoid the practice of allowing red circle rates of pay (paying wages above the range maximum) or green circle rates of pay (paying wages below the range minimum).

Training and Development

This is considered a function concerned with organizational activity aimed at bettering the job performance of individuals and groups in organizational settings.

Training is the process of teaching new employees the basic skills they need to perform their jobs. Programs that are more present-day oriented and focus on an individual's current jobs, enhancing specific skills and abilities to immediately perform their job, is called *training*.

Development is the act of encouraging employees to acquire new or advanced skills, knowledge, and viewpoints by providing learning facilities and avenues where such new ideas can be applied.

Health, Safety, and Security

As defined by the World Health Organization (WHO), "occupational health deals with all aspects of health and safety in the workplace and has a strong focus on primary prevention of hazards."

HR Research

This is simply a kind of research conducted in the field of human resources. HR research also offers detailed analysis on the current development and management issues with the real-life case studies to enable the formulation and implementation of the strategy practice within the current organization.

HR Generalists and Specialists

HR professionals generally take one of two career paths: specialist or generalist. As the term implies, the human resource specialist develops expertise in a specific HR discipline. The generalist, on the other hand, is the HR jack-of-all-trades. The question often arises as to which path is best for you.

HR generalists have a broad spectrum of responsibilities that will require them to draw upon everything they've learned in a master's program in human resources. As its name suggests, duties are comprehensive and diverse and may include the following:

- Staffing and recruitment
- Employee training and development
- Compensation and benefits
- Personnel policies and procedures
- Employee relations
- Workplace safety and security

The following is a sampling of some types of specialist HR jobs:

- Workforce planning and employment specialist
- HR development specialist
- Total rewards specialist
- Employee and labor relations specialist
- Risk management specialist
- Metrics management specialist
- Human resource information systems specialist
- Global human resources specialist
- Organizational development specialist

After receiving a human resource management degree, many human resource graduates begin their careers as human resource generalists, discover an area that's particularly interesting to them, and then pursue it as a human resource specialist. By comparison, HR specialist jobs require a tremendous attention to detail, and you'll be viewed as an authority in a particular field.

HR Manager, Director, or Officer

In businesses large or small, those with multiple layers of authority within the HR department might have several different positions and classifications to fill. The positions range from HR representatives, who represent the lowest level of HR positions, to chief HR officers, who are members of the executive leadership team. Title doesn't always determine the layers of hierarchy in the department. Small companies sometimes give their sole HR department contact the HR director title, even if they don't have employees to supervise.

HR Support System

HR support systems are the various activities, programs, and initiatives used by organizations to assist in the development of human resources. In general, these systems, which are typically operated by an organization's HR department, include training and development, performance appraisal and feedback, career management, formal mentoring, and various types of employee services and assistance programs. The primary goal of these activities is to assist in the growth of the employee as a means of improving individual and organizational performance. In addition, these activities are intended to enhance employee work attitudes and increase employee commitment to the organization.

HR Education and Certification

Numerous programs offer education and professional certification for the individual, ranging from academic programs offered in colleges and universities to various certification programs offered by professional HR organizations. Some of these programs include the following:

- **Human resource certificate programs** Certificates are the easiest credential to achieve and can help you gain practical, tactical knowledge about day-to-day HR issues. Typically, these one- or two-day events are a great way to learn about new technologies, such as online psychological screenings and corporate education programs. They're also a good way to explore a potential specialty. Certificates in state regulations and mandates are valuable because they let employers know you are familiar with important state government requirements.

    Most certificate programs are open to anyone; degree and certification programs have stricter admissions requirements.

- **Human resource degree programs** Undergraduate and graduate degree programs in HR offer deeper learning opportunities but tend to focus more on theory than practical skills. According to the Society for Human Resource Management (SHRM), there are more than 260 HR-focused undergraduate degree programs at U.S. colleges and universities.

    Because an understanding of business operations is crucial for those wanting to advance to a human resource management role, experts say a master's of business administration (MBA) carries the most weight among advanced degree programs. SHRM estimates that U.S. universities offer more than 120 graduate programs, including MBAs, that feature concentrations in human resources.

- **Human resource certifications**   The most valuable educational option is certification because it truly demonstrates mastery of the subject. The three main designations in the HR profession granted by the HR Certification Institute (HRCI®) are
  - Professional in Human Resources (PHR), which focuses on operations and is best for people early in their careers
  - Global Professional in Human Resources (GPHR), which is designed for people who manage HR in multiple countries
  - Senior Professional in Human Resources (SPHR), which covers strategic issues and is designed for experienced professionals

  The Society for Human Resource Management (SHRM) has developed its own competency-based certification program. Designed for early-career and senior HR professionals, these certifications are based upon SHRM's rigorously validated competency model composed of the knowledge and behavior needed to succeed in human resources management.

- SHRM's certification program includes two certifications:
  - SHRM Certified Professional (SHRM-CP) for HR professionals who implement policies and strategies, serve as points of contact for staff and stakeholders, deliver HR services, and perform operational HR functions
  - SHRM Senior Certified Professional (SHRM-SCP) for HR professionals who develop strategies, lead the HR function, foster influence in the community, analyze performance metrics, and align HR strategies to organizational goals

HR Networking

For many HR professionals, networking is assumed to relate to the activity of external consultants who need to network to find work. It isn't something that they think they do or indeed need to do. This is not a good assumption when the ability to perform your HR job well is an underlying expectation of competency. HR professionals need to be far more than just competent; the ability to build and nurture relationships, have advocates, build reputation and credibility, demonstrate openness and trust, and implement fantastic interpersonal skills is a must. This is everything that a good professional networker takes for granted.

There are a number of reasons why HR professionals should network within and outside of their organization. These include the following:

- Do your job well
- Build reputation and credibility
- Gather advocates
- Facilitate trust

Networking can do wonders for your company's performance and your career. There are many ways to network, but the method that will work best is one that is value driven, has integrity, and is open and transparent. Enabling others to succeed, as well as having a strong reputation and credibility, will enable you to attract advocates, thus enabling you to become a more effective HR professional.

Organizational Accountability

This is the obligation of an individual or organization to account for its activities, accept responsibility for them, and disclose the results in a transparent manner. It also includes the responsibility for money or other entrusted property.

Multifunctional HR Department

The typical multifunctional HR department deals with the following six functional areas:

- Recruitment
- Employee relations
- Compensation and benefits
- Compliance
- Safety
- Training and development

An effectively run multifunctional HR department provides the organization with structure and the ability to meet business needs through managing the company's most valuable resources, its employees. Several HR disciplines, or areas, are involved in running an effective multifunctional department, but HR practitioners in each discipline may perform more than one of the more than six essential functions. In small businesses without a dedicated HR department, it's possible to achieve the same level of efficiency and workforce management through outsourcing HR functions or joining a professional employer organization.

Sole HR Practitioner

Those who manage an HR department of one are some of the hardest working in our industry because they must cover everything, including recruiting, benefits, training, employee relations, strategic planning, and more. Putting out daily HR fires can make it difficult to set aside the time it takes to focus on bigger-picture tasks. One of the biggest challenges is balancing both the administrative side of human resources and the long-term strategy. What will drive the most significant impact is the strategy, but small tasks must get done to accomplish the larger goals. While a sole HR practitioner needs to be ready to switch gears at a moment's notice, they can also block off time during the week to deal with specific tasks. Not everything has to be handled right away.

PART II

It is important to read about the latest HR and employment law trends. This is especially true for sole practitioners. Many employment law firms have blogs and also provide updates through e-mail newsletters. There are also countless free and low-cost webinars and in-person seminars put on by HR professionals and employment attorneys.

It is important for a sole HR practitioner to know their limits and ask for help when things get challenging. Consider hiring an HR consultant that can be on call to help. When in a serious or complex pickle, always call your employment attorney. Even small businesses should have a relationship with an employment attorney in case a situation is big enough to warrant legal help.

HR Call Center Operations

Human resource call centers are set up to help employees access human resource information, such as benefit and retirement packages and payroll. The call center is cost effective for companies by serving as a one-stop-shop to answer employee questions and may help increase worker productivity by decreasing the time spent by employees looking for information in a variety of places. For a small business, this may help alleviate the stress of administrators by delegating these questions to a call center so administrators can focus on more demanding tasks.

Call center calls are typically prescreened through an automated system that redirects calls to certain paths based on the caller's selection or area of concern. The prescreening process controls the lines for situations where there may be a lot of callers. This also allows the caller to be directed to the most appropriate HR professional who specializes in a particular area. An HR call center tracks how many callers and how frequently callers choose certain prerecorded answers and particular prescreening paths, such as the location of the HR department office.

Organizational Strategy

An organizational strategy is the sum of the actions a company intends to take to achieve long-term goals. Together, these actions make up a company's strategic plan. Strategic plans take at least a year to complete, requiring involvement from all company levels. Top management creates the larger organizational strategy, while middle and lower management adopt goals and plans to fulfill the overall strategy step by step.

Mission

A mission is a written declaration of an organization's core purpose and focus that normally remains unchanged over time. Properly crafted mission statements

- Serve as filters to separate what is important from what is not
- Clearly state which markets will be served and how
- Communicate a sense of intended direction to the entire organization

A mission is different from a vision in that the former is the cause and the latter is the effect; a mission is something to be accomplished, whereas a vision is something to be pursued for that accomplishment.

Vision

This is an aspirational description of what an organization would like to achieve or accomplish in the mid-term or long-term future. It is intended to serve as a clear guide for choosing current and future courses of action.

Values

Values are important and lasting beliefs or ideals shared by the members of a culture about what is good or bad and desirable or undesirable. Values have a major influence on a person's behavior and attitude and serve as broad guidelines in all situations. Some common business values are fairness, innovation, and community involvement.

Goals and Objectives

Objectives define strategies or implementation steps to attain the identified goals. Unlike goals, objectives are specific and measurable and have a defined completion date. They are more specific and outline the "who, what, when, where, and how" of reaching the goals.

Organizational Culture

This is a system of shared assumptions, values, and beliefs, which governs how people behave in organizations. These shared values have a strong influence on the people in the organization and dictate how they dress, act, and perform their jobs.

Tradition

Tradition is an inherited, established, or customary pattern of thought, action, or behavior (such as a religious practice or a social custom). It is a belief or story or a body of beliefs or stories relating to the past that are commonly accepted as historical though not verifiable.

Unwritten Procedures

These are behavioral constraints imposed in organizations or societies that are not voiced or written down. They usually exist in unspoken and unwritten format because they form part of the logical argument or course of action implied by tacit assumptions. Examples involving unwritten procedures include unwritten and unofficial organizational hierarchies, organizational culture, and acceptable behavioral norms governing interactions between organizational members.

PART II

Confidentiality

Personal information shared with an attorney, physician, therapist, or other individual generally cannot be divulged to third parties without the express consent of the client. While confidentiality is an ethical duty, privacy is a right rooted in common law.

Privacy

In general, privacy is the right to be free from secret surveillance and to determine whether, when, how, and to whom one's personal or organizational information is to be revealed. Specifically, privacy may be divided into four categories:

- **Physical** Restriction on others to experience a person or situation through one or more of the human senses
- **Informational** Restriction on searching for or revealing facts that are unknown or unknowable to others
- **Decisional** Restriction on interfering in decisions that are exclusive to an entity
- **Dispositional** Restriction on attempts to know an individual's state of mind

Employee Records

Employee records are defined to include the application for employment and records that are used or have been used to determine an employee's qualifications for promotion, compensation, termination, or disciplinary action.

Company Data

There are four different areas a company can gather internal data from: sales, finance, marketing, and human resources. Internal sales data is collected to determine revenue, profit, and the bottom line. The finance department supplies cash flow reports, production reports, and a budget variance analysis. Human resource data is information relative to the company's employees.

Personal Data

According to the law, personal data means any information relating to an identified or identifiable individual; an identifiable person is one who can be identified, directly or indirectly, in particular by reference to an identification number (e.g., Social Security number) or one or more factors specific to his or her physical, physiological, mental, economic, cultural, or social identity (e.g., last name and first name, date of birth, biometrics data, fingerprints, DNA, etc.).

Business Functions

EXAM TIP One of the common complaints of executives is that human resource people do not understand the business; they do not know what is required to make a profit or how to speak the language of business.

A business function is defined as any set of activities performed by the department that is initiated by an event, transform information, materials or business commitments, and procedures and output (e.g., order fulfillment, invoicing, cash management, manufactured batch, customer response tracking, regulatory submissions, etc.).

Finance and Accounting

1) The accounting department is part of a company's administration that is responsible for preparing the financial statements, maintaining the general ledger, paying bills, billing customers, managing payroll, doing cost accounting, performing financial analysis, and more. 2) The financial function is the part of an organization that manages its money. The business functions of finance typically include planning, organizing, auditing, accounting for, and controlling its company's finances. The finance department also usually produces the company's financial statements.

Operations

Operations management refers to the administration of business practices to create the highest level of efficiency possible within an organization. It is concerned with converting materials and labor into goods and services as efficiently as possible to maximize the profit of an organization. The outcome of business operations is the harvesting of value from assets owned by a business. Assets can be either physical or intangible. An example of value derived from a physical asset such as a building is rent. An example of value derived from an intangible asset, such as an idea, is a royalty.

Sales

The sales department can be defined as the division of a business that is responsible for selling products or providing services, according to Reference.com. It is also known as the *sales division* and is partnered with marketing in a reciprocating relationship within the world of business.

Marketing

Marketing is the management process through which goods and services move from concept to the customer. It includes the coordination of four elements, called the 4 Ps of marketing:

- Identification, selection, and development of a *product*
- Determination of its *price*

- Selection of a distribution channel to reach the customer's *place*
- Development and implementation of a *promotional strategy*

Business Reporting

A business structure, otherwise known as an *organizational structure,* defines how activities such as task allocation, coordination, and supervision are directed toward the achievement of organizational aims. It can also be considered the viewing glass or perspective through which individuals see their organization and its environment.

There are four main types of organizational structure: flat, functional, divisional, and matrix structure.

- **Flat**   A flat organization (also known as a *horizontal* organization or delayering) has an organizational structure with few or no levels of middle management between staff and executives. The advantages of this type of structure are it elevates the employees' level of responsibility in the organization. It removes excess layers of management, which improves the coordination and speed of communication between employees. Fewer levels of management encourage an easier decision-making process among employees. The disadvantages are employees often lack a specific boss to report to, which creates confusion and possible power struggles among management. Flat organizations tend to produce a lot of generalists but no specialists. The specific job function of employees may not be clear. A flat structure may limit the long-term growth of an organization; management may decide against new opportunities in an effort to maintain the structure. Larger organizations struggle to adapt the flat structure, unless the company divides into smaller, more manageable units. Eliminating the salaries of middle management reduces an organization's budget costs.

- **Functional**   A functional structure is set up so that each portion of the organization is grouped according to its purpose. In this type of organization there may be a marketing department, a sales department, and a production department. The functional structure works well for small businesses in which each department can rely on the talent and knowledge of its workers and support itself. One of the drawbacks to a functional structure is that the coordination and communication between departments can be restricted by the organizational boundaries of having the various departments working separately.

- **Divisional**   A divisional structure typically is used in larger companies that operate in a wide geographic area or that have separate smaller organizations within the umbrella group to cover different types of products or market areas. The now-defunct Tecumseh Products Company was organized divisionally, with a small engine division, a compressor division, a parts division, and divisions for each geographic area to handle specific needs. The benefit of this structure is that needs can be met more rapidly and more specifically; however, communication is inhibited because employees in different divisions are not working together.

Divisional structure is costly because of its size and scope. Small businesses can use a divisional structure on a smaller scale, having different offices in different parts of the city, for example, or assigning different sales teams to handle different geographic areas.

- **Matrix**   The matrix structure is a hybrid of divisional and functional structure. Typically used in large multinational companies, the matrix structure allows for the benefits of functional and divisional structures to exist in one organization. This can create power struggles because most areas of the company will have a dual management—a functional manager and a product or divisional manager working at the same level and covering some of the same managerial territory.

 EXAM TIP   The advantage of functional departmentalization is that it promotes skill specialization; the disadvantages are that it reduces communication and cooperation between departments.

HR Policies and Procedures

Human resource policies are continuing guidelines on the approach the organization intends to adopt in managing its people. It represents specific guidelines to HR managers various matters concerning employment. HR policies provide the outline by which employees are likely to behave in the workplace. These policies are written statements of the company's standards and objectives and include all areas of employment. They contain rules on how employees must perform their jobs and interact with each other.

 EXAM TIP   Human resource policies serve three major purposes: to reassure employees they will be treated fairly and objectively, to help managers make rapid and consistent decisions, and to give managers the confidence to resolve problems and defend their decisions.

ADA HR Policy

The duty to provide reasonable accommodation is a fundamental statutory requirement under the Americans with Disabilities Act (ADA), as amended by the Americans with Disabilities Act Amendments Act (ADAAA). The Rehabilitation Act has similar requirements applicable specifically to federal contractors. (See Chapter 2 for more ADA details.)

Title I of the ADA requires an employer to provide "reasonable accommodation" to qualified individuals with disabilities who are employees or applicants for employment—unless such accommodation would cause the employer an "undue hardship." The law requires reasonable accommodations so that employees with disabilities can enjoy the "benefits and privileges of employment" equal to those enjoyed by similarly situated employees without disabilities. The ADAAA broadens the concept of disability under the ADA by statutorily rejecting Supreme Court decisions that took a narrower view.

PART II

To comply with the ADA and ADAAA, attain diversity goals, access a larger labor pool, and take advantage of tax incentives, most employers adopt a written policy with a formal, comprehensive approach to employing people with disabilities.

EEO HR Policy

Compliance with federal antidiscrimination laws requires covered employers to inform employees of their right to be free from workplace discrimination and retaliation. The Equal Employment Opportunity Commission (EEOC) under Title VII of the Civil Rights Act of 1964 requires employers to post workplace notices, and covered employers typically include a policy statement on equal employment opportunity (EEO) in employee handbooks and other sources of workplace policies distributed to employees. EEO policies also apply to vendors, contractors, and other third parties with whom the employer conducts business. Employers with government contracts or that receive government funding may have additional notice of rights requirements. State or local laws may expand the list of protected categories.

Progressive Discipline Policy

Progressive discipline generally includes a series of increasingly severe penalties for repeated offenses, typically beginning with counseling or a verbal warning. Progressive discipline policies can be a useful tool for warding off potential unionization in the non-union setting, given that most unions typically point to unfair disciplinary actions to promote the benefits of unionization. Such procedures also help ensure uniformity and consistency in the administration of disciplinary action and thus minimize exposure to discrimination claims.

However, in states where an employee handbook or manual creates contractual or enforceable rights, the existence of a progressive discipline policy might be construed to require employers to follow that policy no matter the circumstances. Moreover, if a progressive discipline policy requires the employer to follow a series of steps before certain terminations occur, the policies may hinder an employer's ability to take swift termination action.

When a progressive discipline system is used, it must be designed carefully, backed up by clear procedures and administered by well-trained supervisors.

Employee Handbooks and Policy Manuals

An employee handbook is an important communication tool between you and your employees. A well-written handbook sets forth your expectations for your employees and describes what they can expect from your company. It also should describe your legal obligations as an employer and your employees' rights. This summary will help you write an employee handbook, which typically includes the following topics:

- **Nondisclosure agreements (NDAs) and conflict-of-interest statements** Although NDAs are not legally required, having employees sign NDAs and conflict-of-interest statements helps to protect your trade secrets and company proprietary information.

- **Anti-discrimination policies** As a business owner, you must comply with the equal employment opportunity laws prohibiting discrimination and harassment, including the Americans with Disabilities Act. Employee handbooks should include a section about these laws and how your employees are expected to comply.

- **Compensation** Clearly explain to your employees that your company will make required deductions for federal and state taxes, as well as voluntary deductions for the company's benefits programs. In addition, you should outline your legal obligations regarding overtime pay, pay schedules, performance reviews, salary increases, time-keeping records, breaks, and bonuses.

- **Workers' compensation** Clearly describe applicable employee rights and benefits as provided for under your workers' compensation program.

- **Work schedules** Describe your company's policies regarding work hours and schedules, attendance, punctuality, and reporting absences, along with guidelines for flexible schedules and telecommuting.

- **Standards of conduct** Document your expectations of how you want your employees to conduct themselves, including dress code and ethics. In addition, remind your employees of their legal obligations, especially if your business is engaged in an activity that is regulated by the government.

- **General employment information** Your employee handbook should include an overview of your business and general employment policies covering employment eligibility, job classifications, employee referrals, employee records, job postings, probationary periods, termination and resignation procedures, transfers and relocation, and union information, if applicable.

- **Safety and security** Describe your company's policy for creating a safe and secure workplace, including compliance with the Occupational Safety and Health Administration's laws that require employees to report all accidents, injuries, potential safety hazards, safety suggestions, and health- and safety-related issues to management.

  Safety policies should also include your company's policy regarding bad weather and hazardous community conditions.

  Add your commitment to creating a secure work environment and your employee's responsibility for abiding by all physical and information security policies, such as locking file cabinets or computers when not in use.

- **Computers and technology** Outline policies for appropriate computer and software use and steps employees should take to secure electronic information, especially any personal identifiable information you collect from your customers.

 EXAM TIP Employers need to use caution in using employee handbooks to prohibit undesirable behavior, especially with respect to social media.

HR Metrics

HR metrics are measurements used to determine the value and effectiveness of HR initiatives, typically including such areas as turnover, training, return on human capital, costs of labor, and expenses per employee. To measure and determine the real cost of employee grievances, organizations should gather and store notes and records about employee complaints in a central location so that the time spent on each case—and the cost associated with that time—can be measured and minimized.

The following are five employee relations metrics you should be tracking:[1]

- Number of grievances per month, quarter, and year using a constant measure, such as the number of grievances per 100 or 1000 employees. This data can be "sliced and diced" by manager, department, region, and facility, she said.

- Cost of grievances by calculating—in a consistent manner over time—the time spent by managers, HR, and legal counsel investigating and handling complaints, the cost of lost productivity, and any legal expenses.

- Root cause of grievances. "Just like with safety and quality, if there's a defect or issue we've got to figure out why," she explained. In the case of employee grievances, she noted, such problems can arise as a result of supervisor errors, unclear policies and procedures, lack of management training, and bad hiring decisions.

- Average close time. Similar to "time to fill," a measure used in recruiting, the average close time is a measure of the efficiency of the grievance resolution process that is based on how many days it takes to resolve an issue from the day it is identified as a problem.

- Return on investment (ROI). "Eventually we want to look at how much money— over time—the employee relations program has saved the organization," she noted. Measures such as revenue per employee and profit per employee can be monitored to see whether there is any impact after effective grievance resolution processes are implemented.

Data Compilation Tools[2]

Historically, many organizations have built data storehouses of employee skills, knowledge, and capabilities by capturing data from employees using various checklists and then inputting the raw data or codes into databases. Unfortunately, most of these databases have had limited search and/or retrieval capabilities, and these data compilation efforts have been less than successful in matching employee skills and talent with company needs in a timely manner. So why not revise the process?

Technological innovations such as scanning, data mining, and enterprise-wide software now enable an organization to capture, cross-utilize, and retrieve information from diverse sources. Documents including résumés, employment applications, project management records, capability statements, workflow documents, department records, workforce forecasts, business development plans, performance appraisals, succession plans, and employee wish lists can be organized in the company's data warehouse to aid in the identification of employee talent, skills, knowledge, and capabilities.

Once this veritable mother lode of data has been mined, it is amenable to being sorted, categorized, and assessed to meet organizational needs. The organization can then begin to build its own detailed histories of each employee's relevant skills, knowledge, and capabilities, using the data in a format that is business friendly. Employees can attest to the accuracy of the data by including this as a step in the existing processes for performance appraisal and succession planning.

A far larger universe of information coupled with the organization's development of its own business-driven histories of employee capabilities could result in a giant step forward in matching employee skills with business requirements.

Data mining and warehousing techniques can serve not only as a useful strategic tool in meeting business needs but also as a tool for enhancing task and team performance, recognizing talent capabilities and development, and furthering business development goals.

Data Collection Methods[3]

Determining what metrics to measure and report will depend on an organization's strategy and goals. When high-level executives ask the HR team to start measuring the department's performance, some HR staffers scramble to figure out what they should measure. Measurement just for the sake of providing statistics is never a good idea. As business writer Peter Drucker stated, "What gets measured gets managed," so implementing an HR reporting system should be carefully planned.

A good approach is to focus on the metrics that affect progress toward business goals. However, assessing what data is meaningful, determining how to measure is, and choosing appropriate communication methods can seem daunting.

For help in choosing what HR metrics to focus on, HR professionals may want to consider the following:

- Review business strategy and both long- and short-term goals with C-suite executives to ensure HR is aligned with these objectives. Identify how HR will contribute to achieving those goals, and pinpoint which measurements will provide targeted, relevant information about how those functions affect business objectives and strategies.

- Define each HR metric and its formula. Not all organizations define metrics the same way or use the same formulas. For example, some companies measure the cost for each new hire without including payment for recruiters as a related expense. SHRM offers several calculators[4] for commonly used metrics.

- Determine what data must be collected, what collection methods are available, and how the data will be gathered. For instance, will all data for cost-per-hire be captured in human resource information systems? Or will some data need to be obtained from another department?

- Decide how often HR metrics information will be collected and reported. Will it be monthly, quarterly, or annually?

- Choose what format will be used to report the data and who will receive the report. Will the data be part of a regular operations report or scorecard? Will it be a stand-alone document? Who will receive the report?

- Review what is being measured on a regular basis to ensure that HR is providing relevant information. Have goals changed? Does HR need to be providing different metrics to support business objectives?

 EXAM TIP Reliability refers to the consistency of a measure; validity refers to whether the research effort actually measures what it is supposed to measure.

Surveys[5,6]

A carefully designed and conducted employee survey can reveal a great deal of information about employee perceptions that management can use to improve the workplace. Organization responsiveness to employee feedback leads to higher retention rates, lower absenteeism, improved productivity, better customer service, and higher employee morale. The simple fact that the organization is conducting a survey can send a positive message to employees that their opinions are valued. In addition, managers can gain insights into issues affecting their departments or business units that allow them to manage more effectively. Conversely, if the senior management team is not fully committed and ready to really listen to and, most important, act on what employees are saying, then conducting a survey can falsely raise expectations among employees, leading to an employee relations disaster.

The three most common types of employee surveys include employee opinion and satisfaction surveys, employee culture surveys, and employee engagement surveys.

- Employee opinion and satisfaction surveys measure employee views, attitudes, and perceptions of their organization (also known as *climate surveys*).

- An employee culture survey measures the point of view of employees and is designed to assess whether it aligns with that of the organization or its departments.

- Employee engagement surveys measure employees' commitment, motivation, sense of purpose, and passion for their work and organization.

Interviews

Job analysis and evaluation, performance evaluation, and employment interviews are just some of the circumstances when data is collected by an interview method. Interviewing is a widely used data collection technique. Interviewing is an important step in the employee selection process. If done effectively, the interview enables the employer to determine whether an applicant's skills, experience, and personality meet the job's requirements. It also helps the employer assess whether an applicant would likely fit in with the corporate culture. In addition, preparing for an interview can help clarify a position's responsibilities.

Moreover, to the extent that the interview process leads to the hiring of the most suitable candidate, it can help contain the organization's long-term turnover costs. Applicants also benefit from an effective interview, as it enables them to determine whether their employment needs and interests would likely be met.

Observation[7]

A key advantage of conducting observations is that you can observe what people actually do or say, rather than what they say they do. People are not always willing to write their true views on a questionnaire or tell a stranger what they really think at an interview. Observations can be made in real-life situations, allowing the researcher access to the context and meaning surrounding what people say and do. There are numerous situations in the area of criminology and related disciplines where approaching people for an interview or questionnaire completion is unlikely to yield a positive response but where observations could yield valuable insights on an issue.

On the other hand, there are a number of important problems associated with observational research. An important one relates to the role of the observer and what effect the observer has on the people and situations observed. This is difficult to gauge. There is also the problem of being able to write an account, as a researcher, when one is immersed in a situation or culture. This latter situation can mean that the research is dismissed as too subjective. Observation can be time consuming. Some well-known observational pieces of research took some years of observation and immersion in a situation or culture. However, it is more common in modern research to reduce the observation time substantially. Observation time may be further reduced in experimental conditions (laboratory or simulation), in other words, controlled settings. An important potential disadvantage in conducting observational research is the ethical dilemmas inherent in observing real-life situations for research purposes.

Reporting and Presentation Techniques

There are many ways to present your data so that it can be easily understood by your stakeholders. No matter which reporting method you choose, simplicity will ensure that the results of your evaluation are both accessible and understandable.

There are two broad categories of reporting methods: those that are written (annual reports, fact sheets, etc.) and those that are oral/visual (PowerPoint presentations, exhibits, news release, etc.). No matter the reporting method you choose, the report should take into account your audience and be both accessible and understandable. In this section we will discuss the use of histograms and bar charts.

Histogram

A histogram or Pareto chart (sorted histogram) is a column chart that shows frequency data. Figure 3-1 is a typical example.

To create a histogram in Excel, you can use the Histogram tool of the Analysis Tool-Pak. It uses two columns of data to create a histogram, one for data you want to analyze and one for bin numbers that represent the intervals by which you want to measure the frequency. The major difference is that a histogram is only used to plot the frequency of score occurrences in a continuous data set that has been divided into classes, called *bins*. Bar charts, on the other hand, can be used for a great deal of other types of variables including ordinal and nominal data sets.

Bar Chart

A bar chart or bar graph is a chart or graph that presents grouped data with rectangular bars, with lengths proportional to the values that they represent; Figure 3-2 shows an example. The bars can be plotted vertically or horizontally. Pie charts are best to use when you are trying to compare parts of a whole. They do not show changes over time. Bar graphs are used to compare things between different groups or to track changes over time.

EXAM TIP Bar charts compare variables by plotting categorical data, whereas pie charts show how categories make up parts of a whole.

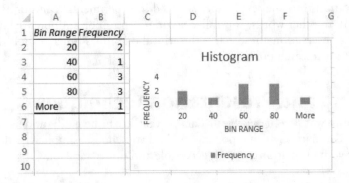

Figure 3-1 Histogram

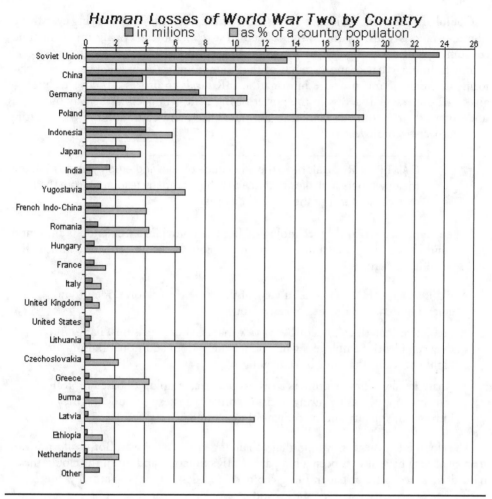

Figure 3-2   Bar chart

Impact of Technology on Human Resources[8]

Rapid changes in technology have affected businesses in more ways than we can count, from globalization and organizational adjustments to a workforce clamoring for remote and mobile job opportunities, and human resources has had to adapt swiftly. If HR wants to continue to play a critical role in helping businesses anticipate and manage organizational change, it must have technology at its core.

With millennials making up more than half of the current workforce, and predicted to make up 75 percent by 2020, HR is going to have to embrace and build on technological advancements to meet both employee expectations and business requirements. Talent analytics and workplace analysis will become more commonplace, and companies using the data available to them will be far more competitive.

Compliance and risk avoidance are essential principles for HR, underlying every function and task. Because of this, HR has earned a reputation for being mired in time-consuming duties with significant amounts of paperwork.

But technology has changed much of that monotony via new HR portals and platforms that digitize much of the information HR needs to process. Today's technology gives HR professionals access to the power of Big Data—impacting the way businesses understand their customers, market to new audiences, and communicate with existing and prospective employees.

 EXAM TIP HR portals have the advantage of allowing employees to monitor their own personal information and other company resources from their own computers or other mobile devices.

When combined with other technologies, Big Data provides a tremendous amount of insight and allows HR professionals to make decisions backed by concrete information and more efficient processes.

- Big Data gives HR a fact-based view of the current workforce, identifying emerging trends so businesses can adapt.

- Predictive analytics allow for better risk-management decisions. For example, they can identify employees who could benefit from additional training or highlight teams that may be struggling.

- Analytics also allows recruiters to assess potential employees based on real information; by basing hiring decisions on facts instead of hunches, they can improve the quality and placement of new hires.

The cloud is another innovation that's changing HR in a big way. Both collection and storage of data have always been a big part of HR's function and, until the cloud, meant hard drive space, piles of paper, filing cabinets, and desk drawers. Naturally, this led to inefficiencies, security issues, data loss, and chaotic office spaces.

Today, all of this information can instead be stored in the cloud; documents and other pertinent information can be easily accessed online while data can be collected through simplified forms and automated processes. Employee information—like tax forms, payroll data, performance reviews, and contact information—can be archived and organized in one secure location.

Cloud-based systems and Big Data go hand in hand. All this data can provide valuable insight if you know how to interpret it, which has already made a tremendous impact on HR. However, in the future, HR's challenge will include the need for higher levels of interpretation and broader application of the insights cloud-based systems and Big Data provide.

Cloud security makes it easy to limit access to information. At the same time, cloud-based mobile platforms allow individuals to access their information more readily than ever before.

Imagine if you didn't need to e-mail HR every time you had a question about your benefits or paycheck; instead, you'd log on to a portal where all that information was at your fingertips. Imagine if you could use the same portal to request time off, change your mailing address, or confirm contributions to your 401(k).

Mobile HR apps make it easy for employees to access this kind of information anywhere and anytime. And that makes life easier for HR workers, too.

Despite the potential impact, many companies still haven't made the switch to modern HR systems, but I think it's only a matter of time. As we barrel into the future of technology in the workplace, HR has a lot to look forward to; cloud computing, easier storage, better insights, and greater transparency are only the beginning. Because of efficiencies, cost savings, employee expectations, and the power of Big Data for HR and organizations as a whole, technology is just too business critical to ignore.

Statutory Reporting Requirements

Federal laws and regulations typically include statutory recording and reporting requirements in their legislation. The following are a summary of these requirements for the Occupational Safety and Health Act (OSHA), the Employee Retirement Income Security Act (ERISA), and the Affordable Care Act (ACA).[9]

The Occupational Safety and Health Act (OSHA)[10]

The Occupational Safety and Health Administration (OSHA) is revising its rule addressing the recording and reporting of occupational injuries and illnesses (29 CFR parts 1904 and 1952), including the forms employers use to record those injuries and illnesses. The revisions to the final rule will produce more useful injury and illness records, collect better information about the incidence of occupational injuries and illnesses on a national basis, promote improved employee awareness and involvement in the recording and reporting of job-related injuries and illnesses, simplify the injury and illness recordkeeping system for employers, and permit increased use of computers and telecommunications technology for OSHA recordkeeping purposes.

The Employee Retirement Income Security Act (ERISA)[11]

The Reporting and Disclosure Guide for Employee Benefit Plans is prepared by the U.S. Department of Labor's Employee Benefits Security Administration (EBSA) with assistance from the Pension Benefit Guaranty Corporation (PBGC). It is intended to be used as a quick reference tool for certain basic reporting and disclosure requirements under the Employee Retirement Income Security Act of 1974 (ERISA). Not all ERISA reporting and disclosure requirements are reflected in this guide. For example, the guide, as a general matter, does not focus on disclosures required by the Internal Revenue Code or the provisions of ERISA for which the Department of the Treasury and Internal Revenue Service (IRS) have regulatory and interpretive authority. For information on IRS notice and disclosure requirements, please visit the IRS web site at http://irs.gov/Retirement-Plans/Retirement-PlanReporting-and-Disclosure. The guide contains, on page 23, a list of EBSA and PBGC resources, including agency Internet sites, where laws, regulations, and other guidance are available on ERISA's reporting and disclosure requirements.

PART II

The Affordable Care Act (ACA)[12]

Employers subject to the Affordable Care Act's 2015 information reporting requirements were given extra time to give these forms to employees and file them with the government. In Notice 2016-4, issued by the IRS on December 28, the agency extended the information reporting due dates.

With transition relief ending, reporting deadlines for filings in 2017 will be months earlier than in 2016.

Subsequently, for year 2016 information filing, the IRS extended the deadline for furnishing forms to employees to March 2, 2017, but left the deadlines for filing forms with the IRS intact (February 28 for paper/mail submissions or March 31 for electronic filing).

Purpose and Function of Human Resources Information Systems (HRISs)

Effective and successful human resource management is required for a business to compete in the marketplace. HR managers coordinate a wide variety of employee management activities that involve large amounts of data over time. A human resource information system provides data management and accurate and timely information for decision-making; it also streamlines HR operational, managerial, and executive support processes.

A human resource information system functions as a productivity tool for HR operational processes. Increased speed and accuracy result when HR transactions are performed with computer software rather than manually, and routine transactions such as employee headcount, payroll tracking, and time and attendance reporting become automated and more cost effective. HR representatives enjoy increased productivity and accomplish more in their work week when manual processes take up less of their time.

An HRIS functions as a managerial information system to gather and provide key data about staffing, turnover, benefits, and regulatory compliance issues. Human resource personnel can provide reports on total number of employees, cost to hire, vacant positions, benefits costs, required reports such as EE03, and cost of raises and bonuses. HR managers can more easily present analysis of compensation, recruiting, accidents, and injuries.

A company's HRIS functions as an executive information system to aggregate high-level data for long-range planning such as succession planning. The system provides executive planning information for strategic needs such as forecasting, staffing needs assessment, and employee skills assessment.

An HRIS also can function as an office automation system to design employee management documents such as applications and job requisitions, to schedule shared resources, and to schedule and track employee training and recognition. HR reports can be automated and set to run and distribute right from the system, getting information to the people who need it in real time. An HRIS reduces the amount of time the staff spends on daily transaction activities, such as tracking employee status changes, and frees them to work on more planning and strategy aligned with corporate goals.

Job Analysis Methods and Job Descriptions

Job analysis is a process to identify and determine in detail the particular job duties and requirements and the relative importance of these duties for a given job. Job analysis is a process where judgments are made about data collected on a job.

Legal Aspects of Job Analysis

An important concept of job analysis is that the analysis is conducted of the job, not the person. While job analysis data may be collected from incumbents through interviews or questionnaires, the product of the analysis is a description or specifications of the job, not a description of the person.

Job analysis can be used in selection procedures to legally identify or develop the following:

- Job duties that should be included in advertisements of vacant positions
- Appropriate salary level for the position to help determine what salary should be offered to a candidate
- Minimum requirements (education and/or experience) for screening applicants
- Interview questions
- Selection tests/instruments (e.g., written tests, oral tests, job simulations)
- Applicant appraisal/evaluation forms
- Orientation materials for applicants/new hires

Job Analysis and the ADA

With the passage of the Americans with Disabilities Act (1990), job analysis has taken on an increasing importance. A job analysis can be used to define the essential elements of the job, including the physical demands that the work requires. The ADA specifically states that no covered entity shall discriminate against a qualified individual with a disability because of the disability of such individual in regard to job application procedures; the hiring, advancement, or discharge of employees; employee compensation; job training; and other terms, conditions, and privileges of employment. The ADA requires that handicapped individuals be given "reasonable accommodation" in the workplace so that they will not be unreasonably excluded from employment. Job analysis is a process to identify the tasks and duties performed on the job as well as the equipment used. This information may be helpful in determining what "reasonable accommodations" could be made for an individual to perform the job.

Job Analysis and the FLSA

The FLSA requires that most employees in the United States be paid at least the federal minimum wage for all hours worked and overtime pay at 1.5 times the regular rate of pay for all hours worked more than 40 hours in a workweek.

The FLSA provides an exemption from both minimum wage and overtime pay for employees employed as bona fide executive, administrative, professional, and outside sales employees.

Job Analysis and Affirmative Action

On August 27, 2013, the Office of Federal Contract Compliance Programs (OFCCP) announced new rules outlining how federal contractors should handle their affirmative action and nondiscrimination obligations for protected veterans and for individuals with disabilities. The changes/new requirements include the following:

- Applying the "Internet applicant" rule to the new rules so that electronic applications and inquiries will be handled the same way they are handled for other groups covered by affirmative action (race, color, religion, sex, or national origin)
- Changing the 2-year recordkeeping requirement to 3 years
- Removing the requirement in the disabilities rule to review all physical and mental job qualification standards on an annual basis and replacing it with a requirement for contractors to establish their own schedule for reviewing job qualifications
- Requiring employers to achieve specific numeric goals to document compliance
- Requiring that contractors compare the number of individuals with disabilities (IWDs) who apply to the number of IWDs who are hired and keep those records for 3 years for audit purposes
- Maintaining an applicant flow log showing the name, race, sex, date of application, job title, interview status, and the action taken for all individuals applying for job opportunities
- Maintaining records pertaining to company compensation design and system
- Filing EEO-1 and VETS 4212 reports annually

Competency Analysis

Competency-based interviews are one form of competency analysis that is an effective means of screening candidates who qualify for the job by targeting the specific competencies required for the position. A skills analysis identifies the major responsibilities of a job and breaks down each major responsibility into its job skills or tasks. A full competency analysis or competency map also describes the subskills, supporting knowledge and abilities, attitudes and behaviors, and tools required to perform the job. Skills gap analyses can identify gaps in training programs and employees' skills.

Job Descriptions and Job Specifications

Job descriptions describe a broad, general, and written statement of a specific job, based on the findings of a job analysis. It generally includes duties, purpose, responsibilities, scope, and working conditions of a job along with the job's title and the name or designation of the person to whom the employee reports. A job specification is a statement of the essential components of a job class, including a summary of the work to be performed, the primary duties and responsibilities, and the minimum qualifications and requirements necessary to perform the essential functions of the job.

Job Description Components

A job description need not account for every task that might ever be done. Here are the most critical components of a good job description:

- **Heading information** This should include job title, pay grade or range, reporting relationship (by position, not individual), hours or shifts, and the likelihood of overtime or weekend work.

- **Summary objective of the job** List the general responsibilities and descriptions of key tasks and their purpose; relationships with customers, co-workers, and others; and the results expected of incumbent employees.

- **Qualifications** State the education, experience, training, and technical skills necessary for entry into this job.

- **Special demands** This should include any extraordinary conditions applicable to the job (for example, heavy lifting, exposure to temperature extremes, prolonged standing, or travel).

- **Job duties and responsibilities** It's more important to list what must be performed and accomplished than how, if there is more than one way to do it. Being too specific on how to accomplish a duty could lead to ADA issues when an employee asks for an accommodation.

Why Use Job Descriptions

The following are reasons job descriptions are important:

- It ensures that you're hiring the right people to fill the right position.

- Writing concise and effective job descriptions is a crucial component for setting your organization apart from the competition in order to attract the best candidate.

- Well-written and effectively developed job descriptions are communication tools that allow both employees and candidates to clearly understand the expectations of the role, its essential duties, the competences and responsibilities, and the required educational credentials and experience.

- As individual roles change over time, the job descriptions should change with them. There are few positions that do not evolve. Most change. Systems and processes evolve. The job descriptions should be continually updated as the duties change over time. The job description needs to evolve and continue to be correctly classified.

FLSA Job Classifications

The U.S. Department of Labor divides jobs into two categories, exempt or nonexempt. Employees whose jobs are governed by the FLSA are classified as either exempt or nonexempt. Nonexempt employees are entitled to overtime pay. Some jobs are classified as exempt by definition. For example, executive employees are exempt. These employees are not protected by the Fair Labor Standards Act (FLSA).

Exempt

The FLSA provides an exemption from both minimum wage and overtime pay for employees employed as bona fide executive, administrative, professional, and outside sales employees. Section 13(a)(1) and Section 13(a)(17) also exempt certain computer employees. To qualify for exemption, employees generally must meet certain tests regarding their job duties and be paid on a salary basis at not less than $455 per week. Job titles do not determine exempt status. For an exemption to apply, an employee's specific job duties and salary must meet all the requirements of the department's regulations.

Nonexempt

Most employees are entitled to overtime pay under the Fair Labor Standards Act. They are called nonexempt employees. Employers must pay them 1.5 times their regular rate of pay when they work more than 40 hours in a week.

Independent Contractors

For the FLSA's minimum wage and overtime provisions to apply to a worker, the worker must be an "employee" of the employer, meaning that an employment relationship must exist between the worker and the employer. The FLSA defines "employ" as including to "suffer or permit to work," representing the broadest definition of employment under the law because it covers work that the employer directs or allows to take place. Applying the FLSA's definition, workers who are economically dependent on the business of the employer, regardless of skill level, are considered to be employees, and most workers are employees. On the other hand, independent contractors are workers with economic independence who are in business for themselves.

External HR Service Providers

Small and midsize companies are increasingly looking to outsource HR functions to focus on core operations and growing the business. Companies have been moving that way as HR has become more complex; it's no longer an HR person sitting in an office planning social events. There are complicated employee and compliance issues to address. Besides HR consultants who are third-party service providers, today's marketplace also includes recruiting firms, benefits brokers, and staffing agencies. Each is described more in the following sections.

Recruiting Firms

Recruiting firms are a type of company that recruits new talent for open positions in the workforce. For example, if there is an open position for an accountant and they have an accountant in their database, they will set that person up with an interview for the company hiring.

Staffing Agencies

A staffing agency, also called a temp agency, can help bridge the gap for people stuck between jobs or for businesses that need to fill out the ranks but are having difficulty finding qualified employees. A temp agency has an army of workers with a variety of skills at its disposal.

Benefits Brokers

A health insurance broker's job is to provide clients with the most appropriate health insurance policy. Authorized by specific insurance companies to act on their behalf, the broker essentially guides clients through the process of selecting a policy for themselves or for employees.

Communication Techniques

Communication skills are critical in all walks of life, but communicating effectively in the workplace is critical to professional success. Whether interacting with colleagues, subordinates, managers, customers, or vendors, the ability to communicate effectively using a variety of tools is essential.

Workplace communication is the process of exchanging information, both verbal and nonverbal, within an organization. An organization may consist of employees from different parts of the society. They may have different cultures and backgrounds and can be used to different norms. To unite activities of all employees and restrain from any missed deadline or activity that could affect the company negatively, communication is crucial. Effective workplace communication ensures that all the organizational objectives are achieved. Workplace communication is tremendously important to organizations because it increases productivity and efficiency. Ineffective workplace communication leads to communication gaps between employees, which causes confusion, wastes time, and reduces productivity.

Effective communication with clients plays a vital role in the development of an organization and the success of any business. When communicating, nonverbal communication must also be taken into consideration. How a person delivers a message has a lot of influence on the meaning of this one.

Tips for e-mail etiquette include the following:

- Start on a personal note.
- Tame the emotions.
- Keep it short and sweet.

- Read it twice.
- If it's a critical e-mail, *do not* under any circumstances send it right away.
- Master the subject line.

Chapter Review

This chapter is as multifaceted as its heading, HR Operations. It started with a brief review of employee relations in the workplace and briefly reviewed some laws and regulations particularly important as you address HR functions in an employee relations environment.

After employee relations, the chapter covered other basic HR functions such as staffing; compensation and benefits; training and development; and health, safety, and security. Along the way, we talked about records management.

You also learned about the type of work typically done by HR generalists and specialists. In fact, the chapter covered the whole HR support system, including career development options and opportunities.

You spent time examining organizational accountability as well as organizational strategy, finally reviewing the role of organizational culture in the workplace. This led to an examination of traditions and unwritten procedures. Confidentiality and privacy were covered next.

Then the chapter covered business functions as well as organizational structure and examined the role and importance of well-drafted employee handbooks and policy manuals. This led to a look at data collection methods, reporting and presentation techniques, and an examination of the impact that technology plays in our daily HR activities.

The chapter examined the function of an HRIS and its impact in all aspects of our HR functions. Before closing this chapter, we examined the legal aspects of job analysis, distinguishing job analysis from job specifications.

Finally, our travels through this varied and complex world ended with a brief look at third-party HR services and closed with a look at various communications techniques and some e-mail tips.

Questions

1. Beverly is setting up the human resource systems for her newly formed organization. She wants to write a policy about employment at will but isn't sure what it is. How would you explain it to her?

   A. Employment at will means either the employee or the employer can end the relationship at any time for any reason.

   B. Employment at will means the employer can terminate an employee when necessary, but the employee must give 2 weeks' notice.

   C. Employment at will means the employee can quit at any time, even without notice.

   D. Employment at will doesn't exist anymore because of state and federal labor laws.

2. A statement that describes what the organization does and its customer base is a:

   A. Vision statement

   B. Statement of position

   C. Lofty statement

   D. Mission statement

3. Taylor is the Quality Assurance director at her organization and reports to both the Division VP at her facility and the VP of Quality Assurance located at the headquarters office. This is an example of what type of organizational structure?

   A. Span of control

   B. Formalized

   C. Matrix

   D. Chain of command

4. True behavioral engagement is considered to be when:

   A. Employees appear engaged.

   B. Employees work longer hours.

   C. Employees think and feel engaged.

   D. Employees actively support local community activities.

5. To which of the following job evaluation methods does the paired comparison method belong?

   A. Ranking

   B. Job classification

   C. Point-factor

   D. Factor comparison

6. Task identity, task significance, and feedback are examples of what?

   A. Job enrichment

   B. Job enlargement

   C. Key productivity indicators

   D. Performance appraisal criteria

7. The statement "We aspire to be a great place to work for all employees" is an example of:

   A. A values statement

   B. A vision statement

   C. A mission statement

   D. A core competency

8. Which of the following is true of training needs assessments?

   A. They are concerned with skill gaps, not attitudes.

   B. They can be eliminated if management knows what training is needed.

   C. They serve as a baseline for evaluating training effectiveness.

   D. They do not consider the conditions under which training is conducted.

9. For which of the following groups does the short test that determines exempt or nonexempt status contain no criteria related to salary?

   A. Executives

   B. Professionals

   C. Administrative employees

   D. Outside salespeople

10. Under OSHA, employees do *not* have the right to

    A. Request OSHA inspections if violations exist in the workplace

    B. Accompany the OSHA compliance officer on an inspection

    C. Apply to OSHA for a temporary variance from a safety standard

    D. Receive training and information on workplace health and safety standards

11. According to behavioral theories, which of the following is an example of employee-centered leadership behavior?

    A. Managers meet with team members to explain recent management decisions.

    B. Managers use their authority to screen the information they give to employees.

    C. Managers develop rules for employees to follow.

    D. Managers set roles and monitor their progress.

12. A manager assigns tasks to an employee that are beyond the scope of the employee's job. When the employee complains, the manager increases the workload and sets unrealistic deadlines. Out of frustration, the employee finally resigns even though he has an employment contract. This situation is an example of

    A. Coerced termination

    B. Constructive discharge

    C. Retaliatory discharge

    D. Voluntary termination

13. According to the FLSA, which of the following would be considered time worked for the purposes of overtime?

   A. A nonexempt employee spends 10 minutes at the end of the day cleaning up the work area.

   B. A nonexempt employee is given a meal break of 45 minutes when working additional hours in the evening.

   C. An exempt employee spends an hour traveling to and from the airport for a 1-day trip.

   D. A nonexempt employee travels from home to a client site after hours in response to an emergency call.

14. A candidate's ability to complete an actual job task is best tested through a(n):

   A. Predictive index

   B. Work sample test

   C. Aptitude test

   D. Achievement test

15. An AAP must include:

   A. A strategy to retain a percentage of older workers

   B. The name and qualification of the EEO coordinator

   C. Descriptions of reasonable accommodations for disabled employees

   D. An analysis of current employees in protected groups by job categories

16. Which of the following is *not* a provision of the ADA?

   A. Buildings financed with public funds must be accessible to the disabled.

   B. New public facilities must be readily accessible to and usable by people with disabilities.

   C. Pre-employment medical exams may be required before an employment offer has been made.

   D. The act applies to employers with 15 or more employees.

17. Which common-law concept protects an employee from being fired for reporting a criminal activity by an employer?

   A. Implied contract

   B. Public policy

   C. Constructive discharge

   D. Implied covenant of fair dealing

18. An HR professional has been assigned to communicate specific policies and procedures to line managers on how to deal with employee grievances. Which of the following HR roles does this task represent?

   A. Advisory

   B. Evaluation

   C. Control

   D. Service

19. Red-circle rates result when a worker is paid

   A. More than the maximum for the pay range

   B. A low salary plus bonus

   C. Slightly more than a new employee with no experience

   D. Less than the minimum for the pay range

20. Disparate treatment occurs when

   A. Only women applicants are required to take a personality test before being offered a position

   B. A policy perpetuates a discriminatory hiring practice

   C. All applicants take a test that only white males perform well on

   D. All workers must meet the same standards, but the consequences are different

21. Employers should obtain which of the following before extending a contingent offer of employment?

   A. A polygraph test

   B. Medical records and a physical exam

   C. Written authorization from the candidate to check work references

   D. Verbal permission from the candidate to check work references

22. Which type of organizational structure would be *most* effective for maintaining centralized authority and accountability of specialized departments?

   A. Line and staff

   B. Functional

   C. Divisional

   D. Matrix

23. Employers with fewer than this many employees are not covered by Title VII.

   A. 500.

   B. 100.

   C. 15.

   D. All companies are covered by Title VII.

24. Which of the following is not a BFOQ?

    A. A synagogue hiring a new rabbi requires that the rabbi be Jewish

    B. A lingerie store hires only female models

    C. A retail store in a predominately Asian neighborhood advertises for Asian clerks

    D. A swimming club requires that the men's changing room attendant be male

25. An employer established an EAP relationship with a social service agency with the employer paying costs up to a preestablished limit. Which of the following programs would most likely be included?

    A. Alcohol and drug abuse counseling

    B. Health risk appraisal

    C. Smoking cessation programs

    D. Nutrition education

Answers

1. **A**. Either party can end the relationship with or without notice, subject to some limitations on the employer created by various laws barring illegal treatment.

2. **D**. A mission statement contains a description of both organizational products/ services and the customer base for which it exists.

3. **C**. When the organization calls for reporting to two or more supervisors, the organization is known as a matrix organization.

4. **C**. Employee engagement is a broad concept of employee satisfaction that leads to behaviors that positively influence business-level performance.

5. **A**. Ranking is one of the simplest to administer. Jobs are compared to each other based on the overall worth of the job to the organization. The "worth" of a job is usually based on judgments of skill, effort (physical and mental), responsibility (supervisory and fiscal), and working conditions.

6. **A**. Job design consists of several factors related to how work gets done, broken into two categories: job enrichment and job enlargement. Task identity, task significance, and feedback are examples of job enrichment activities that can significantly influence job satisfaction through job design.

7. **B**. A vision statement is an aspirational statement that answers the questions of what the company does, who for, and what the company aspires to be in the future.

8. **C**. An effective needs assessment allows a company to both design and evaluate a training program against the specific needs uncovered.

9. **D**. For executives, administrative employees, and professionals, there is a $455 per week salary requirement.

10. **C**. Employees do not have the right to apply for relief from any of the OSHA standards, but they do have the right for any of the other options.

11. **A**. Employee-centered behavior, also known as consideration, refers to leadership behavior that is aimed at meeting the social and emotional needs of group members.

12. **B**. Constructive discharge occurs when an employer makes working conditions so intolerable that an employee is forced into an involuntary termination.

13. **D**. A nonexempt employee called back to work is paid for the time spent getting to the job and handling the emergency.

14. **B**. A work sample test requires candidates to complete an actual work task in a controlled setting. The other tests measure a person's general capacity to learn or ability to relate to others.

15. **D**. An AAP includes a workforce analysis that provides data on the proportion of current employees in protected groups, an availability analysis that provides information on the number of protected group members available in the relevant labor force, and an analysis of incumbency to availability that compares the number of women and minority employees to their availability.

16. **C**. Preemployment exams are permitted only after an employment offer has been extended. The offer may be conditional on passing the exam.

17. **B**. Public policy, an exemption to the employment at will concept, states that employees generally cannot be fired for disclosing illegal, immoral, or illegitimate practices under the control of their employers to organizations that can take corrective action.

18. **A**. In an advisory role, HR trains line managers in the management of human resources.

19. **A**. Red-circle rates are those in which the pay rate is above the range maximum.

20. **A**. Disparate treatment occurs when protected groups are intentionally treated different than other groups.

21. **C**. Because so many firms have been sued by applicants who discovered they had been given poor recommendations, many organizations refuse to supply information without a signed release from the past employee.

22. **B**. Functional organizations are centralized and have specialized departments such as finance, marketing, HR, and manufacturing.

23. **C**. Title VII specifies that any employer engaged in an industry affecting commerce that has 15 or more employees for each working day in each of 20 or more calendar weeks in the current or preceding year, and any agent of such company, is covered by Title VII.

24. **C**. According to the EEOC, there are limited circumstances when race or color is a BFOQ. In this question, A is incorrect because religious organizations are allowed to give preference to members of their religion. The other choices are incorrect because Title VII allows sex as a BFOQ if it is "reasonably necessary" for business operations.

25. **A**. Alcohol and drug abuse counseling would most likely be included because its objectives impact the individual and family. The other choices primarily benefit only the individual.

PART II

Endnotes

1. Penny C Wofford, South Carolina Supreme Court Certified Specialist in Employment and Labor Law, Ogletree Deakins

2. https://www.shrm.org/hr-today/news/hr-magazine/pages/0107hrsolutions.aspx

3. https://www.shrm.org/resourcesandtools/tools-and-samples/hr-qa/pages/metricsmosthelpful.aspx

4. https://www.shrm.org/ResourcesAndTools/tools-and-samples/Pages/Spreadsheets.aspx

5. https://www.shrm.org/resourcesandtools/tools-and-samples/toolkits/pages/managingemployeesurveys.aspx

6. Additional information addressing the use of surveys can be found in Chapter 7.

7. http://compass.port.ac.uk/UoP/file/664e8001-f121-4e5d-aa06-6c95c797e8af/1/Observations_IMSLRN.zip/page_04.htm

8. http://www.huffingtonpost.com/meghan-m-biro-/the-impact-of-technology-_1_b_9294208.html

9. The ACA is under review by Congress with the stated purpose by the House and Senate to pass new legislation to replace the ACA. We recommend you carefully update yourself on the current status of the ACA before coming to a conclusion regarding the current status of this legislation.

10. https://www.osha.gov/pls/oshaweb/owadisp.show_document?p_id=16312&p_table=FEDERAL_REGISTER

11. https://www.dol.gov/sites/default/files/ebsa/about-ebsa/our-activities/resource-center/publications/rdguide.pdf

12. https://www.shrm.org/resourcesandtools/hr-topics/benefits/pages/aca-reporting-tips.aspx

Recruitment and Selection

The functional area Recruitment and Selection will be 15 percent of the Associate Professional in Human Resources (aPHR) exam weighting. Understanding the hiring process, including regulatory requirements, sourcing of applicants, formal interview and selection processes, and onboarding of a new hire, are responsibilities with tight controls on legal requirements imposed by laws. This includes federal laws, which are discussed in this book, as well as the state laws in which your organization operates. While your labor attorney will be your legal guide for your journey through the human resource (HR) profession, you must be able to apply the laws in practical terms so managers can select and hire the best applicants.

The Body of Knowledge statements outlined by the HR Certification Institute (HRCI) for the functional area Recruitment and Selection by those performing early HR career roles are as follows:

Knowledge of

- **01** Applicable laws and regulations related to recruitment and selection, such as nondiscrimination, accommodation, and work authorization (for example, Title VII, ADA, EEOC Uniform Guidelines on Employee Selection Procedures, Immigration Reform and Control Act)

- **02** Applicant databases

- **03** Recruitment sources (for example, employee referral, social networking/ social media)

- **04** Recruitment methods (for example, advertising, job fairs)

- **05** Alternative staffing practices (for example, recruitment process outsourcing, job sharing, phased retirement)

- **06** Interviewing techniques (for example, behavioral, situational, panel)

- **07** Post-offer activities (for example, drug testing, background checks, medical exams)

Laws and Regulations

Twenty-three federal laws impact the functional area Recruitment and Selection. Be sure to refer to Chapter 2 for in-depth information about each of these crucial laws impacting hiring activities. Understanding them is critical to professional performance in the HR profession. HR professionals must be able to apply these laws and guide hiring managers to do the same. You may expect that any or all of these laws will be subjects on the aPHR certification exam.

EXAM TIP   You can expect that the exam will have several questions about the interviewing and applicant processes along with their legal compliance issues.

Federal Laws

Here are the federal laws that you will be responsible for understanding when you have job responsibilities associated with Recruitment and Selection:

- The Fair and Accurate Credit Transactions Act (FACT) (2003)
- The Fair Credit Reporting Act (FCRA) (1970)
- The Fair Labor Standards Act (FLSA) (1938)
- The Immigration and Nationality Act (INA) (1952)
- The Immigration Reform and Control Act (IRCA) (1986)
- The Personal Responsibility and Work Opportunity Reconciliation Act (1996)
- The Service Contract Act (SCA) (1965)
- The Vietnam Era Veterans Readjustment Assistance Act (VEVRAA) (1974), as amended by the Jobs for Veterans Act (JVA) (2008)
- The Wagner-Peyser Act (1933), as amended by the Workforce Investment Act of 1998
- The Work Opportunity Tax Credit (WOTC) (1996)
- Americans with Disabilities Act (ADA) (1990)
- The Civil Rights Act (Title VII) (1964) and (1991)
- The Drug-Free Workplace Act (1988)
- The Equal Employment Opportunity Act (EEOA) (1972)
- The Genetic Information Nondiscrimination Act (GINA) (2008)
- Uniform Guidelines on Employee Selection Procedures (1976)
- The Age Discrimination in Employment Act (ADEA) (1967)

- Executive Order 11246 – Affirmation Action (1965)
- The Congressional Accountability Act (1995)
- The False Claims Act (1863)
- The Homeland Security Act (2002)
- The Employee Polygraph Protection Act (EPPA)
- All the various employment visas for foreign nationals

Applicant Databases

Applicant databases track applicants' information for job openings and are standard for the type of recordkeeping needed in both small and large organizations. Applicant tracking systems (ATSs) provide an automated method for monitoring and tracking the information on applicants from the time they first apply to selection or nonselection, and beyond (such as when a future opening occurs). These systems range from simple Excel spreadsheets to elaborate and sophisticated modules of the human resource information system (HRIS). They provide reports that can be used for EEO-1 reporting and affirmation action plans (AAPs). Federal contractors and organizations with 100 or more employees are required to maintain records of job applicants.

ATSs are helpful for the enormity of the administrative tasks and communications associated with hiring. A hiring management system (HMS) takes the technology up a notch. An HMS integrates with recruiting web sites by moving the candidate's information directly from input into a database. This reduces the errors and allows for faster communication responses via the prescreening capabilities of the HMS. An HMS also provides additional recruitment support with using templates, auto-responders, and standardization of communications. Most HMSs will have advanced report-writing capabilities that can be customized. Table 4-1 provides the typical information that an ATS will track.

Résumés vs. Job Applications

So far, no state or federal law or regulation requires employers to use job applications or résumé forms in their employment process. That means employers are left to their own devices about how to process job applicants. Evaluating differences among job applicants is the primary task. Carefully crafted job application forms can help HR professionals in that evaluation process.

What is required by state and federal law is that employers meet the requirements of equal employment opportunity laws and be able to demonstrate that they made their employment decisions without regard to any of the protected categories. Some organizations prefer to use résumés rather than job applications, and in some companies neither is a requirement.

Information Element	Element Content
Applicant name	Applicant name.
Address	Applicant's current mailing address.
Telephone number	Applicant's current telephone number (home, cell, work).
E-mail or other method of contact	Applicant's e-mail address.
Self-identification of race and sex	This information should not be passed on to the selecting manager (or managers).
Self-identification of protected veteran and disabled status	This information should not be passed on to the selecting manager (or managers).
Source	How did this person get information about your job opening?
Position applied for	Always insist on applicants identifying the specific job opening they are interested in. This might be a job requisition number or a job title.
Job location	If more than one location is available, ask for a preference.
Qualifications for the job	This could be satisfied by a résumé or CV. Alternatively, you can require every applicant to complete your specific job application form.
Availability	How soon will the candidate be available to start work?
Compensation desired	While many people won't answer this question, it is good to ask it anyway. If someone replies with a number significantly above your budget range, you do not need to waste more time on their candidacy.
References	Be sure to track references provided by the job applicant, including educational institutions (and degrees), former employers (with job titles and compensation amounts), and personal references.

Table 4-1   Applicant Tracking Data

If a job application is used, it can be designed by the employer to contain requests for information the employer deems to be necessary in making the employment decision. Obviously, information categories should not include things such as birth date, race, sex, marital status, or other reference to protected categories.

Race and gender/sex are required data points for employees. Employers must either capture that information through employee self-identification or by best guess (via observation). Affirmative action employers (federal goods and service contractors) must invite job applicants to self-identify their race and gender/sex when they submit their application. That information is supposed to be diverted from view of the hiring manager or recruiter. Normally, it is routed to the HR professional responsible for accumulating and analyzing the database it will be entered into.

There are countless ways to write a résumé, and not all of them will contain the same data elements. Further, résumés almost never provide written authorization for employers to gather information from previous employers. Job application forms can be designed with those authorizations and liability release statements to facilitate background checking.

Advantages of Job Application Forms

While there is no requirement for employers to use job application forms, they can be enormously helpful. As an employer, you might expect to gain some or all of these benefits:

- Consistently gather the same data in the same format from each prospective employee. With an employment application, employers gain standardization of the information requested.

- Gather information about the applicant's credentials that candidates would not usually include in a résumé or cover letter. Examples include reasons why the applicant left the employ of a prior employer, felony or misdemeanor crime convictions, and names and contact information for immediate supervisors.

- Obtain the applicant's signature attesting that all statements on the employment application are true.

- Obtain the applicant's signature enabling a potential employer to check the veracity of all data provided on the employment application, including employment history, education history, degrees earned, and so forth. Fraudulent claims and information on application materials, including fake degrees, exaggerated claims about former job responsibilities or compensation, fake dates of employment, and other falsehoods, are a significant problem.

- Get the applicant's signature to attest that the applicant has read and understands certain employer policies and procedures that are spelled out on the employment application. These typically include the fact that the employer is an at-will employer; that the employer is an equal opportunity, nondiscriminating employer; and any other facts that the employer wants the applicant to read and understand on the employment application. When applicable, this may include the requirement that the applicant must pass a drug test prior to hire.

- Obtain the applicant's signature agreeing to a background check, including criminal history, creditworthiness (for certain jobs), driving record (for certain jobs), and anything else required by the job.

- Obtain voluntary self-identification data about race, sex, disability, and veteran status to enable proper reporting to government organizations as required and analysis of employment data by the employer.

These days, it is more a function of employer policy and organizational preference as to which type of record format will be used.

PART II

Online vs. Hard Copy

There are many folks today who prefer to dispense with paper copies of documents, and there are legitimate environmental reasons for moving to electronic copies. There are advantages to each approach.

Hard-Copy Records   Job applications and résumés can provide an insight into the candidate's organization and language skills. Sloppiness and misspellings can be readily detected on paper records, particularly on résumés. Asking applicants to fill out a form can offer some insights into their reading skill, penmanship, written articulation, and inner work standards. When such records are converted to electronic format, the same types of information may not be as obvious.

Online Records   The most obvious advantage of electronic records is that they can be shared by multiple people at the same time. In the case of group interviews, this can be particularly nice. Many years ago there were problems with the legality of electronic signatures on e-documents. The Uniform Electronic Transactions Act of 1999[1] remedied that problem for the most part.

Self-Identification

Invitations to self-identify as part of the application process should be treated as confidential, just as all other HR data is considered confidential. We know from the Fair Labor Standards Act (see Chapter 2) and the EEOC requirement for annual filing of the EEO-1 report that many employers are required to establish and maintain records of employee demographics. The categories of information are for race, gender/sex, veteran, and disabled status.

Race and Gender/Sex

All employers with 100 or more employees and all federal contractors with 50 or more employees and contracts of $50,000 or more (or a construction contract valued at $10,000 or more) must maintain sex and ethnic identification of each employee.

There are seven race/ethnic categories on the EEO-1 form. So, an invitation to self-identify given to employees and job applicants should contain all seven categories. They are as follows:

- White (not Hispanic)
- Black or African-American (not Hispanic)
- Hispanic
- Asian (not Hispanic)
- Native Hawaiian or other Pacific Islander (not Hispanic)
- American Indian, Native American, Alaska Native (not Hispanic)
- Two or more races (not Hispanic)

In the public sector, the EEO-4 report has not expanded its list of five race/ethnic categories. They are as follows:

- White (not Hispanic)
- Black or African-American (not Hispanic)
- Hispanic
- Asian (including Hawaiian and other Pacific Islander, but not Hispanic)
- American Indian, Native American, or Alaska Native (not Hispanic)

 EXAM TIP Be sure to note the category names. The exam's multiple-choice selection may include a question about EEO-1 category names with an answer selection that seems apparent in today's world, such as transgender; however, that is not one of EEO-1 categories.

When an employee fails to self-identify, the employer is responsible for making an observation and best guess as to the race category in which the employee should be reported. If the employee later decides to report their race/ethnicity, that information should be accepted and recorded by the employer.

The government has decided that for tracking and reporting purposes, the Hispanic ethnicity trumps all race categories. That is to say, someone who says they are Hispanic as well as some other race should be recorded as Hispanic. Race categories are used only for non-Hispanic individuals.

The invitation to self-identify should also ask for identification of gender/sex, either male or female. Again, if the individual refuses to self-identify, the employer is obligated to make a selection based on observation.

Veteran and Disabled Status

Federal contractors with $25,000 or more in contract value must abide by regulations related to affirmative action requirements for disabled and veterans. As of 2014, all federal contractors are required to invite self-identification as disabled and veteran from both applicants and employees. When talking about veterans, we mean U.S. veterans. Someone who has served in the armed forces of a foreign country is not included in the government's definition.

The EEOC has determined that it is acceptable to request identification of disability prior to an employment offer being extended as long as the invitation form is the one specified by the Office of Federal Contract Compliance Programs (OFCCP) and it is in an effort to comply with affirmative action obligations. Of course, any request for accommodation during the application process should be handled as required by the Americans with Disabilities Act.

Each of the four categories of veteran should be clearly identified on the self-ID request form. The applicant or employee should be able to choose from that list. Also, a brief explanation of each category should be given so the form user can understand what they mean.

The disability identification should be available as a selection, along with an opportunity to request any job accommodation or applicant accommodation that might be desired.

Pre-employment Testing

Some companies test their applicants before in-depth interviews; others do this afterward. It all depends on the nature of the job. As an example, a job vacancy in IT may have applicants taking a coding test to determine whether they possess the coding skill.

Because of EEO concerns, many organizations ceased testing in the 1970s. Pre-employment testing may involve the risk of litigation on the grounds that the tests discriminate against minorities, the disabled, or other classes of protection if improperly conducted. However, if property conducted, nondiscriminatory formal tests can be of great benefit in identifying and screening good candidates.

A general guideline that is followed for pre-employment testing is like that of any other phase in the hiring processes: the test must be a valid, reliable, job-related predictor. Care must be taken to comply with the Civil Rights Acts of 1964 and 1991 as well as the ADA and any state laws that may apply and be restrictive to pre-employment testing.

 EXAM TIP Monitoring of all required pre-employment testing and making every effort to avoid tests that have adverse impact on minority applicants is a major responsibility of HR. You can expect questions on the aPHR to address the Civil Rights Act.

Recruitment Sources

Often, employers search both inside and outside their organizations for someone who can fill a job opening.

Internal

Some organizations overlook their own workforce as a legitimate source of qualified candidates when job openings occur. Internal recruiting can be handled either formally or informally. In union-represented organizations, a procedure for internal job postings is usually specified in the Memorandum of Understanding (MOU) or union contract (Collective Bargaining Agreement—CBA). Details within union contracts (CBAs) might specify what information should be included in job postings and how long job openings will remain posted. Sometimes internal recruiting must happen for a specified number of days prior to any external recruiting efforts being made. In the absence of unions, the employer will have the opportunity to develop its own policies and procedures in this staffing area.

Often there are internal resources that might fill the needs of the job opening in question. Current employees are constantly changing, through education or temporary job assignments. They may be working on certifications that would better qualify them for a different job. It is important to consider these resources because they represent less expensive candidate pools than those built with external candidates. And it begs the question of whether it is necessary to have a database that tracks current employee skills and certifications. Training accomplishments, new educational achievements, and demonstrated skill performance should all be identified periodically (annually or more often) and the data entered into these types of databases.

One tool that can assist the internal recruiting process is an employee skills database. Information tracked in this database will be confidential to a large extent. Yet it can help you identify qualified candidates for internal placement when the need arises. Your list of data content will likely be different from that created by other HR professionals in different types of organizations. Some of the basics could include the following:

- Typing (rate and accuracy)
- Specific software application skills (Microsoft Office, accounting programs)
- Driving (automobiles, trucks, forklifts)
- Licenses (attorney, physician, pharmacist, private investigation, nursing)
- Certifications (CPA, PHR, SPHR, surveyor, architect)
- Computer programming (languages)
- CPR/first aid
- Credentials (teaching specialty)
- Craft specialty (welding, plumbing, electrician, carpentry)
- Advanced degree (MBA, functional specialty)
- Executive training
- Task force leadership
- Languages (specific language fluency)

Internal recruiting can contribute substantially to your overall placement needs. Generally speaking, internal candidates are less expensive to obtain than external candidates.

Employers often find it is less expensive to recruit job candidates from internal sources. When people are already on the payroll, transferring them to a new job assignment reduces the costs associated with recruiting, hiring, and even sometimes Social Security and Medicare tax.

Job Posting

Internal job posting is an internal job announcement, typically posted on an organization's web site that is accessed only by employees. Basic job description and duties are included along with a deadline for applications. Usually, morale is positively affected when workers see the employer is making opportunities available to the existing workforce before searching outside for job candidates. The job posting might also encourage employee referrals.

Former Employees

Former employees can be a good source for recruitment, especially those who previously held the position. Inviting former employees to apply for re-employment is a viable option, especially with former employees who may have left the workforce because of family care needs or even those who may have had their jobs eliminated because of downturns in the organization's financial picture. If the employee was a top contributor and exited the organization on good terms, inviting a former employee to reapply for an opening can send a positive message to the current workforce and lessen the time required to learn the nuances of the job and company.

External Recruitment Sources

In contrast to internal recruiting is external recruiting, which is just as it sounds: you source candidates from outside the organization. External recruiting sources are covered next.

Public Employment Services

The following are all types of public employment services:

- **State employment services**   Each state has an agency dedicated to providing job search services to job seekers, which includes free posting for job openings of all types of jobs. Many include job search centers where formerly employed workers can have a one-stop place to view openings, obtain assistance with their interviewing skills, and get help with résumés.

- **Veterans' organizations**   Most state employment agencies have linkages to veterans' organizations and often have veteran coordinators on their staff to maintain those relationships. Get to know these people and how they can help with your recruiting efforts.

- **Organizations for the disabled**   Many qualified job seekers are classified as disabled for one reason or another. In many cases, the disability will have no impact on that person's ability to perform the essential job functions. Don't overlook a valuable resource.

- **Local educational institutions**   High schools, community colleges, and universities will usually be glad to post job opening information so their graduating students can find employment in their chosen field of work.

Employment Agencies

With the growth of technology, employment agencies have basically gone away, much like travel agencies. They still exist yet mostly for the most skilled or executive management types. Tech recruiting agencies are still vibrant and necessary for some employers. They recruit and perform as a matchmaker for the applicant and employer. Generally these days, it is the employer that pays a contractual fee, typically paid when a successful hire is made. For the executive and senior levels of management recruiting, these agencies are known as *headhunters,* and it is customary to have the recruiting agency paid on retainer.

Outplacement firms also provide a level of assistance, generally for management-type employees, but not always. When there is a large layoff or facility closure, an outplacement firm may open up a job search center at the organization to assist displayed workers with seeking new employment. This source of potential employees can make recruitment efforts highly cost effective in having a pool of qualified candidates that may know your industry and simply need to be instructed on the nuances of how your organization does business. Several outplacement firms may also provide retraining for different jobs.

Employee Referral

Potential applicants can be referred by current employees, which are great resources. Recommendations from existing employees can result in long-term hires because studies have shown that employees will remain longer with a company where they have established a strong bond of friendship. Moreover, a referral program that provides a monetary cash incentive encourages such referrals and helps with the cost-per-hire expense.

College and University Recruiting

A good source of entry-level hires is college and university recruiting. Large organizations have an entire HR group devoted to nothing but college recruiting. This type of recruitment can be highly effective when capitalizing on school ties, using existing employee alumni to join recruiters on campus during recruitment fairs. Delivering presentations and talking about the culture of your organization and the career path opportunities are going to be highly valued with this resource. With today's technology, many recruitment activities include Skype information webinars and videos that showcase the organization—very much like the colleges and universities themselves use when attracting students to their school.

Professional and Trade Associations

If the employer is a member of an industrial association, there are frequently job posting services offered by such associations, and they are usually free. Also, if the employer sponsors its professional employees with membership in their professional trade associations, here again is another source of posting a job vacancy. These can also include alumni associations.

Diversity Groups

Diversity groups are sometimes called employee affinity groups. They typically are organized along race, gender, disability, or veteran status (for example, African-American Employees Association, Women Engineers Club, or AB Trucking Veterans Association). Sometimes they are sponsored by employers; sometimes they are not. Often, employers provide meeting space and refreshments in exchange for conversations with the groups on topics of diversity management, employee relations, employee development, and so on. Such groups can be a valuable resource for employer human resource management. Diversity groups should be included in external recruiting efforts, encouraging further referrals of job candidates from minority, women, disabled, and veteran populations.

Supplies and Vendors

Although it's often an overlooked source, your organization's vendors and suppliers can "spread the word" about your vacancies. A word of caution, though, if you use a monetary referral incentive—you don't want to necessarily be known as a poacher or a client that hires away the vendor's/supplier's own employees. That might cause you a greater headache for your materials management.

Previous Applicants

This is where the value of the APS comes into play—having a database coded with prospective applicants who may have interviewed for other positions, or perhaps even the current vacancy, who are already interviewed and determined qualified for the position and a candidate for cultural fit. Perhaps they were not selected for a previous position because there was only one position and yet they came in a close second. Previous applicants represent a pool of talent that your organization can quickly and easily identify and contact when a new opening occurs. Courting this group of applicants, in a manner similar to how marketing would court prospective customers and clients, will have a big payoff in cost effectiveness, not to mention the goodwill it leaves with applicants.

Labor Unions

Labor unions, especially those related to your industry, are a source of applicants. Members will have access to announcements at their local union web site and hiring hall. This source can be a great place to attract cross-pollination of talent and skills to cross over to other industries. Of course, if your organization is unionized, pay special attention to the requirements and restrictions that the union contract may have related to hiring for vacancies, particularly the notification to union members first before going externally to the public at large.

Walk-Ins

This used to be a reliable method for attracting applicants. Nowadays if a prospective applicant were to walk in to give their résumé for future openings, they are most likely met with the receptionist advising them that they accept résumés only via their online platform and to please visit their web site. Most walk-ins are reserved for the small mom-and-pop business or other retail associated establishments that are service oriented such as restaurants, nonchain retail stores, and other services. This method is not to be completely discounted, though, because hanging a big sign on your organization's building stating "Now Hiring" still has a big impact, especially for frontline vacancies and seasonal labor. However, you could provide a kiosk in your lobby for the walk-ins to complete their application online rather than using a pencil-and-paper application process.

Recruitment Methods

There are a variety of recruiting methods to attract applicants from the outside. Finding ways to effectively reach the targeted skilled candidates requires you to put on a marketing and sales hat, because this is exactly what it takes. You must figure out how to reach your candidates using the marketing tools and methods available, all at a cost that is within your recruitment budget.

Advertising

Advertising takes many forms. There is the use of traditional media in advertising, and then there are the new frontiers of utilizing the many facets of social media They both have their advantages and disadvantages. It truly takes knowing your applicant base, and that requires research. Talk to your current employees, and keep an eye on where your most recent applicants were generated from if coming to you externally. You will most likely have a budget to stay within, and that requires you to get the most exposure for your budget dollar.

Traditional Media

Newspaper and magazine print advertising can take the form of classified ads or display ads. These days, magazines and newspapers have companion editions online. Buying advertising in one format can also provide the same advertising in the other format. There are also free job search newspapers that can be found in dispensing racks at local supermarkets, on street corners, and at newsstands. These list only job openings within a given geography. They are sustained by paid advertising related to job opportunities and placement, such as those related to training institutions and universities, for example.

Radio and television are other forms of traditional media advertising and can be highly effective when trying to fill a number of positions, such as seasonal labor or a new facility opening. Ads can be created and used at a theater during the previews, on grocery carts, on metro buses, and even on the local sports arena billboards. The creativity is never-ending—where do your desired applicants go, what do they do, and where would you reach them?

Internet and Social Media

The Internet offers several avenues for recruiting, ranging from entry-level and hourly job posting vacancies to professional and management-level openings. HR staff members are integral to directing and managing the online recruitment presence and tools used in organizational hiring. As an early-career HR professional, you will most likely be managing the company's job opportunity section of the web site, which will be a totally separate platform devoted to careers and job opportunities. You'll be intimately involved and have knowledge of all the various generic job boards and sites such as Indeed.com, CareerBuilder.com, Monster.com, ZipRecruiter.com, and others. You'll be browsing how other organizations are posting their vacancies.

Today, more than half of all white-collar jobs are being filled through LinkedIn. LinkedIn.com is a paid resource for employers. Posting job openings on LinkedIn, as of this writing, requires payment of a fee, and that is typically true of the other Internet job boards. Craigslist.com, as of this writing, is still a free service for employers. Social media is growing new tentacles and reaching far and wide as it is quickly becoming a cost-effective and fast method to recruit for a variety of staffing positions. Today companies are investing dollars into creating mobile applications to make recruiting easier for prospective applicants to apply via smart phones. Your organization will likely have a presence on Facebook and use a Twitter account to announce its job vacancies and at the same time request its current workforce to retweet a job posting or announce on its own social media accounts such as Facebook and Nextdoor. It's no longer the Wild West, yet it's still a frontier to be expanded and creatively used to broaden your outreach and quest in attracting applicants.

Job Fairs and Open Houses

Job fairs are designed to bring in a number of employers and job seekers alike into a large hall for quick meet-and-greet interviews, exchanging résumés, and first impressions. This format provides employers a chance to meet a number of potential candidates in a short period of time. HR employment representations and line hiring managers are typically available. These job fairs can be for entry- to mid-level positions. Open houses are where the employer invites job applicants to visit and do the same meet-and-greet as a job fair; only it is at the employer's facility. This allows for a noncompetitive atmosphere for the employer and a chance to provide a tour of the working environment. For both a job fair and open house, this is a cost-effective method for seasonal hiring, positions that have high turnover such as sales, and new plant/facility openings.

Alternative Staffing Practices

The following sections cover alternative staffing practices.

Flexible Staffing

Traditionally, full-time employment was thought of as one of the three 8-hour periods in a workday: 8 A.M. to 5 P.M., 4 P.M. to 1 A.M., or 12 A.M. to 9 A.M. (Each is nine hours long because of a planned meal period of 1 hour.) These days, we don't have quite the lock-step approach to staffing that used to exist, and there are many alternatives to full-time employees.

Temporary Employees

One change to full-time employment is the use of temporary employees. It is not necessary to hire people by putting them on the payroll. Employers can expand their workforce quickly and easily by contracting with temporary talent agencies to satisfy their need for additional people. Temporary workers can be used on production lines, in accounting departments, or in any other portion of an organization experiencing a workload that cannot be handled by the permanent staff. Agencies pay their employees, take care of payroll withholding and tax reporting, add a profit margin, and then pass the final rate to the employer contracting for that help.

Job Sharing

Job sharing is an employment technique that you hear about more and more these days. It offers two or more workers the opportunity to collectively constitute one full-time equivalent employee. One person works the job in the morning, and another works the same job in the afternoon. Considerations involve briefing the "job sharing partner" on the current issues to be dealt with during the next portion of work time. There are some financial considerations, too. Each employee will require the employer's full contribution toward Social Security and Medicare. That may cost the employee more than if one person were to occupy the position.

Part-Time vs. Full-Time

In addition to contributions toward Social Security and Medicare, there are many financial considerations related to full-time versus part-time workers. Where local employment taxes are based on head count, part-time workers can cost more than a full-time staff.

Under the Affordable Care Act, employers can escape paying for benefit coverage of some workers if they maintain a part-time status. By policy, other benefit programs may or may not be available to part-time workers. It is not uncommon to have access to an IRA or other retirement programs based on the number of hours worked each week. The amount of supervision available can also impact the ratio of full-time to part-time workers.

Project Hires/Contract Labor/Gig Employees/Floaters

Using project hires and contract labor is another alternative to full-time employment. Project hires are people who are recruited and placed on the payroll with the understanding that their employment will be terminated once the project is completed. It is common in organizations that seek out projects from client organizations. A staff is hired for the project and then let go when the project comes to an end.

Contract labor refers to people who are hired for a specific period of time. An organization may believe that the workload will last until this time next year. So, it contracts with people to handle that workload for the year. At the end of the contract, those folks will come off the payroll, whether or not the project has concluded. They could be "extended" (payroll status maintained) for a designated period of time if the workload has not diminished.

Gig employees are contracted employees who are utilized for a specific project and then not again until that type of project occurs again. An example would be a concierge type of skilled worker who is employed for only new store openings.

Floaters are employees who are on the organization's payroll who work on a temporary basis for a specific period of time such as vacation relief and may rotate among several positions or departments. A floater is helpful for an on-call basis, able to fill in for temporary assignments such as illness and vacation or leave-of-absence basis, and are ideal for former employees such as early retirees.

Retiree Annuitant

A resource who is already trained, has organizational knowledge, and is experienced in job requirements should not be overlooked. It may be cheaper in the short run to bring back a retired worker to "fill in" temporarily than to hire another type of temporary worker.

Retiree annuitants are folks who have retired from the organization but are called back to work because of emergencies, unexpected workload, or other unforeseen need. They are defined by the Internal Revenue Service (IRS)[2] as people who are entitled to be drawing benefits from their retirement program while earning compensation from their employer for continuing employment whether or not they are continuing to pay into the retirement program.

Phased Retirement

As opposed to instant full-time retirement, phased retirement is another alternative to full-time employment, which allows an individual to take partial retirement while continuing to work a reduced schedule. It can take the form of job sharing, part-time, seasonal, temporary, or project work. A major advantage of phased retirement is that it allows employees to get used to working less and having more time to themselves. It prevents the sudden shock of not having a work routine that comes with traditional retirement.

Contractor Payrolling

When a job needs to be done and the organization does not want to hire someone onto its own payroll to do that job, an alternative is to contract with a vendor who will hire someone to do the job at the client organization. Contractor payrolling is used when you need to adjust to seasonal fluctuations, fill a vacancy while searching for a permanent replacement, bridge the gap in personnel when there is unexpected growth, or use interns for a set period of time. It has many applications, and the greatest benefit is in protecting against charges that the person hired is not an independent contractor but an employee, a problem that cost Microsoft just under $100 million dollars in payroll taxes, penalties, fines, and legal fees. This is usually a process used for less than an entire workforce. When single employees or small groups of employees are needed, payrolling services can solve the need.

Employee Leasing and Professional Employer Organizations (PEOs)

Similar to payrolling, employee leasing is a process of moving employees to another company's payroll as a service for a client organization. Typically, professional employer organizations will take over the entire workforce in a client company. PEOs provide payroll services, tax tracking and depositing, retirement program management, healthcare benefit program management, and even employee counseling and support services. In essence, employee leasing is the outsourcing of the human resource department and the payroll function together. Employees usually become employees of both organizations: the client where they perform their work and the vendor (PEO) that handles the payroll and HR functions for the client. It means both employers are liable for legal compliance.

Outsourcing and Managed Service Providers (MSPs)

Another alternative is outsourcing. Outsourcing is shifting a workload out of the organization through a contract with another employer organization, either here in this country or somewhere else in the world. Managed service providers offer to manage functions as part of a strategic decision to move operations or support functions out of an employment organization to a vendor that can perform them less expensively. Such a decision is designed to allow the client company to focus on key activities within its core business while a vendor handles support activities for the client.

Temp-to-Lease Programs

When a need exists for employees on a seasonal basis or for jobs that will last longer than a few days or weeks, it is possible for employers to lease their workers from a vendor organization. The vendor provides the underlying employment relationship with the worker. When temporary needs stretch into longer-term needs, it still may not be wise to increase payroll in the client organization. That's when contracting for temporary agency workers can be converted into long-term employee leases. These workers often have no benefits provided to them. The client organization pays an employment agency a fee in addition to the pay received by the worker assigned to the client. All payroll operations are maintained by the temporary service agency.

Rehires and Transfers

When workloads rise unexpectedly, it is sometimes difficult to bring in new hires quickly enough to respond to that increased demand. Rehiring laid-off workers and bringing in transfers from other portions of the organization can sometimes be good solutions. Rehired workers are already trained and can be productive immediately. Transfers from other portions of the organization have the advantage of already knowing the culture and, if coming from similar or identical types of work, can also be productive rather quickly.

Interviewing Techniques

Interviewing is an important part of the selection process. A large portion of the workforce is hired only after one or more interviews with the prospective employer. Some organizations conduct a series of interviews ranging from short prescreening interviews to long and in-depth interviews that might last an entire day. The key is to spend sufficient time with the applicant to be able to not only judge their skills and behaviors but also assess whether a "fit" is apparent for the candidate and your company.

Types of Interviews

Employers can select from several primary types of interviews. The types of interviewing styles that you will be using, or the hiring managers who you will be coordinating for, will depend upon the preference of the interviewer (or interviewers), the situation, and the required consistency that must be kept for legality purposes.

 EXAM TIP The various types of interviews are more than likely going to be a question on the aPHR exam.

Prescreening

Prescreening interviews are helpful when there is a high volume of candidates for a job vacancy. HR usually conducts the prescreening interview, which puts them in the role of "gatekeeper." A series of prequalification questions are selected to screen out candidates who do not have the minimal qualifications or whose salary expectations do not fit the organization's salary range.

Structured

An interviewer asks every applicant the same questions along with follow-up probes that may be different depending on the initial response. Structured interviews make it possible to gather similar information from all candidates.

Patterned

In the patterned interview, sometimes called a targeted interview, an interviewer asks each applicant questions that are from the same knowledge, skill, or ability (KSA) area; however, the questions are not necessarily the same. They differ depending on the candidate's background. For example, questions asked of a recent college graduate may differ from those asked of a candidate with years of related experience.

Directive

In this type of interview, an interviewer poses specific questions to the candidate, maintaining tight control; it is a highly structured interview. Every candidate is asked the same questions.

Nondirective

In this type of interview, the interviewer asks open-ended questions and provides only general direction; the interviewer allows the candidate to guide the process. A response to one question dictates what the next question will be.

Behavioral

In a behavioral interview, an interviewer focuses on how the applicant previously handled actual situations (real, not hypothetical). The interviewer probes specific situations looking for past behaviors and how the applicant handled those experiences. The questions probe the knowledge, skills, abilities, and other personal characteristics identified as essential to success on the job. The interviewer looks for three things: a description of an actual situation or task, the action taken, and the result or outcome. The principle behind behavioral interviewing is that past performance is the best predictor of future performance.

Stress

In this type of interview, an interviewer creates an aggressive posture—in other words, deliberately creating some type of stress to see how the candidate reacts to stressful situations. For example, using a room where the candidate has to face an open window with the sun in his or her eyes can put the candidate under stress. This type of interview is used more often in law enforcement, air traffic control, and similar high-stress occupations. The stress interview was more common in the 1970s and 1980s. Today, it is not recommended because of the likelihood that it will be interpreted as personal bias.

Situational

In a situational interview, the interviewer elicits stories and examples that illustrate the applicant's skills and qualifications for the job. Situational interviewing is similar to behavioral interviewing; the only difference is that in a behavioral interview, the interviewer is probing for actual past experiences, whereas in a situational interview, the interviewer develops hypothetical situations and asks the applicant how he or she would handle them.

Group/Panels

Group interviews happen when multiple job candidates are interviewed by one or more interviewers at the same time. Group interviews are used in specific situations where a number of candidates are being considered for the same job in which the duties are limited and clearly defined, such as a merry-go-round operator. A *fishbowl interview* brings multiple candidates together to work with each other in an actual group activity or exercise. It is similar to an in-basket exercise except it involves a group of candidates. A *team interview* typically involves a group of interviewers with a perspective of the actual interactions associated with the job. This might include supervisors, subordinates, peers, customers, and so on. It is like a 360-degree exercise. Finally, in a *panel interview*, questions are distributed among a group of interviewers, typically those most qualified in a particular area. At the conclusion of the panel interview, the panel caucuses with the purpose of coming to a group consensus regarding the result.

Panels can be structured or unstructured. In the public sector, consistency is often a key factor in selection decisions, so structured interviews are conducted by panels. Panel members will sometimes ask the same question of each candidate, and sometimes the panel members will alternate their selection of questions to be asked. Panel size also varies from two to something more. It is common to see panels composed of three to four individuals. Because this is an expensive approach to interviewing (it requires multiple people to spend their time), it is usually reserved for professional and managerial job selections.

Interviewing Skills and Techniques

Conducting effective interviews requires a range of abilities and skills. The following sections cover guidelines that are known to be effective.

Plan Ahead

Be clear on what the job requirements are by reviewing the job and its description with the hiring manager. Observe the job or interview an incumbent. Ask hiring managers what they plan to change about the job from what the predecessor was doing. This provides an opportunity to help plan the standardization of questions.

Create Rapport

Creating a rapport early in the interview process allows applicants to feel more at ease and allows them to open up with dialogue. Remember, the interview is a two-way street—the applicant is also interviewing your organization.

Listen

Reflective listening is a technique that comes in handy in interviewing. Paraphrase or summarize what the candidate said to ensure you have the correct impression. Be sure you are asking open-ended questions so that the interview offers a 70/30 split—by that we mean the candidate is speaking 70 percent of the time and you are speaking 30 percent of the time.

Nonverbal Behavior

Gestures, expressions, eye movement, and body positions are all helpful in the interview. You should be looking for inconsistencies between applicants' verbal and nonverbal cues. Of course, a nonverbal behavior is going to have a filter of your subjective interpretation, yet it should be noted if they have difficulty in coming up with examples when asked or appear uneasy about certain inquiries.

Be Inquisitive

Ask questions. The more open-ended questions you can ask, the better the information will be in helping you determine whether you have a viable candidate. Plan your questions; this is not the time to wing it. Also, for the safety of legalities, do follow the list of questions with all your candidates who are interviewed. Start off with questions such as "Tell me about a time when you (fill in the blank)." Or ask "Describe time when you were required to (fill in the blank)."

Paint a Realistic Picture

As mentioned earlier, the interview is a two-way dialogue where the candidate will also be interviewing the organization, determining whether this is the job they would like to accept if it is offered. To that end, be sure to provide realistic information about the job, the company, and the expectations that the applicant can expect if employed. Culture and values would be ideal to discuss. Be honest and forthright in answering the candidate's questions, yet avoid making promises or making predictions.

Take Notes

It's perfectly fine to jot down notes using an electronic pad, keyboarding, or good old pen and paper. Avoid writing on the applicant's résumé/application, and never make a note that would be construed as discriminatory in some fashion. Notes will help you document the qualifications and the responses when comparing all the applicants who are being interviewed.

Be Courteous

Be prepared, be on time, be professional, minimize any disruptions, and be sure you've reviewed the applicant's résumé *before* they sit in the chair across from you. You are providing an impression about your organization, and having respect for the applicant and their time to interview should be a lasting impression you'll want to make for your organization.

Interviewing Bias

Hiring managers who interview will inadvertently create EEO problems or make ill-fated selection choices without the proper training and guidance from HR. Hiring is typically not a frequent responsibility of a line manager; it may have been several years since they had to hire an employee. A discussion of some common factors that may create problems in interviewing would be helpful from HR. They include the following:

- **Stereotyping**   This involves forming a generalized opinion about how candidates of a particular gender, religion, or race may think, act, feel, or respond. An example would be presuming a woman would prefer to work indoors rather than outdoors.

- **Inconsistency in questioning**   This involves asking different questions of different candidates. An example would be asking only the male candidates to describe a time when they used critical-thinking skills in their last job.

- **First-impression error**   This is when the interviewer makes a snap judgment and lets their first impression (be it positive or negative) cloud the entire interview. An example is where credence is given to a candidate because the person graduated from an Ivy League college.

- **Negative emphasis**   This involves rejecting a candidate on the basis of a small amount of negative information. An example is when a male candidate is wearing a large earring plug and in the interviewer's judgment this is inappropriate, yet the job that the candidate is interviewing for is a phone customer service position—there is no customer visual contact.

- **Halo/horn effect**   This is when the interviewer allows one strong point that he or she values to overshadow all other information. Halo is in the candidate's favor, and horn is in the opposite direction.

- **Nonverbal bias**   An undue emphasis is placed on nonverbal cues that are unrelated to potential job performance. An example is a distracting mannerism such as biting nails.

- **Contrast effect**   This is when a strong candidate has interviewed after a weak candidate and it makes them appear more qualified than they actually are—only because of the contrast.

- **Similar-to-me error**   The interviewer selects candidates based on personal characteristics that they share, rather than job-related criteria. An example would be that both interviewer and candidate attend the same local NFL sports team home games.

- **Cultural noise**   This is when a candidate is masking their response, providing what is considered as "politically correct," and not revealing anything or being factual.

 EXAM TIP   Cultural noise is not associated with a particular geographical location's culture—be sure to not be fooled by the word *cultural*.

Post-Offer Activities

You have a candidate, and they have accepted all the job conditions you have explained; it is now time to put the offer in writing. The offer letter will detail the compensation, start date, job title, organization, and immediate supervisor. You should have a signature block at the bottom of the letter for the candidate to sign as acceptance of the terms. One copy should be returned to you with the signature. It is wise to attach a copy of the job description to the offer letter. It is now time to begin the transition from candidate to potential employee.

The following are activities that an early HR career professional will most likely be responsible for carrying out.

Medical Examinations

Under the Americans with Disabilities Act, employers may require medical examinations only if the exams are job related and consistent with business necessity and only after an offer of employment has been made to the candidate. The purpose of the exam is so it can be used to determine whether the candidate can perform the essential job functions and/or whether a reasonable accommodation is necessary.

Medical examinations can be completed by a physician specified by the company or, in the case of large employers, in their on-site medical centers. Employers have a right to conduct a medical exam, and it is normally limited to "fitness for duty" situations. Examples are an operator of heavy equipment, an air traffic controller, and a first responder. In some organizations, a particular level of management is required to take a physical exam.

Drug Testing

Employers risk the torts of negligent hiring if they knowingly hire a drug or alcohol abuser who causes harm to someone while on the job. That along with federal mandates for some employers and/or occupations is the purpose behind pre-employment drug testing.

Validated studies by OSHA have proven that drug-screening pre-employment tests reduce job-related accidents. Drug screening tests are specifically excluded from the ADA's medical exam requirement. The successful passing of a drug test may be required prior to extending an offer of employment.

Privacy and Legal Issues

Access to information about applicants should be strictly limited to those people in your organization with a need to know the information. Many states are aggressive protectors of employee and applicant privacy; there are severe penalties for a lack of privacy. Make sure you store an applicant's medical exam results and drug testing results in a secure location and that they are not left unattended on your PC screen. Only those people with a need to access the content of the files should be allowed access.

Background Checks

Job offers are often conditioned upon successful completion of background checks, reference checks, and sometimes even credit checks. In some instances, a job offer could be conditioned on passing a medical evaluation or a drug screen.

Before conducting background checks or credit checks, review the current legal limitations on their use. The EEOC has issued guidelines on consideration of conviction records because the population of convicted felons is so heavily skewed with people who are African-American or Hispanic. Considering conviction records has a disparate impact on those two racial groups.[17] Thus, only if the conviction has a direct relationship to the job content will considering it in the hiring decision be permitted by the EEOC.[3]

References

There may be several types of references your organization requires. They may include the following:

- **Employment references**   Information that you ascertain from previous employment of the applicant to verify dates of employment, job titles, and type of work performed. Many employers are reluctant to provide more information than name, rank, and file number for privacy reasons, but as long as the information is factual and provided in good faith, most states consider it "qualified privileged," which protects the reporting employer.

- **Educational references**   Verifying the applicant's degrees or educational attainment, including years of attendance and requests for transcripts.

- **Financial references**   Generally used only when candidates will be handling financial transactions, cash, or other financial resources. Financial references are obtained through one of the three credit reporting bureaus and are subject to requirements of the federal FCRA.

Employment Authorization – Form I-9

The Immigration Reform and Control Act of 1986 (see Chapter 2) introduced the requirement for all employees in the United States to provide proof of identity and proof that they have the legal right to work in this country. That law brought us the Form I-9. Every person hired after November 30, 1986 must furnish information on a Form I-9, and the employer must complete the document citing the specific identification presented by the new worker. The employer must also cite the document used to prove the new employee has authorization to work in this country. This form changes from time-to-time, so employers should visit www.uscis.gov/files/form/i-9.pdf to be sure they are using the most current version of the form.

- **Proof of identity**   Also required for employment is a photo identification of some variety, issued by a governmental agency that contains the individual's name as well as a current or recent image. This can be a U.S. passport (Passport Book or Passport Card), or in most cases, a driver's license issued by the state in which the person lives. All states will issue a non-driver identification card if requested to do so. A list of acceptable documents is included on the instructions for Form I-9. The employer must accept any document listed on Form I-9.

- **Proof of work authorization**   A Social Security Card number is the usual form of authorization offered by new employees. It does not provide proof of identity because it does not have a photo of the card owner, but it does offer proof that the owner is authorized to work in this country. Documents accepted for work authorization include visas of various types and any other form specified on the instructions for Form I-9. Refer to Chapter 2 for a detailed outline of visa types related to employment.

Employers have three work days from the time of hire to complete the Form I-9 and have it ready for inspection by any authorized federal investigator. If, at the end of three days, the newly hired employee has not provided the required documentation, the employer is instructed to remove the worker from the payroll. Retaining someone who is not properly documented will represent a violation of the federal law. There are fines of up to $1,000 per error on Form I-9 and court-imposed fines for retaining illegal aliens on the payroll.

E-Verify System

E-Verify began life as a voluntary program offered by the government as a way for employers to get online verification of new employees' Social Security numbers. It has evolved into a combination voluntary/involuntary program as federal and state governments mandate portions of the employer community to participate. The program was intended to reduce the number of false positives received when the Social Security Administration was checking new hire reports for invalid Social Security number matches.

The Department of Labor now requires federal contractors who are subject to the affirmative action regulations to participate in E-Verify. And, as time has passed, the accuracy of the Social Security number database has improved.

As of August 2013, nine states require all employers to participate in the E-Verify program. There is pending legislation in 11 additional states that would require some or all employers to participate in the program. In addition to that, there are many states that require state agencies to participate in the program, and some local jurisdictions that have their own requirements. The message here is that HR professionals should check their local and state requirements frequently so they remain in compliance.

Social Media Searches

Not so long ago the idea of checking a candidate's social media as part of the hiring process was not even considered. Doing so was thought of little value to understanding an applicant's professional viability. In the last few years, however, that has vastly changed, and checking has since become the norm. In a recent survey by the Society for Human Resource Management, 43 percent of organizations reported using social media to screen job candidates—an increase from 2013.[4] How a candidate acts on social media isn't just a reflection of their professionalism and personality. Their online behavior can also be a sign of how they will represent your business as an employee. HR recruiters have learned how to tap into this mecca of information and how it can damage a potential candidate's credibility. Rants about former employers are a red flag for a prospective employer. Social media sites and searches can provide a treasure trove of behavioral information that may be used as part of the criteria for a hiring or not-hiring decision.

The evaluation potential of social media is obvious, and many employers are already incorporating it into their recruiting strategy. Others are more hesitant. Some hiring managers wonder if social media checks are on shaky ground legally. Is looking at a candidate's Facebook and Twitter accounts the same as asking them about religion or marital status? Is there a good reason firms shouldn't check social media during the hiring process? In most cases, the answer is no. You still need to proceed cautiously with social media checks, but proceed.

Credential Verification

As with educational references, credential verification may be necessary when a job requires a credential, such as a license or certification. Negligent hiring could occur if an employer did not verify professional or technical certification. Such would be the case of a physician whose license expired or was revoked and still performing a procedure that was unsuccessful on a patient.

Public Records

Public records such as criminal records can uncover information about violent behavior, substance abuse, and property crimes such as theft or embezzlement. It can be difficult to extract this level of information if your organization is a private employer, so many times you'll need to employ an investigative third party that does have the ability and credentials to obtain a public record. Criminal record checks are considered consumer investigations and must comply with related FCRA requirements.

Legal and Privacy Issues

The use of polygraph tests in the employment process is limited by the Employee Polygraph Protection Act (EPPA). As discussed earlier, there are privacy issues related to reference checks just as there are with medical examination information. Keep the information confidential. Only those people having a need to access the content of the results should be allowed access. Records should be secured at all times so passersby cannot pull open a file drawer and remove documents.

Onboarding and Orientation

It is a common belief that the first 90 days of a worker's experience on a new job will determine how the relationship goes for the balance of his or her employment. One way to get off on the right foot is to provide a quality orientation program (also referred to as *onboarding*) to every new employee.

A strong orientation program will include such things as follows:

- **Welcome by the CEO/senior executive**   Providing evidence that senior management cares about employees can begin during orientation. Senior executives who believe it isn't worth their time convey a strong message also.

- **Discussion about culture**   This is an opportunity to discuss "the way we do things around here." What does the employer value? What gets rewarded in the organization? What type of image does the employer want to project to the world? What are expectations of ethics?

- **Enrollment in benefit programs**   This is an opportunity to complete payroll tax forms, benefit enrollment forms, and self-identification forms for race, sex, disability, and veteran status.

- **Tour of employee common areas**   This can include the cafeteria or break room, the location for labor law compliance posters, and restrooms.

- **Safety equipment and emergency exits**   This is often overlooked when it should be on the orientation agenda. If there are emergency breathing apparatus, eye-wash stations, emergency shutdown switches, first-aid stations, or other important safety points of interest, this is the time to show each new worker where they are. Safety training in how to use emergency equipment will come later.

- **Introduction to co-workers and supervisors**   Guide the employees to their new work locations and introduce them to their new co-workers and supervisors, even if they may have met some of them during the interviewing process. Have someone designated to explain where to get office supplies, how to access computer terminals, and who to ask when questions come up. These things are just common employment courtesy.

PART II

Records Retention

The management of employment-related records concerning the legal requirements for retention can be daunting and confusing. The confusion is often a result of the complexity and variety of restrictions imposed by the many laws. Some requirements apply to most employers hiring; others apply to just government contractors and subcontractors. Same or similar records are often required by more than one law, but the periods of retention may vary. Some requirements depend on the industry or the location, and federal as well as state laws in which an employer exists apply. Table 4-2 provides a reference for HR professionals to use when considering documentation that is associated

Type of Record	Relevant Law	Years to Be Kept	Records Covered
Selection, hiring, and employment records	Age Discrimination in Employment Act (20 or more employees) Americans with Disabilities Act (15 or more employees) Civil Rights Act of 1964 (Title VII) (15 or more employees) Section 503 of the Rehabilitation Act of 1973 (federal contractors) Vietnam Era Veterans Readjustment Assistance Act (federal contractors) Executive Order 11246 (applies to federal contractors) Service Contract Act, Davis-Bacon Act, Walsh-Healey Act (apply to federal contractors)	1 year after creation of the document or the hire/no-hire decision, whichever is later (3 years for federal contractors)	Job applications, résumés, job ads, screen tools/tests, interview notes, and other records related to hire/no-hire decisions Records related to promotions, demotions, transfers, performance appraisals, terminations, reasonable accommodations, and/or requests, training records, incentive plans, merit systems, and seniority systems AAP records relating to hiring benchmarks and utilization goal analyses, hiring metrics analyses, and self-identification records for veterans and individuals with disabilities Copy of EEO-1 survey and intake forms if applicable
Form I-9	Immigration Reform and Control Act (one or more employees)	3 years after date of hire or one year after date of termination, whichever is later	

Table 4-2 Federal Record Retention for Recruitment and Selection Records *(continued)*

Type of Record	Relevant Law	Years to Be Kept	Records Covered
Polygraph test records	Employee Polygraph Protection Act (one or more employees)	3 years	Polygraph test result(s) and the reason for administering
Affirmative action plan/data	Executive Order 11246 (applies to federal contractors) The Uniform Guidelines on Employee Selection Procedure (100 or more employees)	2 years	
Credit reports	Fair and Accurate Credit Transactions (one or more employees)	No retention requirement; law requires shredding of all documents containing information derived from a credit report; however, don't discard for at least 1 year (see "Selection, hiring, and employment records" in this table)	
Drug test records	Department of Transportation (DOT)–covered safety-sensitive transportation positions; aviation, trucking, railroads, mass transit, and pipelines	1 year from test date (up to 5 years for records relating to drug testing for DOT positions; see §382.401 for specific DOT retention requirements) https://www.gpo .gov/fdsys/pkg/ CFR-2011-title49-vol5/xml/CFR-2011-title49-vol5-part382 .xml#seqnum382.401	

Source: U.S. Department of Labor and the EEOC.

Table 4-2 Federal Record Retention for Recruitment and Selection Records *(continued)*

with the recruitment and selection function. A wise approach in considering which documents to retain is to answer the following three questions:

- What records must be kept under each federal law?
- What is the retention period for those records?
- What is the applicability for each federal law?

EXAM TIP Recordkeeping is a usual responsibility of the early-career HR professional. Expect to see a question on the aPHR exam about record retention in both the pre- and post-employment phases.

Chapter Review

The recruiting and selection process covers a wide swath of knowledge and responsibility. Many laws impact this area of HR responsibility that the early HR career professional will need to follow. There will also be a great deal of skill to be developed. It takes some time for HR professionals to acquire the skills for effective interviewing. Just as important is the level of creativity that is needed for the functions of sourcing viable candidates for job vacancies.

From job postings to reference checks and from illegal employment discrimination to legal hiring practices, HR professionals have extensive responsibilities and knowledge requirements. The laws impacting this function area will be an important foundation to understanding the methods and techniques utilized in recruitment and selection.

Questions

1. Lebron serves his employer as the HR director. It is a startup company, and his bosses want him to hire people fast, so they have given him some tests to use in the screening process. He was told to hire the applicants with the best scores. Are these tests something Lebron should use?

   A. It is OK to use tests if they are job specific in their measurement.

   B. No way. He should not use any tests that he hasn't bought from a legitimate test publisher.

   C. Tests are just fine. He should be sure the passing scores are set so they can get the best people.

   D. If the boss says to use the tests, he has little choice. He just has to be sure to score them properly.

2. AB Trucking has had a policy that nobody will be hired unless they complete the company's job application. Now, all of their job applications are being processed online, and some applicants want to submit their résumés instead of a job application form. What can AB Trucking do about the résumé vs. application controversy?

   A. It is entirely up to the company how it wants to handle the policy. Application forms are not a legal requirement, but using them is generally considered a best practice in the employment arena. Job candidates can be forced to go through the company's process of completing an application form, online or offline.

   B. The government has set up regulations that say employers have to accept résumés if they are submitted in a job search. The company doesn't really have any choice but to accept them.

    C. Job applications are old-school. Almost no employer uses them these days. The company should change its policy and use only résumés in the future.

    D. Résumés don't have all the information that can be gathered on a job application, and people lie on résumés anyway. That alone is reason for the company to continue using its job application forms.

3. An employee in Cortez's organization came to him and suggested that she and her co-worker could consolidate their duties into one job and each work part-time. What is this arrangement known as?

    A. Part-time jobbers

    B. Job sharing

    C. Impossible

    D. Double duty

4. Abel has been having trouble selecting quality accounting people. Everyone claims to be able to use Excel spreadsheets, but few actually can once they get on the job. In the end, he has had to terminate people because of poor performance. He is thinking he will use a test he saw at the local office-supply warehouse. As Abel's HR recruiting liaison, what advice would you give him about his plans for testing?

    A. It sounds like a good idea. It certainly could control the cost of turnover. We should try it.

    B. It sounds like a good idea. Will he be able to show that the test actually predicts success on the jobs he wants to use it for? If not, he should find a different screening tool.

    C. It doesn't sound like a good idea. With everyone talking about the liability of written tests these days, we can't take that risk for any job.

    D. It doesn't sound like a good idea. It is going to create more paperwork for HR, and we can't stand any workload increase.

5. Which of the following is the best online recruiting source for finding passive candidates?

    A. The company's web site

    B. Personal online networks such as LinkedIn

    C. Job fairs

    D. Employment agencies

6. Which of the following is an in-person recruiting method?

    A. Job board

    B. Job bidding

    C. Job fair

    D. Posting on company web site

7. What should your organization do if the requirements for the same record differ between three laws?

   A. Keep duplicates of each record in different files according to the differing requirements

   B. Make a judgment about the maximum retention based on the law that has the most importance

   C. Retain the information for the longest period of time required

   D. Keep the records for the shortest time required unless it involves a federal contractor

8. Which of the following statement is *true* about medical examinations?

   A. Temporary employees can be required to submit to a medical exam before employment.

   B. Pre-employment health checklists can be requested before an employment offer is made.

   C. Exams must be job related and can be required only after an employment offer is made.

   D. The exam must be completed for the company's medical staff.

9. As the employment coordinator for your organization, you have been requested to arrange interviews with three of the top qualified candidates for a customer service position. The interviewers will be a select group of employees from the customer service department who would be the candidate's co-workers. This is an example of what type of interview?

   A. Stress interview

   B. Group/panel interview

   C. Situational interview

   D. Rapport interview

10. A job offer letter should be sent to a selected candidate immediately after:

    A. The hiring decision is made

    B. All contingencies are addressed

    C. Both parties review the employment contract

    D. Both parties verbally agree to any relocation expenses

11. Leslie is reviewing the list of interview questions the hiring manager has submitted. Which interview question on the hiring manager's list has the potential to be discriminatory under federal law?

    A. "Are you legally blind?"

    B. "Do you have any relatives who work for our headquarters?"

    C. "The job requires you to lift a 30-pound package once a month and place it on a shelve in the supply closet. Can you do that?"

    D. "Are you older than 18?"

12. Leslie notices another question on the hiring manager's list. Which additional question is not allowed because of its discriminatory manner under federal law?

    A. "Did you graduate from high school?"

    B. "Have you ever filed a workers' compensation claim?"

    C. "Do you have proper documentation to work in the United States?"

    D. "Did you receive any training in the military?"

13. Which of the following statements indicates a nondirective interview?

    A. The hiring manager asks all applicants the same questions.

    B. The hiring manager purposefully creates a high level of stress.

    C. Each candidate interviewed is asked different questions about the same skill and ability.

    D. The hiring manager's next question is formulated by the candidate's response to the previous open-ended question.

14. What is *not* a characteristic of a realistic job preview (RJP)?

    A. Taking a candidate on a tour of the facility

    B. Having the candidate job shadow

    C. Having a panel interview with a group of employees who are currently performing the job

    D. Completing a pre-employment assessment test

15. Under which of the flexible staffing options would a professional employer organization (PEO) be most likely to provide temporary workers with benefits?

    A. Payrolling

    B. Master vendor contract

    C. Outsources or managed services

    D. Temp-to-lease arrangement

16. "Floater" employees are:

    A. Scheduled to work less than a regular workweek on an ongoing basis

    B. Self-employed independent contractors hired a contract basis for specific functions

    C. People who are employed by the organization receiving a W-2 who fill in on a short-term basis for a temporary period of time and may rotate among several positions or functions

    D. Long-term contracted temporary employees assigned to one department

17. A benefit of job posting within an organization first is that it:

   A. Provides a cost-effective manner to target a desired pool of applicants at one time

   B. Provides an easy way to create a database for job vacancies

   C. Allows individuals to maximize their career opportunities within a company

   D. Allows existing employees to indicate interest in an opening

18. Deidre was disappointed in the lack of qualified responses to a recent print media advertisement, causing several of her open vacancies to exist for longer than anticipated. To expand her recruiting efforts, Deidre should utilize all of the following *except* which one?

   A. College/universities and job fairs

   B. The state employment agency

   C. Employee referrals

   D. Job bidding

19. Which federal agency is used to investigate charges of discrimination in hiring practices under Title VII?

   A. NLRB

   B. EEOC

   C. Pre-employment hiring board

   D. ADA board

20. What type of interviewing bias is being applied when the hiring manager is making a judgment about the applicant based on the manner in which they are dressed?

   A. Stereotyping

   B. Negative emphasis

   C. Contrast effect

   D. Cultural noise

21. Which of the following selection practices is illegal under federal law?

   A. Obtaining information from references without a candidate's written permission

   B. Requiring a job-related test that has adverse impact on minority groups

   C. Determining whether an applicant has ever filed a workers' compensation claim

   D. Requiring applicants to submit to a pre-employment drug test

22. Which of the following recruitment methods offers the opportunity for potential applicants to discuss opening with employers without having a job application/résumé on file?

   A. Job fairs

   B. Employee referrals

   C. Outplacement firm job search centers

   D. State employment agencies

23. When can the Trustworthy Bookkeeping and Tax Preparation organization require a polygraph test of a new employee?

   A. When a candidate is applying for an HR recruiting position

   B. When a candidate is applying for a clerical position

   C. When an accountant candidate is applying for a job in a function that has embezzlement potential

   D. When a candidate is a recovering substance abuse user

24. Which of the following documents from List C verifies a potential candidate's identity and right to work for Form I-9?

   A. A Native American tribal document

   B. A state driver's license with photo ID

   C. A U.S. birth certificate

   D. A U.S. military card

25. When the hiring manager stated to the applicant in the interview, "I notice that you are applying for our job and yet you have a lot more knowledge, experience, and skill than is required for the job. How do you feel about working in a job that is lower than your experience indicates you can perform?" The candidate responds with the statement, "I have always admired and wanted to work at your organization." What interviewing bias is the candidate portraying?

   A. Halo/horn effect

   B. Underachiever effect

   C. Cultural noise

   D. Similar-to-me error

Answers

   1. A. Remember that it is the user of a test that holds the liability, not the publisher of the test. If a test has been validated to properly predict success in specific jobs with specific knowledge and skill requirements, it can be used for those jobs. Using it for *all* jobs is not a good idea. If the boss insists, he needs to be told what the consequences can be.

2. **A**. The company is not constrained by the government on how it designs its job application process. If it wants to have a certain form completed, it can establish that policy. A decision should be made about what documents it will accept from job applicants. Consistency in how the process is applied is critical in avoiding complaints of bias.

3. **B**. Job sharing is where two or more workers collectively work a job on a part-time basis to constitute one full-time equivalent employee.

4. **B**. The test should measure Excel skills because those are the predictors of success for Abel's accounting positions.

5. **B**. Personal online networks are excellent sources for finding passive candidate. A passive candidate is a person who is not seeking employment but may have the background that matches the vacancy of the organization.

6. **C**. Job fairs are designed to bring in a number of employers and job seekers alike into a large hall for quick meet-and-greet interviews.

7. **C**. When the same or similar records are required by more than one law but the period of retention varies, retain the record for the longer period of time.

8. **C**. Only after a job offer is made can an employer require a job candidate to have a medical exam to determine fitness for duty. Only the medical examiner's conclusions about job fitness may go to the employer, not the actual test results.

9. **B**. Group and panel interviews happen when multiple job candidates are interviewed by one or more interviewers at the same time.

10. **A**. Time is of the essence. Put it in writing so that the candidate has assurance and understanding of what the job offer parameters are and they can give notice to their current employer when necessary.

11. **A**. You may ask questions associated with the applicant's ability to perform the identified functions of the job. You cannot ask about the nature or severity of a disability or recent or past surgeries.

12. **B**. Asking about previous workers' compensation claims is considered potentially discriminatory and is not relevant to the job. Asking instead if the applicant can perform all the identified job functions and physical requirements, line by line if necessary, is acceptable. A medical exam for fitness to do the job might be a next level of verification.

13. **D**. With nondirective interviews, the hiring manager will ask open-ended questions and provide only general direction. A response to one question by the candidate dictates what the next question will be.

14. **D**. A pre-employment assessment test will measure skills and/or knowledge to perform the functions of the job, not provide the candidate with a realistic visual preview of what the job actually entails.

15. **D**. An organization contracts with a temp service assigning a long-term temporary worker who, after a period of time of working for the employer, transfers to the employer's payroll.

16. **C**. Employees who are on the organization's payroll and fill in for temporary short-term assignments among several positions or departments are known as *floaters* who provide continuity of knowledge and experience.

17. **C**. It is a morale booster and retention method to offer the existing workforce the opportunity to apply for job vacancies before an employer seeks candidates externally.

18. **D**. Job bidding is only for internal existing candidates from the current workforce.

19. **B**. The EEOC is the agency that is responsible for investigating all charges of discrimination under Title VII, rather than pre-employment hiring practices or post-employment activities.

20. **B**. Negative emphasis often happens when subjective factors such as dress or nonverbal communication taint the hiring manger's judgment.

21. **C**. Be careful not to violate an individual's privacy or other rights. Checking to see whether an applicant has filed a workers' compensation claim is most likely a violation of privacy rights.

22. **A**. Job fairs bring together a number of job seekers with employers in a group setting such as a hall for quick meet-and-greet interviews, exchanging résumés and first impressions.

23. **C**. Although the Employee Polygraph Protection Act of 1988 prohibits employers from requiring or requesting pre-employment polygraph exams under most circumstances, if the position has been identified as a high risk for possible embezzlement, this test can be administered as long as all candidates for the same function are examined.

24. **A**. A Native American tribal document can establish both identity and employment authorization on Form I-9 according to the U.S. Citizenship and Immigration Services.

25. **C**. Cultural noise is when the candidate skirts the question and is reluctant to tell the interviewer unacceptable facts about themselves.

Endnotes

1. Uniform Law Commission, "The Uniform Electronic Transaction Act," www .uniformlaws.org/ActSummary.aspx?title=Electronic%20Transactions%20Act, accessed on February 8, 2014

2. Internal Revenue Service, "Retiree Annuitants," www.irs.gov/Government-Entities/Federal,-State-&-Local-Governments/Rehired-Annuitants, accessed on February 8, 2014, from

3. U.S. Department of Justice, Bureau of Justice Statistics, "Prisoners in 2012—Advance Counts," July 2013. www.bjs.gov/content/pub/pdf/p12ac.pdf

4. Jonathan A. Segal and Joyce LeMay, "Should Employers Use Social Media to Screen Job Applicants?" Nov. 1, 2014. https://www.shrm.org/hr-today/news/hr-magazine/pages/1114-social-media-screening.aspx

Compensation and Benefits

The functional area Compensation and Benefits weighs in at 14 percent of the Associate Professional in Human Resources (aPHR) exam.

Compensation and benefits, collectively identified as *total rewards,* are management functions that are valuable to owners of a business, helpful to managers, and significantly important to employees, all collectively identified as *stakeholders.* As a human resource (HR) practitioner, at some point you should expect to be involved in a wide range of compensation and benefits activities that will require your basic knowledge and understanding of the rules and regulations that apply to compensation and benefits in your organization regardless of whether you are directly involved in the management and administration of compensation or benefits programs. This chapter will provide an overview of basic compensation and benefits requirements that you will need to know for success in your job. Be sure not to overlook their importance in your preparation for the aPHR exam.

The Body of Knowledge statements outlined by HR Certification Institute (HRCI) for the Compensation and Benefits functional area by those performing early HR career roles are as follows:

Knowledge of

- **01** Applicable laws and regulations related to compensation and benefits, such as monetary and nonmonetary entitlement, wages and hours, and privacy (for example: ERISA, COBRA, FLSA, USERRA, HIPAA, PPACA, tax treatment)

- **02** Pay structures and programs (for example: variable, merit, bonus, incentives, noncash compensation, pay scales/grades)

- **03** Total rewards statements

- **04** Benefit programs (for example: healthcare plans, flexible benefits, retirement plans, wellness programs)

- **05** Payroll processes (for example: pay schedule, leave and time-off allowances)

- **06** Uses for salary and benefits surveys

- **07** Claims processing requirements (for example: workers' compensation, disability benefits)

- **08** Work-life balance practices (for example: flexibility of hours, telecommuting, sabbatical)

Laws and Regulations

The following federal laws impact almost every employer in the United States in a significant way, but they are only a start. Understanding them is essential to every HR professional whether you are just starting out or have years of experience. Many of these laws will be on your aPHR exam. You can find additional information on these laws in Chapter 2.

Davis-Bacon Act

The Davis-Bacon Act applies to contractors and subcontractors working on federally funded or assisted contracts in excess of $2000 for the construction, alteration, or repair (including painting and decorating) of public buildings or public works. Contractors and subcontractors must pay their laborers and mechanics employed under the contract no less than the locally prevailing wages and must pay fringe benefits for corresponding work on similar projects in the area.

Copeland Act

The Copeland "Anti-Kickback" Act is divided into two sections. Section 1 is a criminal statute prohibiting anyone from inducing by any means any person employed on the construction, prosecution, completion, or repair of a federally assisted building or work to give up any part of his or her compensation to which he or she is otherwise entitled. Section 1 applies to all construction contracts irrespective of amount. Section 2 is a civil statute requiring certain employment records to be maintained. Section 2 is administered by the U.S. Department of Labor and applies to construction contracts exceeding $2000.

Walsh-Healey Public Contracts Act

The Walsh-Healey Public Contracts Act (PCA) establishes minimum wage, maximum hours, and safety and health standards for work on contracts in excess of $10,000 for the manufacturing or furnishing of materials, supplies, articles, or equipment to the U.S. government or the District of Columbia. All provisions of the PCA are administered by the Wage and Hour Division of the U.S. Department of Labor, except the safety and health requirements, which are administered by the Occupational Safety and Health Administration (OSHA), also part of the DOL.

Fair Labor Standards Act (FLSA) (1938), as Amended

The FLSA establishes minimum wage, overtime pay, recordkeeping, and youth employment standards affecting employees in the private sector and in federal, state, and local governments. Covered nonexempt workers are entitled to a minimum wage of not less than $7.25 per hour effective 2009. Overtime pay at a rate not less than one-and-a-half times the regular rate of pay is required after 40 hours of work in a workweek.[1]

- **FLSA minimum wage**   The federal minimum wage is $7.25 per hour. Many states also have minimum wage laws. In cases where an employee is subject to both state and federal minimum wage laws, the employee is entitled to the higher minimum wage.

- **FLSA overtime**   Covered nonexempt employees must receive overtime pay for hours worked over 40 per workweek (any fixed and regularly recurring period of 168 hours, which is seven consecutive 24-hour periods) at a rate not less than one-and-a-half times the regular rate of pay. There is no limit on the number of hours employees 16 years or older may work in any workweek. The FLSA does not require overtime pay for work on weekends, holidays, or regular days of rest, unless overtime is worked on such days.

- **Hours worked**   Hours worked ordinarily include all the time during which an employee is required to be on the employer's premises, on duty, or at a prescribed workplace.

- **Recordkeeping**   Employers must display an official poster outlining the requirements of the FLSA. Employers must also keep employee time and pay records.

- **Child labor**   FLSA provisions are designed to protect the educational opportunities of minors and prohibit their employment in jobs and under conditions detrimental to their health or well-being.

Equal Pay Act (EPA)

The Equal Pay Act requires that men and women be given equal pay for equal work in the same establishment. The jobs need not be identical, but they must be substantially equal. It is job content, not job titles, that determines whether jobs are substantially equal. Specifically, the EPA provides that employers may not pay unequal wages to men and women who perform jobs that require substantially equal skill, effort, and responsibility and that are performed under similar working conditions within the same establishment.

Pregnancy Discrimination Act (PDA)

The Pregnancy Discrimination Act (PDA) amends Title VII of the Civil Rights Act of 1964. Discrimination on the basis of pregnancy, childbirth, or related medical conditions constitutes unlawful sex discrimination under Title VII. Women affected by pregnancy or related conditions must be treated in the same manner as other applicants or employees who are similar in their ability or inability to work.

Family and Medical Leave Act (FMLA), as Amended

The FMLA entitles eligible employees of covered employers to take unpaid, job-protected leave for specified family and medical reasons with continuation of group health insurance coverage under the same terms and conditions as if the employee had not taken leave. Eligible employees are entitled to the following:

- Twelve workweeks of leave in a 12-month period for any of these reasons:
  - The birth of a child and to care for the newborn child within one year of birth
  - The placement with the employee of a child for adoption or foster care and to care for the newly placed child within one year of placement
  - To care for the employee's spouse, child, or parent who has a serious health condition
  - A serious health condition that makes the employee unable to perform the essential functions of his or her job
  - Any qualifying exigency arising out of the fact that the employee's spouse, son, daughter, or parent is a covered military member on "covered active duty"
- Twenty-six workweeks of leave during a single 12-month period to care for a covered service member with a serious injury or illness if the eligible employee is the service member's spouse, son, daughter, parent, or next of kin (military caregiver leave)

On February 23, 2015, the U.S. Department of Labor's Wage and Hour Division announced a Final Rule to revise the definition of *spouse* under the Family and Medical Leave Act in light of the United States Supreme Court's decision that found the Defense of Marriage Act to be unconstitutional. The Final Rule amends the definition of *spouse* so that eligible employees in legal same-sex marriages will be able to take FMLA leave to care for their spouse or family member, regardless of where they live.[2]

Health Insurance Portability and Accountability Act (HIPAA)

HIPAA is federal legislation that provides data privacy and security provisions for safeguarding medical information. The act contains five sections, or *titles*:

- Title I protects health insurance coverage for individuals who lose or change jobs.
- Title II requires the U.S. Department of Health and Human Services to establish national standards for processing electronic healthcare transactions.
- Title III includes tax-related provisions and guidelines for medical care.
- Title IV further defines health insurance reform.
- Title V includes provisions on company-owned life insurance and treatment of those who lose their U.S. citizenship for income tax purposes.
- **Patient Protection and Affordable Care Act (PPACA)**   Also known as Obamacare, the PPACA is the landmark health reform legislation passed by the 111th Congress and signed into law by President Barack Obama in March 2010.

- **Employee Retirement Income Security Act (ERISA)**   ERISA establishes minimum standards for pension plans in private industry and provides for extensive rules on the federal income tax effects of transactions associated with employee benefit plans.

- **Consolidated Omnibus Budget Reconciliation Act (COBRA)**   COBRA provides continuing coverage of group health benefits to employees and their families upon the occurrence of certain qualifying events where such coverage would otherwise be terminated.

Compensation

Compensation is the lifeblood of the employment relationship between the worker and the employer. But this relationship reaches beyond the scope of compensation alone. Rather, it includes recognition programs and assorted fringe benefits; thus, *total rewards* has become a popular term that best defines this important aspect of the employment relationship.

Financial Inducements

People are willing to work in exchange for rewards they receive from the work they do. The objective is to provide a balance between what work is performed and the reward received for doing the work. Total rewards includes the financial inducements and rewards (direct pay, cash-based incentives, and benefits), as well as nonfinancial inducements and rewards such as the value of good job content as well as a good working environment.

Direct Compensation (Cash)

This term applies to a variety of pay programs that are, in one way or another, cash based, whereas indirect compensation (in other words, benefits) applies to programs primarily designed to provide recognition and benefits and therefore are indirectly cash based. Table 5-1 lists examples of these two types of compensation.

Direct Compensation (Cash)	Indirect Compensation (Benefits)
Base pay (wages and salary)	Social Security
Commissions	Unemployment insurance
Bonuses	Disability insurance
Merit pay	Pensions
Piece rate	401(k) and other similar programs
Differential pay	Healthcare
Cash awards	Vacations
Profit sharing	Sick leave
Gainsharing	Paid time off

Table 5-1   Direct and Indirect Compensation

Some of the direct compensation programs are discretionary (i.e., cash awards, differential pay, and certain bonuses), while others are mandatory and governed by federal, state, and, in some cases, local law and regulation (base pay and incentives). Some of the indirect compensation programs are also discretionary; that is, they are used at the option of the employer. They include paid vacation, sick leave, paid time off, 401(k) and similar retirement plans, and pensions. Finally, some benefits are mandatory and governed by federal law and regulation. Social Security, workers' compensation, and unemployment insurance are examples. Even discretionary programs are subject to regulation when they are employed.

Nonfinancial Inducements

Nonfinancial rewards can have an even more substantial impact on employee satisfaction and motivation than traditional financial rewards. A study by the Hay Group involving about 4 million employees found that employees listed work climate, career development, recognition, and other nonfinancial issues as key reasons for leaving a job. Even well-compensated employees may leave a company if dissatisfied with these aspects. Companies with excellent nonfinancial incentive plans can attract, motivate, and retain talented people.

Job Content

Workers, who are dynamic in nature, do not show preference for routine jobs. They are always ready to accept challenging assignments, which can be brought through mentoring, job redesigning, job enlargement, and job enrichment. It is important to understand the capabilities of every individual in the organization and assign work to him or her accordingly.

Job Environment

A good job environment includes employee recognition. Employees who receive recognition for their work accomplishments tend to have increased morale and positive workplace attitudes. Employee recognition is an incentive employers utilize to offer feedback and encouragement to employees. Employee recognition rewards include verbal praise, award ceremonies, and public announcements for a job well done. Workplace recognition rewards occur frequently such as at the end of the day, at the end of the week, or at the conclusion of the sales month.

Compensation Ethics

In an organization, workplace behavior ethics should be a core value. Aside from doing the right thing, conducting ourselves ethically has great rewards and returns. Being ethical is essential to fixing problems and improving processes. It is needed to establish baseline measures and increase efficiencies. Most importantly, it is essential to having strong working relationships with people. On the other hand, covering up unethical behavior does the opposite of these important workplace practices and impedes the individual's ability to grow as a worker or as a leader.

Wages or Salaries

Wages are primarily associated with employee compensation based on the number of hours worked multiplied by an hourly rate of pay. By contrast, salaries are primarily associated with the employer's assessment of job worth; that is the value of the job to the organization.

Salaries are fixed amounts of pay by regulation and practice. Since the salary is the same amount for each pay period, salaried employee paychecks will likely cover the work period through the date of the paycheck, whereas the hourly paid employee will receive a paycheck at a regular point in time. Many organizations classify all cash-based income, whether from a salary or paid hourly, as wages.

Secrecy or Transparency?

The debate over the question of how open an organization should be about its compensation program is an age-old one that has challenged most total rewards professionals at some point in their career. These are some points to consider when thinking about this topic:

- The essential elements of individual employee pay/benefits should be considered and treated as confidential. Employees should expect that the organization will maintain appropriate controls/access to sensitive employee data and information.

- Notwithstanding the previous bullet point, some leakage of information is difficult to avoid because of the inevitable sharing of information, whether that be from the employees themselves or a business unit leader (or occasionally even an HR staff member).

- A primary objective of any total rewards program should be to attract, motivate, and retain a workforce that can advance the organization's mission and key business objectives. Keeping the key components and drivers of that program a secret from employees will seriously limit an organization's ability to achieve this objective.

- Communication is the foundation of an effective strategy of program transparency, should one be adopted. Communicate early, often, and in multiple media formats.

- In the absence of any official communications, employees are apt to fill the void with rumors and conjecture on any topic, pay related or otherwise.

That said, federal contractors are prohibited from banning discussions about compensation among their employees. Executive Order 13665 (signed by President Obama on April 8, 2014) amended Executive Order 11246. It says, "The contractor will not discharge or in any other manner discriminate against any employee or applicant for employment because such employee or applicant has inquired about, discussed, or disclosed the compensation of the employee or applicant or another employee or applicant...."[3] Be sure to check your state laws because some state laws also speak to this issue.

Wage Surveys

Paying people fairly is good for business. If you underpay, employees will eventually look for a better offer. If you overpay, the payroll budget and profitability will suffer. That's why companies use market data to research the value of their jobs. But what is "market data" anyway?

To determine the prevailing rate for a job, a company can "benchmark" jobs against compensation surveys that are detailed and specific to the company's industries and regions. A good compensation survey uses standard, proven methods of data gathering and statistical analysis to determine how much companies pay for a specific job in a specific industry. A number of types of organizations conduct salary surveys, including compensation information businesses, compensation consulting firms, industry associations, educational institutions, and state and federal governments.

Job Evaluation

Job evaluation is the systematic process for assessing the relative worth of jobs within an organization. A comprehensive analysis of each position's tasks, responsibilities, knowledge, and skill requirements is used to assess the value of the job's content to the employer and provide an internal ranking of the jobs. Job ranking, point factor, job classification, and factor comparison are four of the most common methods used.

Job evaluation methods can be nonquantitative or quantitative. The primary objective of a nonquantitative method is to establish a relative hierarchy of jobs based on each job's relative worth. Nonquantitative methods often are referred to as *whole-job* methods because they rank jobs as a whole based on their perceived worth without placing a numerical value on each job. An example of a nonquantitative method would be to rank a clerical job below a supervisory job on the basis of their relative, nonquantitative worth.

 EXAM TIP   Ranking and classification job evaluation systems are considered non quantitative whole-job systems because they do not produce a specific numerical score; rather they measure the position of the "whole job" as compared to other jobs.

Quantitative job evaluation methods include *point-factor* and *factor comparison* methods. Quantitative methods evaluate factors on a defined measurable scale and provide a score as a result that is a measurable comparison of one job to another (see Table 5-2).

	Nonquantitative Methods	Quantitative Methods
Job-to-job comparison	Job ranking	Factor comparison
Job-to-predetermined-standard comparison	Job classification	Point-factor

Table 5-2   Job Evaluation Methods

Job Ranking Method

The job ranking method is often called a *whole-job* comparison because it is a comparison of the whole job compared to another whole job rather than a comparison based on each job's measurable factors. Job ranking using the whole-job method is quick and easy but not very precise. It is easy to explain, which is why it is popular, but it leaves unanswered why one job is worth more than another, as well as how much of a "gap" exists between jobs.

When there are a large number of jobs to evaluate, a paired-comparison method of ranking can be used. This method enables each job to be compared with every other job. Jobs are methodically compared to the next job and, depending on the perceived worth, moved up or below the next job. Ultimately, the job with the highest number of upward movements is the highest ranked. Other jobs are ranked accordingly.

In a job ranking method, jobs are arranged in order of their value or merit to the organization. Accordingly, the jobs at the top of the list provide more value to the organization, and the relative importance keeps decreasing as you move down the list.

The worth of a job is usually based on judgments of the following:

- Skill

- Effort (physical and mental)

- Responsibility

- Working conditions

Because of its simplistic nature, this method works well for small organizations but is not very effective for big organizations where the jobs are large in number, and thus this becomes a complex process.

Job Classification Method

Jobs can be compared to an outside scale. This also can be done on a whole-job basis called a *job classification* method. Job classification is the result of grouping jobs into a predetermined number of grades or classifications. Each classification has a class description. The federal government has a classification system known as the General Schedule (GS). The GS is the predominant pay scale for federal employees, especially employees in professional, technical, administrative, and clerical positions. The system consists of 15 grades, from GS-1, the lowest level, to GS-15, the highest level. There are also ten steps within each grade. The grade level assigned to a position determines the pay level for that job.

Classes can be further identified by using benchmark jobs that fall into each class. Benchmark jobs have the following characteristics:

- The essential functions and knowledge, skills, and abilities (KSAs) are established and stable.

- They represent the entire range of jobs in each class.

- A significant percentage of workers are employed in these jobs.

- External market rates for these jobs are an acceptable basis for setting wages.

The job classification method is a nonquantitative job evaluation method. In the job classification method, a job may be compared to a similar job or to other jobs in the General Schedule to determine its relative ranking. This is considered a nonquantitative method called a *job-to-predetermined-standard comparison*. Job classification comparisons are a good method when evaluating a large number of jobs and are understandable by employees, but may not be effective when jobs overlap, as they look only at whole jobs.

Job classification is most frequently formally performed in large companies, civil service and government employment, nonprofit agencies, and colleges and universities. The results of a job classification analysis are designed to create parity in job titles, consistent job levels within the organization hierarchy, and salary ranges that are determined by identified factors. These factors include market pay rates for people doing similar work in similar industries in the same region of the country; pay ranges of comparable jobs within the organization; and the level of knowledge, skill, experience, and education needed to perform each job.

Point-Factor Method

The most commonly used job evaluation method is the *point-factor method*, which uses specific compensable factors as its reference points to measure relative job worth. Compensable factors are significant job characteristics that contribute to the value of the work and the organization as a whole. The following are two well-known systems used to identify compensable factors:

- **The Hay plan**   Uses a standard criteria comprising three compensable factors: know-how, problem-solving, and accountability.

- **The factor evaluation system (FES)**   Determines levels of duties and responsibilities using a point rating system to evaluate selected positions. FES uses weighted factors to address the major position characteristics of responsibility, education/experience, job conditions, physical requirements, supervision, training, and so on.

These are the five steps in the point-factor method of job evaluation:

1. Identify key jobs. These are benchmark jobs, not necessarily the most important jobs in the organization, but jobs that are equitably paid, stable, and well defined.

2. Identify the compensable factors. These are the factors that will be used to distinguish one job from another. Six to eight factors are generally sufficient. Experience, responsibility, and education are most often used. Other factors that can be considered, depending on their general applicability, include physical demands, mental requirements, skill, working conditions, and supervisory responsibilities.

3. Weight the factors according to their overall worth. Usually, the most heavily weighted factors are knowledge, responsibility, experience, education, degree of difficulty, and supervisory responsibilities.

4. Divide each job factor into degrees that range from high to low. Assign points to each degree. The number of points assigned to each degree should correspond with the weighting of the factors. As an example, if the factor for skill is weighted 40 percent, the factor of working conditions is weighted 10 percent, and both factors have 5 degrees, then degree 2 for skill should have 4 times as many points as degree 2 for working conditions.

5. The final result will be a table (see Table 5-3) that gives a complete range of points from 50 (the least number, column 1) to 200 (the most, column 5). Based on the assigned point values, the job in this example is 126 on a scale of 50 to 200 points. Points usually determine the pay grade to which the job will be assigned.

Factor Comparison Method

The factor comparison method is more complex than ranking, classification, or the point-factor methods and is only occasionally used. It involves ranking each job by each compensable factor and then, as an additional step, identifying dollar values for each level of each factor to develop an actual pay rate for the evaluated job.

The factor comparison method is most often used in union negotiations as part of a labor contract and in limited cases where wages are steady over a period of time and the organization uses a flat rate for each job.

Factor comparison breaks down a job into a small number of key factors, such as skills, effort, knowledge, and responsibilities. The next stage is to identify benchmark jobs, which are well-known positions that retain consistency across different companies and organizations. Each job is then assigned a salary, which is further broken down for each factor.

Point-Factor Job Evaluation Method						
Compensable Factor	**Weighted Percentage**	**Degrees/Points**				
		1	2	3	4	5
Skill	(40%)	20	32	48	72	100
Responsibility	(30%)	15	24	36	54	75
Effort	(20%)	10	16	24	36	50
Working Conditions	(10%)	5	8	12	18	25
Example: **Machine Operator**	**Compensable Factor**	**Degree**		**Points**		
	Skill	3		48		
	Responsibility	2		24		
	Effort	4		36		
	Working Conditions	4		18		
	Total points			126		

Table 5-3   Point-Factor Job Evaluation Method

Advantages of factor comparison include its broad application; it can be applied to a wide range of job roles and industries and can also be applied to new roles in order to compare them to similar positions. Distilling the value of the job in monetary terms can also help organizations make sure their recruitment methods provide a decent return on investment (ROI). One of the main disadvantages is that someone has to make a decision on the relative worth of each factor; for example, someone may believe knowledge is worth more than skills and give this factor "too much" salary.

Hay Group Guide Chart/Profile Method

Hay job evaluation is a proprietary point-factor job evaluation methodology developed by the Hay Group and used by organizations to map out their job roles in the context of the organizational structure. The general purpose for using this job evaluation method is to enable organizations to map and align their roles/jobs. Typically, Hay evaluations are carried out in a series of steps within any organization that chooses to use the method. These steps are as follows:

1. Train representatives from major departments and HR functions in the use of the method.

2. Revise all job descriptions across the organization with HR assistance.

3. Create job evaluation boards, which includes a mix of line management, HR, and experts deciding on the plotting of jobs.

4. HR works with senior management to put together a banding proposal expressed in Hay points by grading staff and describing the benefits that will be attracted by each band.

5. Once the jobs are all rated and mapping is completed, the company board of directors (or equivalent) reviews the summary, the banding proposals, and cost (if any) with the company and recommends for the activities to go live. If approved, the project manager then moves to implement the changes.

Pricing and Pay Rates

Compensation surveys are essential tools for establishing the pay level of positions and staying competitive in the marketplace. In the "golden gilded age" of comp management (1990s to early 2000s), HR was delighted with the increased availability and access to market data, thanks to technology. Compensation information enabled companies to balance their internal equity pay structures with what the local market was providing for high-demand talent. The data was imperfect, but it was credible when HR would wave a ream of data to support their conclusions for talent bleeding (the loss of key and high-potential employees). That was the good: ease of accessing data in a timely manner and directly. The cost savings were great as well because high-powered consultancy firms were no longer needed to gather information.

In more recent decades, the focus of compensation surveys has shifted to calibrating pay levels primarily with the external market, and that in turn has created enormous pressure to obtain and ensure the data is accurate, timely, and "apple-to-apple" in terms of usefulness. Today there are thousands of published surveys that an HR professional can obtain for various job families, industries, geographical areas, and just about everything else you can sort data on. So, there is a wealth of information at your fingertips, yet beware: just because you read it on the Internet doesn't mean it's true. Here comes the bad news: only a fraction of companies participate in surveys. There are millions of organizations, large and small, in the United States, yet a very low percentage participate in compensation surveys. A survey that has 2500 participants might sound great, yet 2500 participants represent less than 1 percent of all companies that have more than 500 employees. What is most disturbing is that more companies use compensation survey data than contribute to the surveys as participants. Additionally, those companies participating are normally participating in multiple surveys, causing data to be two-dimensional.

Pay Grades and Ranges

After an organization has determined its relative internal job values (i.e., through a job evaluation analysis) and collected appropriate market survey data through pay surveys, work begins on developing the organization's pay structure, including creating pay grades and establishing pay ranges.

Pay grades, or job groups, are the way an organization organizes jobs of similar values. The valuation is a result of the job evaluation process. Jobs of the same or comparatively the same value, even though dissimilar in function, are paid within the same pay grade.

No fixed rules apply to creating pay grades; rather, the number of pay grades and their structures are more a reflection of organizational structure and philosophy. Issues that should be considered include the following:

- The size and structure of the organization
- The "distance" between the lowest and highest jobs in the organization
- The organization's pay increase and promotion policy
- The grouping of nonexempt and exempt jobs as well as job families (i.e., clerical, technical, professional, supervisory, and management jobs)
- Creating sufficient grades to permit distinguishing difficulty levels but not so many that the difference between adjoining grades is insignificant

Well-structured pay grades enable management to develop a well-coordinated pay system rather than having to create a separate pay range for each job. Pay ranges establish the upper and lower boundaries of each pay grade. Market data for a benchmark job (ideally, a "key" job that will link to market value) in each pay range helps to determine the range midpoint. The range spread reflects the equal dispersion of pay on either side of the midpoint to the lower and upper range boundary. Quartiles and percentiles show dispersion of data throughout a range. These are commonly recognized reference points an organization uses to measure its position against the market as well as for internal compensation management purposes.

The range spread is the dispersion of pay from the lowest boundary to the highest boundary of a pay range. Range spread is calculated by subtracting the range minimum from the range maximum and dividing that figure by the range minimum. Range spread is expressed as a percentage.

$$\frac{\text{Maximum} - \text{Minimum}}{\text{Minimum}}$$

For example, the range spread for a pay range with a $30,000 minimum and a $45,000 maximum would be as follows:

$$\frac{\$45,000 - \$30,000}{\$30,000}$$
$$= 50\%$$

Typical range spreads in organizations are as follows:

- Nonexempt jobs: 40%
- Exempt jobs: 50%
- Executive jobs: 60%

Generally, lower-level jobs have a narrow range between minimum and maximum pay ranges. Jobs at a lower level tend to be more skill based, which provides for more movement opportunity than higher levels where jobs are more knowledge based and progression is slower.

Ranges should overlap so that progression is steady within a pay grade; as a worker's pay increases with movement to a higher-range quartile, the opportunity for managed movement is possible in a measured way.

There also should be a large enough distance between range midpoints so that pay compression between a lower pay grade and a high pay grade does not occur.

Broadbanding is a recent concept that combines several pay grades or job classifications that have narrow range spreads with a single band that has a wider spread. Organizations usually adopt broadbanding as a way to simplify their pay levels and reduce management oversight requirements. As a result, broadbanding typically is more popular in large organizations than in smaller ones.

While broadbanding has some advantages, it also has some disadvantages. In some cases, broadbanding does not work well with the organization's compensation philosophy. This is particularly true in organizations that focus on promotional opportunities. The reduction of pay grades as a result of broadbanding correspondingly reduces the number of opportunities for promotion.

Broadbanding can also be used against an organization in equal pay analysis. If it is assumed that all jobs are equal within a broadband, the government has claimed that all jobs should be paid the same. If the jobs are not paid the same, differences can be computed and analyzed for statistical significance. Excesses can be claimed to represent illegal pay discrimination. For example, an HR manager, an accounting manager, and a facilities manager are all in the same broadband. They are not all paid the same, however. Differences can be hard to defend against discrimination charges. Broadbanding should be used with care, particularly in an organization that is a federal contractor.

Compa-ratios are indicators of how wages match, lead, or lag the midpoint and are normally an indicator of market value. Compa-ratios are computed by dividing the worker's pay rate by the midpoint of the pay range.

The compa-ratio formula is as follows:

$$\text{Compa-ratio} = \frac{\text{Pay rate}}{\text{Midpoint}}$$

Compa-ratios less than 100 percent (usually expressed as a "compa-ratio less than 1.00") mean the worker is paid less than the midpoint of the range. Compa-ratios greater than 100 percent (1.00) mean that wages exceed the midpoint.

 EXAM TIP Compa-ratios can be used for budgetary controls as well as to investigate discrimination in that a difference between one group and another can indicate the possibility of discrimination.

Variations in Pay: Red and Green Circle Rates

Pay ranges must be periodically evaluated and adjusted to reflect organizational and market changes. Red circle rates, green circle rates, and cost-of-living adjustments are some of the techniques used to adjust to these changes.

Red Circle Rates

Organizations use red circle rates as a method to increase an employee's pay to a new rate higher than the maximum for the assigned pay range. This situation occurs more often in smaller organizations where promotional opportunities may be limited. When this happens, an employee's next pay raise indicated by the organization's merit guidelines might place the new pay level above the maximum for the applicable pay range.

An example of this is the accounting manager who is paid $95,000 per year, a point less than 5 percent from the top of the range. Based on job performance, the manager would be entitled to a 7 percent increase. The next promotion step is the chief financial officer (CFO) job. In this case, the company may decide to process the 7 percent increase as a red circle rate 2 percent above the range maximum for an accounting manager. Typically when this is done, the new pay level is frozen until the maximum of the pay range moves upward to exceed the accounting manager's pay level. This would usually happen when the comparative market numbers increase, thereby allowing a change to the pay range.

Green Circle Rates

Green circle rates occur when a new employee is hired at a pay rate lower than the minimum rate for the applicable grade. It can also happen when a "fast track" employee is promoted to a new job in a high pay grade under circumstances where the percentage pay increase needed to reach the new grade is excessive and might create an unwanted precedent. In this case, the pay increase may result in a pay level below the minimum level of the new pay grade, thus creating a green circle rate.

Situations such as this should be avoided whenever possible and should be allowed only as a last resort because they can create serious morale issues and, even worse, may create an arguable case of pay discrimination. In any case, such actions should be carefully considered and justified in writing after all of the possible consequences are considered.

Base Pay Systems

After an organization has analyzed, evaluated, and priced its jobs, as well as designed its pay structure, the next step is to determine a type of base pay system that will help attract, motivate, and retain employees. In most cases, employees receive some type of base pay, either as an hourly wage (paid to hourly employees) or as a salary (a fixed wage that doesn't change regardless of the hours worked). Base pay system choices include single or flat-rate systems, time-based step rate systems, performance-based merit pay systems, productivity-based systems, and person-based systems. Each of these systems is designed to best achieve the objectives of attracting, motivating, and retaining employees under a different set of circumstances.

Single or Flat-Rate System

In the single, or flat-rate, system, each worker in the same job has the same rate of pay regardless of seniority or job performance. This pay system is most commonly found in elected public-sector jobs or in a union setting. The single pay rate (or flat pay rate) usually is directly linked to an applicable market survey. This system is also used as a training rate under circumstances when the worker is being trained for a job.

Time-Based Step Rate Systems

The time-based step rate system bases the employee's pay rate on the length of time in the job. Pay increases are published in advance on the basis of time. Increases occur on a predetermined schedule. This system has three variations, as described in the sections that follow.

Automatic Step Rate System

In the automatic step rate system, the pay range is divided into several steps, each a predetermined range apart. At the prescribed time interval, each employee with the required seniority receives a one-step pay increase. This system is common in public-sector jobs and in a union environment.

Step Rate with Performance Considerations

The step rate with performance considerations system is similar to the automatic system except that performance can influence the size or timing of the pay increase.

Combination Step Rate and Performance

In the combination step rate and performance system, employees receive step rate increases up to the established job rate. Above this level, increases are granted only for superior job performance. To work, this system requires a supporting performance appraisal program, as well as good communication and understanding by the workers paid under this system.

Performance-Based Merit Pay System

The performance-based merit pay system is based on an employee's individual job performance. A performance-based pay system is often referred to as *merit pay* or *pay for performance*. In this system, employees are typically hired at or near the minimum for their applicable pay range. Pay increases are normally awarded on an annual basis (or annualized if awarded on other than an annual basis) and influenced by the individual's overall job performance. A document identifying the percent pay increase linked to levels of performance and the individual's position in the applicable pay range is communicated to employees as an incentive to increase their performance, thereby earning a higher percentage increase. This document is known as Merit Guidelines. Table 5-4 illustrates a Merit Guidelines example.

To be effective, the merit pay system must be understood by employees affected by the system. In addition to the merit pay system, a clearly stated performance appraisal program is required to support the merit pay system. Key points that should be addressed in designing and implementing an effective merit pay system include those depicted in Table 5-5.

Performance Rating	1st Quartile	2nd Quartile	3rd Quartile	4th Quartile
Exceeds Performance Objectives	6–7%	5–6%	4–5%	3–4%
Meets Performance Objectives	4–5%	3–4%	2–3%	1–2%
Needs Improvement	2–3%	1–2%	0–1%	0%

Table 5-4   Merit Guidelines Example

Merit Pay System	Performance Appraisal Program
Merit pay figures within quartiles can be either a range or a single number depending on the experience of the raters.	Performance ratings should clearly link to documented pre-agreed performance objectives.
Use a range for experienced raters; use a single number for inexperienced raters.	Performance ratings are for overall performance.
Use one standard (range) or the other (single number) for the entire program.	Not more than three performance levels should be used.
The gap between one performance level and the next should be at least 2 percent in order to be a significant incentive.	"Needs Improvement" ratings should be placed into a Performance Improvement Program with a defined period (usually not more than 90 days) to improve overall performance.

Table 5-5   Merit Pay and Performance Appraisal Key Points

Productivity-Based System

In the productivity-based system, pay is determined by the employee's output. This system is mostly used on an assembly line in a manufacturing environment. The following sections describe two types of productivity-based systems.

Straight Piece-Rate System

With the straight piece-rate system, the employee receives a base rate of pay and is awarded additional compensation for the amount of output produced.

Differential Piece-Rate System

In the differential piece-rate system, the employee receives one rate of pay up to the production standard and a higher rate of pay when the standard is exceeded. Both the straight piece system and the differential piece-rate system focus on quantity rather than quality. As a result, other quality control programs may be required to ensure the required quality standard is met.

Person-Based System

In the person-based system, employee capabilities, rather than how the job is performed, determine the employee's pay. For example, two employees do the same work, but one employee with a higher level of skill and experience receives more pay. There are three types of person-based systems, as described next.

Knowledge-Based Systems

In the knowledge-based system, a person's pay is based on the level of knowledge he or she has in a particular field. This system is often used in the learned professions such as lawyers and doctors.

Skill-Based Systems

Employees paid in the skill-based system are paid for the number and depth of skills that they have that are applicable to their job. Heavy-equipment operators are typically paid in this system.

Competency-Based Systems

In the competency-based system, pay is linked to the level at which an employee can perform in a recognized competency. In HR, a professional with specialty skills in organizational development or labor relations will typically be paid for his or her competency; an example is organizational development or labor relations in the HR field.

Financial Incentives

Financial incentives are a monetary benefit offered to organizations, employees, and consumers to encourage behavior or actions that otherwise would not take place. A financial incentive motivates actions that otherwise might not occur without the monetary benefit.

Differential Pay

A pay differential is additional compensation paid to an employee as an incentive to accept what would normally be considered adverse working conditions usually based on time, location, or situational conditions. The same pay differential is paid to all employees under the same circumstances or conditions. Pay differentials benefit the employer by incentivizing employees to accept work they might not otherwise accept; they benefit the employee as additional compensation for accepting the work.

Overtime Pay

The Fair Labor Standards Act requires employers to pay nonexempt employees one-and-a-half times their regular rate of pay when they work more than 40 hours in a single workweek. Some employers pay more than the legally required time-and-a-half rate for overtime. The FLSA allows employers, at their discretion, to pay more than the FLSA requires; they may not pay less. (Note that a workweek is a fixed and regularly recurring period of 168 hours, or seven consecutive 24-hour periods.)

Regular Rate of Pay

The FLSA requires employers to pay overtime based on an employee's regular rate of pay. Where an employee in a single workweek works at two or more different types of work for which different straight-time rates have been established, the regular rate for that week is the weighted average of such rates. That is, the earnings from all such rates are added together, and this total is then divided by the total number of hours worked at all jobs. In addition, section 7(g)(2) of the FLSA allows, under specified conditions, the computation of overtime pay based on one-and-a-half times the hourly rate in effect when the overtime work is performed. The requirements for computing overtime pay pursuant to section 7(g)(2) are prescribed in 29 CFR 778.415 through 778.421.

Where noncash payments are made to employees in the form of goods or facilities, the reasonable cost to the employer or fair value of such goods or facilities must be included in the regular rate of pay.

Hazard Pay

The hazard pay type of differential pay occurs when employees are called to work under adverse conditions either caused by the environment or due to the circumstances. Work generally considered putting an employee at risk for safety or health purposes would typically qualify for a hazard pay differential.

Shift Pay

Shift pay is a time-based differential pay that rewards the employee who works hours normally considered undesirable such as a night shift or hours that are in addition to the employee's regular work schedule (i.e., overtime). Time-based differential pay may be a specified amount per hour or a percentage of the employee's regular rate of pay. Except for overtime, federal law does not legally require employers to pay a differential rate of pay, although state requirements may differ.

On-Call Pay

An employee who is required to remain on his or her employer's premises or so close to the employee's work location that he or she cannot use the time effectively for his or her own purposes is working while on-call. Whether hours spent on-call are hours worked is a question to be decided on a case-by-case basis. All on-call time is not hours worked.

On-call situations vary. Some employees are required to remain on the employer's premises or at a location controlled by the employer. One example is a hospital employee who must stay at the hospital in an on-call room. While on-call, the employee is able to sleep, eat, watch television, read a book, and so on, but is not allowed to leave the hospital. Other employees are able to leave their employer's premises but are required to stay within so many minutes or so many miles of the facility and be accessible by telephone or by pager. An example of this type of employee is an apartment maintenance worker who has to carry a pager while on-call and must remain within a specified number of miles of the apartment complex.

Callback Pay

Callback pay applies when employees are "called back" to perform work beyond regularly scheduled hours. The Fair Labor Standards Act does not guarantee employees a minimum number of hours of work when they are called back. However, FLSA guidelines require that the hours they do work must be paid for at the employees' base rate or at the applicable overtime rate. This rule is not limited to situations that are designated report-in time by an employment agreement. It applies to any situation where the employee performs work outside his or her regular working hours, is guaranteed pay for a minimum number of hours, and does not work the number of hours covered by the guarantee.

Geographic Differentials

Geographic differentials are differences in pay for similar or identical jobs that are based on variations in costs of living in labor markets in particular geographic regions. Large cities, notably New York and San Francisco, often include a portion of an employee's wages, typically a percentage of the basic salary, as a supplement to cover the increased costs of living in a "high-cost" city.

Weekend and Holiday Pay

An employer is required to pay hourly employees only for time actually worked. On the other hand, exempt employees (salaried employees who do not receive overtime) who are given the day off must be paid their full weekly salary if they work any hours during the week in which the holiday falls.

Team and Group Incentives

Team-based incentive plans are initiatives designed to encourage and reward exceptional levels of professional achievement. Employers use incentives in business as motivators for staffers to work collectively to earn monetary and nonmonetary rewards. It is also a way for business owners to boost overall productivity and earnings while simultaneously rewarding employees for a job well done. The objective of team incentives is to encourage group goal setting, collaboration, and teamwork.

Organization-Based Pay

Often referred to as *pay-for-performance plans* (PFPs), these plans tie compensation directly to specific business goals and management objectives. In PFP systems, employees' compensation is composed of a fixed base salary and a variable component. The most commonly used variable components are profit-sharing and gainsharing plans, described next.

Profit Sharing

A profit-sharing plan, also known as a *deferred profit-sharing plan,* is a plan that gives employees a share in the profits of a company. Under this type of plan, an employee receives a percentage of a company's profits based on its quarterly or annual earnings. The company contributes a portion of its pretax profits to a pool that will be distributed among eligible employees. The amount distributed to each employee may be weighted by the employee's base salary so that employees with higher base salaries receive a slightly higher amount of the shared pool of profits.

Gainsharing

Gainsharing is best described as a system of management in which an organization seeks higher levels of performance through the involvement and participation of its people.

As performance improves, employees share financially in the gain. It is a team approach; generally all the employees at a site or operation are included. The typical gainsharing organization measures performance and through a predetermined formula shares the savings with all employees. The organization's actual performance is compared to baseline performance (often a historical standard) to determine the amount of the gain. Employees have an opportunity to earn a gainsharing bonus (if there is a gain) generally on a monthly or quarterly basis.

 EXAM TIP The difference between gainsharing and profit sharing is that gainsharing is reward based on improved productivity, whereas profit sharing is reward based on a percentage of profits.

Employee Benefits

Benefit programs, also referred to as *indirect compensation* (compared to compensation, which is a direct benefit), are designed to promote organizational loyalty, reward continued employment, enable employees to live healthy lives, help them care for their families, and help provide for retirement benefits.

In addition to helping employees, benefits programs help employers by

- Attracting and retaining talent
- Increasing an employee's loyalty and commitment to the organization
- Providing tax-advantaged health and welfare benefits to employees

Table 5-6 lists the most significant employee benefit programs.

Leave-of-absence benefits	Healthcare benefits
• Family and Medical Leave Act (FMLA)[4]	• Managed healthcare programs
• Military service leave (USERRA)[5]	• Fee for service
• Paid holidays	• Preferred provider organization (PPO)
• Paid vacations	• Point of service (POS)
• Paid sick leave	• Health maintenance organization (HMO)
• Paid personal leave	• Group health cooperatives
• Sabbaticals	• Consumer-directed healthcare
• Jury duty	• Flexible health benefit plans
• Bereavement leave	• Flexible spending accounts (FSAs)
• Union activities	• Health reimbursement accounts (HRAs)
• Recognition and achievement awards	• Health savings accounts (HSAs)
Social Security	
Workers' compensation	
Unemployment compensation	

Table 5-6 Employee Benefits

Paid Holidays

Most small businesses have six or seven holidays a year. The most common paid holidays in the United States are the following:

- New Year's Day
- President's Day
- Memorial Day
- Independence Day (4th of July)
- Labor Day
- Thanksgiving Day
- Christmas Day

Paid Vacation

No law requires employers to give their workers paid vacation days, but most companies do pay for some vacation days. More than 90 percent of all full-time employees in private industry receive paid vacation days, according to 2015 figures from the federal Bureau of Labor Statistics.

Paid Sick Leave

Momentum for a federal paid sick leave requirement is growing. There are currently only a few states, sometimes limited to specific cities within these states, in which employers are required to provide paid sick leave to qualified individuals. Because paid sick leave is a rapidly developing subject, we recommend that you check first with your local and state authorities to stay on top of this rapidly evolving set of requirements. The current areas are as follows[6]:

- California
- Emeryville, California
- Oakland, California
- San Francisco, California
- Connecticut
- Massachusetts
- Oregon
- Portland, Oregon
- District of Columbia
- Vermont
- New Jersey cities of Bloomfield, East Orange, Irvington, Montclair, Newark, Passaic, Patterson, and Trenton
- Jersey City, New Jersey

- Seattle, Washington
- Tacoma, Washington
- New York, New York
- Montgomery County, Maryland

Paid Personal Leave

In the United States, requirements vary from state to state, but some leaves of absence are required by federal laws. Examples of a legally required unpaid leave of absence are time allotted by the Family and Medical Leave Act and time allotted by the Uniformed Services Employment and Reemployment Rights Act (USERRA). Bereavement time and jury duty are examples of a paid leave of absence.

Sabbaticals

Some professions or industries allow long-term employees to take a paid leave of absence as a way to complete a course of study, do research, or engage in other learned pursuits. This practice is particularly evident in the teaching profession although not restricted to that profession. Some organizations allow its long-term employees with high-balance sick leave accounts to take extended unpaid time off with the opportunity to use a portion of their sick leave for paid time off during this absence.

Jury Duty

Jury duty is any action or other proceeding of a judicial nature, but does not include an administrative proceeding (a summons or subpoena to serve as a witness from an administrative law judge). Administrative proceedings do not have juries; they are not informational or preliminary in nature, and the judge makes the ultimate decisions.

When a person is called for jury duty in the United States, that service is mandatory, and the person summoned for jury duty must attend. Failing to report for jury duty is not technically illegal and usually results in the individual simply being placed back into the selection pool to be called for another trial. However, repeatedly ignoring a jury summons can result in strict penalties, which may include being fined or jailed for contempt of court. Employers cannot fire an employee for being called to jury duty, but they are typically not required to pay wages during this time.

Bereavement Leave

Most organizations have policies that provide for paid time off to attend a funeral of a family member. In some cases, this benefit is available to extended family members as well as close friends.

Union Activities

Employees covered by the National Labor Relations Act (NLRA) are afforded certain rights to join together to improve their wages and working conditions, with or without a union. Employees have the right to attempt to form a union where none currently exists or to decertify a union that has lost the support of employees.

Examples of employee rights include the following:

- Forming, or attempting to form, a union in the workplace
- Joining a union, whether or not the union is recognized by the employer
- Assisting a union in organizing fellow employees
- Refusing to do any or all of these things
- Being fairly represented by a union

Employees who are not represented by a union also have rights under the NLRA. Specifically, the National Labor Relations Board protects the rights of employees to engage in *concerted activity*, which is when two or more employees take action for their mutual aid or protection regarding terms and conditions of employment. A single employee may also engage in protected concerted activity if he or she is acting on the authority of other employees, bringing group complaints to the employer's attention, trying to induce group action, or seeking to prepare for group action.

Some examples of protected concerted activities are as follows:

- Two or more employees addressing their employer about improving their pay
- Two or more employees discussing work-related issues beyond pay, such as safety concerns, with each other
- An employee speaking to an employer on behalf of one or more co-workers about improving workplace conditions

Recognition and Achievement Awards

Communication is the exchange of information verbally and nonverbally between two or more people. In the workplace, communication includes between management and employees that rewards them for reaching specific goals or producing high-quality results in the workplace. Recognizing or honoring employees for this level of service is meant to encourage repeat actions through reinforcing the behavior you would like to see repeated.

Social Security

Administered by the United States Social Security Administration (SSA), Social Security is a social insurance program consisting of retirement, disability, and survivors' benefits. The U.S. Social Security Administration is an independent agency of the U.S. federal government that administers the Social Security program. To qualify for most of these benefits, most workers pay Social Security taxes on their earnings; the claimant's benefits are based on the wage earner's contributions. Otherwise, benefits such as the Supplemental Security Income (SSI) program are given based on need. Social Security is the largest social welfare program in the United States. For the year 2014, the net cost of Social Security was $906.4 billion, which accounted for 21 percent of government expenditure.

SSA administers the retirement, survivors, and disabled social insurance programs, which can provide monthly benefits to aged or disabled workers, to their spouses and children, and to the survivors of insured workers. The programs are primarily financed by taxes that employers, employees, and the self-insured pay annually. These revenues are placed into a special trust fund. These programs are collectively known as Retirement, Survivors, Disability Insurance (RSDI). SSA also administers the SSI program, which is needs based, for the aged, blind, or disabled. SSI recipients are paid out of the general revenue of the United States. In addition, some states pay more SSI funds. Today, 7 million people are covered by SSI.

The administration of the Medicare program is a responsibility of the Centers for Medicare and Medicaid Services, but SSA offices are used for determining initial eligibility, for some processing of premium payments, and for limited public contact information.

Workers' Compensation

Workers' compensation is a form of insurance providing wage replacement and medical benefits to employees injured in the course of employment in exchange for mandatory relinquishment of the employee's right to sue his or her employer for the tort of negligence.

Workers' compensation will pay hospital and medical expenses that are necessary to diagnose and treat the injury. It also provides disability payments while the employee is unable to work (typically, about two-thirds of the regular salary) and may pay for rehabilitation, retraining, and other benefits as well.

 EXAM TIP The basic concept behind workers' compensation is that the basis of workers' compensation laws is "liability without fault," that is, the injured employee is entitled to reasonable compensation regardless of who causes the accident.

Unemployment Compensation

Unemployment insurance provides workers whose jobs have been terminated through no fault of their own monetary payments for a given period of time or until they find a new job. Unemployment payments are intended to provide an unemployed worker with time to find a new job equivalent to the one lost without financial distress. Without employment compensation, many workers would be forced to take jobs for which they were overqualified or would end up on welfare. Unemployment compensation is also justified by sustaining consumer spending during periods of economic adjustment.

In the United States, unemployment insurance is based on a dual program of federal and state statutes. The program was established by the federal Social Security Act in 1935. Much of the federal program is implemented through the Federal Unemployment Tax Act. Each state administers a separate unemployment insurance program, which must be approved by the secretary of labor, based on federal standards. The state programs are applicable to areas normally regulated by laws of the United States. There are special federal rules for nonprofit organizations and governmental entities. A combination of federal and state law determines which employees are eligible for compensation, the amount they receive, and the period of time benefits are paid.

Healthcare Benefits

This term refers to healthcare items or services covered under a health insurance plan. Covered benefits and excluded services are defined in the health insurance plan's coverage documents. In Medicaid or CHIP, covered benefits and excluded services are defined in state program rules.

Marketplace Plans Under the Affordable Care Act (ACA)

The ACA requires organizations to minimally cover the following categories, called *essential health benefits*:

- Ambulatory patient services (outpatient care provided without being admitted to a hospital)

- Emergency services

- Hospitalization (surgery and overnight stays)

- Pregnancy, maternity, and newborn care (both before and after birth)

- Mental health and substance use disorder services, including behavioral health treatment (includes counseling and psychotherapy)

- Prescription drugs

- Rehabilitative services and devices (services and devices to help people with injuries, disabilities, or chronic conditions gain or recover mental and physical skills)

- Laboratory services

- Preventive and wellness services and chronic disease management

- Birth control coverage

- Breastfeeding coverage

- Pediatric services, including oral and vision care (but adult dental and vision coverage aren't essential health benefits)

- Medical management programs (for specific needs such as weight management, back pain, and diabetes)

Managed Healthcare Plans

Managed healthcare plans are a type of health insurance. They have contracts with healthcare providers and medical facilities to provide care for members at reduced costs. These providers make up the plan's network.

Fee-for-Service Plans

Fee-for-service (FFS) is a payment model where no services are unbundled and paid for separately. In healthcare, it gives an incentive for physicians to provide more treatments because payment is dependent on the quantity of care, rather than the quality of care.

PART II

Preferred Provider Organization (PPO)

PPO plans are one of the most popular types of plans in the individual and family market. PPO plans allow members to visit any in-network physician or healthcare provider without first requiring a referral from a primary-care physician.

Members of PPO plans are encouraged to use the insurance company's network of preferred doctors and usually won't need to choose a primary-care physician. No matter which healthcare provider a member chooses, in-network healthcare services will be covered at a higher benefit level than out-of-network services. It's important to check whether the provider accepts a health plan in order to receive the highest level of benefit coverage.

Members usually have an annual deductible to pay before the insurance company starts covering their medical bills. They may also have a copayment of about $10 to $30 for certain services or be required to cover a certain percentage of the total charges for medical bills.

Point of Service (POS)

A POS plan has some of the qualities of HMO and PPO plans with benefit levels varying depending on whether a member receives care in or out of the health insurance company's network of providers.

POS plans combine elements of both HMO and PPO plans. Like an HMO plan, members may be required to designate a primary-care physician who will then make referrals to network specialists when needed. Depending upon the plan, services rendered by a member's primary-care physician are typically not subject to a deductible, and preventive-care benefits are usually included. Like with PPO plans, members may receive care from non-network providers but with greater out-of-pocket costs. Members may also be responsible for copayments, coinsurance, and an annual deductible.

Health Maintenance Organization (HMO)

HMO plans offer a wide range of healthcare services through a network of providers who agree to supply services to members. With an HMO members will likely have coverage for a broader range of preventive healthcare services than they would through any other type of plan.

Members of HMOs are required to choose a primary-care physician (PCP). The PCP will take care of most of the member's healthcare needs. Before seeing a specialist, members need to obtain a referral from their PCP.

Though there are many variations, HMO plans typically enable members to have lower out-of-pocket healthcare expenses. They may not be required to pay a deductible before coverage starts, and the copayments will likely be minimal. Members also typically won't have to submit any of their own claims to the insurance company. However, keep in mind that they will likely have no coverage for services rendered by out-of-network providers or for services rendered without a proper referral from the PCP.

Group Health Cooperative

Formerly known as Group Health Cooperative of Puget Sound, Group Health Cooperative, now more commonly known as Group Health, is a nonprofit healthcare organization based in Seattle, Washington. Established in 1945, it today provides coverage and care for about 600,000 people in Washington and Idaho and is one of the largest private employers in Washington. Patients who receive care at its medical centers are provided web access to their medical records, secure e-mailing with doctors and nurses, and the ability to fill prescriptions online that are mailed to homes without a shipping charge. On December 4, 2015, it was announced that Group Health would be acquired by Kaiser Permanente, forming the latter's eighth region.

Consumer-Driven Healthcare

Consumer-driven healthcare (CDHC), defined narrowly, refers to third-tier health insurance plans that allow members to use health savings accounts (HSAs), health reimbursement accounts (HRAs), or similar medical payment products to pay routine healthcare expenses directly, but a high-deductible health plan protects them from catastrophic medical expenses. High-deductible policies cost less, but the user pays medical claims using a prefunded spending account, often with a special debit card provided by a bank or insurance plan.

Flexible Spending Account (FSA)

A *flexible spending account* (also known as a *flexible spending arrangement*) is a special account you put money into that you use to pay for certain out-of-pocket healthcare costs. You don't pay taxes on this money. This means you'll save an amount equal to the taxes you would have paid on the money you set aside.

FSAs are limited to $2600 per year per employer. If you're married, your spouse can put up to $2600 in an FSA with their employer too.

You can use funds in your FSA to pay for certain medical and dental expenses for you, your spouse if you're married, and your dependents. You can spend FSA funds to pay deductibles and copayments, but not for insurance premiums. You can spend FSA funds on prescription medications, as well as over-the-counter medicines with a doctor's prescription. Reimbursements for insulin are allowed without a prescription. FSAs may also be used to cover costs of medical equipment such as crutches, supplies like bandages, and diagnostic devices like blood sugar test kits.

Health Reimbursement Account (HRA)

A health reimbursement arrangement, commonly referred to as a *health reimbursement account,* is an IRS-approved, employer-funded, tax-advantaged employer health benefit plan that reimburses employees for out-of-pocket medical expenses and individual health insurance premiums. An HRA is not health insurance. A health reimbursement arrangement allows the employer to make contributions to an employee's account and provide reimbursement for eligible expenses. An HRA plan is an excellent way to provide health insurance benefits and allow employees to pay for a wide range of medical expenses not covered by insurance. Because of federal legislation passed in December 2016, there exists a new HRA available to small businesses.

HRAs are notional arrangements; no funds are expensed until reimbursements are paid. Through HRAs, employers reimburse employees directly only after the employees incur approved medical expenses.

Like a health savings account, there is a limit to the amount of money an employer can contribute to certain HRAs. Annual employer contributions for small-business HRAs are capped at $4950 for a single employee and $10,000 for an employee with a family.

However, for other HRAs, such as an integrated HRA or a one-person stand-alone HRA, there are no annual contribution limits.

An HRA may reimburse any expense considered to be a qualified medical expense under IRS Section 213 of the Internal Revenue Code, including premiums for personal health insurance policies. Within IRS guidelines, employers may restrict the list of reimbursable expenses in any way they choose for their HRA plan.

HRA balances may roll forward from month to month or from year to year, depending on which HRA plan an employer chooses. Small-business HRAs may roll forward from month to month only; no annual rollover is permitted.

Health Savings Account (HSA)

A health savings account is a tax-advantaged medical savings account you can contribute to and draw money from for certain medical expenses tax-free. HSAs can be used for out-of-pocket medical, dental, and vision. HSAs can't be used to pay health insurance premiums. HSAs can be used with only high-deductible health plans that count as minimum essential coverage (MEC).

The funds contributed to an HSA account are not subject to federal income tax at the time of deposit. Unlike a flexible spending account, HSA funds roll over and accumulate year to year if they are not spent. HSAs are owned by the individual, which differentiates them from company-owned HRAs that are an alternate tax-deductible source of funds paired with either high-deductible health plans or standard health plans.

Employee Benefit Account Administration

Benefits administration is the process of establishing, maintaining, and managing benefits for the employees of an organization. Employee benefits typically include medical insurance, pension plans, individual retirement accounts (IRAs), vacation time, sick time, and maternity leave. Numerous vendors offer software that can assist benefits administrators.

A good benefits administration program creates and maintains an enrollment profile for every employee, keeping track of information such as the date hired, marital status, number of dependents, total hours worked, and attendance records. The program offers flexibility, taking into account special employee needs, part-time and temporary hires, and changes in government regulations. The benefits administration program can function in tandem with tax preparation software, ensuring that all allowable deductions are taken and maintaining detailed records for reference in case of an audit.

Retiree Benefits[7]

Over time, the share of large employers (with 200 or more employees) offering retiree health benefits has declined, and employers that continue to offer benefits have made changes to manage their costs, often by shifting costs directly or indirectly to their retirees. Since 1988, the percentage of large firms offering retiree health coverage has dropped by more than half from 66 percent in 1988 to 28 percent in 2013, according to the 2013 Kaiser/HRET Survey of Employer-Sponsored Health Benefits. The biggest drop occurred between 1988 and 1991, after the Financial Accounting Standards Board (FASB) required private-sector employers to account for the costs of health benefits for current and future retirees. But ever since, there has been a more or less steady erosion in the percentage of firms offering retiree health coverage, dropping from roughly 40 percent of large employers in the mid-to-late 1990s to 28 percent of firms in 2013. Some firms elected to stop offering benefits (usually to future retirees first), while newer firms and firms in the service and technology sectors, for example, never established the financial commitment to provide health benefits to their retirees. As a result of these changes, fewer than one in five workers today are employed by firms offering retiree health benefits.

Benefits: Legal Compliance

Employee benefits fall into two categories: taxable and nontaxable benefits. Both categories include direct compensation and indirect compensation (employer-paid coverage or reimbursements). Table 5-7 identifies some of the benefits we've discussed in this chapter in each category (the list is only generally indicative; it is not all-inclusive).

	Taxable Benefits	Nontaxable Benefits
Direct Compensation	Base pay Differential pay Severance pay Paid time off	Wages paid after death in a new year
Indirect Compensation (Employer Paid or Reimbursed)	Disability benefits when employer pays the premium Life insurance when employee pays with pretax dollars Gifts, prizes, and awards over certain dollar amounts Personal use of a company vehicle Sick pay	Work-related expense reimbursements Childcare (subject to limitations) Company vehicle use (only work related) De minimis ($25 or less) Group life insurance plans ($50,000 or less coverage) Educational expenses (subject to annual limits) Medical, dental, health plans (employer contributions) Employee-paid disability benefits when purchased with after-tax dollars

Table 5-7   Taxable and Nontaxable Benefits

HR's responsibility is to know whether an organization's compensation and benefits program is effective. Key questions that HR must be able to answer include the following:

- Is the system in legal compliance?
- Is the system compatible with the organization's mission and strategy?
- Does the system fit the organization's culture? Is it appropriate for its workers?
- Is the system internally equitable?
- Is the system externally competitive?

The following are measurements and analysis needed to determine whether an organization's compensation and benefits program is meeting its goals and objectives:

- Does the system meet ERISA nondiscrimination requirements?
- Is there adverse impact on protected groups?
- Are the organization's EEO and affirmative action objectives supported?
- Is the system compatible with the organization's mission and strategy?
- Does it meet the organization's mission, goals, and objectives?
- Does it help the organization attract and retain employees?
- Does it motivate employee performance?
- Does the system fit the culture? Is it appropriate for the workers?
- Is the organization entitlement oriented or contribution oriented?
- Does the system support the organization's orientation?
- Does the system have programs that meet employee lifestyle needs?
- Is the system internally equitable?
- Does the mix (fixed versus variable, cash versus benefits, retirement versus health/welfare) fit?
- Do the employees understand the system?
- Do employees perceive the system to be fair and adequate?
- What is the organization's turnover rate?
- Is the system externally competitive?
- How does this system compare to the competition?
- Are dollars spent generating a meaningful return?

Benefits: Communication Requirements

ERISA-required reporting and communicating requirements that must automatically be distributed to every employee include the following:

- **Summary plan description (SPD)** Contains information on what the plan provides in layperson terms. Distribution is required within 120 days after the plan's establishment or 90 days after eligibility. The SPD must be updated no less frequently than every 5 years.

- **Summary annual report (SAR)** Contains financial information about the plan. Distribution is required within 7 months after the end of the plan year.

- **Summary of material modifications (SMM)** Required whenever any of the plan's features have been significantly changed or within 201 days after the end of the plan year.

Other required or highly recommended communications include the following:

- An FMLA policy statement in all employee handbooks (for employers with 50+ employees)

- General notification of federal (and state if applicable) COBRA rights (employers with 20+ employees)

- Notice of special HIPAA enrollment rights and privacy rights

The preceding list is not all-inclusive. Due diligence is required so that all organizations understand the requirements of applicable laws, regulations, and instructions for any official forms or other official guidance.

Developing Employee Self-Service (ESS) Technologies

The communication requirements described in this section are influenced by the introduction of self-service technologies that are rapidly improving the communication abilities of organizations. Self-service technologies will continue to improve the ability of the organization to effectively implement its communication responsibilities. Employee self-service (ESS) applications will play a more active role in payroll and benefits by providing quick and easy access to information, which benefits the organization by

- Increasing the accuracy of employee data
- Improving the timeliness of employee transactions
- Reducing HR costs associated with the handling of traditional delivery channels

Chapter Review

In this chapter, we examined the important role of compensation and benefits in all aspects of the organization. This is an important topic to know and understand for the exam and because of its direct impact on all of the organization's stakeholders.

You learned that compensation is a systematic approach to providing value to employees in return for the work they perform for the organization. This "system" provides methods for maintaining a balance between the organization's needs while attracting, developing, retaining, and rewarding employees. As part of exploring the "system," we reviewed the purpose of job evaluation as a systematic way of determining the value or worth of a job in relation to other jobs in an organization. We reviewed different methods of job evaluation, including job ranking, job classification, the point-factor method, the factor comparison method, and the Hay plan.

We also examined the theory behind pay grades and ranges along with the basis of pay rates. We reviewed financial incentives, including differentials, team and group-based incentives, and organization-based pay such as profit sharing and gainsharing.

Going hand in glove with a good compensation program is a good benefits program. Although expensive, there are many intrinsic benefits to providing employees with a comprehensive benefit program. For most, the ability to find and keep highly qualified staff is the key driver. The more progressive the organization, the more flexible the structure is in response to today's challenges. Employers who continue to provide a more traditional and limited program will likely find it more difficult to attract and keep different types of employees.

In "Employee Benefits," we reviewed various leave-of-absence formats, as well as their purpose and value to employees as well as the organization. Some of these leaves are mandated by law, while others are prescribed by policy. Either way, they will be an important part of your practice as a human resource management professional. Also, we reviewed Social Security, workers' compensation, and unemployment compensation. Finally, we looked into healthcare benefits, including managed healthcare and consumer-directed healthcare, and closed with a look at the administration of benefits accounts and programs.

All of these topics are important to you, not only because some will likely appear as subject matter on your exam, but also because they are basic concepts you need to know as you move forward in your professional HR management career.

Questions

1. A window manufacturer guarantees its installers a base wage plus an extra $25 for each job completed to specifications. The employer is using a

   A. Merit pay system

   B. Productivity-based pay system

   C. Competency-based system

   D. Flat-rate system

2. Under the factor comparison method, jobs are evaluated through the use of

   A. Predetermined wage classes

   B. A wage/salary conversion table

   C. A scale based on compensable factors

   D. A comparison with market pricing

3. Which of the following is not a pay differential?

   A. Hazard pay

   B. Shift pay

   C. Base pay

   D. Overtime

4. If a leave under FMLA can be reasonably anticipated, how much notice must the employee give the employer?

   A. 7 days

   B. 14 days

   C. 30 days

   D. 90 days

5. Which of the following terms refers to collapsing multiple pay ranges into a single-wide pay range?

   A. Wide banding

   B. Pay compression

   C. Green circle rates

   D. Broadbanding

6. Which of the following laws does not directly relate to a company's compensation or benefits program?

   A. Equal Pay Act

   B. Fair Labor Standards Act

   C. Port-to-Portal Act

   D. Uniform Guidelines on Employee Selection Procedures

7. Social Security, COBRA, and Medicare are examples of

   A. Medical benefits

   B. Social benefits

   C. Government-regulated benefits

   D. Employer-sponsored benefits

8. _____ is the right of employees to receive benefits from their retirement plans.

   A. Transference

   B. Portability

   C. Social Security

   D. Vesting

9. Which job evaluation method is most difficult to use?

    A. Factor comparison method

    B. Ranking method

    C. Classification method

    D. Point-factor method

10. The simplest method of job evaluation is the

    A. Job ranking method

    B. Point-factor method

    C. Classification method

    D. Factor comparison method

11. A(n) _____ system is a productivity-based system in which an employee is paid for each unit of production.

    A. Incentive

    B. Merit

    C. Results-oriented

    D. Piece-rate

12. The Equal Pay Act prohibits wage discrimination on the basis of

    A. Race

    B. Sex

    C. Seniority

    D. Merit

13. Which of the following determines the relative worth of each job in an organization?

    A. Job analysis

    B. Job specifications

    C. Job content

    D. Job evaluation

14. Which of the following is a nonquantitative method of job evaluation?

    A. Factor comparison

    B. Point-factor method

    C. Job ranking

    D. Job qualification

15. Which of the following compensates employees who arrive at work but find that no work is available?

   A. On-call pay

   B. Reporting time pay

   C. Premium pay

   D. Travel pay

16. Which of the following statements about workers' compensation is true?

   A. It covers all of workers' health problems.

   B. It is funded by employers and regulated by the federal government.

   C. It is paid even if an accident is the employee's fault.

   D. It pays all injured workers the same benefits.

17. Which of the following managed-care plans will not cover any services outside of the network?

   A. EPO

   B. PPO

   C. POS

   D. PPA

18. The concept of broadbanding was developed to

   A. Limit the autonomy of line managers

   B. Reduce employee mobility with the organization

   C. Work with flatter organization structures

   D. Provide narrower salary ranges

19. A worker is paid $8.50 an hour when the pay range for that assigned grade is $7 to $8 an hour. This is referred to as a

   A. Green-circle rate

   B. Pay differential

   C. Red-circle rate

   D. Compressed salary

20. Which of the following statements about a single-rate pay system is true?

   A. It provides opportunity for progression within a single grade level.

   B. It is typically used for exempt jobs.

   C. It disregards performance or seniority.

   D. It is not applicable in a union environment.

21. Which of the following is *not* regulated by the FLSA?

    A. Exempt status

    B. Employee benefits

    C. Minimum wage

    D. Overtime pay

22. Which job evaluation method is commonly used by the government and the public sector?

    A. Ranking

    B. Classification

    C. Point-factor

    D. Factor comparison

23. The process of adjusting salary data to keep pace with market movement is referred to as

    A. Aging

    B. Leveling

    C. Benchmarking

    D. Compressing

24. A bonus paid to an employee based on his or her performance at the end of a period of time is referred to as

    A. Performance-based

    B. Discretionary

    C. Formula-based

    D. Service-based

25. Workers' compensation is regulated by the

    A. U.S. Department of Labor

    B. States

    C. Private insurance companies

    D. Social Security Administration

Answers

1. **B.** The employer is using an incentive program based on performance results, which is considered a productivity-based system. A merit-based pay system does not address incentive pay. A competency-based system addresses capabilities, whereas a flat-rate system establishes a fixed rate of pay.

2. **C.** The factor comparison job evaluation method involves a set of compensable factors identified as determining the worth of jobs. Typically, the number of compensable factors is small. Next, benchmark jobs are identified. Benchmark jobs should be selected as having certain characteristics such as equitable pay and be distributed along a range. The jobs are then priced, and the total pay for each job is divided into pay for each factor. This process establishes the rate of pay for each factor for each benchmark job. The other jobs in the organization are then compared with the benchmark jobs, and rates of pay for each factor are summed to determine the rates of pay for each of the other jobs.

3. **C.** Hazard pay, shift pay, and overtime are all differentials. Base pay is the foundation of an employer's compensation program.

4. **C.** The FMLA allows employers to require 30 days' advance notice when the leave can be reasonably anticipated. The other choices are incorrect.

5. **D.** Broadbanding is a term that refers to pay ranges with a wide spread. This is often done to facilitate the management of pay levels within the pay range. A side effect of broadbanding is to reduce the opportunity for promotions because of a smaller number of ranges. That can adversely affect morale.

6. **D.** In 1978, the Civil Service Commission, the Department of Labor, the Department of Justice, and the Equal Opportunity Commission jointly adopted the Uniform Guidelines on Employee Selection Procedures to establish uniform standards for employers for the use of selection procedures and to address adverse impact, validation, and recordkeeping requirements. The other choices are laws that directly relate to employers' compensation programs.

7. **C.** Social Security, COBRA, and Medicare are all government-regulated benefits.

8. **D.** Vesting is the absolute right to an asset that cannot be taken away by any third party, even though one may not yet possess the asset. The portion vested cannot be reclaimed by the employer, nor can it be used to satisfy the employer's debts. Any portion not vested may be forfeited under certain conditions, such as termination of employment.

9. **A.** The factor comparison method is a systematic and scientific method of job evaluation. It is the most complex method of the four recognized methods. Under this method, instead of ranking complete jobs, each job is ranked according to a series of factors. These factors include mental effort, physical effort, skill needed, responsibility, supervisory responsibility, working conditions, and other such factors. Pay is assigned in this method by comparing the total value of the factors required for each job and dividing the result among the factors weighted by importance. Wages are assigned to the job in comparison to its ranking on each job factor.

10. **A.** The simplest method of job evaluation is the ranking method. According to this method, jobs are arranged from highest to lowest, in order of their value or merit to the organization. Jobs can also be arranged according to the relative

difficulty in performing them. The jobs are examined as a whole rather than on the basis of important factors in the job; the job at the top of the list has the highest value, and obviously the job at the bottom of the list has the lowest value. The ranking method is simple to understand and practice; it is best suited for a small organization. This kind of ranking is highly subjective in nature and may offend many employees.

11. **D.** The piece-rate pay method compensates employees a set amount for each unit of work completed. For example, in a manufacturing setting, an employee receives a set amount for each item he produces, regardless of how fast or slow he works.

12. **B.** The Equal Pay Act requires that men and women be given equal pay for equal work in the same establishment. The jobs need not be identical, but they must be substantially equal. It is job content, not job titles, that determines whether jobs are substantially equal.

13. **D.** Job evaluation is a systematic way of determining the value/worth of a job in relation to other jobs in an organization. A job specification is a statement of employee characteristics and qualifications required for satisfactory performance of defined duties and tasks comprising a specific job or function. Job specification is derived from job analysis. Job content is all that is contained within a job.

14. **C.** Job ranking determines the value/worth of a job in totality with respect to other jobs in an organization. One of the most basic and simple methods of doing this is the ranking method. Factor comparison is designed to rank job roles based on a breakdown of factors rather than the role as a whole. Point-factor analysis is a systemic bureaucratic method for determining a relative score for a job. Jobs can then be banded into grades, and the grades can be used to determine pay.

15. **B.** Reporting time pay is a guarantee of at least partial compensation for employees who report to their job expecting to work a specified number of hours but who are deprived of that amount of work because of inadequate scheduling or lack of proper notice by the employer. On-call pay is pay legally required for time an employee must be on duty, on the employer premises, or at any other prescribed place of work. Premium pay is additional pay provided to employees for working certain types of hours or under certain types of conditions. Travel pay that is home-to-work travel is generally not compensable.

16. **C.** Workers' compensation is a "no-fault" insurance plan that is paid even if an accident is the employee's fault. The other three choices are incorrect.

17. **A.** As a member of an exclusive provider organization (EPO), you can use the doctors and hospitals within the EPO network but cannot go outside the network for care. There are no out-of-network benefits. Preferred provider organization (PPO) plans are one of the most popular types of plans in the individual and

family market. PPO plans allow you to visit whatever in-network physician or healthcare provider you want without first requiring a referral from a primary-care physician. A point-of-service (POS) plan is a type of managed-care plan that is a hybrid of HMO and PPO plans. Like an HMO, participants designate an in-network physician to be their primary-care provider. But like a PPO, patients may go outside of the provider network for healthcare services. The Pension Protection Act (PPA) document restatement is an IRS requirement that employer plan documents be updated and resubmitted for review and approval. The last restatement requirement was April 30, 2016.

18. **C.** Broadbanding is the term applied to having extremely wide salary bands, much more encompassing than with traditional salary structures. Whereas a typical salary band has a 40 percent difference in pay between its minimum and maximum, broadbanding would typically have a 100 percent difference. This is done to reduce an organization's hierarchy that facilitates movement within the organization. The other three choices are incorrect.

19. **C.** When an employee is overpaid, a salary term describes their base pay as a red circle rate, or a rate of pay that is above the maximum salary for a position. A red circle policy is a common approach to addressing this situation and allowing the market to catch up with the employee's pay. A green circle rate denotes any individual employee's salary that falls below the minimum of the organization's pay range. Pay differential is simply a difference in pay in response to external factors. A compressed salary situation occurs whenever the difference in salary levels reaches a minimum difference between one level and the other. This occurs when external factors artificially inflate applicable salary levels.

20. **C.** This is a policy of compensation whereby employees are all paid at the same rate as opposed to being paid within a pay range. This is typical in a situation where the job being performed is so similar that there really isn't room for a wide range of skill level. The other three choices are incorrect.

21. **B.** Employee benefits are regulated by the Employee Retirement Income Security Act (ERISA). The other three choices are regulated by the Fair Labor Standards Act (FLSA).

22. **B.** The classification system is the primary evaluation system used by the government and in the public sector. The other choices are more heavily used in the private sector.

23. **A.** Aging is a process that adjusts the value of salary data from multiple sources and/or over a period of time with the objective of achieving an adjusted result as reflective as possible to the desired moment in time. Leveling is calculating the average amount of money that a particular group of people receive for their work. Benchmarking is a measurement of the quality of an organization's policies, products, programs, strategies, etc., and their comparison with standard measurements or similar measurements of its marketplace.

24. **B.** A bonus is discretionary if it is given at the sole discretion of the employer to award it, not an expectation by the employees. A discretionary bonus is a form of variable pay; the amount, requirements, timing, and announcement of the bonus should not be disclosed in advance, as this may appear to be a motivator or incentive implying that meeting certain levels would guarantee a bonus or reward. Performance-based bonuses are meant to be motivational. They are designed to reward employees for fulfilling their responsibilities and for delivering superior results. Bonus targets and their associated payouts reflect a range of expected levels of performance. Formula-based and service-based bonuses are designed to reward performance, or service on the basis of predesigned measurements. Gainsharing is an example of a formula-based bonus.

25. **B.** Workers' compensation is regulated by the states. At the turn of the twentieth century, workers' compensation laws were voluntary for several reasons. Some argued that compulsory workers' compensation laws would violate the 14th Amendment due process clause of the U.S. Constitution. Many felt that compulsory participation would deprive the employer of property without due process. The issue of due process was resolved by the United States Supreme Court in 1917. After the ruling, many states enacted new compulsory workers' compensation laws. The other three choices are incorrect.

Endnotes

1. United States Department of Labor, Wage and Hour Division, Wages and the Fair Labor Standards Act (FLSA)

2. United States Department of Labor, Wage and Hour Division, Family and Medical Leave Act, Department of Labor, Wage and Hour Division, 29 CFR Part 825, RIN 1235-AA09

3. 79 FR 20749

4. Described earlier in this chapter as well as in Chapter 2

5. Described in Chapter 2

6. Check state and local regulations frequently to be sure you are current with this rapidly evolving set of requirements

7. KFF.org, "Overview of Health Benefits for Pre-65 and Medicare-Eligible Retirees"

Human Resource Development and Retention

While consisting of only 12 percent of the Associate Professional in Human Resources (aPHR) exam, the Human Resource Development and Retention functional area has an important bottom-line impact on any employer organization. Keeping employees' skills and knowledge current is necessary for the effectiveness of the organization, yet retaining productive and key employees is vital to an organization's health. Understanding the techniques and methods for delivering training programs and developing individual employees is what the aPHR will address.

The Body of Knowledge statements outlined by the HR Certification Institute (HRCI) for the Human Resource Development and Retention functional area by those performing early HR career roles are as follows:

Knowledge of

- **01** Applicable laws and regulations related to training and development activities (for example, Title VII, ADA, Title 17 [copyright law])
- **02** Training delivery format (for example, virtual, classroom, on the job)
- **03** Techniques to evaluate training programs (for example, participant surveys, pre- and post-testing, after-action review)
- **04** Career development practices (for example, succession planning, dual-ladder careers)
- **05** Performance appraisal methods (for example, ranking, rating scales)
- **06** Performance management practices (for example, setting goals, benchmarking, feedback)

Laws and Regulations

The following eight federal laws have an impact on this functional area. Be sure to refer to Chapter 2 for more information about each of these laws. Understanding them is critical to professional performance in the HR profession. You may expect that any or all of these laws will be subjects on the aPHR certification exam.

- **The Copyright Act (1976)**   The Copyright Act offers protection of "original works" for authors so others may not print, duplicate, distribute, or sell their work.
- **The Trademark Act (1946)**   The Trademark Act sets forth the requirements for registering a trademark or service mark. HR usually has a role to play in training employees in how to properly handle organizational trademarks and the policies that govern those uses.
- **Uniform Guidelines on Employee Selection Procedures (1978)**   This law provides guidelines to avoid illegal discrimination in hiring decisions particularly with regard to the job requirements and selection devices such as written or oral tests, interviews, and ability testing.
- **Age Discrimination in Employment Act (1967)**   This law bans employment discrimination based on age for those 40 years old or older.
- **The U.S. Patent Act**   This law was established to protect inventions for 20 years. U.S. law grants the inventor the right to exclude others from making, using, or selling the invention.
- **Title VII of the Civil Rights Act (1964)**   Title VII of the Civil Rights Act speaks to employment discrimination and cites five protected classes of people: race, color, sex, religion, and national origin.
- **The Americans with Disabilities Act (1990)**   This act prohibits discrimination in employment, public services, public accommodations, and telecommunications for people with disabilities.
- **Uniformed Services Employment and Reemployment Rights Act (1994)**   This act provides instructions for handling employees who are in the reserves and receive orders to report for active duty. The law also protects the employment, reemployment, and retention rights of anyone who voluntarily or involuntarily serves or has served in the uniformed services.

Training Delivery Format

Training and development (T&D) activities are core value functions of the HR department. The process of training provides skills, abilities, and knowledge that are focused on a specific outcome. The intent is a short-term focus and immediate application for on-the-job use by the trainee.

With development activities, there is a longer-term focus that prepares the intended trainee for future job skill or knowledge needs to increase their effectiveness in the organization.

One of the most widely used standard processes to determine the needs for training, developing the training, and evaluating the outcomes is known as the ADDIE model.

ADDIE represents Assessment, Design, Development, Implementation, and Evaluation. The early-career HR professional will generally have responsibilities associated with the implementation and evaluation phases of ADDIE.

Regardless of the type of training to be conducted, there are a number of methods and approaches that an organization can use to deliver the training. With today's rapid pace of growth in technology, the available choices are expanding exponentially. Whatever the selected approach, there are a variety of considerations when deciding on the methods:

- The subject matter
- Team versus individual training
- Self-guided versus guided
- Number of trainees
- Geographical restrictions
- Resources and costs
- Time frame for the training
- Traditional or e-learning
- Conditions and parameters set by recertification requirements
- Legal issues with the selection of individuals for inclusion in training

There is no one perfect teaching method for every situation. In fact, the method used will depend upon the training circumstances and the material being covered. There are teacher-centered instructional methods and learner-centered instructional methods.[1] According to University of Tennessee's Bob Annon, instructional methods are the manner in which learning materials are presented to students.

Classroom

Facilitator-led classroom training continues to be the most often used approach to training. This traditional mode usually happens internally through the organization with in-house instructors or vendors or through a professional organization. This face-to-face classroom setting permits the use of several learning methods: presentation, case study, reading, role-playing, exercises, demonstration, and group discussion. Table 6-1 explains when to use each method.

An important aspect of classroom training is to recognize that adults in a classroom setting will have different expectations and learning styles than younger students in a school/college classroom setting. The adult learning principles have a single-track focus: trainability. *Trainability* is concerned with the readiness to learn and its associated motivation.

Facilitator Classroom Method	When to Use
Presentation	When information needs to be delivered to a group, especially large groups and perhaps at different locations
Case study	When trainees need to apply the knowledge on the job right away
Reading	When self-reflection is needed to process the information being disseminated
Role-playing	When trainees need to practice in a simulation the information or skills being taught and learn skills quickly
Exercises	When practice is necessary to fully develop the new skills or learning
Group discussion	When trainees need to have an exchange of experience and information sharing with their other trainees
Demonstration	When new information or skills are being presented

Table 6-1 Classroom Learning Methods

Virtual Classroom

With current technology, remote instruction is possible. It all began with a growing number of college and university classes that began using some form of Internet-based training to reach out to a broader number of students, and it quickly caught speed with the advent of new technologies and faster Internet speeds. Today, organizations reach out to their employee groups efficiently and effectively via the virtual classroom. Webinars and programs such as Blackboard are popular Internet programs that allow the trainer and the trainees to have real-time chat and electronic file exchanges. Live streaming video is a sign of the times in the training conference room in many organizations, allowing a trainer in one geographical location to see and respond to a group class in a number of other locations.

As with any delivery of training modality, the coordination of creating the virtual classroom, the materials, the instructor, the intended trainees, *and* the technology (especially the technology) usually involves a number of important elements that will influence the success of the training program. This is the most visible stage of the ADDIE process because success is to be measured by the learning that takes place during the delivery of the training. It would benefit trainers to create checklists to ensure participants have PDF files of handouts and to set up auto-e-mail reminders for participants with time zone information and web links or phone numbers.

Corporate Universities

Corporate universities have been a growing trend in corporations since the 1990s. Large organizations such as Boeing, Walt Disney, and Yahoo! have developed their in-house universities to assist their organizations in achieving their strategic employee development goals and to foster individual and organizational learning and knowledge.[2] McDonald's Corporation has the best-known corporate university, Hamburger University, in Chicago.

For the most part, corporate universities are not universities per se in the strict sense of the term. Not to be confused with accredited universities that may be hosted at an organization's facility, the corporate university does not provide accredited under-graduate and postgraduate degrees. A corporate university limits its scope to providing job and organizational-specific training. They are set up for a variety of reasons, yet most organizations will have the same basic needs:

- Support a common culture, loyalty, and belonging to a company
- Organize training as part of the curricula for employees
- Remain competitive in their industry
- Retain employees
- Start and support change in the organization
- Offer training development to fit the career aspiration goals of employees

These types of in-house universities offer value-added training and education to employees, but they also help organizations retain and promote key employees.

Learning Styles   All adults have a particular learning style that best suits their ability to learn. Understanding these learning styles will assist you in the creation of a learning environment within your organization, allowing you to accommodate each style with the delivery of training.

Additionally, if your job responsibility includes being a presenter or trainer, knowing your own learning style will enhance your ability to adjust your preference of delivery methods, so you won't fall into the comfort of just your style and can shift your delivery to meet the needs of all participants. Also, knowing your own learning style will assist you in your career with problem-solving, managing conflict, negotiations, teamwork, and career planning.

There are three learning styles: auditory, visual, and kinesthetic.

- *Auditory learners* tend to benefit most from lecture style. Present information by talking so they can listen. Auditory learners succeed when directions are read aloud or information is presented and requested verbally because they interpret the underlying meanings of speech through listening to tone of voice, pitch, speed, and other nuances.

- *Visual learners* rely upon a seeing presentation style: "Show me and I'll understand." These learners do best when seeing facial expressions and body language. It helps them understand the content of what is being taught because they think in pictures, diagrams, charts, pictures, videos, computer training, and written directions. These students will value to-do lists, flip charts, and written notes. They need and want to take detailed notes to absorb the information.

- *Kinesthetic learners* are also called tactile learners. They learn via a hands-on approach and prefer to explore the physical aspects of learning. Sitting for long periods of time is difficult for these learners because they need activity in order to learn. Kinesthetic learners are most successful when totally engaged with the learning activity such as in role-playing, practicing, and with topics that can use the senses of feeling and imagining.

Learning Curves   Besides having different learning preference styles, adults also learn at different rates. This is referred to as learning curves. A learning curve is a graphical representation of the increase of learning (vertical axis) with experience (horizontal axis). The factors that determine how quickly an adult will learn are

- The person's motivation for learning
- The person's prior knowledge or experience
- The specific knowledge or task that is to be learned
- The person's aptitude and attitude about the knowledge or skill to learn

The four most common learning curves are

- **Increasing returns**   This is the pattern that comes into play when a person is learning something new. The start of the curve is slow while the basics are being learned. The learning increases and takes off as knowledge or skills are acquired. This curve assumes that the individual will continue to learn as time progresses. An example would be when an IT programmer needs to learn a new coding language. Learning will be slow at first until the programmer grasps the new coding protocol, and after mastering the basics, the learning becomes easier and/or quicker as the programmer learns more about the particular language.

- **Decreasing returns**   This pattern is when the amount of learning increases rapidly in the beginning and then the rate of learning slows down. The assumption with this learning curve is that once the learning is achieved, the learning then stops. This occurs when learning routine tasks and is the most common type of learning curve. An example is when a data entry clerk learns how to enter a sales order—the learning is complete.

- **S-shaped**   This learning curve is a blend of the increasing and decreasing returns curves. The assumption with this learning curve is that the person is learning something difficult, such as problem-solving or critical thinking. Learning may be slow at the beginning until the person learning becomes familiar with the learning material, and at that point, learning takes off. The cycle continues with a slow to faster progression as new material is presented. An example of this is when a production lead is trained on new equipment, yet this equipment has not been utilized in the production of the product before. There might be a trial and error for adjustments until the new production equipment is working as expected and is adjusted to the new product. Then when another product is introduced, the equipment and process need adjusting again until everything works smoothly.

- **Plateau curve**   As the name suggests, learning on this curve is quick in the beginning and then flattens or plateaus. The assumption is that the plateau is not permanent and that with additional coaching, training, and support the person learning can ramp up again. With this curve, it can be frustrating to the learner if they are not getting the support and additional training needed to master the task. An example of the plateau curve is a salesperson who has met quotas in the past, and when a new line of equipment is introduced into the product line, the salesperson is provided with a minimal level of training/knowledge about it but not enough training to answer all the questions of the prospective customers. The anticipation of additional sales with the new product is not being achieved because the salesperson requires more training in order to pitch the new product and convince the customer to purchase.

Figure 6-1 illustrates the four most common learning curves.

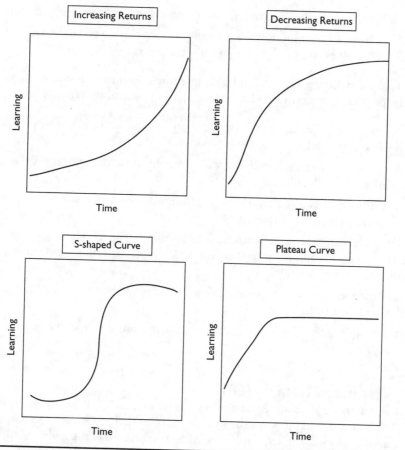

Figure 6-1   Adult learning curves

E-learning

Only a few years ago, e-learning was not an option in the workplace. Learning was accomplished by attending a classroom session lasting from a few hours to several days, weeks, or months. Today, employees are able to log on to a computer access point and participate in training programs at their own pace, on their own schedule. These e-learning systems provide materials, review, and testing to assure the employee has accomplished specific learning objectives before moving to the next training step. They also offer an audit trail to report on who has participated in each program. That is handy when you have to be sure everyone has gone through specific training programs. There is no need for an instructor. Each individual works with the materials presented, and perhaps some reference materials, to meet the training objectives.

E-learning can be synchronous or asynchronous:

- Synchronous learning is when training participants interact together in real time.

- Asynchronous learning is when training participants access information at different times and maybe even in different places.

There are also differences in adult learning in the e-learning classroom. The following are some pointers to keep in mind when conducting e-learning training:

- Screens should be designed with attention to adult learning cognition and retention principles.

- Trainees need to have familiarity with the software and computer equipment being used for the training.

- Ensuring models, simulations, online notepads, tests, and games are created to keep the trainee's attention span.

- Font size, colors, and graphics are used appropriately and allow for easy navigation through the program. Too much rapid movement can cause distraction for the trainee.

- Online and telephone support during the training session for the trainee should be made available.

- Language barriers and other cultural considerations for diversity need to be considered.

Computer-Based Training (CBT)

With computer-based training, employees can participate in training and learning programs from terminals at kiosks in the workplace, from their own desktop computers, and even from their tablets and smart phones. Most computer-based training is self-directed, allowing learners to progress at their own pace, or a timed pace, through a set of training modules. Web-based workbooks and materials are often part of these programs. HR has found that the use of computer-based training programs for compliance and regulatory training needs is not only cost effective, but it also helps with the tremendous amount of recordkeeping requirements.

 EXAM TIP Computer-based training is evolving at a rapid pace and becoming the norm for cost-effective delivery for employers. Expect the exam to have questions related to the benefits and the cons of CBT.

On-the-Job Training (OJT)

On-the-job training is specific training provided to existing employees at the actual job site or desk. It utilizes the actual performance of the task or skill of the job function to be accomplished. Some advantages for OJT include a "just-in-time" demonstration of expectations in the real environment where the employee would be expected to perform. It also provides an opportunity for immediate feedback. OJT training can also be done in groups or one-on-one. A major disadvantage to OJT training can be potential safety issues (for example, with the use of machinery), and it can be distracting to other co-workers.

Skills Training

Skills training generally encompasses specific skill sets associated with jobs as identified in job descriptions. Skill development is a constantly moving target because of the nature of changing workplace requirements. With the added complexity of technology and rules/regulations, most jobs will have changing skill set requirements throughout their existence in the organization. Categories of skills training will normally include the following:

- Sales training
- Technology training
- Technical skills
- Quality training
- Communication skills training
- Emotional intelligence
- Basic on-the-job training

Other skills training may be specifically targeted to supervisory-level positions such as leadership/supervisory skills training, discrimination/harassment prevention training, or diversity and ethics training.

Apprenticeships   Apprenticeships relate to a technical skills type of training for a specific job position or function. Unions and employer groups will have apprenticeship programs with a set of standards that include an on-the-job training period, some form of learning curriculum that may include classroom instruction, and specific operating procedures with timelines. The U.S. apprenticeship system is regulated by the Bureau of Apprenticeship and Training (BAT) of the U.S. Department of Labor. Apprentices are not exempt from the FLSA's minimum wage and overtime rules and regulations or their particular state's. Federal rules on apprentices can be located at the Code of Federal Regulations (https://www.gpo.gov; search for *29 CFR 520*).

Internships   Internships are programs that are normally designed to give students who are in a course of professional studies an opportunity to gain real-time experience in their chosen professional career prior to earning their degree or certification. By providing a learning experience in a real work environment, the student gains valuable exposure to the profession, the industry, and the organization that the internship is at. Organizations benefit by developing low-cost access to potential new graduates and the opportunity to observe the intern's performance and "fit" for potential job openings. They also provide a mode of alternative staffing for the employer.

Job Rotation   Job rotation is the shifting of an employee between different jobs. An example would be where an employee may work one day in the ER of a hospital and then the next day work in the urgent-care unit of that same hospital. Or in the case of a manufacturing plant, the employee may work on an assembly line one day and the next day in the quality control inspection station. This not only provides a lot of flexibility for staffing needs for the employer, but also provides an enrichment for the employee with being multiskilled and has been proven to increase their engagement in their work.

Today, a new form of job rotation has emerged that is related to "gig assignments." Gig workers can be employed for a defined short-term engagement and then rotated to another short-term engagement, such as an employee with several different skill sets that may be assigned to project teams. This is becoming more frequent in technology jobs.

 EXAM TIP   You may not use trending terms such as *gig assignments* and *gig workers* in your organization, but you should know what they mean for the exam.

Cross Training   Cross training happens when employees are trained to do more than one job, sometimes several jobs. As an example, a payroll specialist may know how to process accounts payable and accounts receivables. The advantages of cross training for the organization are flexibility with coverage, such as for vacation relief or job vacancy. Advantages for the employee would be professional development and career growth. It's not uncommon to see employees seeking out cross-training opportunities to prepare them for promotional opportunities. Unions have been known to not be in favor of cross training, as it threatens job jurisdiction and could broaden the job descriptions.

Techniques to Evaluate Training Programs

The final phase of the ADDIE model involves evaluating, which means measuring the effectiveness of the training program. Having training objectives identified before the training is conducted is necessary for measuring the outcome of a training program.

Specific achievement and objective goals so training participants can demonstrate their ability to perform are essential for participants and instructors to use in determining training effectiveness. They also provide a focus for the design of the training, which is a responsibility at a midlevel or specialist organizational development HR position. Nevertheless, the identified objectives are needed to provide what is to be measured and select the appropriate technique to be used for evaluating whether the training objectives were achieved. An example of an objective might be something like this: "With the knowledge and techniques taught in this three-day training course on operating the new widget processor, the participant will be able to operate the widget processor at a 100 percent production capacity." The selected evaluation technique might be observation.

Having a basic understanding of evaluating training and HR programs is helpful for determining the techniques to be used for a particular training program's evaluation. The most widely known model is Donald Kirkpatrick's four levels. Kirkpatrick's model focuses primarily on evaluating the effectiveness of the training presented.[3] Figure 6-2 illustrates the four levels.

The first level measures the reaction of the participant. A survey given at the conclusion of the training is the most common method. Participants detail how they liked the training and their thoughts as to its applicability. This, however, measures the immediate reaction about the training delivery and its environment rather than their level of learning.

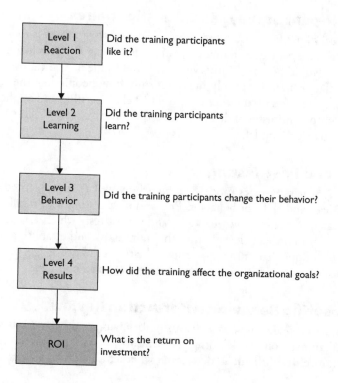

Figure 6-2
Kirkpatrick's four levels of evaluating training

The second level measures how well participants in the training learned facts, concepts, theories, and behaviors. Using this measure normally requires HR professionals or consultants who are trained in statistics and studies to interpret the results. Pre- and post-training measurements are conducted, and control groups may be involved. The results will indicate the effectiveness of the training.

The third level deals with the measurement of behavior and is more difficult to measure than the previous two levels because it can be difficult to determine whether behavior changed solely because of the training program; other outside influences could be involved. In level 3 measurement, observations, interviews, 360-degree feedback instruments, and simulations can be used. Critical incidents performance by the trainee's supervisor might be employed.

The fourth level deals with the measurement of results to determine whether the planned effectiveness of the training delivered the desired results. The difficulty with this measurement is with determining whether the training was the sole factor affecting the results. Typically a cost-benefit of return on investment (ROI) follows to substantiate the level 4 results.

When evaluating the training program's effectiveness, it is important to achieve an objective viewpoint. Choose techniques that will solicit information from all affected sources—not just the training participants and presenter but also the sources affected by the training, which could be other departments, management, and even customers.

Participant Surveys and Questionnaires

One technique to measure the reaction level of the trainees is to administer participant-written surveys or questionnaires immediately after the conclusion of training. Another method would be an oral interview with the trainees. Use caution, though, because the immediate reaction typically measures only how people like the training and the environment that was used rather than their level of learning and application. It is the easiest method to administer and thus is used the most frequently. This is referred to as level 1 in Kirkpatrick's model.

Pre- and Post-Testing

Level 2 of Kirkpatrick's model measures how well trainees learned facts, concepts, theories, ideas, and skills or behavior. Pre- and post-testing would fall into level 2. A pre-test of what the trainee's knowledge is, and a post-test, which is a second measurement of what their knowledge level is after the training, would establish a baseline of knowledge. This technique determines how much the trainee's knowledge, or skill level, has changed because of the training, commonly referred to as reaction and learning.

Measuring Behavior: After-Action Review

After-action review involves measuring behavior, and behavior is more difficult to measure than reaction and learning. The reason why is that it involves the circumstances of the trainee. It's difficult to determine whether a behavior change is related solely to the attendance at a training program. For example, if a supervisor has improved relationships with subordinates, was it through a management training program the supervisor attended or from a recent 360-degree feedback instrument that pointed out a lacking in that area?

Changes in behavior can be evaluated using a variety of techniques. Combining several techniques may provide a truer evaluation of the behavior change. The techniques are performance tests, critical incidents, performance appraisals, 360-degree feedback, observations, and simulations.

Performance Tests

A performance test is administered to training participants and contains actual samples of content that was taught in the training. This type of technique measures behavior changes desired for the work environment. An example of a performance test would be conducting an oral scenario interview after an ethics training course and having the trainee role play the suggested behavior response.

Critical Incidents

With the critical incidents method, a record of both positive and negative incidents is scored to measure the training's outcomes. Normally this would be completed by the trainee's direct reporting supervisor or manager. An example of this method might be where a salesperson concluded their negotiation tactics training, and during an actual new client meeting, the salesperson's manager is present and noting the behaviors that were effective, and least effective, in the negotiation.

Performance Appraisals: 360-Degree Feedback

Performance appraisals will most likely include the critical incidents method, though captured for a longer period of assessment of behavior, such as a year. More effective these days is the use of the 360-degree feedback performance appraisal. This is where trainees, their peers, their direct reports, internal (or even external) customers and suppliers, and other relevant people whose perspectives "count" give feedback about effective behaviors and ineffective behaviors. Perceptions may be right or wrong; what matters is that perceptions count! Which perceptions does the trainee need to change? This type of feedback zeros in on what specific behavior the trainee would benefit from changing and, over time, measures how well they changed it. This is a popular technique used in management and supervisory training in organizations and is an administrative-intense process that HR is normally intimately involved with.

Observations

Observation can be one of the most validated of the techniques in evaluating changed behavior, that is, if the behavior has been observed both pre- and post-training. The difficulty is in determining the conditions of the observation period and the length of the observation and then pinpointing whether the observer is subjective or biased. Observations can assess complex performance that is difficult to measure or evaluate by the other techniques. External executive coaches are often hired by organizations for senior management and utilize the observation tactics of their coachee to assess where improvement has occurred (e.g., facilitation of meetings) or behavior has changed (e.g., body language in meetings).

Simulations

With simulations as a training evaluation technique, the training participant performs a simulation of what was learned and applies it in real time on the job. This is an experiential bridge between the training and its actual application in the world of the trainee's work. How well the trainee performs the simulation can be a measurement of the training's effectiveness on the trainee. Simulations that accurately reflect the work conditions and environment can be costly to construct by way of resources and time.

Career Development Practices

Career development is the lifelong individual process that involves planning, managing, learning, and transitions at all ages and stages in work life. In organizations, it is an organized approach used to match employee goals with the business's current and future needs. An individual's work-related preferences and needs continuously evolve throughout life's phases. At the same time, organizations are also continuously adapting to economic, political, and societal changes.

It is not just the individual employee and HR involved in career development. The direct line of management and the organization's leaders have roles to play, too.

Individuals bear the primary responsibility for their own careers. Today, individuals are required to be proactive in planning their career progressions and not rely on an organization to direct their career paths. Being keenly aware of currently assessed traits and skills, along with needs for increased knowledge, skill, and experience associated with the individual's career ambitions, is largely the responsibility of an individual employee. Figure 6-3 illustrates the stages of an individual's career development.

The direct line of management normally serves as support in helping an individual assess his or her current effectiveness and potential and provides a broader view of the organization's career paths. The direct supervisory management will wear many hats, including coach, appraiser, guidance counselor, and resource referral, in the employee's career development planning.

HR professionals are involved in the development of career pathing, personal development programs, and skill development training in order to enable employees to achieve their career aspirations and goals. Creating a skill inventory database along with work and educational experience of the current workforce is needed in helping the organization assess its current workforce talent. Additionally, HR professionals monitor training and development needs and create programs to meet those needs, along with the communication of job progression opportunities.

The organizational leader's role in career development includes communicating the organization's mission and vision to the workforce to link the organization's initiatives and changes with the anticipated talent needs. Fostering a culture of support and internal opportunity for career development is another important function of the organizational leader's role.

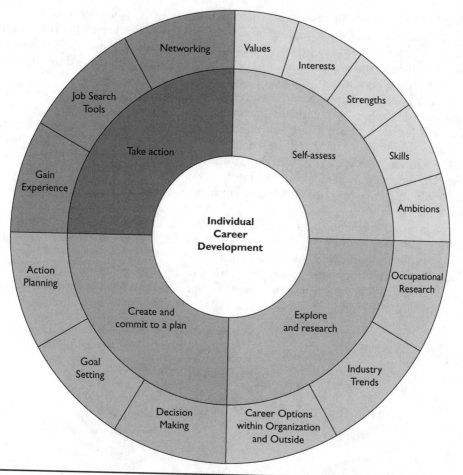

Figure 6-3 Individual career development

In the role of early-career HR, the HR professional will most likely have responsibilities associated with tracking, monitoring, and providing or aligning resources with regard to the organization's career development practices.

Succession Planning

Succession planning systematically identifies, assesses, and develops talent as a key component for business success. It is an ongoing process that enables an organization to plan or recover when critical talent is lost. An effective succession plan includes a focus on identifying, developing, and preparing the placement of high-potential employees for future opportunities. It is foolish to assume that key players would provide adequate notice of resignation. Succession planning is not just for the planned events such as retirements; it serves for replacement planning such as when a key player is relocating because of family or perhaps perished in an accident. Succession should be developed to anticipate managerial staffing needs or key employee positions that would interrupt the business process if an incumbent were to vacate.

A succession plan contains an identification of high-risk positions along with those positions with known or potentially known vacancy dates (as with retirements). Competencies for those positions are identified, and a gap analysis is performed using the current workforce to review potential candidates. Individuals within are identified as high-potential employees, which might include their interest/aspiration in the position. After all, not every individual may be interested in moving into a position with more responsibility. Tentative plans are created for shortages, which may include seeking outside candidates.

HR is typically responsible for maintaining a candidate database of skills and career development plans, along with the monitoring of development activities. This function is generally one that is handled by early-career HR professionals. Additionally, HR is responsible for the sourcing or creation of training needs for candidates and monitoring their continued interest. Figure 6-4 provides a typical progression of steps in succession planning.

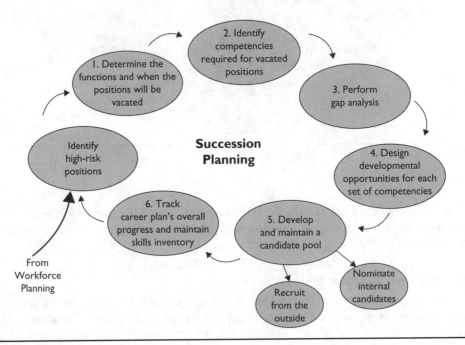

Figure 6-4 Succession planning

Career Pathing

Career pathing is a practice in which an employee charts a course within their organization for his or her career path and career development. Using HR as an example, an early-career HR employee, who may have started out in the organization as an HR intern during their college studies, may have decided that the area of HR that most interests them and aligns with their talents is associated with the functions of compensation. The HR employee will research the responsibilities and requirements for the differing positions within the HR compensation function. They may plan to attend an outside course of study to attain a certification credential in compensation. Or they may apply for voluntary positions with the union to learn the aspects of union salary negotiations.

Additionally, with career pathing, a formalized employee self-assessment tool may be used to assist employees in understanding their areas of strengths and where to hone their areas of development needs or weaknesses. Self-assessments will identify where the employee is now in the career, where they intend to grow, and, more importantly, what gaps they need to fill. Creating a plan that gains the employee the exposure, experience, and knowledge to move through the various levels of the career aspiration goals is career pathing.

 EXAM TIP The importance of career pathing is that employees design and drive their chosen career progression with input from others. It is vastly different from formal in-company career development programs where selected individuals may be fast tracked in a career progression such as management training development programs.

Dual-Ladder Careers

Dual-ladder career development programs allow mobility for employees without requiring that they be placed into the managerial enclave. Mostly associated with technical, medical, engineering, and scientific occupations, this type of program is a way to advance employees who are not interested in pursuing a management track. These individuals exhibit one or more of the following characteristics:

- Have substantial technical or professional expertise beyond the basic levels
- Have licensure or required credentials
- Are known for innovation
- May or may not be well suited for management or leadership roles

An objective within a dual-ladder development program is to increase complexity and value to the organization, enabling the organization to increase employee salaries to improve employee retention and satisfaction. Lateral movement may occur within a dual-ladder program such as team membership, internal consultative roles, mentorships, or larger facility rotation. Figure 6-5 shows an example of a dual-ladder career path.

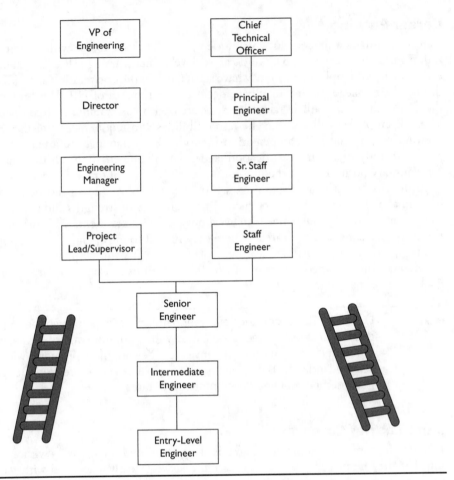

Figure 6-5   Dual-ladder career path

Career Counseling

Whether in a large or small organization, HR will generally receive a knock on the door from employees who are seeking guidance for their careers within an organization. Sometimes having a crystal ball sitting on your desk can have metaphoric value. *"Let's have a look at the crystal ball and see what it indicates for you."* Seriously, with career counseling and coaching, the foremost skill that all levels of HR professionals must utilize is helping the employee take ownership and accountability for their careers, not expecting the organization to map out or hand them their personalized career plan on a silver platter. Individual counseling and coaching involves one-on-one discussions about specific direction and needs between an aspiring employee and experienced individuals within the organization who are normally in the career path the employee is intending to pursue. This can be a supervisor, a mentor, a retiree, or a hired career consultant. HR's role is to help the employee sort out their options and engage the resources available to them.

PART II

Performance Appraisal Methods

A regular feedback system discussing individual employee performance is at the core of a good organization. It ensures that employees are on course for the completion of tasks and goals that are aligned with the organization's goals and that resources and support are provided for the employee to perform such functions.

Employees need to know and understand what specific performance is expected of them in performing their jobs and the acceptable behavior. This communication begins with the very first discussion in a job interview and certainly with the job offer and new-hire onboarding orientation. The discussion continues on a consistent basis, both with the reinforcement of organizational standards that are outlined in employee handbooks and other written material and with performance appraisal review sessions. The clearer the expectations set for employees, the greater the success in having expectations met.

Performance appraisals satisfy three purposes:

- Providing feedback and coaching
- Justifying the allocation of rewards and career opportunities
- Helping with employee career planning and development plans

For the organization, performance appraisals can foster commitment and align people to contribute to initiatives with their upcoming performance contributions. The most common performance appraisal method involves just two people: the employee and a direct supervisor. In some companies, others are asked to be involved in the appraisals such as peers, another level of management, and sometimes colleagues in the organization whose job function interacts with the employee. These are known as 360-degree feedback appraisals.

Methods for rating the performance can be completely narrative, management by objectives (MBO), behaviorally anchored ratings (BARS), category rating, and comparative ratings with others in like functions. No single method is best for all situations. Therefore, a blended combination of methods may be the best choice in certain circumstances and offset the disadvantages with some methods and highlight the advantages in others.

EXAM TIP   Most employers use a blended method approach to performance approvals, and using the MBO method does not require an employee to be in a management job.

Category Rating

The least complex of the methods is the category rating method where the evaluator simply checks a level of rating on an evaluation form. Three types of rating formulas are typically used in category rating methods, covered next.

Forced Choice

With the forced-choice rating method, the evaluator is required to check two out of four statements on the evaluation form, one that the employee is "most like" and one that the employee is "least like." The statements on the form are normally a combination of positive and negative statements. The biggest limitation of this appraisal rating method is the creation of the valid statements. The creation of the statements would typically not be part of the early-career HR professional role.

Graphic Scale

This is the most common type of category rating, where the appraiser checks a place on the scale for the categories of tasks and behaviors that are listed. A typical scale is 5 points, where 1 means not meeting expectations or low, and 5 means exceeding expectations or high. These types of performance appraisals normally have a comments section that the appraiser completes that provides justification for the rating.

Checklist

Another common appraisal rating method is one in which the evaluator is provided with a set list of statements/words to describe performance. The appraiser selects the one word or statement that best describes the performance—for example, "Employee consistently meets all deadlines" or "Employee consistently misses deadlines."

Comparative Methods

With comparative methods, employee performance is compared directly with others in the same job, group, or function. The evaluator will rank the employees in a group, causing a forced distribution known as a bell curve. Ten percent will fall in the highest and lowest areas of the rating scale, another 20 percent will fall on either side, and then 40 percent will meet job standards and expectations. An obvious fault with this type of system is suggesting that a percentage of employees will fall below expectations. Figure 6-6 displays a bell curve distribution.

Figure 6-6
Bell curve distribution

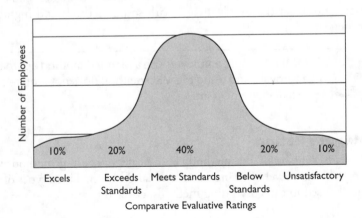

Ranking

Using a ranking method, the evaluator lists all the employees in the same job or function, from highest to lowest, performance-wise. If there are ten employees, the evaluator will rank them with a number in order of best performance (#1) to poorest in performance (#10). This method is restrictive in that the difference between the employees ranked and their performance output is not described. There may be little difference between rankings 3 and 4 and yet a huge difference in performance results and output between 7 and 10. The bias of the evaluator comes into play with this method's effectiveness, and it forces a conclusion of better to worse. What would you do if all employees in the group were adequately performing or perhaps were an exemplary group of key contributors? Ranking would not be appropriate.

Paired Comparison

In paired-comparison evaluation methods, each of the employees in a group is paired with every other employee and compared, or "toggled," one at a time, using the same scale of performance. Although this method provides more information about individual employees than pure ranking, it has its limits in that the time required to evaluate each pair of employees can be significant within large employee groups.

Narrative

Narrative evaluations are time consuming for an evaluator to complete, yet they can be the most meaningful to the employee being evaluated. Three methods are the most common for the narrative appraisal.

Essay Format

Basically, the evaluator writes a short essay type of narrative describing each employee's performance. There may be structures with specific categories to comment on, such as attendance, teammanship, achievements, and development plans. Some are free form, without guidelines. This method allows the evaluator a lot of flexibility than the other methods mentioned. But it is time consuming and normally difficult to get supervisory management to comply with this method in a timely fashion. Today, most performance appraisals have blended an element of the essay format with the other methods.

Critical Incidents

With this method, the evaluator is noting dates and details of both good and not-so-good performance incidents throughout the evaluation period. This method requires the appraiser to keep detailed notes on a regular basis during the appraisal period and not rely solely on an employee's most recent performance.

Field Review

In the field review method, this will directly involve the HR professional. The HR person will interview the supervisor of the employee group, taking notes about the performances of the supervisor's direct reports. After the information is compiled, the HR group will gather and do a comparison ranking for all like positions/employees. An example would be all lead widget producers in the district at five manufacturing facilities.

 EXAM TIP   When reading the exam questions pertaining to evaluation methods, read the scenario closely to determine the job function that would best be evaluated using a narrative versus ranking method.

Behaviorally Anchored Rating Scale (BARS)

This appraisal method describes desirable behavior and undesirable behavior. Examples are then compared with a scale of performance levels for the rating. BARS works well in circumstances in which several employees perform the same function. A BARS appraisal system requires extensive time to develop and maintain to keep the performance dimensions up to date as the job functions change. This is a prime reason why those in early-career HR roles will be involved in the administration and monitoring of the performance appraisal system when BARS is employed. The BARS method offers a more accurate gauge of performance measurement, provides clearer standards to employees, and has more consistency in rating.

BARS is best suited for situations where many employees are performing the same function. However, a unique BARS must be created for each like occupation/job. As an example, an accounts payable clerk function would have its unique BARS, and so would a payroll clerk.

Management by Objectives (MBO)

Management by objectives is often used by the supervisor and employee to mutually identify specific performance goals. The goals are derived and aligned with the overall goals and strategies of the organization. Other names used for MBO include *appraisal by results, performance objective setting,* and *mutual goal setting.* Frequently MBO is associated with compensation incentive programs. The advantage of this method is it helps align an employee's performance and actions with the organization's goals, measuring the accomplishment of goals with quality and quantity as a scorecard. It is a highly effective manner in tying results to goals and is used in HR interventions such as performance improvement programs (PIPs).

The term MBO was first introduced in Peter Drucker's 1954 book *The Practice of Management.*[4] It is a management model that aims to improve the performance of an organization by clearly defining objectives that are agreed to by both the individual and the line management. According to Drucker, when people have a say in goal setting and action plans, it ensures better participation and commitment on the part of the individual and alignment to organizational goals. Thus, many performance appraisal systems include MBO, and incentive bonus awards are linked with an MBO list of organizational goals.

To use the MBO method in performance evaluation, a foundation must be in place within the organization that includes the following:

- A strategic plan
- A high level of commitment from employees who are willing to plan and set their own goals
- Clearly defined objectives that are not ambiguous
- Measureable performance objectives that specify the desired outcome

Organizations adopting the MBO method need to ensure that the goals are not unachievable or even too easy to reach. That can work against the intention of MBO and actually turn into a demotivator.

Performance Management Practices

Performance management is the process in which the organization maintains or improves employee job performance utilizing performance tools, coaching/counseling, and feedback. Because individual contribution drives the business results in an organization, the practices involved in performance management are of great interest to the growth and sustainability of the organization. People (including their skills, their knowledge, their contributions, and their innovations) are the soul of the performance management system and practices.

Figure 6-7 shows the elements of a performance management system. They must incorporate the following:

- Delegating and planning work
- Setting expectations for performance results
- Continually monitoring performance
- Developing a capacity to perform to new levels for personal and professional growth
- Periodically rating performance in a summary fashion
- Providing recognition and rewarding good performance

Organizational Values and Goals

Values and goals reflect the organization's philosophy and structure. As mentioned earlier in this chapter, when organizations establish and clearly communicate their values and strategic goals, employees gain a sense of purpose and have a better understanding of where their job fits in to the priority line.

Values are principles and create standards of behavior; they are what is most important in how the organization will conduct business and shape its culture. Values can be positive drivers of behavior (treating everyone with respect) or negative drivers causing

Figure 6-7
Performance
management
system

behavior that may be less than desirable in the workforce (i.e., being tethered to your smart phone 24/7 to respond to work texts or calls), which in this example causes an unbalance in work/life.

It is an important role of both management and the HR group to consistently and clearly communicate the organization's goals and strategic direction. Goals and their milestone achievements are the signs that reflect the success of the organization, assisting the workforce in perceiving the organization's progress and how their performance plays a part.

Performance Management Standards

It's important that employees know and understand what specific performance is expected of them in performing their jobs and associated acceptable behavior. For example, if putting the customer first is expected as a high standard of behavior, each employee's job needs to have identified and measured clear examples of what represents "putting the customer first." Performance standards will include behaviors (what does the organization want employees to do?) and results (what does the organization want employees to produce?).

Setting and communicating a job's performance standards is an ongoing process. It begins during the initial interview when filling the position with a candidate, and during the onboarding phase. It continues on a frequent and regular basis as the employee learns and grows in the job, and as changes occur to the job's functions. This is one of the most important supervisory functions of management—being clear on what the expectations are of each employee in their job role and as an employee at the organization. The clearer the expectations, the greater the chances of the employee understanding them and being able to meet the standards.

Employee Performance/Behaviors

For employees to meet expectations, there should be a direct correlation for them between their job description and the job competencies required, along with the performance plan's goals and behaviors *before* the work is performed. Basically performance standards (which are benchmarks and targets) define what satisfactory job performance is for the employee. Employees need to understand what aspects of their job are critical to its success, in priority order. We've discussed the value of clear expectations so that employees completely understand the outcome their job functions are to produce and the importance of having employees and their supervisor develop their goals jointly along with a plan to achieve those goals. This is the foundation part. The next part, and just as impactful, is what motivates and keeps the employee engaged in producing the expectations of their job. This includes interacting with their supervisor, receiving timely feedback, and feeling personally connected to their work and the organization.

Ways that organizations can foster this level of performance from employees include the following:

- Nurture a positive work environment.

- Have employee engagement activities.

- Be sure management is trained in good performance management methods and understand the legal issues surrounding the methods.

- Provide continual feedback (the good, the not so good, and the ugly). Hold monthly performance appraisal meetings rather than just an annual meeting.

- Provide the resources and tools needed for employees to do their jobs and exceed standards.

- Be consistent in management practices.

- Show sincerity toward employee development and assist employees with resources.

These are just a couple of ways to set the stage for employee performance and behaviors to thrive. As an HR professional, your role is to support these functions for management and the employee group. This can be the innovative part of your job, so get creative!

Goal Setting

When involving employees in setting and creating goals for their performance and development programs, using the SMART method will ensure that the goals selected stand a chance of actually being achieved. Here's an example of an achievable goal:

Implement the ABC time management approach to reduce customer call wait time by 5 percent by the end of the third quarter.

SMART stands for the following:

- **Specific** Be specific on what the outcome or end result is to be ("reduce customer call wait time.")

- **Measurable** Have a yardstick to measure the specific intention ("by 5 percent").

- **Attainable** Make the goal achievable ("using the ABC time management approach to").

- **Realistic** Make the goal realistic to achieve in the time frame and relevant to the person's job.

- **Timed** Specify whether this goal has an implementation date or is ongoing ("by the end of the third quarter").

Composing goals with the SMART outline and using action verbs such as *identify*, *describe*, and *define* will guide the objective of the goal's learning.

A word of caution when assisting employees and/or management with goal setting: be careful of the smorgasbord effect, which means getting so excited about creating SMART goals that too many are put into the employee's goal sheet. This can dilute all other goals.

Performance Improvement Plans (PIPs)

Like with any type of relationship, in the employment relationship there will be instances where disagreements and conflict arise, especially in the form of perception and expectations related to job performance. When an employee is not meeting the minimum requirements of their job, or perhaps their behaviors are producing issues within the workgroup, it is the supervisor's responsibility to have a "painfully honest discussion" that shifts the supervisory tactics to the disciplinary realm. HR's role is to help provide the guidance and expertise needed to set up the disciplinary process to be fair and equitable and to make sure it is applied uniformly and consistently throughout the organization.

A PIP is not an automatic "nail in the coffin" sentence for the employee; it is a de facto document in writing that makes no misunderstanding as to what it is the employee is to correct and by when. The employee has a chance to make a course correction to the results produced to meet the plan's expressed standards or to shift their behavior to align with the plan's expressed perception. A must for a PIP is the consequence: "if this is not corrected by a certain time frame, then this will be the consequence" (up to and including losing the position or employment). The HR professional will be skilled in asserting what the appropriate consequence is and determining whether the time frame and requested changes are reasonable and attainable. HR acts as a broker in a sense to help the parties ensure a successful completion of the PIP.

 EXAM TIP Though normally used as a last resort to correct deficient performance and behavior, PIPs are an opportunity to make it perfectly clear to the employee what performance is expected in order to maintain their employment in the current job.

Employee Retention

Once you've hired a new employee or developed existing employees who are contributors to the progress of your organization, you want to keep them. Retention is the collection of programs and techniques that result in good and productive employees staying at your organization, engaged. Retaining employees means the employer does not have to undertake the expenses involved with recruiting, hiring, training, and possibly relocating.

According to the Society for Human Resource Management's "Future of the U.S. Labor Pool Survey Report,"[5] three out of ten employees in the workforce are retiring each year for the next 12 years. That creates a large knowledge gap and an emphasis on passing institutional knowledge to employees via replacement/succession planning. Yet a plan is only going to work as designed if the identified candidates remain employed with the organization. Retention is the ability to keep talented employees. The importance of retention has moved to the top of the priority list in today's global competitive marketplace because of the following factors:

- An improved economy rebounding from a recession, causing the job market to improve
- Retirement of the Baby Boomers and a likely shortage in skills/knowledge-based labor
- An increase of global competition
- Economic factors resulting in cost of living substantially increasing
- Technological advancements
- Generational motivation differences

Methods for Employee Retention

Many management members believe that money is the prime retention factor. That would be true if an individual's hierarchical needs[6] are not being met with their compensation. Yes, competitive pay and benefits are important methods for retention of talent, as discussed in Chapter 5. Yet it is the employee relationships to the organization, including its structure, management, job recognition, and culture, that are mostly connected to retention. Having tangible forms of recognition for a job well done and milestones of commitment are good and necessary, though providing employees with sincere feedback and appreciation that the work they do makes a difference is a reward that tops the retention reasons lists.

Additional forms of relationships for employee retention involve even the HR department, its policies, the perceived fairness, and assistance to the employee. HR could be administering a program on work and family life balance, which might be a key program that is high on the priority list for a group of employees. Identifying what your key contributors in your workforce value and then matching those needs to programs, rewards, and benefits that your organization is willing to offer is a successful retention objective.

Employee Suggestion Systems

Having an employee suggestion system is an employee engagement and involvement strategy that goes along with employee retention. When employees feel their opinion counts, or their perspective is "heard," they are more likely to turn away from third-party representation.

Employee suggestion systems, anonymous or not, can provide management with a way to "hear" the workforce for both positive ideas and negative issues or perceptions. Many improvements are discovered through employee suggestion systems that are considered at upper management levels in an organization. Often, HR is the gatekeeper responsible for screening or compiling the employee suggestions. It's important that employee suggestions are acknowledged and given serious consideration and that responses are provided in a timely manner.

Employee Focus Groups

When a large cross-section of employee opinions or perspectives is needed, an employee focus group from various units, functions, and facilities in an organization is used. Surveys can solicit the input from the entire employee population, and there are survey instruments that can compile this input for HR, but a focus group offers the opportunity to have two-way dialogue for clarity and probing purposes. The employees, however, must feel safe providing candid and honest feedback, which is a reason why either HR or an outside consultant will conduct employee focus groups.

When an organization is bleeding from key and high performers exiting, a focus group of existing employees might be needed in order to learn what the root cause of the exodus is.

Chapter Review

HR development and retention is the integrated use of training, organizational development, and career development efforts to improve individual, group, and organizational effectiveness for the purpose of retaining top talent. This HRCI functional area focuses on the methods and tasks that the HR department is responsible for in order to support management and employees in evaluation and development, in an effort to further the organization's goals. The aPHR professional will have various methods and processes to follow that support the integration of programs that help develop, select, and implement human resource programs and activities into the workforce.

HR has a prominent role to play in helping employees acquire skills and knowledge and in assisting with the changes and outside influences through the development of training and development programs, change management, performance management, employee career planning, and job enhancement.

Questions

1. Your company decided to review the exit interviews from the past two years for the finance department to determine the reasons why turnover was higher than other departments. From the analysis of the interviews, the HR consulting firm found that exiting employees for the most part left for a promotional opportunity in other organizations. It was suggested that a formal career counseling program be implemented to reverse the perception of lacking promotional opportunities. Which answer *best* describes the kind of program HR will be developing?

    A. Knowledge management program

    B. Succession planning program

    C. Career pathing program

    D. Talent management program

2. Which term best describes the manner in which adults learn?

    A. Kinesthetic

    B. Emotional intelligence

    C. Andragogy

    D. Pedagogy

3. HR has been asked to facilitate a companywide training for all forms of harassment (sexual, bullying, etc.). Which would be the *best* training delivery for the employees located in remote locations?

    A. In-person, groups of ten each

    B. Corporate university course

    C. E-learning course

    D. Virtual classroom

4. At the completion of an eight-module computer-based training course, the trainees are being asked to complete an assessment about what they learned. What evaluation method is this known as?

    A. Learning

    B. Reaction

    C. Results

    D. ROI

5. ADDIE is an instructional design tool. What is not part of ADDIE?

   A. Delivery

   B. Implementation

   C. Design

   D. Development

6. According to Maslow's hierarchy theory, which need must first be met?

   A. Esteem

   B. Security/safety

   C. Self-actualization

   D. Belonging/loving

7. Rx Pharmaceuticals is a company that employs both technical and scientific professions. What could it provide to have the most effective impact on retention for its employees?

   A. An employee work/life balance program

   B. A validated succession planning program

   C. Dual-ladder careers

   D. Differing telecommuting options

8. What performance evaluation method increases employee engagement and dialogue the most?

   A. Management by objectives (MBO)

   B. Behaviorally anchored rating scale (BARS) method

   C. A forced-choice method

   D. Paired comparison method

9. Which of the following is *not* an example of a narrative evaluation method?

   A. Behaviorally anchored rating scale (BARS)

   B. Forced distribution

   C. Management by objectives (MBO)

   D. Essay

10. HR is modifying the supervisory trainee program and has decided that a case study should be added to the program, one that trainees would work on in a group. Which stage of the ADDIE model is HR currently in?

    A. Analysis

    B. Implementation

    C. Decision

    D. Design

11. The customer service manager in your company maintains an online log of her employee's weekly results along with praises or criticism from customers. She uses this information in the quarterly performance reviews. This is an example of what type of performance appraisal method?

    A. Behavior observation

    B. Forced distribution

    C. Critical incident

    D. Supervisory logging

12. Headquarters in Virginia Beach, Virginia, has decided that all management employees who have direct responsibility for directing the work of subordinates will have their annual evaluations include feedback not only from their direct report but also from a selection of their peers and subordinates. Which evaluation method is headquarters adopting?

    A. Management by objectives (MBO)

    B. Peer review

    C. 360-degree review

    D. Internal customer rating scale

13. MaryLou has decided that she will give a presentation at her professional association chapter's annual conference, based on the best practices her marketing department uses. She expects to have anywhere from 150 to 300 attendees at her breakout session. Which of the following instructional methods would be best for MaryLou to use?

    A. Group discussion in pairs

    B. Case study

    C. Presentation

    D. Demonstration

14. Your branch manager is given a set of effective sales traits and is being asked to rate his salespeople on each of them on a scale of 1, being unsatisfactory, to 5, which represents outstanding. Which of the following does this appraisal method describe?

    A. Paired comparison

    B. Behavior observation

    C. Forced distribution

    D. Graphic rating scale

15. Pita holds an advance degree in chemical engineering and works in research and development in the Paris facility of a large global company. Pita is solely responsible for developing a new type of removable adhesive for picture hangers, which she discovered while working on improvements for an existing elastic chalking product her company produces. Who will be the owner of the patent for the new adhesive?

   A. Pita, because she is the researcher and developer of the product

   B. Pita's company because Pita is an employee and is paid to research and develop products

   C. Pita, because her discovery of the new adhesive had nothing to do with the product she was working on

   D. The French government due to an agreement with the company having an R&D facility in Paris

16. What appraisal method approach is the IT manager using when she details the strengths, weaknesses, and development recommendations for her employees?

   A. Management by objectives (MBO)

   B. Critical incident

   C. Ranking method

   D. Narrative essays

17. The ADDIE model is an acronym that describes the five elements of _____ design.

   A. Interactive

   B. Development

   C. Instructional

   D. Talent management

18. Which of the following is a comparative method of performance appraisal?

   A. BARS

   B. Ranking

   C. Critical incident

   D. Rating scale

19. When creating SMART goals, what does the acronym SMART stand for?

   A. Smart, Meaningful, Action-oriented, Relevant, and Timed

   B. Specific, Measureable, Attainable, Realistic, and Timed

   C. Smart, Measureable, Accurate, Relevant, and Timed

   D. Specific, Measurable Accurate, Responsible, and Timed

20. The training specialist at a chain of retail stores is conducting a training evaluation after the new customer service VIP training that took place last quarter. He is analyzing data from observations, interviews, tests, and surveys to assess whether new skills were successfully transferred to the job by the trainees. The analysis he is completing is an example of what type of evaluation?

   A. Behavior

   B. Results

   C. Learning on the job

   D. Reaction

21. Your organization has a six-page performance evaluation form that management is using to evaluate employee performance annually. The requirements are to evaluate and mark a box for each performance category, selecting (1) unsatisfactory not meeting expectations, (2) inconsistent in meeting expectations, (3) consistently meets expectations, (4) exceeds expectations, and (5) above and beyond expectations. What kind of performance appraisal method is this?

   A. Ranking

   B. Checklist

   C. Comparison

   D. Graphic rating scale

22. What is *not* a benefit of job rotation?

   A. Engagement in work for the employee

   B. Flexibility for employer staffing needs

   C. Multiskilled workforce

   D. Reduced benefit cost

23. Performance improvement plans (PIPs) are:

   A. Used when an employee is transitioning to a new job via promotion

   B. Used when existing employees are no longer meeting standards

   C. Used in career pathing

   D. Used at the end of the apprenticeship program

24. Girish is a recruiter, and his company is opening several new retail facilities within the next six months in a metropolitan area. He is having difficulty locating interested candidates for their new opening project teams that will work for the first four weeks at each facility. Which program should he propose to his HR director to address the staffing need?

   A. Internships

   B. Job rotation

   C. Gig workers

   D. Cross-training

25. Which statement is not true about in-house corporate universities?

    A. Offer collegiate-accredited degree programs

    B. Support a common culture and loyalty

    C. Offer training and education to employees

    D. Help organizations promote from within

Answers

1. **C.** Career pathing is a practice in which an employee charts a course within their organization for his or her career path and career development. By creating a program in which employees can perceive other possibilities for their career, it broadens their career progression opportunities and is a helpful practice for retention of talent.

2. **C.** Andragogy is the process of learning associated with people who are older than 18 to 25 and generally referred to as nontraditional learners.

3. **D**. Virtual classroom training has been proven to be more cost effective and timely in reaching a multitude of employees in differing geographical locations

4. **B.** The easiest method to administer and the most frequently used, the reaction evaluation method, is level 1 of Kirkpatrick's model. It measures how participants in the training felt about the training program immediately following the conclusion of the training.

5. **A**. ADDIE is an instructional design model that follows the phases of assessment, design, development, implementation, and evaluation.

6. **B.** Abraham Maslow's 1943 paper "A Theory of Human Motivation" created a framework in sociology extending to management training and adult development theories and describing the stages of human growth through varying needs beginning with physiological, safety, belonging, love, esteem, and then self-actualization. This is the pattern that human motivations generally move through.

7. **C.** Dual-ladder careers provide opportunities for a parallel occupational track that recognizes and rewards different skill sets. This allows organizations to retain their technical and professional employees at a similar rate as their managerial track employees.

8. **A.** Management by objectives (MBO) is often used by the supervisor and employee to mutually identify specific performance goals, offering a two-way dialogue and agreement on what goals should be and a discussion of self-assessment by the employee. Employees are more engaged in their work goals when they have a say in setting them.

9. **B.** Forced distribution is when employee performance is compared directly with others in the same job, group, or function. The evaluator will rank the employees in a group, causing a forced distribution known as a bell curve.

10. **D**. During the design phase, the course developer is involved in activities related to determining which tasks participants need training on, and in this case, they have determined a case study would be the delivery method.

11. **C**. This example best describes the critical incident appraisal method. The critical incident method refers to when a rater logs over a period of time both desired and effective behaviors with their results and ineffective behavior incidents.

12. **C**. More organizations are having their employees participate in perception evaluations on their bosses, peers, and co-workers, known as 360-degree evaluations. This affords an opportunity for the employee to become aware of how their behaviors and actions affect others they interact with on the job. The input offers focused areas of behavioral effectiveness and ineffectiveness for leadership and personal development plans.

13. **C**. Presentation style will allow MaryLou to present her best practices to a large group of attendees at the same time, with minimal disruption.

14. **D**. A graphic rating scale is used when an evaluator is given a set of traits and asked to rate the employee on each of them. The ratings are on a scale, typically 1 to 5.

15. **B**. Pita's employer pays her for this R&D work as a part of her normal job duties, and as long as this discovery occurred while Pita was on the job, the patent and discovery belong to the employer. HR needs to ensure this information is imparted to all employees, new and existing, in functions like R&D.

16. **D**. Narrative essay methods allow a short written description of the performance of the employee in a free-form fashion.

17. **C**. The ADDIE model is an acronym that describes five elements of instructional design.

18. **B**. Ranking, paired comparison, and forced ranking are all comparative methods of performance appraisals.

19. **B**. Goal setting using the SMART format requires that goals be specific, measureable, attainable, realistic, and timed.

20. **A**. Having observations, conducting interviews, giving tests, and conducting surveys describe the behavioral evaluation method.

21. **D**. Graphic rating scales are the oldest and most popular performance appraisal method. They assign a simple rating by using a scale describing acceptable performance to unacceptable performance.

22. **D**. Job rotation is the shifting of an employee between different jobs and does not usually correlate with reduced benefit costs.

23. **B**. When an employee is no longer meeting the specific requirements of their job, a performance improvement plan is created that specifically describes what needs to be improved and by when, along with a consequence (including termination of employment) if the performance level is not brought up to standards by the specified time frame.

24. **C.** Gig workers are independent workers employed by an organization for short-term engagements; they have the skills and/or knowledge for a particular function.

25. **A.** In-house corporate universities are not credentialed "universities" that provide academic-accredited degrees.

Endnotes

1. University of Tennessee, http://edtech2.tennessee.edu/projects/bobannon/in_strategies.html, accessed on July 25, 2014.

2. Annick Renaud-Coulon, *Corporate Universities: A Lever of Corporate Responsibility.* (Global CCU Publisher, 2008).

3. Don Kirkpatrick: The Father of the Four Levels (*Chief Learning Officer Magazine*, November 2009)

4. Peter Drucker, *The Practice of Management* (Harper Business, 2010).

5. SHRM, "Talent Management Future of the U.S. Labor Pool Survey Report" (2013), www.shrm.org/india/hr-topics-and-strategy/strategic-hrm/talent-development-strategy.

6. Abraham Maslow, "A theory of human motivation" (*Psychological Review* 50 (4): 370–96, 1943).

Employee Relations

The functional area Employee Relations will be 16 percent of the Associate Professional in Human Resources (aPHR) exam weighting. As you can see from the list provided in Chapter 2 of this book, there are 66 federal laws each HR professional must be able to recite. HR professionals are protectors of the employer's liability, while also being protectors of employees' rights. Those responsibilities can be met only if there is mastery of the legal requirements imposed by these laws and all similar state laws in addition. While your labor attorney will be your legal guide for your journey through the HR profession, you must be able to apply the laws in practical terms so managers and employees alike are able to perform their functions appropriately. We wish you a successful journey.

The Body of Knowledge statements outlined by HR Certification Institute (HRCI) for the Employee Relations functional area by those performing early HR career roles are as follows:

Knowledge of

- **01** Applicable laws affecting employment in union and nonunion environments, such as laws regarding antidiscrimination policies, sexual harassment, labor relations, and privacy (for example: WARN Act, Title VII, NLRA)

- **02** Employee and employer rights and responsibilities (for example: employment-at-will, privacy, defamation, substance abuse)

- **03** Methods and processes for collecting employee feedback (for example: employee attitude surveys, focus groups, exit interviews)

- **04** Workplace behavior issues (for example: absenteeism, aggressive behavior, employee conflict, workplace harassment)

- **05** Methods for investigating complaints or grievances

- **06** Progressive discipline (for example: warnings, escalating corrective actions, termination)

- **07** Off-boarding or termination activities

- **08** Employee relations programs (for example: recognition, special events, diversity programs)

- **09** Workforce reduction and restructuring terminology (for example: downsizing, mergers, outplacement practices)

Laws and Regulations

As with all the other chapters, you will find more details about laws that apply to employee and labor relations in Chapter 2. Look to that chapter for information each time you come across a reference to a law you don't understand or have yet to hear about.

Federal Laws

Here are some of the federal laws that you will be responsible for understanding when you enter the HR profession:

- The Consumer Credit Protection Act (1967)
- The Copeland "Anti-Kickback" Act (1934)
- The Copyright Act (1976)
- The Davis-Bacon Act (1931)
- The Dodd-Frank Wall Street Reform and Consumer Protection Act (2010)
- The Economic Growth and Tax Relief Reconciliation Act (2001)
- The Electronic Communications Privacy Act (1976)
- The Employee Polygraph Protection Act (1977)
- The Employee Retirement Income Security Act (ERISA) (1974)
- The Equal Pay Act (EPA—amendment to the FLSA) (1963)
- The FAA Modernization and Reform Act (2012)
- The Fair and Accurate Credit Transactions Act (FACTA) (2003)
- The Fair Credit Reporting Act (FCRA) (1970)
- The Fair Labor Standards Act (FLSA) (1937)
- The Foreign Corrupt Practices Act (1997)
- The Health Information Technology for Economic and Clinical Health Act (HITECH) (2009)
- The Health Insurance Portability and Accountability Act (HIPAA) (1996)
- The Immigration and Nationality Act (INA) (1952)
- The Immigration Reform and Control Act (IRCA) (1976)
- The Labor-Management Relations Act (LMRA) (1947)
- The Labor-Management Reporting and Disclosure Act (LMRDA) (1959)
- The Mine Safety and Health Act (MSHA) (1977)
- The National Industrial Recovery Act (1933)
- The National Labor Relations Act (NLRA) (1935)
- The Needlestick Safety and Prevention Act (2000)
- The Norris-LaGuardia Act (1932)
- The Occupational Safety and Health Act (OSHA) (1970)

- The Omnibus Budget Reconciliation Act (1993)
- The Pension Protection Act (2006)
- The Personal Responsibility and Work Opportunity Reconciliation Act (1996)
- The Portal-to-Portal Act (1947)
- The Railway Labor Act (1926)
- The Rehabilitation Act (1973)
- The Retirement Equity Act (1974)
- The Revenue Act (1977)
- The Sarbanes-Oxley Act (SOX) (2002)
- The Securities and Exchange Act (1934)
- The Service Contract Act (1965)
- The Sherman Anti-Trust Act (1790)
- The Small Business Job Protection Act (1996)
- The Social Security Act (1935)
- The Tax Reform Act (1976)
- The Taxpayer Relief Act (1997)
- The Trademark Act (1946)
- The Unemployment Compensation Amendments Act (1992)
- The Uniformed Services Employment and Reemployment Rights Act (USERRA) (1994)
- The Vietnam Era Veterans Readjustment Assistance Act (VEVRAA) (1974) (as amended by the Jobs for Veterans Act in 2007)
- The Wagner-Peyser Act (1993) (as amended by the Workforce Investment Act in 1997)
- The Walsh-Healey Act (1936)
- The Work Opportunity Tax Credit (1996)
- The Americans with Disabilities Act (ADA) (1990) (as amended by the ADA Amendments Act in 2007)
- The Civil Rights Act – Title VII (1964)
- The Civil Rights Act (1991)
- The Drug-Free Workplace Act (1977)
- The Equal Employment Opportunity Act (1972)
- The Genetic Information Nondiscrimination Act (2007)
- The Lilly Ledbetter Fair Pay Act (2009)
- The Pregnancy Discrimination Act (1977)
- The Uniform Guidelines on Employee Selection Procedures (1976)

- The Age Discrimination in Employment Act (ADEA) (1967)
- The American Recovery and Reinvestment Act (ARRA) (2009)
- The Consolidated Omnibus Budget Reconciliation Act (COBRA) (1976)
- The Older Workers Benefit Protection Act (OWBPA) (1990)
- Executive Order 11246: Affirmative Action (1965)
- The Family and Medical Leave Act (FMLA) (1993)
- The National Defense Authorization Act (2007)
- The Patient Protection and Affordable Care Act (PPACA) (2010)
- The Worker Adjustment and Retraining Notification Act (WARN) (1977)

State Laws

Each state can pass its own labor and employee relations laws. And many have. At the state level you will find such coverage as these, governing the following topics:

- Expansion of benefits beyond those provided for in federal law
- State disability insurance programs
- Unemployment insurance programs
- Paid sick leave
- Equal employment opportunity protections for classes beyond those in federal law
- Wage and hour requirements for overtime rates and rules of application

Federal Regulations

When Congress passes a law, it is up to the appropriate department (or agency) such as the U.S. Department of Labor (and the National Labor Relations Board) to develop and publish proposed regulations that will implement the new law. Once the proposed regulations are published, there is a requirement for a public comment period. At the close of the public comment period, the department will review the comments, make any changes it believes appropriate in the regulation proposal, and publish either the final regulations or a revised proposal with a new public comment period. Once published as final, the regulations will carry an implementation date (or dates for individual components of the law's requirements). Once that date has arrived, all employment organizations subject to the new law and regulations will be obligated to comply.

Rights and Responsibilities

As with any relationship, each party must meet certain rights and certain responsibilities for the relationship to continue in a healthy and productive way.

Employer

Employer responsibilities include such things as treating employees in accord with the principle of "good faith and fair dealing." It is more than an ethical requirement. Good faith and fair dealing is a legal covenant. Employers are expected to honor commitments made to employees when employees are convinced to act based on those employer promises. For example, when a manager interviews the best qualified job candidate and says, "We really want you to move out to our state and be part of this organization. We will have a job for you for as long as you want it," the employer has enticed the candidate into action based on the promise of permanent employment. If the employer cuts the new employee off the payroll when downsizing the organization, it has broken its obligation under the covenant of good faith and fair dealing. The result can be a lawsuit based on contract law.

Employer rights include the expectation that employees will work for a full 8 hours each day they are scheduled for 8 hours. The employer has a right to ensure worker behavior while on the job meets with policy requirements, and the employer has the right to inspect employee work product, work space, and communication related to work.

Employee

Employees have the right to expect they will be treated with good faith and fairly by their employer. They have the right to proper wage calculation and prompt payment. They have the right to full benefit provisions as provided by organizational policy and contract provisions.

Employees also have responsibilities. Those include the responsibility to give a full 8 hours of effort for an 8-hour workday, compliance with all employer policies, and treatment of everyone in the workplace with civility.

Employee Feedback

Employee feedback is necessary to assess many conditions in the workplace, including morale, job satisfaction, and ideas for innovation and improvements. The communication cycle depends on feedback to assess the quality of the communication. Without feedback, there is only uncertainty about the effectiveness of the communication effort.

 EXAM TIP   Since employee feedback is so critical to successful business operations today, you can expect that the certification exam will contain questions about the methods of collecting employee feedback and how it can be used.

Employee Surveys

There are a host of methods for assessing employee morale, work satisfaction, and communication quality and effectiveness. One method that is held as extremely helpful in providing direct feedback is the survey format. Employee surveys are a tool that can gather information directly from the employee body and can be applied in a timely way immediately following a major employment event. For example, when new benefit programs are introduced, surveys can be used to identify employee reactions to the new offerings and the ease with which they have access to those programs. Surveys are most commonly used to determine how engaged workers are within the organization.

Attitude Surveys

Employee attitude surveys can be done by telephone, by mail, or online. Surveys that assess employee attitudes are usually prepared by professional consultants (psychologists) to assure that information can be gathered that will actually be useful. *Employee attitude surveys* are used to improve morale, productivity, and engagement and to reduce turnover by gathering actionable feedback on job experiences.

Topics covered in employee attitude surveys can include job-related training, supervisor treatment, employment policies and their impact on individual employees, satisfaction with compensation programs, and satisfaction with benefit programs such as healthcare insurance and vacation policies. At some time, it is generally helpful to get feedback about employee attitudes on all topics that touch the lives of workers.

360/180-Degree Surveys

Taken literally, 360-degree surveys ask everyone around an employee to provide feedback about that person's competencies, behaviors, and contributions. In one common application, management people use these surveys to get feedback from their subordinates as well as their peers and supervisors. Usually feedback is provided anonymously.

Nonmanagement individuals can't literally be the subject of a 360-degree feedback program because they have no subordinates, so 180-degree surveys are used where only their manager, co-workers, and internal customers are asked to provide input. Peers and supervisors can offer input to nonmanagement people that can help with interpersonal skill development and grooming for promotional opportunities.

Stay Interviews

A stay interview is a one-on-one meeting between a manager and a highly valued employee who may be at risk for leaving the organization. The purpose is to identify the factors that will entice the employee to stay with the employer rather than change jobs. If it is possible to identify conditions or "triggers" that might cause the employee to leave, they may be preventable. These meetings can be used by any sized organization to increase retention of people who are major contributors to achieving objectives. While it is not always possible to meet all conditions, just listening to the employee can go a long way to making them feel that they are valued by the employer.

Processes for Obtaining Feedback

There may be dozens of ways to collect feedback from employees. Here are some of the most common processes used today. All have been used for decades. Yet they remain the best tools for gathering input from groups of people.

Paper Surveys

Paper and pencil seem like the most basic approach to recording opinions. Yet that process is still one of the most effective. Properly prepared questions will yield a wealth of information that can be digested and then produce actionable items. If there is a new policy to be considered, employee attitudes about such a change can be invaluable before the change is made. Avoiding the negatives of decisions that employees view as undesirable is much preferable to correcting the bad decision after it has been implemented.

Even though we live in a digital age, there are many employees, and even entire work-places, that lack computers. Factory workers are a good example. In some cases, computers may be brought in and set up on kiosk displays to overcome that deficiency. In other instances, introducing computers may not be an option. So, paper and pencil surveys remain the standard. Employees may be allowed work time to complete the surveys, or they may be allowed to take them home and return them later. Making survey responses anonymous can be achieved if employees return them by mail to an address that is not a company work location. Having a third party summarize the responses can create a wall against identifying individual responses.

Paper surveys can cover a wide range of issues. And responses can be offered on a scale such as "more likely" to "less likely" or "strongly agree" to "strongly disagree." Some vendors offer standard attitude surveys that can lower the cost of gathering input. Others offer support in creating customized surveys that can raise the cost but also increase the value of specific information about workplace issues.

Computer-Based Surveys

When computers are available, presenting surveys digitally can be a good option. Advantages include the speed of response summaries and the ability to track which employees have responded and which have yet to log on and take the survey. That isn't the same as tracking individual responses. Just knowing who has yet to participate can increase the feedback percentage substantially.

Computer-based surveys can be made available on employee personal computers so the surveys can be accessed from home. Usually, when computers are made available to workers on the job, the survey is taken at work during work time.

Computer-based surveys can often be accessed from smart phones, laptops, tablet computers, or desktop computers. That flexibility of access can increase initial participation rates substantially.

Focus Groups

For an in-depth exploration of issues and testing of alternatives, focus groups offer an excellent opportunity to probe initial responses and go into more detail. With a properly skilled facilitator, focus groups can provide excellent information about employee beliefs. For example, when options exist for increasing employee benefits, getting employee input about preferences can be extremely helpful in the decision-making process. Perhaps the company has budget available to increase either paid-vacation allotment or retirement pay computations. Which would employees prefer? How strongly do they feel about their preference? Would they actually like a third or fourth alternative? Focus groups provide the environment in which to probe those choices. The downside of focus groups is that they are not anonymous. So, they do not apply in every situation.

Workplace Behavior

Behaviors are things that we do or say. Behaving is the act of saying something or doing something. There are good behaviors and bad behaviors from the viewpoint of an employer. Workplace policies usually include a description of acceptable behaviors and/or unacceptable behaviors. Workplace behavior is a factor to be considered in a work performance evaluation.

PART II

Attendance and Absenteeism

Actually showing up to work and being on time is viewed as a requirement by many employers. An employee who can't do one or the other may not be acceptable in the eyes of the employer.

Identifying Standards

Each employer must establish its own standards for attendance and punctuality. That means it must answer questions like "How many minutes after the beginning of a work shift should be allowed before an employee is considered tardy?" Standards for employee absence can be developed by using questions like "How many days will we allow an employee to be missing from work without proclaiming them to have an absenteeism problem?"

Establishing standards is a key step in managing these two behaviors that have a great impact on work performance. Even in organizations that have adopted an "unlimited vacation" policy, there must be some limit. If not, the standard is wide open, and employees can be absent for as much of their work year as they wish. The policy then is really a "not to exceed" limit that can be substantial. For example, an "unlimited vacation policy" can permit up to 90 days in any given calendar year. And, the quantity of days that will be paid can be determined based on company tenure, like in other circumstances. If an employee decides to take 6 or 7 months off work, is that permissible under the policy? If not, when does it cross the line we know as behavioral standard?

Violation of Standards

So, when the standard is not met, what happens? Sometimes nothing. Appropriately, what should happen is disciplinary action. That means beginning with a discussion and working through the progressive discipline process until the problem is solved because the behavior has changed. When the employee begins showing up for work again and/or begins arriving on time each day, the behavior has changed, and it is no longer necessary to move further on discipline progression.

As with all other disciplinary programs, these should be consistent from one situation to another when circumstances are the same. Treating employees inconsistently can result in charges of illegal discrimination.

Improvement Programs

An improvement program is a formalized approach to correcting inappropriate behavior. If an employee needs to improve attendance, then it may be necessary to create an improvement program for his or her attendance problem. It might look something like this:

Attendance Improvement Program

1. Have the initial meeting with the employee to review the attendance record.
2. Compare the attendance record with the standard expected of all employees.

3. Explain that the employee will be expected to have no absences (paid or unpaid) during the coming 30 days.

4. Any absence in the next 30 days will result in an unpaid suspension of two days and a job-in-jeopardy warning.

5. After the suspension, a new 30-day period will begin. Any absence during that 30-day period will result in termination of employment.

6. It is common for the supervisor to have the employee sign the improvement program, making a contract out of the expectations for improved behavior.

Violation of Code of Conduct

A Code *of Conduct* is a list of behavioral expectations the employer has for each employee. Violations of the code of conduct can fall along a spectrum from "minor" to "worthy of immediate dismissal." All of these relationships should be identified in the employer's policy manual. That way there are no surprises for any employee.

EXAM TIP   Even in today's work environment of greater sensitivity to employees and their needs, it is still necessary for employers to establish and maintain employee codes of conduct. You should expect that there will be questions on the exam about what a code of conduct is and how it should be administered.

Employee Behavior

We have already reviewed the nature of behavior. When someone does or says something that is unacceptable, there should be consequences of some sort. Minor violations of a code can include the following:

- Frequent tardiness
- Frequent absence (excused, unexcused, or both)
- Minor insubordination
- Pilferage from employer supplies
- Frequent incomplete or inaccurate work product
- Abuse or misuse of office equipment
- Arguments with co-workers

Moving up along the scale of unacceptable behavior, serious code of conduct violations might include the following:

- Bringing weapons to work
- Threats of violence or actual violence against others in the workplace

- Blatant insubordination
- Embezzlement or misappropriation of company funds
- Theft of equipment
- Filing false reports

Serious infractions of the code of conduct can result in discipline that could even include immediate termination for the most serious of violations. Workplace violence is an example of behavior that can result in immediate termination. Less serious infractions can result in progressive discipline that begins at a written warning or even a job-in-jeopardy warning.

Ethics

Unethical behavior is something most employers abhor. Given the U.S. laws that prohibit kickbacks to government representatives or bribes to foreign institutions, ethics is a high-level expectation in the employment relationship. It is not only compliance with the letter of the law but the intent of the law that counts.

Here are some examples of employer expectations that might be included in a code of conduct. Each of these would be a violation of that code of conduct.

- Misusing company time (not focusing on work production for the entire workday)
- Bullying or other abusive behavior
- Theft of any kind (from supplies to misusing a company car)
- Lying to anyone in the workplace about anything
- Taking credit for work done by someone else
- Undermining or sabotaging someone else's work
- Following your boss' instructions even though you know it to be wrong
- Deliberate deception of a customer, vendor, media representative, boss, or co-worker

Employee Conflicts

It is natural that people will disagree from time to time. This happens in the workplace as well as at home, in clubs, and at the ballpark. When these disagreements happen at work, it is incumbent upon all parties to work civilly with one another to resolve the problem.

Work Assignments Conflicts

If a boss tells a worker to do something that is considered a bonus or premium assignment, another employee may actually prefer that work assignment. It is possible that an argument can arise between the two employees over the work assignment.

No matter what the argument is about, the employer's expectation should be that it will be resolved without resorting to bad behavior on the part of any participant.

Personal Conflicts

Sparks can fly when two people have a conflict resulting from personal involvement either in or out of work. If two co-workers want to date the same person, it is easy to imagine that such a conflict can result in heated arguments or worse. When two or more people want the same special work assignment, it is easy to imagine another argument. It doesn't have to be that way, but often is. It is the responsibility of all employees to act in a civil manner to every other person in the workplace. Allowing escalation of emotions during such conflicts is unacceptable to most employers. That is because escalating emotions lead quickly to escalating behavior issues. First, words are said that carry strong impact, and then an actual physical knock-down, drag-out fight takes place with physical impact. None of that is desirable or permitted by most employers.

Workplace Harassment

Harassment can take many forms. What started as sexual harassment has expanded to include racial harassment, religious harassment, national origin harassment, and even veteran harassment. All are illegal, not just undesirable. Under federal laws, it is the employer's responsibility to address the harassment problem with the offending employee. Under some state laws (such as California), it is the employer's responsibility to be sure the harassing behavior does not occur again. That goes beyond simply addressing the problem.

Both employees and job applicants are included in the legal protections against harassment on the job.

Sexual Harassment

Sex discrimination is prohibited by the Civil Rights Act of 1964. And nowhere in that law will you find "sexual harassment" as prohibited behavior. Sexual harassment has been defined by the U.S. Supreme Court over the years since the law was enacted. (The U.S. Equal Employment Opportunity Commission [EEOC] guidance also offers a great deal of employer information regarding sexual harassment.) Now we know that sexual harassment is behavior of a verbal or physical nature that is unwelcome. There are two types of sexual harassment defined in case law, as shown in Table 7-1.

Quid Pro Quo	Hostile Environment
• Submission to sexual advances is made a condition of employment.	• Sexual advances are unwelcome by the victim.
• Demands of sexual favors are made in exchange for a job benefit (pay raise, good work assignment, promotion, or not being fired).	• Sexual advances interfere with the employee's work.
• Most often the offender is a supervisor of the victim.	• Sexual advances create a hostile or intimidating work environment.
• It represents an abuse of power (the victim must acquiesce or pay the penalty).	• Behavior can be verbal, physical, or visual.

Table 7-1 Types of Sexual Harassment Defined in Case Law

The emergence of sexual harassment as a workplace problem has resulted in the elimination of cheesecake and beefcake photographs from office walls, prohibition of sexually explicit cartoons from corkboards, and banning of sexually explicit jokes and stories in the workplace.

Sexual Orientation Harassment   Also defined in case law is the issue of sexual orientation harassment. When lesbian, gay, bisexual, transgender, or queer (LGBTQ) individuals are harassed because of their sexual orientation, the behavior is illegal. (See Appendix B, "Federal Case Laws." Look for *Oncale vs. Sundowner Offshore Services* and *Price Waterhouse vs. Hopkins*.) All forms of sexual orientation are protected from harassment. That includes heterosexual, homosexual, and bisexual.

Transgender Harassment   When people strongly identify with a different gender than they were assigned at birth, they may dress as their rightful gender or even have surgery to physically switch genders. Harassment of transgender employees is illegal. Employers should recognize their responsibility to protect these workers from such attacks.

EXAM TIP   While sexual harassment is important and must be prevented in the workplace, it is by no means the only type of harassment. Expect that the certification exam will also have questions dealing with the other types of workplace harassment hazards.

Male vs. Female Harassment   While it might seem pretty basic, harassment because of sex still happens in our American workplaces. In fiscal year 2015 the EEOC received 26,396 charges of sex-based discrimination in the workplace. Of those, 3.7 percent following the agency's investigation had reasonable cause, and 62.1 percent were closed with the agency having found no reasonable cause. The balance of the cases were closed administratively or through conciliation. Some peripheral issues are reproductive protections on the job, compensation differences, and caregiver responsibilities.

Racial Harassment

Disparate treatment based on race causes resulted in 31,027 EEOC charges in fiscal year 2015. Employment actions that were covered in alleged discrimination cases included the gamut from hiring and firing to work assignments, training, and promotions. That represented 34.7 percent of the charges received by the EEOC in fiscal year 2015.

Religious Harassment

In fiscal year 2015 the EEOC received 3,502 charges of illegal religious discrimination. That is 3.9 percent of all charges that year. When an employee is harassed and can't complete their work assignments because they are a target of jokes and other harassing behavior due to their religion, there may be illegal discrimination going on. Religious harassment has seen a slight increase since September 11, 2001. The same types of problems result in verbal, visual, and physical representations that are unacceptable in the workplace.

National Origin Harassment

National origin harassment amounted to 9,437 EEOC cases in FY 2015. This includes behaviors that poke fun at people because of their heritage. It has frequently involved poor treatment of Middle Easterners and Mexicans. It results from the visual appearance of individuals in most instances.

Other Types of Harassment

Over time, the EEOC has been sculpting definitions of harassment that are broader and broader. It began with sexual harassment and has since grown to include race, religion, and the following categories as well.

Bullying behavior on the job can constitute harassment if it is persistent and interferes with an employee's ability to perform his or her job duties. Bullying can be described as browbeating, intimidating, antagonizing, heckling, persecuting, pestering, or tormenting. It's all bad any way you look at it. Management has a responsibility to intervene and end the bullying behavior. Progressive discipline is usually recommended in such cases.

Disability Harassment   While arguably the cruelest of all harassment, disability harassment can be aimed at either mental or physical disability. Remember that disability status can include any of us at any time. It is usually the most transmutable category on the list. People don't change their race, color, or national origin. They can change their religion, but it isn't common. They can change their sex, but it is infrequent in our population. But anyone can be disabled by accident or illness at any time. Jokes, snide remarks, cartoons, graffiti, practical jokes, or other teasing or criticizing based on disability status is illegal under federal law for covered employers according to the EEOC.

Age Harassment   Age jokes are thought to be the most benign among other possible targets. That is unless you happen to be the older person to whom the joke would apply. Then it's not so funny. A persistent pattern of such jokes can constitute harassment, and employers have an obligation to stop such behavior without delay. Any of the other forms of age harassment are also inappropriate and illegal under EEOC rules.

Veteran Status Harassment   When someone has served the country by placing themselves in harm's way as a member of the military, it is hard to imagine that they would become the target of harassing behavior on the job. Yet, it happens. It happened a lot at the conclusion of the Vietnam War. And it still happens today. HR professionals are responsible for training managers and employees on the prevention of such behavior in the workplace. There is nothing funny about harassment, regardless of the intent of those participating.

Harassment Based on Other Factors   The EEOC says any individual characteristic protected by one of the federal equal opportunity laws can be the basis for a complaint of workplace harassment. Just because it isn't sexual harassment doesn't mean there is a green light for the behavior. It is still not welcome behavior in the workplace, and HR professionals play an important role in helping control it. Medical conditions fall into this category, even if they do not rise to the level of a disability.

PART II

Complaints and Grievances

Several conditions impact how employee complaints and grievances are handled within an employer's organization. One large determining factor is whether the employer has labor unions involved in the workplace. Labor agreements/contracts (or memorandum of understanding) will usually contain a structured method for dealing with employee grievances. They designate steps for handling complaints about working conditions or other provisions of the labor union contract. Complaints about issues outside of working conditions are not usually addressed within the confines of a labor union contract. Those are handled by other employer policies.

Methods of Investigation

Investigations are appropriate in several circumstances within an employer's organization. They can be helpful in a grievance handling effort and are essential in determining the validity of discrimination complaints. Whenever there is a need to determine facts surrounding a complaint, an investigation should be conducted.

Internal HR professionals are almost always given authority in state and federal law to conduct an investigation on behalf of the employer. If the organization wants to have an external investigator handle the fact finding, there are some limitations imposed by certain state laws. In California, for example, external investigators who are not licensed attorneys must be licensed private investigators. Other states have different requirements.

Legal advisors suggest that internal attorneys are not the best people to conduct investigations because they could be placed in the position of having to testify to their investigative activities while still providing legal advice to their employer.

Whoever is designated as the investigator should normally follow these steps:

1. **Written complaint** The employee should write out a complaint that states he or she was treated differently from others in similar situations based on a legally protected category and that category should be identified. If he or she can do this, he or she will have provided a prima facie case, which means it sounds good on its face.

2. **Interviews** Next it is necessary to interview the complaining employee, the supervisor or management person who is named as the offending decision maker, and any witnesses the employee says were there at the time. Sometimes, it is a peer who has been the offending party. When that is the case, at least one interview of the offending party should be scheduled. The investigation should follow whatever leads are uncovered until the investigator is satisfied that all the facts have been uncovered that can be uncovered. Each step of the process should be documented in writing and maintained in a complaint investigation file.

3. **Determination** Once the facts have been determined as best as possible, a determination should be made about the validity of the complaint. If the complaint is valid, a remedy should be sought based on both legal and reasonable requirements. If the complaint is determined not to have valid grounds, that will be the determination. The decision should be documented in writing and included in the investigation folder.

4. **Feedback**   The employee who filed the complaint should be given feedback about the investigation results and any decisions made as a result. It may or may not be advisable to provide specific information about disciplinary action taken against an employee. Your legal advisor can give you guidance about that in your specific circumstances.

Use an Internal Investigator (HR or Legal Professional)

It is usually less expensive to use internal personnel than hire someone from outside to conduct an investigation. Whether to spend the extra money will depend on the sensitivity of the situation and the availability of internal people who would otherwise do the work.

HR professionals should be trained by a legal expert in the process of investigation. HR professionals should not be asked to conduct investigations without proper training. Employee complaints can sometimes jump from simple and basic to complex and legally challenging in a brief time. Without proper training, an investigator can bring liability to the employer rather than offer resolution with the lowest possible cost.

Hire an Outside Investigator
(Consultant, Private Investigator, Attorney)

There are some circumstances when an outside investigator is appropriate. That investigator can be an attorney or a licensed private investigator. HR consultants are sometimes used when a licensed private investigator is not required. Some states, such as California, require that the investigator be licensed by the state if the work to be done is an "investigation." Using lawyers is a good idea if the investigation is legally sensitive and the lawyer used will not also be handling the case as company attorney. Be guided in choosing which outside resource is best for you in your circumstance by your internal HR management and company legal department.

Expert witnesses are sometimes hired by employers and their legal representatives to support their position in lawsuits. When that happens, the people hired as experts offer knowledge and experience that fit the issues being disputed.

Using an attorney can be beneficial in many ways. One key benefit is the potential for attorney-client privilege. Communication between an attorney and a client can be protected from disclosure if the attorney is dispensing legal advice in that conversation. The communication could be verbal or written. When consultants prepare fact-gathering documents or reports under the instructions of an attorney, those documents may be protected because they were prepared for use by legal counsel. Critical self-analysis, such as preparing statistical testing for disparate impact in employee hiring or promotion, can be helpful to a plaintiff in a legal challenge. If the analysis is prepared for use by legal counsel, it may be protected from disclosure even when specifically requested by the plaintiff. Your attorney can provide more help in understanding how to guard against disclosing documents containing sensitive or proprietary information.

 EXAM TIP   Grievance processing within provisions of a union contract is usually highly structured. Handling employee complaints in a nonunion environment will also take the same type of steps, but may not be quite as structured.

Grievance Processing

Grievance handling will always be a segment of a union agreement (Memorandum of Understanding – (MOU) or a Collective Bargaining Agreement – (CBA)). It will specify the grievance steps and how each will be handled.

Here are the typical grievance-handling steps you will find in most organizations:

1. **Written complaint**   The employee describes in writing what is causing the upset or discontent.

2. **Supervisor-level discussion**   The employee's supervisor (or another group's supervisor) will discuss the complaint with the employee, reviewing facts and reasons for the decision that resulted in the complaint. If the explanation is sufficient, the grievance ends here. If the employee presents information that causes the decision to be changed, the grievance can also end here.

3. **Management or HR-level discussion**   If the supervisor and employee can't agree, the next discussion is with a management person and/or the human resource department. If an agreement is reached, the matter is settled. If not, it can go to a final step with senior management.

4. **Senior management**   The final step is usually with a senior management official. Sometimes that is the chief executive officer, but it can be with any other designated official who has authority to make any adjustments or decisions deemed appropriate in settling the grievance. If no agreement is reached at this step, the employee will have to either drop the complaint or seek legal advice in a potential civil suit.

Union Grievance Procedures

If your union contract grievance procedures differ from these four stages, be sure to follow your required steps. If other requirements exist in your union contract, you should follow those provisions also. Get help from senior HR managers or your company legal staff if you need it. See the four basic steps outlined earlier for typical stages of grievance processing. Union representation can be sought to provide third-party oversight and a fair outcome for both the employee and company.

In 1975, the U.S. Supreme Court handed down an opinion in a case that said employees have a right to union representation at investigatory interviews. Those have become known as Weingarten Rights.[1] The supervisor has no responsibility to advise the employee of his or her rights. The employee must claim the right to have representation.

Nonunion Grievance or Complaint Procedures

Remember when we discussed the doctrine of good faith and fair dealing? Well, the same principles should apply to any system an employer develops to handle nonunion complaints. In every instance, the company should be seen as treating employees fairly and in good faith. The steps can easily follow those used in union grievance handling:

1. Submit a written complaint.

2. Conduct a supervisor-level discussion of the complaint.

3. Have a discussion with HR or the supervisor's management level.

4. Have a resolution reached by senior management.

If there is a provision either in the union contract or in company policy for arbitration, that would be the final step in both discussion ladders.

Progressive Discipline

Progressive discipline is an organized process that permits employers to meet the obligation for good faith and fair dealing with employees.

Identifying Steps of Discipline

Although each situation will be assessed based on its own requirements, there are generally four major steps in progressive discipline. Sometimes, a situation will require more than one oral warning or more than one written warning. Be sure that each employee is treated as others in similar circumstances have been treated in the past. Length of service (time with the employer) will influence the steps to be taken in progressive discipline. Generally speaking, the longer someone's service, the more time should be permitted for demonstrating acceptable behavior and meeting of standards.

Oral Warning

When some behavior has been unacceptable, a supervisor has an obligation to address the employee and issue an oral warning. This is a statement such as "This is a formal warning that your attendance is unacceptable and any other absences on your part will result in further disciplinary treatment." Rather than say "will result," it is acceptable to say "may result" to permit greater flexibility in handling things as they develop further. Sometimes, more than one oral warning will be appropriate. This is particularly true when the infraction is minor in nature.

Written Warning

When the time has come and behavior has not improved since the oral warning, the next step is a written warning. It can be a simple memo, handwritten or electronically generated, as company systems dictate. It should include a statement such as "This is a formal written warning that further disciplinary action will/may result if you have additional absences during the coming 60 days." Saying "may" will permit management to make allowances if there is death in the employee's family or a leave of absence is required for medical reasons. It is sometimes necessary to use this step more than once. Presume that the employee maintains perfect attendance during the 60-day improvement period but then slips back into the old pattern of absence after that. Rather than begin again with oral warnings, it is possible to issue another written warning with expectations for a new improvement period.

Suspension

Following a written warning, a suspension is sometimes the next step. Suspensions are usually issued in a "without pay" condition. That is to deprive the employee of some income to bring home the seriousness of the problem. Suspensions can be influenced by state laws that govern treatment of exempt versus nonexempt workers. Pay treatment may not be impacted in some states for exempt employees.

The length of a suspension will depend on how others have been treated in similar circumstances in the past and whether a union contract has influence in the situation. The length of a suspension should match the level of infraction and be mitigated by the employee's length of service.

It is common for a "job in jeopardy" warning to be issued along with the notice of suspension. It can say something like "This is a final warning that your job is in jeopardy and you may be dismissed from the payroll if you do not meet the company's attendance standards during the coming 60-day period." Almost always a final warning needs to be issued even if there is no suspension. A final warning puts the employee on notice that they will be removed from the payroll if they don't meet expectations for behavior in the future.

Termination

The final step in any disciplinary sequence is termination from the payroll. There are fancy terms used for it, but the end result is always the same. The employee is fired, sacked, terminated, or let go. It all means the same. The employee is being released for cause. The cause is failure to meet behavioral standards of the job and the employer. Termination for cause can influence the eligibility of an employee for unemployment insurance, depending on the state and its rules for benefit payment.

Documenting Progressive Discipline

The holy grail for HR professionals is documentation. That is the single most important component of any supervisor and management training program. Regardless of the training topic, documentation expectations should always be on the agenda. As the saying goes, "If it isn't documented it didn't happen." Think about the likelihood that a jury will side with an employer over the employee when the employer didn't take the time to properly document the discipline that was applied to the situation. It's the big guy against the little guy, and juries usually like the little guy. So, the employer must be prepared to support its actions with appropriate documentation of its good faith and fair dealing.

 EXAM TIP Progressive discipline is a key example of how employers meet their requirement for "good faith and fair dealing" under U.S. law. Knowing the application of progressive discipline is only part of your exam preparation. Knowing why it is important is even more critical.

These days no one thinks twice about video recording events and posting them on social media. Audio and video recordings are covered by federal and state law. In employment terms, it takes only one party to permit recording of a conversation. That is known as the one-party consent rule. Federal law requires only one-party consent.[2] When you hear a telephone message that says, "This call may be monitored or recorded for training and quality purposes," that is designed to achieve two-party consent. If you don't object to the recording, you are consenting to it being done. Eighteen states and the District of Columbia have their own laws about recording voice or video. Many of them require two-party consent.[3]

Timing of Documentation

Documentation should ideally be prepared immediately after the event. If a supervisor has a conversation with a worker to point out a safety violation, that conversation should be documented in writing as soon after the conversation as possible.

Some people think it is alright to prepare documentation only when a formal complaint or lawsuit has been filed. Worse, some people believe it is alright to post-date the documentation. That is never OK. If documentation was not prepared when the event took place, prepare it as a reflective document with the current date to provide an honest picture of when it was created.

Content of Documentation

Complete documentation can be brief. It doesn't have to go on for pages if that is not necessary to log what happened. All documents that meet the following content requirements will be considered satisfactory:

- **Who?** What were the names of individuals involved in the incident?
- **What?** What happened?
- **When?** When did this happen?
- **Where?** Where and under what conditions did this event take place?
- **How?** How did it happen? Were there events that led up to the one being documented?

Answer those primary questions in your documentation and you will have touched all the bases. The only remaining requirements are the date the documentation is being prepared and the name/signature of the person creating it.

Retention Requirements

"EEOC Regulations require that employers keep all personnel or employment records for 1 year. If an employee is involuntarily terminated, his/her personnel records must be retained for one year from the date of termination.

"Under ADEA recordkeeping requirements, employers must also keep all payroll records for 3 years. Additionally, employers must keep on file any employee benefit plan (such as pension and insurance plans) and any written seniority or merit system for the full period the plan or system is in effect and for at least one year after its termination.

"Under Fair Labor Standards Act (FLSA) recordkeeping requirements applicable to the EPA, employers must keep payroll records for at least 3 years. In addition, employers must keep for at least 2 years all records (including wage rates, job evaluations, seniority and merit systems, and collective bargaining agreements) that explain the basis for paying different wages to employees of opposite sexes in the same establishment.

"These requirements apply to all employers covered by Federal anti-discrimination laws, regardless of whether a charge has been filed against the employer."[4]

Federal contractors subject to affirmative action regulations must retain all employment records for at least 3 years unless they have fewer than 150 workers on the payroll. Then, the retention requirement is 2 years.[5] Be aware that "employment records" include all documents related to employment such as job requisition, resumes, job applications, interview notes, supervisor notes, and personnel files.

State retention requirements can vary substantially from federal requirements. It is best that you determine the retention periods in states where you have work locations. Seek help from your labor attorney if you need it.

When to Escalate Corrective Action

There comes a time when it may be necessary to move corrective action approval to a higher level. For example, when an employee has a given number of years of service, the employer may place a policy requirement on progressive discipline that more senior management approval is needed before implementation of the discipline.

When a case arrives at a deadlock in attempting to gain consensus agreement, it may be necessary that someone more senior in management will be needed to break that deadlock.

If there appears that there may be a conflict of interest or a desire to avoid a conflict of interest, senior management approval or intervention might be the right action to request.

Escalation can be within the employee's own chain of command, or it could be within the HR department's chain of command. The larger the organization, the more need there is for such policies to be prepared and published. Escalation is a policy issue, not a legal issue. However, the more senior people involved, the greater the employer's weighted consideration of events and consequences.

Standard Practices and Procedures

When events move in a normal, expected fashion, a normal response can be sufficient. In other words, standard circumstances require standard responses. It is normal to have written policies and procedures that deal with how things normally happen. That is because most instances will require similar treatment. It is when things jump out of the "normal" box and into the "unusual" box that you must make adjustments.

Unusual Circumstances

It is when circumstances fall outside the routine that escalation to higher management may be required. Cases such as these might fall into that category:

- A 25-year veteran of the company suddenly develops an absence problem. (Requiring senior management approval on any disciplinary program would acknowledge the duty the company has to this senior employee.)

- A relatively new employee has passed the training period but now has a child who was seriously injured in a bicycle accident. Senior management approval may be required to lift the normal leave of absence qualification threshold.

- An employee with 5 years of service has had a confrontation with her supervisor over work quality requirements. Later it is discovered that she has cancer and the stress of her treatment and its medication is causing behavioral changes. A more senior management person may be needed to approve less severe treatment of the insubordination incident.

Termination

When the company is going to initiate the involuntary termination of a person's employment, it is a good idea to require management review and approval. The level of approval required for the review will in large part depend on the size of the organization.

Termination should be taken reluctantly by any employer. It should be the final result of rehabilitation efforts. And, it can also be the immediate reaction to such serious behavior that there is no possible way the employee can be allowed to remain on the payroll. An example of such behavior is violation of the no weapons policy. If an employee walks into the workplace with a hunting knife in hand, waves it around, and threatens people, that is behavior that should usually result in immediate dismissal.

Voluntary Terminations

Voluntary terminations are payroll separations that are initiated by the employee without employer intervention. These include employee death, resignation, and retirement.

Death Death may not seem like a voluntary separation from the payroll, but it is most often not initiated by the employer, either. Death is treated as voluntary when it comes to payroll separation.

Resignation Resignation is voluntary unless it constitutes a constructive discharge. Constructive termination occurs when the employer makes working conditions so intolerable the employee has no alternative but to resign. In fact, constructive discharge is not a resignation but a forced involuntary termination.

A true resignation is voluntary. It results from personal needs like a relocation brought on by a spouse's change in employment, return to school as a full-time student, or a simple desire to travel and see more of the world. It could also result from the employee receiving a job offer from a different employer. If the resignation is truly voluntary, it can be recorded that way.

Retirement Another departure that is considered voluntary is employee retirement. It is possible for employees to separate themselves from the payroll by accepting benefits under the employer's retirement program. Retirement benefits are frequently enhanced as part of a reduction in force (RIF). It is usually advantageous to have voluntary acceptance of an enhanced retirement package than having involuntary layoffs.

Involuntary Terminations

Involuntary terminations are those over which the employee has no control. These include layoffs; performance terminations; and injury, illness, or disability.

Layoffs   A layoff is a reduction in force by an employer when revenues have dropped and payroll expenses must be cut or when work levels have shifted without an employer's ability to reclaim them. It is inappropriate for an employer to claim someone is being laid off to avoid dealing with performance or other behavioral problems that should result in a dismissal for cause.

Performance Terminations   When employees are unable to successfully complete a performance improvement program, the result is performance termination. It is an involuntary separation from payroll. Not meeting the standards of production quantities or quality is the reason.

Injury, Illness, or Disability   None of us expects to become disabled, but it happens. Automobile accidents, accidents in the home, and industrial accidents are just a few examples of how that can come to pass. When an injury is long term, or even permanent, it may not be possible for the individual to continue performing their job, even if an accommodation of some kind could be made. Illness can strike that requires long-term treatment and prevents the person from working a normal schedule. Any or all of these circumstances can result in the employer concluding that keeping the employee on the payroll is inappropriate when filling the job vacancy would be a better business decision.

Off-Boarding and Termination

We used to say "removal from payroll." Now we say "off-boarding." The result is the same. It is a process of ending someone's working relationship with an employer. It is termination of that relationship, either voluntarily or involuntarily.

EXAM TIP   You might not use contemporary terms like "off-boarding," but you should know what they mean for the exam.

Payroll Processing—Final Paycheck

Part of removing an employee from the payroll involves changing status in the payroll system. Ending issuance of future paychecks is the objective.

Time may have elapsed since the most recent paycheck was issued to the terminating employee. In that case, it will be necessary to create a final paycheck that covers the as-yet-uncompensated work time. State laws differ in requirements for when final paychecks must be issued. In California, for example, when an employee gives notice of resignation, the employer must provide the final paycheck on the final day of work. If there is no notice given, the paycheck is due within 72 hours of the resignation. Other states have different rules. Be sure you understand the rules where you work.

Benefit Processing

Benefits will sometimes end when an employee separates from the payroll. Health insurance, for example, will usually cease coverage at the end of the month in which the termination occurs. Death benefits sometimes require company involvement for an extended period of time, providing certified death certificates and processing claim requests.

Documenting Reason for Separation

As we mentioned earlier, documentation is a critical part of the process. And separation is actually a series of events that include compliance with federal and state requirements. For employers with 20 or more workers, compliance with the Consolidated Omnibus Budget Reconciliation Act (COBRA) is required (for more about COBRA, see Chapter 2). Layoffs may trigger Worker Adjustment and Retraining Notification (WARN Act) compliance (for more about the WARN Act, see Chapter 2). And, the Internal Revenue Service requires that notices be provided in some circumstances regarding rights to retirement benefits. All of these types of actions should be properly documented, perhaps even in a checklist/action plan that permits entering completion date information.

Supervisor Documentation

Supervisors may or may not have direct involvement in terminations. If they do, it will likely be related to documenting a final performance review or delivering the supervisor's portion of the personnel file to the HR department. Any final supervisory documentation should be completed in a timely way so it can be included with the archived documents.

Exit Interviews

In some organizations exit interviews are standard procedure. They are optional in other companies. Since the objective of an exit interview is to obtain employee opinions about how they have been treated while with the company, supervisors are not a good choice for conducting the interviews. Sometimes, employees are not as honest as they might otherwise be with someone in the HR department, for example. It is standard procedure to have the HR department conduct exit interviews in some organizations. Documenting the answers to specific questions can offer insights into unspoken issues that can be consolidated into summary reports periodically issued to senior management.

Employee Relations Programs

Employee relations programs include communication, benefits, compensation, complaint handling, supervisor relations, and more. The entire culture supports or detracts from a positive employee relations program.

Recognition

The larger an organization grows, the greater the likelihood that its recognition programs will be structured. In small organizations, recognition can be given in many forms, often as events unfold and accomplishments are achieved.

Employee recognition can include service anniversary awards (watches, clocks, plaques, certificates, pins), employee-of-the-month awards (designated parking space, plaque or bulletin board posting, special benefit like a dinner gift certificate), cost savings suggestions, sales achievement awards, team achievement awards, or individual achievement awards. Obviously, that is not an exhaustive list. You can add others and apply them as your organization finds a fit between the recognition and the accomplishment.

Service Anniversary Awards   Employee recognition can include service anniversary awards such as watches, clocks, plaques, certificates, and pins. Obviously, that is not an exhaustive list. You can add others and apply them as your organization finds a fit between the recognition and the length of service.

Employee-of-the-Month Awards   Employee-of-the-month awards can include designated parking spaces, plaques or bulletin board posting, or a special benefit like a dinner gift certificate.

Employee Suggestion Awards   Cost savings suggestions can be rewarded in many ways from cash to paid time off or even paid travel excursions. The larger the organization, the greater the variety of options.

Sales Awards   Sales achievement awards are dependent on reaching certain pre-announced sales goals. Often rewards in this category involve some type of financial benefit to the employee. It can be cash, a paid cruise, or gift certificates that can be spent on something the employee really would like to have.

Team Awards   Team achievement awards come into play when the team of workers has preestablished work goals that will result in a benefit to the company if achieved. It can be a production goal, a safety record, or absence control. The reward can be anything from a pizza party to a free night at the movies or a dinner out. Sometimes, teams are awarded paid time off for their accomplishments. It is something the employer can customize to its own culture.

Individual Achievement Awards   Individual achievement awards are like team awards in many respects. The rewards can be much the same, and they are made because of a special achievement by an individual employee. It could be a production award, an accomplishment in production quality, contribution of suggestions for improving the workflow, or any other personal idea.

Peer-to-Peer Awards   According to the Society for Human Resource Management (SHRM),[6] peer-to-peer recognition systems are used in just under half of the companies surveyed in 2013. One can expect that portion to grow as time progresses. When peers receive recognition from co-workers, it has special meaning. Getting colleague approval is a great motivator.

Special Events

There are many types of special events. They can include company parties, holiday celebrations, company days at the local amusement park, paid excursions at the local ski park, or a night out at the theater. Special events offer "thank you" and recognition to the entire group of employees.

Company Parties

Company parties are a common way of rewarding groups of people at one time.

Company Day at Amusement Park A popular reward is the company day out at the local amusement park. Whether it is a water park in August or Disneyland in January, sponsoring these events is a way for a company to acknowledge the hard work put in by its employees.

Company Picnics Company picnics have been popular since the nineteenth century. They are a great way for an employer to say thank you to its employees by inviting all the families to participate. What is better than a fire-roasted hot dog and ice cream cone after a three-legged race with co-workers? Consumption of alcohol at such events has been reduced in recent years because of liability issues faced by company hosts. Some say that alcohol will not be served just to avoid the liability of people driving while intoxicated.

Holiday Celebrations

Holiday parties happen around the December celebrations of Christmas, Hanukah, and Kwanzaa. They are year-end events that acknowledge all that has happened during the year and all the work put in by employees to help the company achieve its objectives.

Holiday Parties Parties can be held in the office with light refreshments or involve more elaborate celebrations with meals involving employees only or employees and their families. Budget is the main controller of the agenda.

Decorating the Workplace Some people really enjoy decorating for the holidays. Independence Day, Halloween, Thanksgiving, Christmas, Hanukah, and Kwanzaa decorations tend to make a workplace livelier. They help lighten the atmosphere at work. Sometimes, the HR department is placed in charge of decorating, and other times a committee of interested workers can handle the effort. Company funding of the decorative materials is usually provided.

Diversity Programs

Everyone likes to have their personal heritage acknowledged. And modern workforces have representation of many diverse heritages.

Celebration Days

Every culture has its days of celebration. They are all examples of opportunities to put the spotlight on a specific portion of the workforce. Table 7-2 is a current listing of cultural and religious holidays that are sometimes recognized in the United States.

Month	Day	Holiday
January	5	Guru Gobind Singh's Birthday (Sikh)
	6	Three Kings Day (Puerto Rico, Dominican Republic)
	13	Lohri (Buddhist, Hindu, Sikh)
	19	Tu B'Shevat (Jewish, Israel)
February		Black History Month
	3	Chinese Lunar New Year
	5	Constitution Day (Mexico)
	14	Race Relations Day
March		Greek-American Heritage Month, Irish-American Heritage Month
	1	St. David's Day (Welsh)
	17	St. Patrick's Day (Ireland)
April	6	National Tartan Day (Scotland)
	8	Vesak—Buddha's Birth (Buddhist)
	16	Emancipation Day (African-American, United States)
	19	Passover (Jewish)
	24	Easter (Protestant, Roman Catholic)
May		Asian Pacific American History Month, Jewish-American Heritage Month
	1	Yom Hashoah/Holocaust Memorial Day (Jewish)
	2	May Day Bank Holiday (United Kingdom)
	5	Cinco de Mayo (Mexico)
	9	Victory Day (Russia)
	18	Israel's Independence Day
June	2	Ascension Day (Christian)
	7	Shavuot (Jewish)
July	1	Canada Day (Canada)
	4	Filipino-American Friendship Day
	4	Independence Day (American)
	9	Feast of Lanterns (Japan)
	24	Pioneer Day (Mormon)
	31	Feast of St. Ignatius Loyola (Spain)
August	1	Lammas and Lughnassad (Britain, Pagan, United States)
	1–29	Ramadan (Islamic, Muslim)

Table 7-2   Calendar of Some Cultural and Religious Holidays[7] (*continued*)

Month	Day	Holiday
	14	Pakistan's Independence Day
	15	Liberation Day (Korea, South Korea)
	15	India's Independence Day
	26	Lailat-Ul-Quadr (Islamic, Muslim)
September		9/15 to 10/15: National Hispanic Heritage Month (Mexico)
	16	Mexico's Independence Day
	19	San Gennaro Day (Italian-American)
	28	Rosh Hashanah (Jewish New Year)
October		German-American Heritage Month, National Italian-American Heritage Month, Polish-American Heritage Month
	8	Yom Kippur (Jewish)
	9	Cirio de Nazare (Brazil)
	26–30	Diwali (Buddhist, Hindu)
November		National American Indian Heritage Month
	1	Dia de los Muertos: "Day of the Dead" (Latin America)
	26	Continuing through 12/24, Al Hijra (Muslim New Year)
December	6	St. Nicholas Day (International)
	8	Bodhi Day—Buddha's Enlightenment (Buddhist)
	13	Santa Lucia Day (Sweden)
	21–28	Hanukkah (Jewish)
	25	Christmas (Christian, International)
	26	Boxing Day (Canada, United Kingdom)
	26	Kwanzaa (African-American)

Table 7-2 Calendar of Some Cultural and Religious Holidays[7]

There are also many more days of celebration than those listed in Table 7-2, including the following.

Black Holidays   The third Monday in January is a national holiday for Martin Luther King, Jr. March 10 is Harriet Tubman Day. May 19 is Malcolm X Day. The African-American community celebrates each of these anniversaries yearly.

Hispanic Holidays   In addition to those listed in Table 7-2, Cesar Chavez Day is March 31. Cesar Chavez was a hero of Latino people for organizing the farm workers in California's San Joaquin Valley in the 1960s.

Asian Holidays   September 22 is the Autumnal Equinox in Japan. June 9 is the Dragon Boat Festival in China. In addition, 104 days after the Winter Equinox, Ching Ming Day is celebrated in China based on a legend that is 2500 to 2700 years old.

PART II

Culture Programs   November is National American Indian Heritage Month. June is LGBT Pride Month. August 26 is Women's Equality Day. And, our favorite, July is National Ice Cream Month.

Disability Awareness Programs   October is National Disability Employment Awareness Month. It provides an opportunity to highlight or spotlight some of the key achievements of disabled employees and employer programs for job accommodation and support.

Measuring Diversity

Measurements are easy to construct. The important point to remember is that we must be careful about how we define the thing to be measured. What gets measured is what gets done. Whatever the boss emphasizes and keeps coming back to every week or month is what people will spend their days working on. If turnover of a given racial group is extremely high, we should ask why. Measurements give us information that allow further exploration into the reasons things are happening. Some of the most common measurements include workforce representation, turnover rates or longevity, the number of complaints received, and the extent to which senior management is involved in the process of improving diversity of the workforce.

Workforce Representation   Determine the percentage representation of each ethnic group in the workforce. Divide the number of individuals identifying as Hispanic by the total number of people on the payroll. Multiply that by 100, and the result is a percentage. The same can be done for any subset of the employee population.

Turnover Rates (Longevity)   Another measurement of interest is the turnover rate. Again, a percentage is derived by dividing the number of individuals in a given group by the total population and then multiplying the result by 100 to get the percentage. If a given group is leaving the payroll at a faster rate than all others, perhaps there is reason to investigate further.

Complaints Received   Is a given group generating more complaints than other groups? Determine the percentage of complaints for individual groups and compare the percentages.

Management and Executive Involvement   It is up to the executive team in any employment organization to set the pace for others to match when it comes to diversity issues. Accepting people into the workforce along with their cultural background is achieved only when executives demonstrate that acceptance is the way things are done in the organization. Having a policy that is not followed by executives is a recipe for problems.

Workforce Reduction and Restructuring

When in the course of organizational circumstance it becomes necessary to reduce the workforce to reduce the payroll, it must be done in a nondiscriminatory manner. Building a system in advance is the proper approach. How will individuals be identified who must be removed from the payroll? How will that be done without regard to age, race, sex, or another protected group?

Workforce reduction can happen when there is a paradigm shift in the market for the products produced by the employer. When digital watches were introduced, the number of people making analog watches (with hands that circled a watch face) was suddenly reduced. All of a sudden it was necessary to reduce the workforce to save payroll dollars because the old products weren't selling nearly as well as they used to sell.

Restructuring occurs when the business model changes and a portion of the enterprise is no longer needed. It can also be necessary when merging with or acquiring another organization. There is usually not a need for duplicate support staff such as accounting and human resources.

Terminology

It helps to be able to converse in the language of human resources if you are an HR professional. Here are some key terms that you should remember for discussing workforce reduction and restructuring.

Reduction in Force (RIF)   Reduction in force, workforce reduction, and layoff all result in the same thing...fewer employees on the payroll. The Age Discrimination in Employment Act (ADEA) (see Chapter 2) requires certain waiting periods after an employee agrees to be taken off the payroll. During that time, the employee may rescind the decision. The WARN Act (see Chapter 2) can also be at play depending on the number of employees affected.

EXAM TIP   With more employers making use of temporary workers, you might expect that the exam will inquire about the "gig economy" and how it is being implemented. Study the glossary to be sure you will be ready to answer questions about contemporary HR practices.

Temporary Workers   Temporary workers will normally not be employed for longer than 6 months. If they are hired as "project employees," they will work for the life of the project, which could last up to 2 years. Temporary employees must be taken off the payroll at the end of the temporary period or converted to regular employees.

Incentive Programs   When a RIF is necessary, the number of involuntary separations can be reduced by offering an incentive to those in the impacted work groups. If all or some of the required headcount agrees to separate from the payroll voluntarily, it can even prevent any involuntary separations in some cases.

Incentives can involve an enhancement of retirement benefits, a bonus amount for leaving voluntarily, or any other enticement that might be available and that would seduce people into separating from the payroll.

Outplacement Support   Another means of encouraging people to accept separation from the endangered work group is to offer outplacement support. This can involve hiring consultants to work with separating employees in developing resumes, identifying targets for new employment, and even providing office space and telephones from which to implement the job hunting campaign. Sometimes, an employer can simply provide office space and telephones in a work center or the old work location for a period of time in helping the employee find a new job elsewhere.

Downsizing

Downsizing can happen even in the normal course of a budget cycle. If revenues are falling, then expenses will have to fall as well. A very large expense is payroll. Thus, an immediate impact on budget reduction can be achieved by reducing payroll through downsizing.

Work Location Closings

When jobs move from one location to another, it may not be possible for some employees to move with them. An automobile manufacturing plant moves to Mexico, and the people at the old plant will be experiencing a layoff. When the WARN Act applies, there is either a work location (plant) closing or a sizeable reduction in workforce at the work location.[8]

WARN applies to organizations with 100 or more workers, not counting those who have worked less than 6 months in the last 12 months and those who work less than 20 hours per week. Regular federal, state, and local government entities that provide public services are not covered. Employees entitled to notice under the WARN Act include managers and supervisors as well as hourly and salaried workers. The act requires employers to provide notification 60 calendar days in advance of plant closings and mass layoffs. A mass layoff is any group of 50 or more at the same work location. An employer who violates the WARN provisions is liable to each employee for an amount equal to back pay and benefits for the period of the violation, up to 60 days.

Temporary Workers

Temporary workers are hired for temporary periods. They are on the payroll but are subject to being removed from the payroll according to their employment agreement. Sometimes they work under contract for a specific period of time or project longevity. Sometimes they are on the payroll only to help handle a bulging workload. Removing temporary workers from the payroll will depend on their contract provisions. It may be that they can be separated without any due process.

Mergers

Mergers require blending the workforces of two or more organizations. Sometimes that happens quickly, and sometimes it takes years. The United Airlines and Continental Airlines merger is an example of long-term adjustment to a merger. Eventually, duplicate jobs will be identified, and someone will have to either find a new job within the organization or look to a different employer for a new job.

Government Approval

Sometimes it is necessary to obtain government approval for mergers and acquisitions. The United Airlines and Continental Airlines merger is one example. Another is AT&T's purchase of Dish Network. In each case, government agencies needed to review the plans to be sure there would not be a violation of the Sherman Antitrust Act or other federal law.

Blending Policies and Culture

Far more difficult than signing an agreement to merge, the actual implementation requires cultures and policies to be merged. How will union representation be determined? Which policy will prevail when there are two different policies for a given topic? How will a culture of generous work scheduling support be blended with a culture of strict scheduling rules? Those are all difficult questions to resolve.

Duplicate Workforce

When Nation's Bank purchased Bank of America, there were a great many duplicate jobs in the headquarters organization. How can duplicate accounting personnel be reconciled with the ongoing needs for accounting workers? What happens when there are two bank branches just down the street from one another and the market can't support more than one? Duplicate workforce can be absorbed over time by placing surplus employees in other job openings that need filling. It may also involve general outplacement.

Outplacement Practices

The larger the workforce, the more likely the organization will offer outplacement services to people being separated from the payroll.

Internal Programs

Internal support offered by employers during a downsizing can include free office space and telephone service, free computer and Internet access, and free administrative support including receptionist and/or secretarial help. It can even include a career coach and assessment services to aid the employee in identifying the type of target job to be considered.

External Programs

Benefits to be found in external outplacement companies can include job assessment and counseling; connection to large placement service centers; help designing, writing, and reviewing a resume and job application; and office service support such as secretarial help and receptionist support.

Consulting Companies There are some consulting firms that specialize in outplacement service for companies that find it necessary to downsize the workforce. They offer services based on a menu of support that laid-off employees can use.

40 Plus   Founded in 1939, this nonprofit organization was created to help managers and executives older than 40 find new employment after being laid off. It serves as a job clearinghouse and mutual support group. Chapters are run by the volunteer work of members rather than with paid staff. The group holds weekly meetings that are normally free and open to the public. Guest speakers make presentations relevant to the job search process for managers and executives. Training programs are available that teach members the basics of job searching and what to expect during the process.

State Employment Service Centers   Each state has an organization designed to assist unemployed individuals find new employment. You can find your state's service by doing an Internet search with your state's name and *Employment Service Center* in the search. The agency will also process your unemployment insurance claim so you can receive the appropriate benefit. There are classes and referral services available as agency offerings.

Chapter Review

In this chapter we have identified human resource functions related to employee health, safety, and security. We have explored how federal laws and regulations impact these functions and how employers can properly manage each of the impacted areas. From union agreements (union contracts/collective bargaining agreements) to complaint investigations and making adjustments to workforce levels, human resource managers have critical roles to play.

Questions

Select the *best* answer among the alternatives in each question.

1. Collective bargaining agreements are contracts between a union and an employer.

   A. Yup. They are written expressions of a set of workplace rules and benefits the employer will provide in exchange for employee work performance.

   B. Nope. They are guidelines only. The union will work out any deviations in the grievance process.

   C. Hmmm. Maybe. If the agreement says it is a contract, then it is a contract. If it doesn't claim to be a contract, then it isn't.

   D. Arrrrggggg. Never. If the employer tells the union it isn't going to enter into a contract, then the agreement is only an informal set of working rules.

2. Seniority will always be the determining factor in a union agreement.

   A. Not always. Some union contracts will use education as the determining factor overruling seniority in the process.

   B. Seniority is only used by unions that have contracts or subcontracts with federal agencies.

C. Public agencies rely on seniority, and they are the only ones with those agreements.

D. Universally, unions will rely on seniority as the determining factor for all treatment under contract provisions.

3. Dabney is the HR manager negotiating a renewal of the contract his organization has with an international union. Since the union is international, he isn't sure if the National Labor Relations Act applies to his situation. What would you tell him?

A. He's right to be concerned. It is the International Labor Relations Act (ILRA) that governs his situation with the union.

B. When the union is an international organization, they get to choose between the governance of the ILRA and the NLRA.

C. The NLRA governs all union interactions regardless of the union's scope of involvement.

D. If Dabney's organization is negotiating in good faith, there is no law that will tell him what to do. Only if he isn't willing to negotiate will the NLRA take effect.

4. Employment policies as laid out in the employee handbook can take precedence over union contracts.

A. If there is a conflict between the union contract and the employer's policies, the contract will always win.

B. If a conflict arises, then the policy will always prevail.

C. Whenever there are different provisions in a union contract and employer policy, the differences must be arbitrated to resolution.

D. It is up to the manager of the unit involved to determine which will be applied in the given situation.

5. A union contract normally details the process called *progressive discipline*. How would you counsel nonunion employers to deal with the process?

A. Progressive discipline is required only for union-represented organizations.

B. There is no need for nonunion employers to have a progressive discipline process since they are probably "at-will" employers and can terminate employees any time.

C. Progressive discipline is a good process for any employer. It offers "due process" to workers. And, it satisfies the legal covenant called "good faith and fair dealing."

D. Employers can consider using progressive discipline, but absent a union contract, there is little motivation to use the process.

6. Elaine has attended an industry meeting with other HR professionals. She came back to her office with the idea that background investigations of new hires are something she ought to implement. What would you say to Elaine about that idea?

   A. The EEOC has banned background investigations in any form because they discriminate against Hispanics and African-Americans.

   B. The EEOC has only recommended that background checks not automatically eliminate Hispanics or African-Americans because of employment history.

   C. Background checks are still legal and should be conducted on applicants before a job offer is made to be sure there is no history of bad behavior that could bring liability into the new workplace.

   D. Finding anyone these days with no skeleton in the closet is going to be difficult. So, background checks are not really worth the money or time they require.

7. Mary has never before had an employee who caused a physical fight with another employee. The policy in her organization calls for progressive discipline. Mary isn't sure if she should just give the employee a warning or terminate him immediately. What would you recommend?

   A. This is the reason people should learn self-defense. When someone is defending themselves, there should be no reason for employer-imposed discipline. The aggressive employee should be given a written warning, though.

   B. It is hard for someone to start a fight by themselves. Both employees should be written up, skipping the oral warning step of progressive discipline.

   C. It depends on how other aggressive behavior has been treated in the past. Even though there have not been fights per se, the employee treatment should be guided by history.

   D. Violent behavior of any kind is justification for immediate dismissal. Even if there is no policy that says violence can result in immediate termination, that is how this situation should be handled.

8. Woodrow has been awarded a paid day off because he delivered his product development project ahead of schedule. Does this mean every time someone delivers a job in advance of the deadline they should be given a paid day off?

   A. Maybe. If the situations are the same or similar, the reward should be the same.

   B. Maybe. Assuming that the employees had the same amount of service and their projects were similar in difficulty, they should all be given a paid day off.

   C. Maybe. With an eye on illegal discrimination, the employer should err on the side of providing a day off with pay to anyone who completes work ahead of schedule.

   D. Maybe. If the employer can describe the reward as "special" based on the circumstances, it needn't create a precedent that must be followed in each future instance.

9. Harold has heard that it is necessary to have a diversity management program under some new federal law. What would you tell Harold about that requirement?

   A. The new law won't be effective until a year after it was passed. So, there is no immediate requirement for him to worry about.

   B. There is no federal law requiring diversity management programs. Sophisticated employers are moving in that direction because it is the right thing to do and production results often improve.

   C. There is no law requiring diversity management programs, and employers should not consider moving toward such programs unless they are federal contractors.

   D. The new law will require diversity management programs only for employers that have federal contracts to provide goods or services to government agencies.

10. Naji is wondering how he is going to describe the difference between his organization's employee grievance resolution process and the discrimination complaint-handling process. What would you suggest?

   A. There isn't any difference between them. The processes for handling them are the same.

   B. Employee grievances are often regarding workplace rules and work assignment processes. Discrimination complaints have more to do with equal employment opportunity issues.

   C. Grievances happen only in union-represented organizations, so Naji doesn't have to worry about that. He still has to explain how discrimination complaints can be handled in his organization.

   D. Handling grievances is not required by law, but handling discrimination complaints is a legal requirement under federal law.

11. Emma has never had to manage a union contract before. As the HR manager, she is involved with the grievance-handling process as the third step in the process. At her first meeting with the union steward, the steward began yelling at Emma and telling her what she had to do to satisfy the union in this situation. Emma was stunned. What should she do?

   A. She has little choice but to sit there and take it. She is the employer's representative, and if she gets upset, it will only make matters worse.

   B. Emma should call a recess and ask for a management representative to join the meeting with her so she can have some backup in an unpleasant situation.

   C. Emma should recess the meeting and tell the steward that she will not continue their conversation until the steward can conduct herself in a civil manner.

   D. Once the steward has blown off all her steam, Emma should continue the discussion by explaining the employer's position.

12. Sophia makes it a practice to call each applicant's former employers to verify employment claims and determine whether there were any behavioral problems in prior jobs. Her company is now being sued because a new hire had an automobile accident while on a delivery run. It turned out he had a history of reckless driving charges in his past two jobs. But she wasn't told about those when she talked with the former employers. Should Sophia be worried?

    A. Yes. Almost certainly, Sophia will be blamed for negligent hiring. She has little defense. She should have found out about the new employee's previous employment issues.

    B. No. She tried to get information from the previous employers and they wouldn't talk to her. She made a good faith effort. She is off the hook.

    C. Yes. Sophia is going to have to explain to her attorney why she hired this person when there was such a bad history of workplace behavior.

    D. Yes. In this instance, she should also have conducted a search of his driving record before hiring him into a job that required driving for deliveries. She shouldn't have relied on only former employer input.

13. Olivia believes that it is a good idea to conduct an employee survey each year to get input about employee attitudes. Her vice president thinks that employee surveys cost too much money and don't provide much value in the end. What should Olivia tell the vice president?

    A. A well-constructed employee survey can provide information about the types of employment benefits employees would find attractive, how they feel about their managers, and if they believe they are being treated fairly. All of these feedback categories can be assigned dollar values and can be compared over time as budget impacts.

    B. Since the professional HR community is suggesting that employee surveys be conducted each year, it would be wise for Olivia's organization to do that also.

    C. The organization Olivia worked at before did an employee survey, and she thinks it would communicate to employees that the employer is willing to listen to them.

    D. In the modern workplace, employee attitudes are controlling factors. Surveys will help managers regain control of the workplace.

14. Federal regulations are important because:

    A. They give politicians a way to influence how government oversees the private sector.

    B. They implement laws that Congress has passed.

C. They precede congressional action and guide Congress in the law-making process.

D. They offer suggestions to the private sector but really have no strong influence over federal contractors.

15. Employers have the right to:

A. Treat employees any way they want in a democratic marketplace.

B. Hire and fire people without influence from any federal law. State laws apply.

C. Expect employees to work hard during the time they are on the job.

D. Divide the workforce into teams that will all write letters to politicians opposing current legislative action.

16. Employee surveys are a good source of input about morale and can be conducted in any of these ways:

A. Calling each employee into the president's office to discuss their opinions of company policies

B. Telling each employee to appear at a third-party contractor's office to take part in a one-on-one 360-degree feedback session

C. Paper and pencil questionnaires, online surveys, or focus groups

D. Computer psychological testing that will divulge the attitude of individual employees

17. Attendance and punctuality are:

A. Examples of things that drive supervisors nuts

B. Examples of job behavior that can contribute to or detract from company goal achievement

C. Examples of job behavior that should never be reported to another employer in a background check

D. Examples of subjective performance characteristics that supervisors can document

18. Violations of the employer's code of conduct can include:

A. Fighting and insubordination

B. Sickness and excess leaves of absence

C. Failure to meet production requirements

D. Talking with other employees about compensation amounts

19. The following are not examples of unethical behavior:

A. Pilferage from employer supply cabinet

B. Playing *Counter Strike: Global Offensive,* a computer game, during coffee break

C. Scanning a friend's time card when he will be late

D. Calling in sick and then playing a round of golf

20. A private-sector employer does not have the right to:

   A. Examine the contents of employee lockers and desks

   B. Listen in on customer service representative phone calls with customers

   C. Track drivers of company vehicles using GPS devices

   D. Use cameras in the employee restroom to catch smokers who should not be smoking in the bathroom

21. Sexual harassment cannot originate from:

   A. A supervisor on the job

   B. A supervisor off the job

   C. A co-worker who suggests a nice hot-tub relaxation party, swimsuits optional

   D. A neighbor who invites the target employee to participate in a birthday celebration for his wife

22. It is not true that illegal harassment can be based on:

   A. Sexual advances

   B. Racial slurs

   C. Persistent requests for a loan

   D. Persistent jokes about an employee's home country

23. In handling an employee with a disability:

   A. The employer must grant discussion about a job accommodation if asked for one.

   B. The employer must not log an employee as disabled if the employee doesn't want to be identified as disabled.

   C. The employer should not distinguish between a temporary injury and long-term disability.

   D. The employer should file annual disability reports with the U.S. Department of Labor.

24. When an employee complains about unfair treatment by the supervisor:

   A. The HR department should soothe the emotional complaint and encourage the employee to go back to work and pay no attention to the treatment.

   B. It should always be investigated as possible illegal discrimination.

   C. HR should suspend the supervisor for at least 2 days.

   D. The CEO should be notified that a lawsuit is not far behind.

25. Diversity means:

   A. The employer must hire representatives of all backgrounds even if they aren't qualified.

   B. Poor job performers must be retained if they are the last representatives of their cultural background.

   C. Searching for qualified people from many backgrounds so they can be considered for a job opening.

   D. Identifying at least one person from each racial group who can be appointed to a given job title.

Answers

1. **A.** Collective bargaining agreements are contracts between the union and the employer.

2. **D.** We have yet to see a union contract that didn't use seniority as the determining factor for contract provisions.

3. **C.** The National Labor Relations Act has effect regardless of how large the union or employer may be. The key is that operations take place in the United States.

4. **A.** Contract provisions are policy. So, contract provisions will prevail.

5. **C.** Due process is the effort made by employers who want to convey that they are treating employees fairly. And it does demonstrate that the employer is abiding by the covenant of good faith and fair dealing.

6. **C.** Background checks are still legal. The EEOC simply recommends making sure they are job related and that conviction records not automatically disqualifying candidates. Using them to help prevent claims of negligent hiring is a good idea.

7. **D.** It is hard to be absolute in any recommendation; however, this situation sounds like it should result in the immediate termination of at least the aggressive employee. It may be appropriate to also discipline the other employee depending on the outcome of an investigation.

8. **D.** It is not a requirement that each person who completes their project ahead of schedule be given a paid day off. However, if we create a situation where people in similar circumstances are treated differently based on membership in a protected class, we could face a claim of illegal discrimination.

9. **B.** Diversity management programs are not a new idea. And they are not a legal requirement. More and more employers, however, are implementing them because they help with employee satisfaction and marketplace perceptions.

10. **B.** Labor relations issues are usually handled by grievance procedures, and discrimination complaints handle EEO issues.

11. **C.** Emma does not have to sit there and take abuse from the steward. If the steward cannot behave civilly, the meeting should end. Only when the steward can control herself should Emma agree to continue. It might also be a good idea to provide some feedback to the union president about what has happened in the meeting.

12. **D.** A background check should be tailored to the situation. For a job that requires driving, a check of DMV records and history of insurance claims should be routine. Had Sophia conducted such a check, she surely would have uncovered this history and been able to change her hiring decision.

13. **A.** In fact, each category of employee feedback can be assigned a dollar value, and those can be tracked over time as budget impacts. Benefits are only one segment of the employee experience at work. Interpersonal relations with supervisors and managers are another big issue. Generally speaking, employees who feel well treated will be better performers, which also impacts the financial results.

14. **B.** Regulations represent the detailed implementation requirements for laws that Congress passes. They must be published and public comment invited before they may be finalized and made into legal requirements.

15. **C.** If an employee is to be paid for a full day, the employer has the right to expect that employee to work hard for the full day in exchange for the pay.

16. **C.** Paper and pencil questionnaires, online surveys, focus groups, and 360-degree feedback appraisals are all valid methods of conducting employee surveys.

17. **B.** Achieving company objectives depends upon employees being at work on time on each day they are scheduled to work. Absent or tardy employees can cost the company money and detract from the company's chance to meet its objectives for financial performance and product deliveries.

18. **A.** Fighting and insubordination are prime examples of code of conduct violations. They are almost always cited in policy manuals as examples of violations.

19. **B.** Playing a computer game during a work rest break or lunch break is perfectly acceptable as long as it is done in a safe environment. The company lunch room would qualify as a safe environment.

20. **D.** Generally, restrooms or bathrooms are places where cameras are not allowed for privacy reasons. Otherwise, with properly published policies, employees should probably not have an expectation of privacy in the workplace.

21. **D.** Sexual harassment can be based only on unwanted sexual advances in some way connected to the workplace.

22. **C.** Illegal harassment can be based only on a protected category under the law. These include sex, race, national origin, age, pregnancy, color, disability, genetic information, religion, and retaliation are all protections under federal law.

23. **A.** When an employee requests a job accommodation, the employer is obligated to enter into a discussion that may or may not result in the accommodation being approved. It may result in no accommodation or in a different accommodation that will work for the employee and be more favorable to the company.

24. **B.** Any employee complaint that is based on a protected category should be investigated as possible illegal discrimination.

25. **C.** Outreach and recruiting are tools that can help achieve a diverse workforce. Only qualified people should be included in the candidate pool, and selection decisions should be made based on the best qualified.

Endnotes

1. https://www.umass.edu/usa/weingarten.htm, retrieved on 12/5/2016

2. http://www.dmlp.org/legal-guide/recording-phone-calls-and-conversations, retrieved on 12/5/2016

3. http://www.dmlp.org/legal-guide/state-law-recording, retrieved on 12/5/2016

4. https://www.eeoc.gov/employers/recordkeeping.cfm, retrieved on 11/23/2016

5. 41 CFR 60

6. https://www.shrm.org/hr-today/news/hr-magazine/pages/1114-peer-recognition.aspx, retrieved on 12/5/2016

7. Wake Forest University, American Ethnic Studies, http://college.wfu.edu/aes/calendar-of-ethnic-holidays/, retrieved on 11/25/2016

8. https://www.dol.gov/compliance/guide/layoffs.htm, retrieved on 12/5/2016

PART II

Health, Safety, and Security

While consisting of only 5 percent of the Associate Professional in Human Resources (aPHR) exam, the functional area of Health, Safety, and Security has a decided impact on any employer organization in the modern era. From a factual viewpoint, this chapter focuses on some important human resource (HR) requirements. Just because it is only a small portion of the test composition doesn't mean it is something to be passed over quickly. When you are on the job and there is a safety problem, accidental injury, or death, you need to know what to do without spending a lot of time looking up the protocols. In addition, you must know how to fill out all the required reports. Yes, it is an important set of knowledge requirements.

The Body of Knowledge statements outlined by HR Certification Institute (HRCI) for the Health, Safety, and Security functional area by those performing early HR career roles are as follows:

Knowledge of

- **01** Applicable laws and regulations related to workplace health, safety, security, and privacy (for example: OSHA, Drug-Free Workplace Act, ADA, HIPAA, Sarbanes-Oxley Act)

- **02** Risk mitigation in the workplace (for example: emergency evacuation procedures, health and safety, risk management, violence, emergencies)

- **03** Security risks in the workplace (for example: data, materials, or equipment theft; equipment damage or destruction; cyber-crimes; password usage

Laws and Regulations

The following federal laws have an impact on this functional area. Be sure to refer to Chapter 2 for more information about each of these laws. Understanding them is critical to professional performance in the HR profession. You may expect that any or all of these laws will be subjects on the aPHR certification exam.

Organizational Safety and Health Act (OSHA)[1]

 EXAM TIP You can expect there will be questions on the exam about OSHA. It is a major piece of legislation that impacts every employer in the country. Read more in Chapter 2.

What is known as the General Duty Clause provides that "Each employer (1) shall furnish to each of his employees employment and a place of employment which are free from recognized hazards that are causing or are likely to cause death or serious physical harm to his employees; (2) shall comply with occupational safety and health standards promulgated under this Act."

And each employee should "comply with occupational safety and health standards and all rules, regulations, and orders issued pursuant to this Act which are applicable to his own actions and conduct."

The law and its regulations are overseen by an agency in the U.S. Department of Labor (US DOL). Some states have negotiated with US DOL to provide their own safety enforcement organizations under contract. These must all meet Occupational Safety and Health Administration (OSHA) minimum standards or exceed the federal expectations for workplace safety and health.

Nothing will allow an employer off the hook for these responsibilities. When there are no specific regulations addressing a situation in an employer's workplace, the General Duty Clause will still apply. That is the umbrella responsibility all employers must meet.

National statistics are just too big to mean anything of value. Breaking down the numbers into North American Industry Classification System (NAICS) code helps the numbers carry more meaning. (Table 8-1 shows the number of nonfatal injury and illness cases in a few example industries.)

Bloodborne Pathogens[2]

According to OSHA, bloodborne pathogens are infectious microorganisms in human blood that can cause disease in humans, including hepatitis B (HBV), hepatitis C (HCV), and the human immunodeficiency virus (HIV). Needlesticks and other sharps-related injuries may expose workers to bloodborne pathogens. Workers in many occupations,

NAICS Code	Industry	2015 Rate	2014 Rate
92216	Fire protection (local government)	10.2	12.1
92212	Police protection (local government)	10.2	10.6
54194	Veterinary services (private industry)	9.6	10.0
321992	Prefabricated wood building manufacturing (private industry)	7.9	8.6
92214	Correctional institutions (state government)	8.3	8.2
All	Total (including state and local government)	3.3	3.4

Table 8-1 OSHA Nonfatal Occupational Injury and Illness Cases in 2014 and 2015[3]

such as first responders, housekeeping personnel in some industries, and nurses and other healthcare personnel, may be at risk for exposure to bloodborne pathogens.

 EXAM TIP Bloodborne pathogens are receiving more attention these days. The attempt to prevent injury through contamination or puncture injuries is a key OSHA goal. You can expect the exam to have some references to this issue.

Any employer that faces risks of transmitting bloodborne pathogens must meet specific OSHA standards for handling what are called *sharps*. These are syringe needles, surgical needles, knives, and other puncture devices. All must be properly disposed of in puncture-resistant containers known as *sharps containers*. These containers are red with lids that can lock when the container is full.

Also subject to these regulations are used medical sponges, bandages, and any other materials contaminated with human blood. All bodily secretions are included in the list of controlled and hazardous substances. All must be disposed of in a proper way through incineration or in approved medical landfills.

All human blood, urine, and other bodily secretions must be handled as though contaminated with HBV, HCV, or HIV.

There are posting requirements for work areas where employees handle bloodborne pathogens.

Needlestick Safety and Prevention Act[4]

OSHA's Bloodborne Pathogens standard as amended pursuant to the Needlestick Safety and Prevention Act of 2000[5] prescribes safeguards to protect workers against the health hazards caused by bloodborne pathogens.

Self-sheathing needles, sharps with engineered sharps injury protections, and needleless systems are all examples of engineered protections against bloodborne pathogens in the workplace.

If you are in a doctor's office, dental office, medical laboratory, veterinarian's office, hospital, or other such work environment, you need to document all the protections you use against bloodborne pathogens. Also, you need to conduct regular employee training programs to be sure all workers understand the rules and how to protect themselves against infection.

Mine Safety and Health Act (MSHA)

Like the Occupational Safety and Health Act, MSHA addresses the issue of safety and health of employees, but in the mining industry.

Also like OSHA, there is an agency within the U.S. Department of Labor that is assigned responsibility for implementing regulations under the mine safety law. It is known as the Mine Safety and Health Administration. This agency inspects mines in all locations around the country. It tracks statistics based on two categories: coal mines and metal/nonmetal mines. Of course, the agency reports totals also.[6] In 2015 (the latest data available as of this writing), the mine fatality rate was .0099 deaths per number of miners. In 2014, the death rate was .0148; this improvement was just a bit more than 33 percent. Total injuries improved in the same period by 6.5 percent (2.46 percent in 2014 and 2.30 percent in 2015).

Mine Safety and Health Administration inspections resulted in a 24 percent citation rate in both 2014 and 2015. Fines and assessments by the agency against mine operations totaled $65 million in 2015, down from $96.8 million in 2014.

Health Information Technology for Economic and Clinical Health (HITECH) Act

This law, "enacted as part of the American Recovery and Reinvestment Act of 2009, was signed into law on February 17, 2009, to promote the adoption and meaningful use of health information technology. Subtitle D of the HITECH Act addresses the privacy and security concerns associated with the electronic transmission of health information, in part, through several provisions that strengthen the civil and criminal enforcement of the HIPAA rules (Health Insurance Portability and Accountability Act)."[7]

HIPAA applies to health plans, healthcare clearinghouses, and healthcare providers that transmit any health information in electronic form.

Breach of electronic data systems and release of patient information can be costly. The interim final rule (regulation) provides that the Secretary of Health and Human Services (HHS) can penalize employers up to $50,000 per violation if the act was willful, but not more than $1.5 million. For nonwillful violations, penalties start at $100 per violation and go up from there.

Health Insurance Portability and Accountability Act (HIPAA)

This is the grandfather of healthcare data protection legislation. It protects patient privacy in many ways. Electronic systems must be protected from unauthorized persons accessing patient records. Paper systems must provide for the same protections. Disclosing patient information verbally to unauthorized persons is also forbidden.

Covered entities include hospitals, doctor offices, dentist offices, and other medical-care providers. Business associates of these entities are also covered. These include services to a covered entity and are limited to legal, actuarial, accounting, consulting, data aggregation, management, administrative, accreditation, and financial services. All must have systems that protect personally identifiable patient information from disclosure to unauthorized persons.

Americans with Disabilities Act (ADA)

In 1973 the Rehabilitation Act was passed by Congress to require federal contractors to make reasonable job accommodations for disabled people on the workforce or those who are job applicants. In 1990, much of the same content was reapplied to all employers engaged in interstate commerce who have 15 or more people on their payroll. The ADA was amended in 2008. (See the next section.)

EXAM TIP The Americans with Disabilities Act is a key piece of legislation that impacts most employers in the country. You will find questions on the exam about this subject area.

Disabled individuals are defined as people with physical or mental impairments that substantially limit one or more major life activities, people who have a record or history of such impairment, or people perceived by others as having such an impairment.

Employers are not required to make job accommodations until they receive a request for a job accommodation. At that time, the employer is required to enter into a discussion about the specific disability, the accommodation requested by the employee, and any alternative accommodation the employer believes would speak to the individual's request while being more acceptable to the employer.

The Equal Employment Opportunity Commission (EEOC) has published regulations implementing the ADA to prohibit inquiring about disabled status until after a job offer has been extended to a job applicant. Recently, the Office of Federal Contract Compliance Programs (OFCCP) has promulgated regulations that require federal contractors with $10,000 or more in contracts to gather disability status about job applicants as well as employees. To do that, the contractors must inquire about disability status from job applicants. The EEOC has published an opinion letter that grants permission to employers in this situation to ask job applicants about their disability status without fear of penalty.

Americans with Disabilities Act Amendments Act

After it was passed in 1990, the courts tightened the interpretation of *disability* under the ADA, much to the concern of Congress. When Congress passed the ADA Amendments Act, it was intended to "loosen" the interpretation of *disability* so more people would be covered by its protections. Now almost any physical or mental condition that impacts a major life activity can be considered a disability covered under the act.

Mitigating circumstances may no longer be considered in determining disability status. If an employee takes medication for controlling multiple sclerosis (MS) and the disease has been in remission because of that treatment, the individual is still considered disabled under the ADA Amendments Act. Treatment is irrelevant under the new law. The only specifically excluded treatment for determining disability is the use of eye glasses or contact lenses. Only blindness is considered a disability. Eyesight problems that depend on corrective lenses are not considered disabling.

Under the original ADA, an employee whose migraine headaches were controlled by medication was not considered disabled. That is now different under the ADA Amendments Act.

Having more people defined as disabled doesn't necessarily mean there will be more people asking for job accommodations. Since the ADA Amendments Act was passed in 2008, there has been no observable change in the willingness of people to be viewed as disabled. There is still a reticence about being seen as disabled. It will take more education for people to gain more comfort with that identifier.

Genetic Information Nondiscrimination Act (GINA)

In 2008 (a busy year for Congress), the Genetic Information Nondiscrimination Act was passed and implemented. Up until then it was fairly common for employers, and particularly insurance companies, to restrict benefit coverage based on genetic information. Even the basic decision to hire or not hire someone based on their genetic information was not uncommon.

Why? Genetic information can offer indicators of predilection for certain diseases such as cancer, multiple sclerosis (MS), and diabetes. Over time, those are expensive diseases to treat. Avoiding people who would likely have those diseases in the future was a way to control insurance costs and medical expenses.

Genetic science is gaining more sophistication every day. We can tell with more precision what might happen to individuals in the future. Yet that information may no longer be used for employment-related decision-making.

Rehabilitation Act

As previously noted, the Rehabilitation Act was passed in 1973 and applies only to federal contractors and subcontractors with $10,000 or more in contracts. It requires that federal contractors make job accommodations for employees and hiring accommodations for job applicants under certain circumstances.

Additionally, the Rehabilitation Act replaced the Vocational Rehabilitation Act and created support for states to form vocational rehabilitation programs. When the legislation first was published, it used the term *handicapped*. The term has been replaced by *disabled*.

Table 8-2 lists some of the important sections of the Rehabilitation Act.

Pregnancy Discrimination Act

In 1978, 14 years after the passage of the Civil Rights Act of 1964, the Pregnancy Discrimination Act provided some modifications to coverage under the 1964 law. This law defined pregnancy as protected within the definition of *sex* for the purpose of coverage under the Civil Rights Act. It also specifically said that no employer can illegally discriminate against an employee due to pregnancy. It defines pregnancy as a temporary disability and requires accommodation on the job if it is necessary. It guarantees the

Section	Content
Section 501	Requires nondiscrimination and affirmative action in hiring disabled workers by federal agencies within the executive branch
Section 503	Requires nondiscrimination and affirmative action by federal contractors and subcontractors with contracts valued at $10,000 or more
Section 504	Requires employers subject to the law to provide reasonable accommodation for disabled individuals who can perform the major job duties with or without accommodation

Table 8-2 Rehabilitation Act Components

employee rights to return to work to the same or similar job with the same pay following her pregnancy disability.[8]

Family and Medical Leave Act (FMLA)

This law requires some employers to provide unpaid leave of absence when the employee, the employee's spouse, or other family member requires medical attention and the employee must be off work to care for the circumstance. Some states like California have enacted expanded Family and Medical Leave Act legislation that provides for paid time off. Be sure to identify the requirements in the state (or states) where you have employees.

FMLA provides up to 12 weeks of unpaid, job-protected leave per year. The year is a rolling year. It begins when the employee begins using FMLA leave and continues for the next 12 months. It also requires that the employee's group health benefits be maintained during the leave and the employer continue paying whatever portion it would normally pay if the employee were working. Over the years since this was enacted into law, regulations have been developed that provide for the 12 weeks to be taken in increments of a day if required for periodic medical treatment (e.g., chemotherapy). The leave is deemed to be flexible in favor of helping the employee accommodate their medical needs.

FMLA leave may be taken for any of the following reasons:

- For the birth and care of the newborn child of an employee
- For placement with the employee of a child for adoption or foster care
- To care for an immediate family member (spouse, child, or parent) with a serious health condition
- To take medical leave when the employee is unable to work because of a serious health condition

FMLA applies to all public agencies, all public and private elementary and secondary schools, and companies with 50 or more employees.

Mental Health Parity Act and Addiction Equity Act (MHPAEA)

The Paul Wellstone (D-MN, U.S. Senate) and Pete Domenici (D-NM, U.S. Senate) Mental Health Parity and Addiction Equity Act of 2008 is a federal law that generally prevents group health plans and health insurance issuers that provide mental health or substance use disorder (MH/SUD) benefits from imposing less favorable benefit limitations on those benefits than on medical/surgical benefits. MHPAEA originally applied to group health plans and group health insurance coverage but has since been amended to include individual health insurance coverage.

Patient Protection and Affordable Care Act

This landmark legislation was the flagship for the first Obama administration in 2010. It is sometimes called the Obamacare law or the Affordable Care Act because of President Obama's effort to get it passed and implemented.[9]

Key benefits to Americans include the following:

- Improving quality and lowering healthcare costs
  - Free preventive care
  - Prescription discounts for seniors
  - Protection against healthcare fraud
  - Small business tax credits
- New consumer protections
  - Preexisting conditions
  - Consumer assistance
- Access to healthcare
  - Health insurance marketplace in each state
- Benefits for women
  - Providing insurance options
  - Covering preventive services
  - Lowering costs
- Young adult coverage
  - Coverage available to children up to age 26
- Strengthening Medicare
  - Yearly wellness visit
  - Many free preventive services for some seniors with Medicare
- Holding insurance companies accountable
  - Insurers justifying any premium increase of 10 percent or more before the rate takes effect

Risk Mitigation

The HR department is responsible for controlling the risk of financial loss due to safety and health issues in the workplace. Mitigation means to lessen in severity. The following sections cover the key areas in which HR professionals focus their efforts in this regard.

Injury and Illness Prevention Plan (IIPP)

IIPPs are not mandated by OSHA. However, some states do require employers to use them. OSHA endorses the application of IIPPs in every workplace. Key elements of an IIPP include management leadership, worker participation, hazard identification, hazard prevention and control, education and training, and program evaluation and improvement.

EXAM TIP Even if you are not required to have an injury and illness prevention plan, you can expect the exam will ask you something about that topic.

Eight states either require employers to have IIPPs or provide incentives for employers who use them.[10]

- Alaska had an injury and illness plan requirement for more than 20 years (1973 to 1995). Five years after the program was implemented, the net decrease in injuries and illnesses (the statewide reduction in injuries and illnesses over and above the national decrease during the same time period) for Alaska was 17.4 percent.

- California began to require an injury and illness prevention program in 1991. Five years after this requirement began, California had a net decrease in injuries and illnesses of 19 percent.

- Colorado has a program that allows firms to adopt basic injury and illness prevention program components in return for a workers' compensation premium reduction. The cumulative annual reduction in accidents was 23 percent, and the cumulative reduction in accident costs was between 58 and 62 percent.

- Hawaii began to require employers to have injury and illness prevention programs in 1985. The net reduction in injuries and illnesses was 20.7 percent.

- Massachusetts workers' compensation program firms receive a premium credit for enrolling in a loss management program. In the first year of this program, firms participating in the program had a 20.8 percent improvement in their loss ratios.

- North Dakota has a component under its workers' compensation program for employers who have a risk management plan. The incentive is a 5 percent discount on annual workers' compensation premiums. These risk management programs contain many of the elements of an injury and illness prevention program. They resulted in a cumulative decline for serious injuries of 38 percent over a 4-year period.

- Texas had a program under its workers' compensation commission from 1991 to 2005 that identified the most hazardous workplaces. Those employers were required to develop and implement injury and illness prevention programs. The reduction in injuries over a 4-year period (1992 to 1995) averaged 63 percent each year.

- Washington began requiring establishments to have injury and illness prevention programs in 1973. Five years later, the net decrease in injuries and illnesses was 9.4 percent.

Clearly, there are financial benefits to employers who use IIPPs in their workplaces.

Identification of Risks/Dangers

A basic tenant of any safety program is workplace inspection. Identifying hazards, safety issues, and behavior problems that can cause injury are the result of such inspections. Once problems are identified, employees can be coached in how to change the way they behave in their workplace so the hazard can be reduced or eliminated. An example is leaving file cabinet drawers open after adding or removing documents. The potential for someone to walk into the open drawer is high when the cabinet is in the center of the workgroup. Opening more than one drawer at a time is another behavior problem that can result in the file cabinet tipping over onto the user. Only bad things can result.

Figure 8-1 is an example of a simple safety inspection form.

Emergency Evacuation

One important provision of any safety plan is the preparation of emergency evacuation procedures. Employees must understand where the nearest exits are and what alternate exits are available in case the primary route out of the building is blocked. In addition, they need to know where to reassemble outside the building so the emergency operations officer can count noses and be sure everyone is safely away from the hazard.

Emergency Medical Care

When creating an emergency plan, considering emergency medical care is a key element. It is nice when a call to 911 will garner ambulance dispatch, but what if you can't reach 911 or there are no ambulances available when you call? Alternative plans must be made for treating and transporting injured workers to a medical facility where they can receive proper treatment.

Workplace Violence

A growing problem in this country is workplace violence. Everything in this category can cause trauma, physical or emotional. Consider how you will handle issues involving an employee who is upset and yelling at others in the workplace. What about a former employee who feels disrespected and returns to the workplace intent on killing someone? What about people who enter the workplace with weapons to take away valuable property? Any or all of these situations should be on your list of potential workplace violence incidents for which plans should be made.[11]

Health and Safety Monitoring

Human resource professionals are in a unique position to monitor employee health and safety. They usually have access to attendance reports and can identify patterns in employee wellness or illness. They can also detect issues with employee safety that occur in more than one supervisory unit. Perhaps the safety concerns span multiple work shifts within the same unit. Whatever the issue, human resource professionals should identify it and begin interventions that can mitigate the problems.

Sample Office Safety Inspection Form

Date:	Evaluations:	S = Satisfactory
Inspector Name:		**U = Unsatisfactory**
		NA = Not Applicable to Area
Inspector Signature:		
	If an unsatisfactory rating is provided for	
Area Inspected:	**a particular item, company Form 4 must**	
Desks, Work Stations, Chairs	**be completed for that item.**	
	Rating	**Additional Comments**
Pencils stored, points away		
No overhanging objects on desks		
Cords not a trip hazard		
Storage: Knives, letter openers		
Storage: Scissors		
Ashtrays: Not near flammables (If smoking is permitted in the workplace)		
Plants/water not near outlets		
Chair castors function properly		
Chair arm rests function properly		
Chair adjustments function properly		
Broken furniture is not being used		

Form 1 (1/2017)   This sheet is Page _____ of _____ pages

Figure 8-1   Sample office safety inspection form

Workplace Safety Inspections

A key activity in preventing safety (and health) hazards is an active inspection program that covers all areas of the workplace. That means production facilities, office facilities, loading facilities, and shipping facilities. No location within the workplace should be exempt, and the inspections should be conducted on a regular basis. Often organizations find it helpful to apply a quarterly schedule; sometimes monthly inspections are more appropriate. It depends on how high a risk the work location faces. The higher the risk, the more frequent the inspections should be.

Handling Workplace Violence

All employees should be trained in recognizing and handling workplace violence problems. Supervisors must be trained in how to respond to workplace violence behavior and when to sound an alarm to other employees. There needs to be a management person appointed as the emergency response officer who will be responsible for talking with the media when that becomes necessary and for collecting information that can be passed on to senior management on a regular basis until the emergency has ended. Typical emergencies include fire, earthquake, tornado, hurricane, flooding, isolation of the facility due to utility failure, surface road failure, or communication failure. Severe snow storms can cause emergency conditions, and the employer must be prepared for them, knowing that they will come sooner or later.

Handling Emergencies

When emergencies occur, employees need to understand how to respond. There should be some employees trained in first aid so they can provide preliminary treatment to people who have been injured. There should be some people designated to secure the facility by locking doors and closing other access points. Someone should be designated to contact law enforcement or emergency services (fire, paramedics) so employees and others can receive proper treatment. Someone should be designated as the spokesperson for media contacts and senior management briefings. Proper safety training for employees and supervisors can go a long way to reducing injuries and achieving the appropriate emergency response when it is needed.

Security Risks

In the modern American workplace there are a lot of potential security risks. Just in the information services context, cyber-crimes have begun climbing the activity chart. International players are involved in some attacks, and other bad actors are people within our own country. Identifying the risks is a task that should be undertaken as part of the policy development process and procedural planning. The way to do that is to inspect each element of organizational operations and ask yourself what could go wrong, or what is exposed, and then develop your plans accordingly.

If your organization is large enough to enjoy the presence of a security department, you should expect those folks will play a key role in all of the following planning, problem identification, and response implementation.

Data Security/Cyber-Crimes

Data security is critical for human resource professionals. Maintaining a viable HR data system (human resource information system [HRIS]) is important for employee, supervisor, and HR use. Having that access blocked is a serious issue. If it is blocked because of equipment problems, that is one set of problems. If it is blocked because of a cyber-attack from someone intending to do harm, that is a different set of problems. Planning for both is something HR professionals must contribute to and sometimes take the lead in managing. Often, when there is a staff of information service professionals, they will be key allies in the planning and response process. Working with law enforcement officials is another duty that must be assigned to someone in the organization. Supporting organizations that work to prevent cyber-crimes is a consideration for medium to larger-sized employers.

Hacker Theft

What happens when someone hacks into the HRIS and gains access to personal information about employees? HRIS data includes Social Security numbers, home addresses, names and ages of dependents, employee banking information used for direct deposit, and more. When an unauthorized person gains access to that level of sensitive data, there needs to be a rapid response to help employees protect themselves and their families. One type of support is to sponsor coverage by an organization such as the Equifax credit protection service or the LifeLock identity theft protection service. There are many such services in the marketplace. You can get advice about selecting such support from your chief financial officer and legal adviser.

A relatively new problem in the area of cyber-crime is the problem of hackers holding your data hostage. They corrupt your computer disk so that you cannot access or retrieve your data if you don't agree to pay them a fee to unlock your computer. This is emerging as a serious threat to employers. What if you pay and the hackers don't unlock your computer? What if you don't pay and your computer is suddenly worthless? What backup practices do you have for ensuring you can re-create your computer on a different machine with all the current data should that be necessary? Cyber-criminals are becoming very creative in their methods of attack. Almost always, their nastiness is aimed at ways they can extract money from employers for the release of the employers' information.

Employee Cyber-Theft

Disgruntled employees sometimes head for the company's databases with an eye to stealing proprietary information on products or services. They also can seek out access to employee data from payroll systems or the HRIS. You can imagine all the bad things they could do with such data if they got it. An HR professional's first duty is to plan for such problems and create plans to prevent them from happening. The second duty is to determine how to respond once a theft has occurred. Human resources normally plays a lead role in planning and implementing these plans and policies.

Inventory and Supply Security

Large organizations usually have large quantities of raw materials and completed product on hand. They also have large quantities of supplies used for office functions, medical support, employee comfort, and safety. Small organizations don't have nearly the same levels of inventory, but what they have is precious to them and a financial hardship if these supplies should go missing.

HR professionals need to work with operations managers and supervisors who have primary oversight of raw materials and product inventories and identify the risks they face and how those risks can be mitigated. Then, there should be attention paid to how the organization will respond if such a theft should occur. What law enforcement will be needed? What, if any, public announcements should be made and by whom within the company?

Equipment Security

Equipment is expensive. Human resource department computer equipment expands with the size of the organization. The more there is, the greater the investment that must be made to replace the equipment should it be stolen. Many years ago, a human resource consulting firm was the victim of vandals who broke into their offices and removed every computer they had. The criminals were in and out of the facility so fast that no one saw them, and they didn't appear on any video surveillance recording because the firm didn't have any cameras installed. The data was lost. There were no backups. The firm nearly went out of business because of that theft. You can protect your organization from such a disaster if you think ahead to what you would face if someone stole your computers or other essential equipment. How can you protect that equipment? How can you prevent such a theft? What will be your recovery plan if you do experience such an attack?

Theft Prevention/Loss Prevention

In large organizations, entire departments are given the responsibility of preventing loss. There is "shrinkage" of inventory caused by shoplifting and employee theft. There is loss of money from bank accounts due to embezzlement. If it is an asset to the business, it can be stolen. HR professionals have roles to play in loss prevention, whether or not there is an independent department assigned to address those issues.

Employee Theft

Pilfering from the petty cash box in the office manager's desk drawer or diverting customer payments to personal accounts rather than company accounts are both examples of employee theft. In retail establishments, employee theft of products can be an issue.

When individuals have a predilection to stealing, they likely have a record showing they have been in trouble for such behavior in the past. Background checks should be able to unveil the record so it can be assessed and the job candidate rejected from further consideration if that is appropriate. To do that, the historical problem should be relevant to the job in question. If the job involves handling inventory, cash, or financial records, and the background shows convictions for grand theft, that might qualify as a rejection reason.

Customer Theft

Customer theft can involve a "five-finger discount" taken as the customer cruises the aisles of the employer's store. Shoplifting is America's number-one property crime according to pricegun.com.[12] On average there are 550,000 shoplifting incidents every day. They total $13 billion of loss each year, representing a daily loss of $35 million. That is significant reason for employers to address customer theft issues.

Forty-seven percent of high-school students admit to shoplifting in the past year.[13]

HR professionals are involved with policy development and implementation coordination with operations departments and other staff organizations. The tasks HR people may be involved with can include investigation of complaints about management treatment, investigation of policy violations, and training for employees on policy requirements.

Preventing Equipment Damage

One would normally think that preventing equipment damage falls to the operations groups that use the equipment. Yet when arguments turn nasty, employees can resort to sabotage. *Sabotage* means deliberately destroying something so it will not work; the word comes from a century-old employee grievance over employer treatment (literally, throwing a shoe, or *sabot* in French, into the machinery to cause damage or failure of the equipment).

HR professionals can play a preventative role by properly training employees in requirements of organizational policies and investigating employee complaints of unfair or illegal treatment. Feedback to the complaining employee is critical so the communication cycle is fulfilled. The complaining employee must learn what has resulted from the complaint. Without that feedback, employee trust in the employer's handling the issue without bias will diminish substantially.

Securing Passwords

HR professionals can help the organization with securing passwords by reviewing and training employees on the policy requirements. HR can also maintain a master log of passwords issued to each employee for the software access each person needs. If there is an information technology department, that log can be kept by the computer professionals. Preventing people from using sticky notes to write passwords and sticking them onto computer screens is important. Putting passwords on a list taped to the "breadboard" pull-out tray on a desk is also unacceptable. HR can help organizational groups determine the proper method for securing passwords for the employer.

Terrorism

Hardly a day goes by without a news story about terrorism somewhere in the world. Workplace violence is sometimes a result of terrorism and sometimes a result of disgruntled workers. It is obvious that terrorism can sometimes result in harm to employees and sometimes in loss of property. A key method for identifying situations that can involve terrorism is through employee involvement. Employee alerts to a central processing group (text message, voice call, or e-mail message) can start the wheels turning to respond and save injury and damage. Training employees in the policies for handling such incidents and how to report them is often an HR responsibility.

Report Processing

At the beginning of the twentieth century, HR departments as we know them today didn't exist. There were a few reports to track, and often that was done by secretaries in each department. Also, the report content varied from one department to another, usually based on the wishes of the department managers. Then, the personnel department was born. In it were consolidated all of the responsibilities for filling out payroll forms, handling benefits enrollment, and tracking worker attendance. Personnel had little to do with policy. It was a paper-handling group of people that took work off the shoulders of operations supervisors. Late in the twentieth century the HR management group was invented. As it evolved within organizations, it took on more and more strategic importance. In some organizations, HR departments have become profit centers, billing out to organizational units the cost of services provided to those remote groups. In some instances, the HR department has even become a profit center, providing services for a fee to other employer organizations. Strategic planning is a key HR focus these days.

How can benefits planning contribute to the company's profit and loss statement? How can policy development address evolving employee needs while meeting legal and organizational requirements? While entry-level HR professionals won't likely be involved in the policy discussions, they will be expected to conduct one-on-one discussions with employees who have questions about their benefit coverage, savings plans, and even disciplinary treatment. After some initial experience in the HR department, new professionals may even be involved with complaint investigations.

Workers' Compensation

The world of workers' compensation insurance is tightly regulated by state governments. States govern reporting of workplace accidents and follow the treatment for each injured worker from beginning to end. Workers' compensation insurance dictates how much will be paid for treatment and for how long. Yet there are some decisions employers get to make about their involvement with workers' compensation cases.

 EXAM TIP Every employer is required to have workers' compensation insurance. Even though the rules governing workers' compensation are generated by each state, you can expect there will be some questions on the exam about this topic.

Reporting Requirements

Workers' compensation insurance procedures specify what information must be transmitted to the insurance company for an employer with a workplace accident. Also, they specify what administrative information must be sent periodically, along with medical treatment reports. HR professionals are usually tasked with the responsibility to monitor case reports and be sure everything the insurance carrier needs actually gets to them.

Return-to-Work Policies

You might not immediately think there are policy latitudes available to employers in the handling of workers' compensation issues. Yet return-to-work policies are a good example of how employers get to determine certain employee-handling questions.

It is almost never up to the employer how early someone can return to work. That is governed by the medical evaluators. But employers can overlay policies about the conditions under which a person can return to work.

Modified-Duty Assignments
Some people believe that modified-duty assignments are required by workers' compensation rules if there are medical restrictions when an employee is ready to return to work. In fact, employers can determine their own policy about their ability to have someone working with restrictions. That policy may vary by job type and the restrictions specified by the workers' compensation medical determinations.

If someone is going to return to work from a skiing accident with the restriction that they may not carry more than 10 pounds because of a broken leg that is still in a cast, for example, the employer gets to say whether it can have someone on the job with those restrictions. If it is not possible to have the employee lift only 10 pounds in a shipping and receiving job, it is permissible for the employer to delay the worker's return until there are no restrictions required.

Likewise, if the medical restriction involves working only a few hours each day, the employer gets to determine whether it can use someone on the specific job assignment for less than full time each day.

Any decisions about these return-to-work issues should be properly documented to show both the decision and *why* that decision was the best for the circumstances. Employers may not arbitrarily block someone from returning to work without a legitimate business explanation.

Reasonable Accommodation
Reasonable accommodation in workers' compensation cases involves the same obligations that any other job accommodation request would impose on the employer. The employer must be willing to engage in an interactive dialogue process with the employee about the medical restrictions and how the job can be performed with those restrictions.

Safety is one reason for rejecting a job accommodation request. Return-to-work decisions must provide for the safe performance of job duties. If it is not possible for an injured worker to perform the job without significant safety risks, the employer may be justified in delaying the return to work by rejecting the job accommodation request.

Independent Medical Exam
Often the medical advisers on which a workers' compensation case will rely are those hired by the insurance carrier. At any time, the employer and/or the employee can choose to involve different medical people for additional opinions. Those involvements will come at the expense of the party requesting the additional opinion. When medical opinions clash, a decision must be made with concurrence of the workers' compensation insurance carrier, the employer, and the employee.

When an employee doesn't want to return to work under conditions specified by the medical experts, it may be that progressive discipline is the appropriate avenue for resolving the disagreement.

Documentation by the HR organization will be essential in case the employee decides to contest his or her treatment in court. Entry-level HR professionals play a key role in that documentation process, if not by writing it then by ensuring that appropriate parties submit it for the case file.

OSHA Compliance

Federal safety and health laws and regulations begin to impact an employer once the first employee is hired. The Occupational Safety and Health Act contains a General Duty Clause that requires employers to provide safe and healthy working conditions. That duty involves proper observation of workplace safety conditions and correction of any problems identified.

Workplace Safety Inspections

Larger employers have organizations that care for safety issues in all organizational units. Even though a safety department may exist, it is still incumbent upon supervisors, managers, and HR professionals to support safety rules and policies.

In smaller organizations, it may be the HR professional in concert with line supervisors who will handle safety monitoring and reporting tasks. Conducting inspections using a documentation tool such as that in Figure 8-1 (shown earlier) can be helpful to document the safety status of your workplace.

Accident Reporting

Depending on your organizational payroll size, you may have specific requirements for reporting accidents to OSHA. Even if you have only one person on the payroll, you will have reporting requirements under your workers' compensation insurance policy.

For detailed instructions about OSHA injury reporting requirements, you should visit the agency's web site at https://www.osha.gov/recordkeeping/RKforms.html. Any changes the agency might make in the future will be posted on the web site as soon as they are approved for use. Make a habit of checking the site often.

Accidents that require only first aid are not reportable under OSHA regulations. You must identify your company's policy to determine how you should report such incidents internally.

How does OSHA define first aid?[14]

- Using a nonprescription medication at nonprescription strength (for medications available in both prescription and nonprescription forms, a recommendation by a physician or other licensed healthcare professional to use a nonprescription medication at prescription strength is considered medical treatment for recordkeeping purposes)

- Administering tetanus immunizations (other immunizations, such as hepatitis B vaccine or rabies vaccine, are considered medical treatment); cleaning, flushing, or soaking wounds on the surface of the skin

- Using wound coverings such as bandages, Band-Aids, gauze pads, and so on; using butterfly bandages or Steri-Strips (other wound-closing devices such as sutures, staples, and so on, are considered medical treatment)

- Using hot or cold therapy

- Using any nonrigid means of support, such as elastic bandages, wraps, nonrigid back belts, and so on (devices with rigid stays or other systems designed to immobilize parts of the body are considered medical treatment for recordkeeping purposes)

- Using temporary immobilization devices while transporting an accident victim (e.g., splints, slings, neck collars, back boards, etc.); drilling of a fingernail or toenail to relieve pressure; draining fluid from a blister

- Using eye patches

- Removing foreign bodies from the eye using only irrigation or a cotton swab

- Removing splinters or foreign material from areas other than the eye by irrigation, tweezers, cotton swabs, or other simple means

- Using finger guards

- Using massages (physical therapy or chiropractic treatment are considered medical treatment for recordkeeping purposes)

- Drinking fluids for relief of heat stress

How does OSHA define a recordable injury or illness?[15]

- Any work-related fatality.

- Any work-related injury or illness that results in loss of consciousness, days away from work, restricted work, or transfer to another job.

- Any work-related injury or illness requiring medical treatment beyond first aid.

- Any work-related diagnosed case of cancer, chronic irreversible diseases, fractured or cracked bones or teeth, and punctured eardrums.

- There are also special recording criteria for work-related cases involving needlesticks and sharps injuries, medical removal, hearing loss, and tuberculosis.

It can be helpful to prepare a reference list showing your reporting requirements to refer to should there be an accident with one of your workers. It could look like Figure 8-2.

You should customize Figure 8-2 for your organizational policies and expectations. The priority of contact points should be resequenced for your employer. It may be that management wants notification before the workers' compensation insurance company is called.

Contact	E-mail/Phone Number	Date of First Contact
First Aid Injury		
Workers' Comp Carrier	Report Line: Phone #	
Senior Management	Safety Officer Phone # Department Manager Phone #	
Minor or Nonserious Injury		
Workers' Comp Carrier	Report Line: Phone #	
Senior Management	Safety Officer Phone # Department Manager Phone #	
OSHA Incident Report	Local OSHA Office Phone #	
Serious Injury or Death		
Employee's Emergency Contact List	Employee Contact #1: Employee Contact #2:	
Workers' Comp Carrier	Report Line: Phone #	
Senior Management	Safety Officer Phone # Senior HR Officer Phone # Department Manager Phone #	
OSHA Incident Report	Local OSHA Office Phone #	

Figure 8-2   Employee injury reporting contacts

Make this tool fit your requirements. It is better to get these questions answered in advance of any actual injury and a need to use the list.

Incident Reports   OSHA has a series of forms that are important for tracking injuries and illnesses and then summarizing the totals at the end of each year.

OSHA Form 301,[16] Injury and Illness Incident Report, is used to document a reportable injury. It asks for basic information such as name, address, birth date, hire date, who the tending medical provider was, what happened, and what the employee was doing just before getting injured. Current requirements call for retaining each of these incident reports for a minimum of 5 years.

Annual Accident Summary   At the end of each calendar year, employers with ten or more people on the payroll must prepare summary reports called OSHA Form 300 and OSHA Form 300A. These forms contain information about the number of days of work lost because of the accident and the number of days that the employee was on restricted duty or in a different job assignment while recovering. OSHA Form 300 is, in essence, a log of accidents that have happened during the year. This log must be summarized and documented on OSHA Form 300A. It is the summary form (OSHA Form 300A) that must be posted in a conspicuous location within the workplace from February 1 to April 30 each year. This summary does not have any personally identifiable information on it.

That is all on the log (OSHA Form 300), which does not need to be posted. Form 300A must be retained for a minimum of 5 years.

Employee Wellness Programs

Programs that promote employee wellness are considered part of the employee benefit package. A 2012 SHRM survey of 646 HR professionals[17] found that there was a return on investment (ROI) of $1 to $3 for every $1 spent on employee wellness programs. The following are some basic elements that are usually included in all wellness programs:

- Health screenings
- Health risk assessments
- Healthcare coaches or advocates

There are federal requirements for wellness programs governed by three laws.[18]

- The Employee Retirement Income Security Act (ERISA) prohibits discrimination by group health plans based on an individual's health status. ERISA makes exceptions for wellness programs to offer premium or cost-sharing discounts based on an individual's health status in certain circumstances.

- The Americans with Disabilities Act prohibits employment discrimination based on health status and generally forbids employers from inquiring about workers' health status but makes an exception for medical inquiries that are conducted as part of voluntary wellness programs.

- The Genetic Information Nondiscrimination Act prohibits employment discrimination based on genetic information and forbids employers from asking about individuals' genetic information, including information about family members' health status or family history. Like the ADA, GINA allows an exception for inquiries through voluntary wellness programs.

Another federal law—the Health Insurance Portability and Accountability Act—establishes standards to protect the privacy of personal health information, including information that may be collected by some workplace wellness programs. The ADA and GINA also include certain privacy protections.

According to the EEOC, in May 2016, the EEOC, which enforces ADA and GINA, issued new regulations to modify ADA requirements for workplace wellness programs in a manner that reflects both the ADA's goal of limiting employer access to medical information ... and the ACA's provisions promoting wellness programs. A new final rule made similar changes to GINA wellness program requirements.[19]

As Part of Medical Coverage

These days most health insurance providers are well accustomed to the requirements of laws related to employee wellness programs. Often benefit programs such as health insurance will include provisions for wellness programs. The insurance will pay for such things as gym memberships, nutritional education, and smoking cessation. If your health insurance does not currently provide these benefits, it likely will in a short while. Employee wellness programs are the up-and-coming thing in today's workplace.

Employee Assistance Programs

Another benefit of many health insurance programs these days is an employee assistance program (EAP). These are formal structured programs that tap into third-party organizations that are staffed by health management experts. Used for both mental and physical issues, an employee can place a confidential call to the EAP adviser 24/7. The EAP adviser is qualified to dispense counseling and connect the employee with additional resources for their specific need. Usually there is no limit to the number of times an employee can use the EAP advisers. The entire focus of EAPs is early intervention in health issues before they become debilitating to the employee.

Ergonomics

Finally, ergonomics have been gaining ground in health programs for employee populations. Employers have been paying more attention to these needs and allocating budget dollars to helping assure the work environment is contributing to employee wellness. Scientists have studied workplace requirements for human motion and discovered there are ways to reduce the risk of injury by assessing the ergonomic requirements of the job assignment. OSHA has used these studies to create its own ergonomic assessment program.[20] Said simply, "ergonomics is the science of designing the job to fit the worker, rather than physically forcing the worker's body to fit the job."

Musculoskeletal disorders (MSDs) are caused by repetitive use of fingers, hands, arms, legs, and back. Identifying the body part impacted by a given job can help determine whether there are ways to redesign a job so those impacts can be reduced or eliminated. Controlling costs that rise with employee absenteeism and medical treatment expense is another goal of ergonomic programs.

Chapter Review

This chapter covered the importance of employee health, safety, and security issues. Employers are governed by many federal laws in these areas. Those laws require certain documentation and reporting of events. Although collectively they amount to only 5 percent in the test weighting, it is an important portion from a cost management perspective. You also saw how advance planning can help prevent workplace accidents. New developments in the area of cyber-theft and network hacking are becoming more important to HR professionals. Medical benefit programs such as health insurance are embracing more preventative approaches to employee care, including employee wellness programs and employee assistance programs. There are many tasks involved with these facets of HR management. Understanding the impact they have on the organization and its workers is critical to all HR professionals.

Questions

1. The ABC Company owns a gold mine in the California mountains. It has only eight employees. The company is most certainly going to be governed by the federal law known as

   A. MSHA

   B. OSHA

   C. TEPA

   D. SBGP

2. In an insurance company, there are few employee hazards according to its HR manager. In fact, the HR manager believes there are no federal laws that will impact safety in its operations. As the associate HR manager, what recommendation would you make to your boss?

   A. Stay the course. The HR manager is right about the freedom from federal oversight.

   B. Reconsider the conclusion. Federal oversight and office safety laws say that the employer must conduct safety training for all employees.

   C. Stay the course. The employer is specifically exempt. All insurance companies are excluded from coverage under federal safety laws.

   D. Reconsider the conclusions. OSHA requires all employers to provide a safe workplace in compliance with the General Duty Clause.

3. Latisha works for a veterinarian as the office manager. She also serves as the HR manager. It is a small practice with only 12 employees. The boss, veterinarian Jill, is strict about handling needles and other sharp instruments. Also, since they are not dealing with human patients, Dr. Jill says they don't have to worry about bloodborne pathogens. Is she right?

   A. Dr. Jill is wrong. While animal blood may not transfer human diseases, accidental human injury by sharps can cause human blood transfer.

   B. Dr. Jill is wrong. Animal blood can easily transmit most human diseases.

   C. Dr. Jill is right. However, Latisha should ignore the issue until there is need to respond to an accident involving a needle or other sharp instrument. Then she can put together a program.

   D. Dr. Jill is right. Even if someone should get stuck by a needle, there is still no coverage under OSHA's regulations.

4. HIPAA does not apply to which of the following?

   A. Health plans

   B. A healthcare clearinghouse

   C. A healthcare provider that sends medical records electronically

   D. A chiropractor who has retired and sold the practice

5. Morton is your colleague and another Associate Professional in Human Resources. He is wondering if someone who has diabetes under control by using insulin should be considered disabled. What is your advice?

   A. Absolutely not. When a disabling condition is controlled by medication, it is no longer considered a disability.

   B. When the disability is controlled with only limited insulin injections, it is no longer considered a disability.

   C. Even if it is controlled by insulin, diabetes is still considered a disability under the ADAAA.

   D. Unless the diabetes has been treated for more than 5 years, it is not considered a disability.

6. Why was the Genetic Information Nondiscrimination Act passed by Congress?

   A. Employers were being nosy about employee health problems that they had not admitted on their job applications.

   B. Insurance companies were using genetic information to determine who would have expensive diseases in the future.

   C. Insurance companies were finding it useful to know genetic information to defend against lawsuits.

   D. Employers were using the genetic information to determine racial category membership.

7. The Rehabilitation Act and the Americans with Disabilities Act apply to employers

   A. Only one at a time but never both together

   B. Only when the employer is a federal contractor with $10,000 or more in contracts and more than 15 people on the payroll do both laws apply at the same time

   C. Only when there are 15 or more people on the payroll; then ADA takes precedence over the Rehabilitation Act

   D. Only if the federal contractor has a contract of $100,000 or more and at least 50 people on the payroll will both laws apply

8. The Family and Medical Leave Act will apply to an employee who

   A. Is a new father wanting to take time off for bonding with his new son

   B. Is an uncle who wants to travel to the "old country" to see his new niece

   C. Is a mother who wants to take more time off following her vacation

   D. Is a sister wanting to surprise her brother for his 50th birthday

9. An injury and illness prevention plan is a tool for improving safety when

    A. A company receives a letter from OSHA saying they will soon be inspected

    B. An employer wants to cover up hazards that have been bothering people for years

    C. A company wants to communicate with its employees the procedures for handling certain hazards

    D. Personal protective devices are sent out for repair

10. IIPPs have been shown to

    A. Reduce illness and injury by as much as 17 percent

    B. Improve the décor of any modern-day office

    C. Reduce the paperwork associated with injury reports to the government

    D. Increase the amount of supervisor interventions when janitorial staff performance problems arise

11. Workplace hazards are best identified through

    A. Having a working committee to discuss the problems they see

    B. Conducting periodic inspections of each work location and documenting the issues identified as potential hazards

    C. Logging the accidents that employees have

    D. Employee suggestions for fixing problems they see at their workstation

12. One hazard common to all work locations is fire. Consequently, an evacuation plan should be developed and included in the

    A. Material Safety Data Sheets at that location

    B. Illness prevention medical reference maintained at each location

    C. Injury and illness prevention plan

    D. Identification of employee problems that should be addressed

13. Workplace violence is something that most employers

    A. Won't have to worry about

    B. Will address through the IIPP

    C. Should downplay to prevent any self-fulfilling prophecies

    D. Can prevent if they keep their doors locked

14. The following are not considered security risks

    A. Employees who have a worsening attendance problem

    B. Customers who insist on seeing the way their products are assembled

    C. City refuse collection personnel

    D. Managers who travel with laptops containing company databases

15. If you receive an anonymous tip that one of the company employees is stealing employee data for identify theft purposes, you should
   A. Call the police and let them handle it
   B. Confront the employee to get their reaction
   C. Notify senior management and begin an investigation
   D. Dismiss it as an unfounded story

16. Some of the reports created from HR data include
   A. Employee birthdays, new hires, employee training needed, EEO
   B. Training needed, department expense reports, building security access
   C. Performance evaluations, employee absence, profit and loss by department
   D. Payroll account bank reconciliation, EEO, employee longevity, employee terminations

17. HR can influence the company's "bottom line" financially through
   A. Advising senior management
   B. Tracking birthdays
   C. Determining reasons for turnover rates
   D. Checking with colleagues in competing organizations

18. When an employee is injured at work, HR should
   A. Notify the proper federal and state demographic agencies
   B. Notify the bank that there will be more workers' compensation checks needed
   C. Notify the workers' compensation insurance carrier
   D. Notify the parent company

19. When an employee's doctor releases the employee to return to work with restrictions, what should happen?
   A. The employer must take the employee back and find a way to accommodate the restrictions.
   B. The employer can determine whether there is a way to accommodate the restrictions.
   C. The employer is obligated to return the employee to the same job without doing all the heavy lifting.
   D. The employer is required to pay the employee the normal rate even if there is no job available with the required restrictions.

20. An employee is ready to return to work with restrictions lasting 8 months specified by his doctor. The employer

  A. Must make a job available that matches the restrictions for the entire 8 months.

  B. Must pay the employee at the old earnings rate even though the restrictions mean working at a lower-paid level.

  C. Must give up to a full year of restricted-duty assignment to any worker injured on the job.

  D. Must determine whether it is possible to keep the employee working with restrictions for that long a period. If not, the employer may choose not to return the employee to work.

21. All employers are subject to OSHA regulations

  A. As long as they have ten people on the payroll

  B. If they engage in interstate commerce

  C. Regardless of the number of employees

  D. Whenever state regulations don't predominate

22. When someone at work is injured and the injury is treated with Steri-Strips, OSHA classifies it as

  A. A reportable serious injury

  B. A nonreportable serious injury

  C. A nonreportable first-aid injury

  D. A reportable first-aid injury

23. When someone is stuck by a syringe needle accidentally, OSHA says you should

  A. Report the case under special OSHA rules.

  B. Save the reporting until the end of the calendar year for the summary report.

  C. Report the case as a minor incident that didn't require medical treatment.

  D. Ignore the needle stick. It isn't covered.

24. The year-end OSHA summary report must be posted

  A. From January 1 through March 31

  B. From February 1 through April 30

  C. From March 1 through May 30

  D. From April 1 through June 30

25. Employee wellness programs are

    A. A bad idea because they discriminate against disabled workers

    B. A good idea because they can reduce employee rates of illness

    C. A bad idea because the physical stress may cause heart attacks

    D. A good idea because they use genetic information to work around genetic predispositions for illness

Answers

1. **A.** The Mine Safety and Health Administration governs all mining operations in the United States. It has overall authority for safety in mining. Even with only one employee, the company must meet standards prescribed by the Mine Safety and Health Administration.

2. **D.** OSHA's General Duty Clause requires all employers to offer employees a safe and healthy work environment.

3. **B.** Any veterinary facility dealing with known human pathogens must comply with OSHA's regulations on bloodborne pathogens. AVMA strongly recommends voluntary compliance for all veterinary establishments.

4. **D.** Responsibilities for record privacy transfers to the new owner, assuming the chiropractor will not be retaining any medical records after the transaction.

5. **C.** Mitigating treatment used to eliminate disability status, but no more. The ADAAA now says that mitigations may not be considered in determining disability status.

6. **B.** Determining who would be covered by health insurance based on who would have expensive diseases in the future was judged by Congress to be unacceptable.

7. **B.** A federal contractor with 15 employees and a contract or subcontract of $10,000 or more will be subject to both laws.

8. **A.** Time for bonding with a new child is a qualifying event under FMLA.

9. **C.** IIPP is a tool for communicating hazards and the means for handling them in the workplace. It should address the specific workplace in question.

10. **A.** Alaska discovered there was a direct link between having an IIPP and reduction in the number of injury and illness cases.

11. **B.** When supervisors make inspections and record hazardous conditions, they have a record of actions necessary to make the workplace safer. Repair and improvement can be noted in future inspections.

12. **C.** Every IIPP should contain an evacuation plan and directions for reassembly outside the facility so it can be determined whether everyone evacuated successfully.

13. **B.** Both internal and external workplace violence possibilities should be addressed in the IIPP along with the employee training plans for dealing with them.

14. **A.** Employee attendance records have no correlation to security risks.

15. **C.** Even though the allegation is from an anonymous source, you should discuss it with senior management and, with their approval, begin an investigation to determine whether there is any truth to the story.

16. **A.** Each of the four examples can be generated from the HR information system.

17. **C.** Identifying reasons for employee turnover can lead to reducing turnover and the need to hire fewer replacements, which lowers training cost and increases production output.

18. **C.** The workers' compensation insurance carrier will open a case file and begin the process of managing examination, medical treatment, and recovery details.

19. **B.** The employer must evaluate the restrictions and determine whether it is possible to accommodate the employee given the performance limitations.

20. **D.** The employer must evaluate and document its efforts to identify a placement opportunity for that duration, but it is not obligated to create a job for the restricted employee.

21. **C.** OSHA rules apply to all employers. Sometimes states contract with OSHA to perform the same functions in OSHA's place.

22. **C.** First-aid treatment is a nonreportable event under OSHA rules.

23. **A.** OSHA calls needlesticks reportable injuries under special recording criteria.

24. **B.** The summary report must be posted for 90 days from February 1 through April 30 each year.

25. **B.** Employee wellness programs have been shown to reduce employee illness rates.

Endnotes

1. 29 USC 654

2. https://www.osha.gov/SLTC/bloodbornepathogens/, accessed on November 29, 2016

3. www.bls.gov/iif/oshwc/osh/os/ostb4736.pdf, accessed on November 30, 2016

4. https://www.osha.gov/needlesticks/needlefaq.html, accessed on November 29, 2016

5. www.cdc.gov/sharpssafety/pdf/Neelestick%20Saftety%20and%20Prevention%20Act .pdf, accessed on November 29, 2016

6. http://arlweb.msha.gov/mshainfo/factsheets/2016-at-a-glance-legacy.pdf, accessed on November 30, 2016

7. https://www.hhs.gov/hipaa/for-professionals/special-topics/HITECH-act-enforcement-interim-final-rule/, accessed on November 30, 2016

8. www.eeoc.gov/laws/types/pregnancy.cfm, accessed on November 30, 2016

9. www.hhs.gov/healthcare/facts-and-features/key-features-of-aca/benefits-of-the-affordable-care-act-for-americans/index.html, accessed on December 1, 2016

10. https://www.osha.gov/dsg/InjuryIllnessPreventionProgramsWhitePaper.html, accessed on December 1, 2016

11. Jay C. Beighley, CPP, "War in the Workplace: A Practical Guide to a Safer Workplace," *The Management Advantage, Inc.,* 2016

12. www.pricegun.com, accessed on December 23, 2016

13. Ibid

14. https://www.osha.gov/SLTC/medicalfirstaid/recognition.html, accessed on December 26, 2016

15. https://www.osha.gov/recordkeeping/, accessed on December 26, 2016

16. https://www.osha.gov/recordkeeping/RKforms.html, accessed on December 26, 2016

17. https://www.shrm.org/ResourcesAndTools/hr-topics/benefits/Pages/Wellness-Dollars-Saved.aspx, accessed on December 26, 2016

18. http://kff.org/private-insurance/issue-brief/workplace-wellness-programs-characteristics-and-requirements/, accessed on December 26, 2016

19. Ibid

20. https://www.osha.gov/Publications/osha3125.pdf, accessed on December 26, 2016

Early HR Career–Level Tasks

All the previous chapters focused on specific knowledge within the human resource (HR) profession. As a new HR professional, you will need to understand all of that information. In addition, you will need to understand how to apply it on the job. To that end, the Human Resources Certification Institute (HRCI) has developed a list of tasks in the Associate Professional in Human Resources (aPHR) Body of Knowledge that are representative of what is to be found on a typical entry-level HR professional job assignment. There are no priorities assigned to items on this list. Although there will not be any questions on the certification exam about these tasks, you should be prepared to fulfill each of these task assignments if you are asked to do so.

In large organizations, an entry-level HR professional will be expected to focus on only a few of these tasks. In smaller organizations, it may be necessary to perform most of them.

We have brought in a guest contributor for this chapter, Christina Nishiyama, MBA, PHR, SHRM-CP. Christina will be sharing her experiences when she was new to the HR profession and offer some helpful advice in the *In the Trenches* features. We hope this valuable information will help you as you embark on or continue your growth in your HR career.

What follows are the 31 tasks that HRCI has outlined that an individual would likely be expected to perform at the early HR career level.

In the Trenches

Actual HR Experience

Allow me to introduce myself as the contributing author to Chapter 9 of this book with the *In The Trenches* insertions. I am Christina Nishiyama, MBA, PHR, SHRM-CP. Please know that the overwhelming number of commas after my name serve a purpose in our partnership during this chapter. They are the result

(Continued)

of the terror I felt while finishing my undergraduate degree. Upon graduation, I was not prepared to trade leisurely lunches on a grassy knoll in San Diego for a cubicle. Thus, I endeavored to attain a few additional certifications that have served me well in my career. In your chosen field of human resources, these certifications are extremely helpful for both educational and credibility reasons. Thus, you are absolutely making the right decision to take the aPHR exam! The road you are about to endeavor on by taking the aPHR exam is certain to be educational, both professionally and personally. All of the competencies you will learn by using this aPHR study guide will tie back to the same general principle: nurturing a people-driven culture that supports the success of the organization. HR is an important seat at an organization, and continuing your education will demonstrate how important *you* truly are.

Not so long ago, I was in your shoes, starting off on the first phase of my career after completing my educational journey. To be candid, I was terrified. That is why I find great excitement in providing you with a few helpful tips that served me well during this phase in my career. As you read the following 31 early HR career tasks that are part of HRCI's aPHR Body of Knowledge, I have inserted several experiences and tips from my early HR career days. I hope these *In the Trenches* experiences will help you keep an open mind. There are many times you may pause while reading and say "Wait…I've never done this." That is okay, and that is why the authors felt that sharing my experience would be helpful to you.

I remember my first human resource job like it was yesterday. Prior to walking in the door, I spent plenty of time overeducating myself. After so many years of school, education had come naturally to me and was comfortable. Taking on a "real job" was truly the scary part. After all, what in the world would it be like to sit in one place for eight hours every day?

My first job was in recruiting. Thankfully for me, it was a mix of the two disciplines that I knew I liked: human resources and marketing. Beyond that, I had no idea what to expect. For anyone who may feel that way right now, please know that this is a perfectly acceptable feeling. It can take years to determine exactly what you want to do, and your desires and interests may continue to change throughout your career. What is most important is that you make the best of every opportunity you have. Each opportunity you take on will reveal more about you: your interests, your strengths, and your weaknesses.

Moreover, each individual work task within an opportunity can have a profound effect on your career. Let me explain. If anything, I have always been an expert at overcommitting myself; I'm a "yes" person to the core. Whenever my boss asked, "Who wants to help with a project?" I would always be the first to jump at the opportunity. Most of the time, I had no idea what the project was. Thus, I managed to commit myself to a wide range of tasks, from taking trips to the bagel shop with an exhausting list of cream cheese preferences to developing a new performance management system in 24 hours. While these tasks vary greatly in their overall impact to the business, each had a significant impact on my career. From the trips to the bagel shop, I learned that I did not enjoy the event planning function of human resources. While I can get behind any employee engagement initiative 110 percent, it is not my preference to execute them. On the other hand, had I not jumped out of my seat to pull an all-nighter to create a performance management system, I would have never considered a career in talent management. Moreover, my work would not have been noticed by our CEO, and I expect I would not have gotten that promotion as soon as I did.

It is important to be up for any challenge as you grow your career. Sure, some of the tasks that end up in your lap may be mundane, but others can be of great benefit. As another example, I asked a former boss why he made the decision to promote me when I had very little experience. The main reason was my ambition. Being ambitious does not require years of studying or years of work experience. Open yourself up to every opportunity; you never know where it will take you.

And remember, HR is everywhere! Right now, you may be working part-time at a fast-food restaurant, teaching dance lessons, or serving as a file clerk. In any of these situations, human resource knowledge and experience can be applied. At a fast-food restaurant, you can hone your employee relations skills by mediating an argument between co-workers and coming up with a meaningful resolution. As a dance instructor, you can heighten your training acumen and develop the best way to reach your audience and guide them to success. Lastly, as a file clerk, take the extra time to read up on labor and employment laws. In this ever-changing landscape, you can quickly become a trusted authority at the organization, maintaining important documentation in the appropriate manner.

I realize that it may be hard to see these benefits now, especially on a daily basis. But be patient. Landing your first dream HR job takes time and can be frustrating. Taking the first step and attaining your certification is an important way to show that you have the knowledge, commitment, and ambition to be successful in human resources. In conjunction, do not be afraid to show off your skills. Use what you have learned in this certification journey to "wow" your supervisor and your co-workers by going the extra mile on the next project you are assigned. It may not be the first, second, or third time that you receive the recognition and growth you are seeking, but it will come eventually.

As you review the 31 tasks outlined for the early HR career level by HRCI, I'll pop in with a few examples and advice. Remember, you are sealing a brighter future for yourself in human resources by taking this exam. The aPHR foundation you are building can be applied for the rest of your career.

−CN

Task #1—Access, Collect, and Provide Information and Data to Support HR-Related Decisions

As an entry-level HR generalist, you can expect to be exposed to a wide range of HR activities and processes. As a general rule, your responsibilities will be in providing support to a number of HR programs and activities. For example, recruiting, employee relations, training, safety, budgeting, needs analysis, off-boarding, and termination. You will typically work with others to access, collect, and provide information and data to support HR-related decisions.

You may be tasked to provide administrative support, such as by completing forms and documents or assembling new-hire packets (in some cases, assisting new hires as they complete a variety of forms and documents). You may be tasked to research common HR practices and procedures as part of the developing or updating of new HR policies and procedures. There will likely be many opportunities to provide support to your organization's training programs. Here again, you may be tasked to research various subjects as part of assisting instructors in their preparation in presenting important training topics.

Other activities that may call for your support include sitting in on safety meetings and documenting the safety committee's decisions for the formal record and later posting for employees. Almost certainly, you will be tasked to carry out important administrative responsibilities such as organizing and maintaining personnel records in compliance with prevailing legal norms and practices. All the various activities in which you engage are for the most part intended to develop your HR skills and knowledge for the present even as they help prepare you for the future and for successfully taking and passing your certification exam.

Task #2—Comply with All Applicable Laws and Regulations

In Chapter 2 we provided a list of the most common federal laws impacting human resources. Once an employer hires its first employee, it immediately becomes subject to 53 federal laws. We haven't listed all the state laws that kick into effect. Those will be important for you to identify and fold into your HR management plans. There are far too many to include here, and the aPHR exam will focus only on federal laws. So in your study plan, you should give consideration only to the federal laws. On the job, you need to concern yourself with both.

We suggest you plan to comply with all of these requirements. The exam will be constructed with that expectation. Each of the laws carries equal weight in your study preparation. Don't forget that these requirements change from time to time as Congress sees fit to modify them. It is your responsibility to keep track of the changes and new requirements as they evolve.

In the Trenches

aPHR Task #2

One of my favorite things about a career in human resources is that you never stop educating yourself. Lifelong learning comes with the territory. It is so much easier to truly enjoy your career when it is ever-changing. While the responsibility of understanding so many federal and state laws may seem daunting, it becomes easier with practice. It is also important to find great resources such as HRCI and the Society for Human Resource Management (SHRM) to remain fully engaged in changes to the requirements. To boot, you will be the most popular family member at the dinner table when you can provide guidance for any employee relations issue that comes up in conversation.

–CN

Task #3—Coordinate and Communicate with External Providers of HR Services

Times are changing. Years ago, the HR function came from internal HR resources. Often, small organizations combined their resources in such a way as to utilize the capabilities of their accounting function and the HR function to provide a minimal level of capability and support in both functional areas. Unfortunately, more was lost than gained by this approach.

Today, even small organizations see the importance of having qualified knowledge staff in both areas, but it doesn't stop there. The increasingly legal complexity of the organization's many HR functions creates a need for outside third parties to augment the internal HR staff. This provides an excellent opportunity for you as an entry-level HR professional to build on your HR skills and knowledge. In addition, it provides a significant opportunity to learn even more about HR as a profession. Examples of external providers would be recruiters, COBRA administrators, and employee recognition services.

Task #4—Maintain Employee Data in HRIS or System of Record

A key task for entry-level HR professionals is maintaining employee data in the company tracking system. These are referred to as human resource information systems (HRISs). You will be required to learn the HRIS data fields, how to enter data into the database, and how to prepare reports that may be standard or customized, depending on what your boss needs for special projects.

Writing and formatting reports is a critical task requirement. You have heard the adage that databases are only as good as their input. So, "garbage in, garbage out" is an accurate descriptor. Input errors or data gaps will directly influence the accuracy of report output. That does not reflect well on you or the HR organization. Commit yourself to accuracy.

In the Trenches

aPHR Task #4

One of the many benefits to growing up in the millennial generation is the ease with which technical acumen comes to us. Yes, those years of video games do pay off in some capacity. Data entry and system maintenance may not seem like the sexiest task but can be approached in an innovative manner. Don't be shy about going the extra mile to become an expert on your HRIS system. You can add a great deal of value to the HR department and overall operation. Analytics is often not seen as an HR strength area by many executives, and this task is abound with opportunity to leverage that strength.

–CN

Task #5—Maintain, File, and Process HR Forms

HR forms include such things as notices, announcements, new hire forms, salary forms, performance-related documents, termination paperwork, and sometimes payroll documents. Microsoft Excel has become a popular tool for data tracking purposes. When key data elements have been assigned their own column in Excel, they can be sorted and used for database reporting. Pivot tables can be created to summarize the number of entries for each data element. They can also be used to summarize the numeric values that appear in each data element.

Large organizations will have their own programmers who can create and maintain customized HRIS databases. Small, and sometimes medium-sized, organizations will have to use the Excel approach or an off-the-shelf HRIS.

For example, you might need to track the hire date for each employee. So using an Excel spreadsheet, each employee would occupy an individual line on the spreadsheet. Employee names would be entered in the first column, their date of hire into another column, their job title into another column, etc. And yet later, you might want to track the date a specific announcement or notice was provided to each employee, and thus another set of new columns can be added for those elements.

Keeping accurate records of employee information is part of the HR professional's responsibility. While entering data can be done by a clerical person, constructing reports is usually the task of an entry-level HR professional. Be ready to respond to your boss's requests for information. You may even find yourself receiving requests for information from your internal client organizations.

PART II

In the Trenches

aPHR Task #5

The foundation that you build with this task sets the stage for the success of many organizational functions. This is the data that is used for *everything*. You can answer all of your boss's questions: What should we pay our new hire? What are the salary grades and ranges for our compensation plan? Employee X is not performing; when was he hired? What is the history on other separations in this department? What is the overall cost and enrollment in our benefits plan? That's right. All of these questions can be answered by the data that you maintain, so do not take this responsibility lightly.

–CN

Task #6—Prepare HR-Related Documents

In most organizations, there is a schedule for generating standard reports and charts. For example, reports, presentations, and organizational charts. Some are done monthly, some are done quarterly, and others are due on an annual basis. Monthly reports can include the number of job requisitions filled and the length of time they were open. The number of people placed in training slots for essential training programs can also be a monthly report requirement. Quarterly, you may find a need to generate reports on expenses versus budget allocations. There can also be reports required for employee participation rates in benefit programs such as health coverage and life insurance programs. Annually, most organizations have an overall review of their financial performance, which is back to expenses vs. budget.

In some organizations, the HR department bills internal clients for services performed related to HR activities, including recruiting, candidate screening, onboarding, initial training, exit interviews, benefit program reviews, and employee engagement in other programs offered by the employer. There will always be opportunities to practice your skills at report writing.

In the Trenches

aPHR Task #6

HR professionals often face challenges being pigeonholed into a certain stereotype. Being good at working with people does not always translate to technical and financial savvy. Thankfully, this means we have an opportunity to change

(Continued)

that mind-set. Early in my career, I took it upon myself to create a thorough analysis of our benefits plan, including reports and every macro I could Google about in Excel. My boss was so impressed that I was promoted to oversee the finance function. This was an unexpected result from a bit of hard work. Don't be afraid to go the extra mile on this task.

–CN

Task #7—Provide Internal Customer Service by Answering or Referring HR-Related Questions from Employees as the First Level of Support

What better way to learn what to do and how to do it than to do it in a real-world setting? This is the time in your professional career when you will have the opportunity to learn not only the technical skills of HR but also the best personal skills of HR. It is often said that HR, in its best form, can be a "bridge" between an organization's management and its workers, but this doesn't happen by magic. It happens by being where "the rubber hits the road" and using your role of providing first-level support to others in the organization in a way that can only be described as a win-win for everyone.

In the Trenches

aPHR Task #7

Many of us begin a career in human resources because we love helping others. And in this day and age, it is a rarity to resolve a service concern by speaking to an actual person. In HR, we provide service to the most important customer at an organization: its employees and its management. Even if you are not able to answer an employee's question, taking the time to refer the employee to the appropriate party and following up is so appreciated by the workforce. Remember, *human* is the first word in our chosen function, and we should fully embrace the responsibility to be a helpful advocate and voice of balanced reason for the organization we work for.

–CN

Task #8—Communicate Information About HR Policies and Procedures

Effective HR organizations will review their HR policies and procedures each year. In coordination with legal counsel and with input from operations managers, the HR organization is responsible for updating and then publishing the new policies emerging from this process. Once the policies are published, as individual documents or part of an employee handbook or policy manual, it is incumbent on HR professionals to distribute the new policies to employees. As an entry-level professional, you will likely find this responsibility falls to you. Questions must be answered prior to distribution. Will employees be asked to sign a receipt for the updated policies? When will the policies become effective? Will the policy be distributed or simply included by reference in a letter, memo, or e-mail to all employees?

You will probably be asked to draft the letter to employees once more senior management people have provided answers to these questions. Identify the preferred writing style your company uses and craft your letter in that style.

As you gain experience, you may be asked to create procedural statements. Procedures include tasks such as updating employee name changes, registering benefit selections, altering payroll documents (e.g., W-4s), and updating employee data in the HRIS. You can find yourself involved in all of these tasks at some time in your early career.

In the Trenches

aPHR Task #8

One of my first responsibilities in a "real" HR job was developing a policy and procedure manual. I walked out of my first meeting with a list of acronyms to be included, and I did not know what most of them meant. Fast-forward to several days on the Internet educating myself, and I quickly learned that this was more than a work task. I was getting the opportunity to shape the organizational culture and be involved in important decisions about how we would operate as a company. Even the slightest differentiation in how you write an appearance policy can shape your organization. Will there be uniforms? Do we allow tattoos? How should hair be styled? How are we communicating this procedure?

–CN

Task #9—Communicate the Organization's Core Values, Vision, Mission, Culture, and Ethical Behaviors

When you join an organization, specifically in the functions of HR and management, you assume a role model position wherein you support and pontificate the organization's core values, vision, mission, culture, and ethics. You "walk the talk" as your activities and communications align with the defined ethical behaviors and desired culture. Your actions will demonstrate the core values that drive the organization's mission and point it in the direction of its desired future, its vision.

Most organizations have a deeper meaning as to why they exist—that is their mission. Their mission will influence decision-making and behaviors desired at all level of employees, but it isn't well articulated throughout the rank and file. That's where HR comes in as a key contributor with employee communications, establishing a relevance with employees in a way that makes them care about the organization's reason for existing (mission) and what their aspiration is to become (vision). It will be at the core of *all* of your HR communications: simple, redundant, and inspiring messages that always link to mission, ethics, values, and vision. Specific messages linked to mission and vision become tools to help employees connect their day-to-day efforts with the strategies of the company.

Walking the talk in the role of the HR professional will include demonstrating and behaving in alignment with the expressed core values and ethics of the organization. It often requires an HR professional to increase their behavior a notch higher with their actions to demonstrate what is expected of others in the workforce. So if an organization has defined one of its core values to be having high respect for the customer and its employees, gossiping about peers in or outside of a work setting would be the opposite of walking the talk.

The communication of mission, vision, core values, and ethical standards of behavior, along with describing the culture of the organization, will be one of the main objectives in the role of recruiting and on-boarding new hires.

In the Trenches

aPHR Task #9

As the first-born child in a Sicilian family, I have always taken great pride in leading by example. This might explain the glee with which I create these "In the Trenches" for you. The task of communicating core values, vision, mission, culture, and ethical behaviors allows you to breathe life into an organization. Helping others understand the organization is the foundation for developing the employee culture and communicating that culture to the outside world. You also have the opportunity to be a leader on the HR team and within the organization by setting the example for fundamental values and behaviors.

–CN

Task #10—Identify Risk in the Workplace

Risk comes in many forms. There are safety risks, financial risks, image risks, and health risks. You may be asked to perform surveys to identify the specific types of risks in your workplace. Occupational Safety and Health Administration (OSHA) reviews will be necessary as part of the compliance requirements of federal safety law. Depending on your industry, you may have to deal with specific requirements such as bloodborne pathogens and needlesticks. General safety provisions can be identified in a survey form. You may be asked to create or update this form for your organization and then to actually perform the survey. Depending on the size of your organization and the type of workplace you have (e.g., industrial, warehouse, office, or moving work location such as a fishing boat), the survey can take from a few minutes to several days.

Risk identification is important because you must know what risks you face before you can begin to identify ways to eliminate them. You may be required to review your survey results with a safety committee, task force, or upper management. Then you may be asked to document discussions about risk resolution and participate in the implementation of action plans chosen.

In the Trenches

aPHR Task #10

Safety and risk management are deeply connected to other HR functions. For example, serving on the safety committee can generate additional knowledge on employee relations issues, training needs, or ergonomics concerns in the workplace you may have not otherwise been aware of. Even if this task is not assigned to you, be mindful of its importance. Volunteering to serve on a safety committee can help you gain a great deal of insight into the workplace and allow you to spearhead new and exciting initiatives to help the organization.

–CN

Task #11—Minimize Risk by Conducting Audits

Things that get audited in human resource systems can include Form I-9s, workers' compensation records, employee compensation history, and employee records such as the Human Resource Information System (HRIS) or Human Resource Management System (HRMS). Beyond surveys of the workplace, audits of records can uncover risks to the organization. For example, Form I-9 is required of all new employees. Part of the form is completed by the new employee, and part of the form is completed by the employer. If there are errors or omissions on any one of those forms, the organization may be subject to financial penalties of up to $1000 each. While there are fewer I-9 reviews by government agencies these days, it is still possible. Being sure each form is accurately completed is really important.

Workers' compensation records are also important. They must be kept current (updated each time something changes in the case) and protected from disclosure to unauthorized individuals by storage in a secure facility (locked room, locked file drawer, password-protected computer file, etc.). Correspondence in workers' compensation cases is constantly developing; correspondence to employees, insurance carriers, and medical workers must be created and filed immediately upon receipt. Determine the chain of custody and approval your organization uses to process correspondence in these cases. Be sure you follow that chain religiously.

Employee records include a vast array of documentation. The HRIS usually includes information such as name, home address, job title, hire date, job date, performance evaluation rating, training program participation, EEO-1 race or ethnicity, gender identification, department, educational background, and professional certification or licenses. That just touches on the obvious data fields. Some HRIS databases contain only current information. Others contain data history going back to the original employee hire date. Sometimes employees can update their own data records using personal passwords for access. Other times HR is expected to maintain the database. Even when employees update their own information, HR is usually responsible for maintaining the access audit trail and individual password issuance. You will find these duties included in your job list.

In the Trenches

aPHR Task #11

For most people, the word *audit* does not trigger a sense of excitement. However, audits can be extremely valuable. A few years ago, it was time to conduct an audit of our new payroll system to ensure that direct deposit information was entered correctly. After reviewing several records, I learned that zeros in all bank account numbers were not being captured in the system. It was Thursday evening, and this meant that most employees were not going to receive their paycheck on time, resulting in a host of problems. Audits are often recommended at a certain frequency. But when in doubt, audit! Accuracy is an incredibly important part of the HR function.

—CN

Task #12—Document and Update Essential Job Functions with Support of Managers

There are two tasks here. One involves job descriptions for your job, and the other involves job descriptions for other employees. Many employers are required to perform annual reviews of their job descriptions (e.g., federal contractors, both goods and services contractors, and construction contractors). The Americans with Disabilities Act and the Rehabilitation Act have brought employing people with disabilities into the mainstream. When essential job functions change, there may be need for a disability accommodation. You can be expected to keep the job descriptions current. That entails working with management or the supervisor of the job description being updated. It may mean working with incumbents in the job as well.

While no federal law currently requires job descriptions, they are advisable as a communication device and as a defense tool when the company is challenged about job accommodations. You can plan on being involved with this monitoring task.

In the Trenches

aPHR Task #12

The importance of job descriptions resides in many facets of human resources. This task is more than simply drafting a job description; it's about interacting with department heads and developing an accurate baseline for job performance. So often job descriptions lie dormant for years and don't accurately account for responsibilities, leading to recruiting, employee relations, compliance, and even safety challenges. Consider this task an important one and take the time to establish an accurate foundation for your peers in other HR disciplines.

–CN

Task #13—Post Job Listings

Job posting is one of the most frequently required tasks of an entry-level HR professional. Job posting announcements can be posted on a company's web site, on social media sites, or on Internet job boards. In larger organizations, employers will offer internal bidding wherein a job vacancy is posted first within the organization, allowing existing employees to apply for it. This way, an organization can capitalize on the investment it has made in recruiting from current employees and employee referrals. You might use an internal intranet job bidding board that is password protected and seen or accessed by the organization's current workforce. This gives current employees the chance to indicate interest in a position that they feel qualified for before it becomes available, say, in the example of an upcoming retirement.

A posting should provide a brief description of the job, including significant job duties and minimum qualifications, education, experience, and physical requirements.

Posting jobs externally is an important and creative process with the use of social media, Internet job boards, and governmental job sites. The opportunity to reach a qualified audience and to screen out applicants who do not meet the minimum qualifications has its advantages (i.e., assisting in employment branding of the organization to attract the talent it is seeking) and disadvantages (i.e., having an overabundance of applicants or missing out on potentially a cross-pollination of skills, experience, and talents of candidates due to the algorithms in the software system).

Task #14—Manage Applicant Databases

An applicant tracking system (ATS) is a database that keeps track of job applicants from the time they first apply to an organization for employment to the point when the position is filled and sometimes beyond. The database is used to enter data, access and update records, and search for and compile potential candidates for job openings as they occur. Most organizations will utilize an applicant database system software; smaller companies may use Microsoft Access or even just an Excel spreadsheet. The old adage "garbage in, garbage out" couldn't be more applicable than it is with applicant databases. Setting and monitoring the algorithms are important components when managing these systems. Not only do frequently changing laws impact the data that is kept and accessible, the sheer nature of changing employment environments requires that these databases are legally current.

Additionally, the organization's reputation can be at stake if the management of a database is not congruent or misaligned with the intentions of tracking and "courting" potential employees (i.e., sending the wrong e-mail that states "nothing at this time" because of a system coding glitch to a desired college recruit that the organization is courting who is awaiting their graduation).

Task #15—Screen Applicants for Managers to Interview

Frontline HR professionals are given the task of reviewing application forms and résumés to choose those applicants who meet the job specifications and desired candidate profile. This basic function of the recruiting process helps save the hiring manager a lot of time by using the HR professional to screen the pool of applicants. You may find yourself screening applicants via a phone conversation, an e-mail exchange, or a face-to-face interview to gain more clarification about their experience, qualifications, and fit for the job, along with providing some rudimentary information about the job/company.

These screening interviews are generally short: 15 to 30 minutes in length. Your assessment allows you to narrow the pool of candidates to be passed on to the hiring manager those candidates who best fit the job opening's requirements, providing them with a top tier of applicants to interview. You are known to the applicant as the "gatekeeper," in other words, the person to get by in order to reach the hiring manager.

A difficulty to be aware of in the screening processes is to know the pitfalls of interviewing, such as the halo effect. You can find out more information about effective interviewing techniques in Chapter 4, which will help you with the task of screening applicants.

Task #16—Answer Questions from Job Applicants

Typically as the first point of contact for an applicant, and the person who organizes the interviewing process, you will be known as the gatekeeper, the person who buffers the hiring manager. The importance of the impressions you leave with potential applicants, and those that are screened out, is vital to the organization's reputation. Know this important function of your job and remember that all impressions count, especially the first impression. Your organization could be vying for a pool of candidates in a highly competitive profession, or even a large number of seasonal workers that are needed by other organizations at the same time. Your ability to answer applicant questions and to be a good skilled communicator is an artful talent in HR.

At the same time, you must balance the best interests of the organization and the hiring manager by maintaining an ability to know what can and should not be discussed with an applicant. As an example, a job applicant for a mid- or high-level position may want to discuss salary. You should be clear on how to respond so as to not understate a range and avoid losing a sought after candidate. Anticipating what questions might be asked and rehearsing responses are a necessity as the gatekeeper. Coordinating the responses with the hiring manager to be in sync will also be helpful in your gatekeeper role.

In the Trenches

aPHR Task #16

You may not realize this now, but when an applicant speaks to an actual person, it is a big deal. If you have ever applied for a job, you probably know that you'll send many applications over the Internet, and the likelihood of a response is slim. Thus, simply being responsive to applicants can make your company a desirable place to work. People appreciate this humanistic approach to recruiting. Even if you can't answer all the questions an applicant may ask, word will spread quickly that your company cares about its people.

–CN

Task #17—Coordinate Interview Logistics

Although coordinating the interview logistics for the hiring manager and the potential candidates may at first seem to be a function of an administrative assistant, it is much more than just coordinating calendars. For the HR professional, it will involve the review and possibly the preparation of interview questions that the hiring manager will use, ensuring that compliance with legalities and pitfalls of interviewing techniques are avoided. Many times it will most likely involve group interviewing and perhaps even mentoring a supervisor who has had no experience with hiring or interviewing.

Task #18—Interview Job Candidates

In several instances, the interviewing of job applicants and the selection of new employees may be a responsibility of the early-career HR professional. Such will be the case with many organizations that use field HR representatives, such as the retail industry, or when there is a cyclical seasonal workforce such as a distribution center or manufacturing facility that hires temporary workers.

Learning and understanding effective interviewing and selection techniques, as Chapter 4 explains, will be essential for being successful with this task.

In the Trenches

aPHR Task #18

From "Tell me a bit about your work history" to "What song would you choose to make a grand entrance to in front of your co-workers," interview styles can be extremely different. There are always innovations in interview techniques, and undertaking this task provides an opportunity to do some research and find the best technique for your organization. Behavioral interviews can shed a great deal of insight on an applicant's fit for a position. While interviews should always comply with legal requirements, there is an opportunity to develop some helpful tools for an organization through a bit of research and creativity.

–CN

Task #19—Arrange for Tests and Assessments of Applicants

Assessments and tests are used to determine the knowledge and skills that have been identified as essential for a job. A typical job applicant assessment may involve the completion of a created standard test that is given to all applicants to ensure they can demonstrate the skills/knowledge needed. This is common when hiring IT programmers and in the skills trade occupations. Even professional occupations have gravitated to assessments, including HR.

The HR professional may arrange for these prescreening assessments in a controlled environment (not allowing smart phones, for example), with time frames imposed, or may set them up with a third-party testing center. To ensure a successful assessment and test of applicants, it's important they are prepared for the experience and expectations are clearly communicated as to what they will be tested/assessed on.

In the Trenches

aPHR Task #19

The budding psychologist in all of us can rise to the occasion on this task. In this day and age, there is so much more to the hiring process than an interview. There are an array of tests and assessments available that can uncover certain behaviors and predict potential success in certain positions. While you may only start by arranging appointments, you will ultimately have the opportunity to see the results of these tests and the insight they can provide, arming you with additional knowledge that can be applied in the future.

–CN

Task #20—Coordinate the Employment Offer

The interviews have been concluded, the references have been checked, and the assessment or employment tests are in. The hiring decision has been made, and it's time to extend a job offer. Communicating the job offer, which would include start date, salary, benefits, etc., is typically the next step handled, and in most larger organizations, that responsibility belongs to the HR department. The reason that HR would handle the job offer is to ensure again that legality issues are not breached (such as can happen when a hiring manager states, "You will have a job for life in our company") and to be the first line of negotiation representing the organization (such as salary negotiation). Having a checklist of vital information to offer is always recommended and helpful, including the desired start date, the offered salary, the benefits package, and any perks, official job title, etc.). Normally the more senior-level position offerings will be handled by the senior HR leader or even the senior management of the organization and may include employment contracts. You can fully expect to be making job offers to nonexempt position candidates. Offer letters should be approved and immediately prepared upon acceptance of the verbal offer for the candidate.

Task #21—Administer Post-Offer Employment Activities

When the offer has been accepted by the selected candidate, the transition from candidate to employee now begins. Employment relationships in many U.S. states are subject to the law of *employment at will,* meaning that the relationship can be ended at any time by either party, with or without a reason (more information is noted in Chapter 2 and Chapter 7). As a result, few employees will be working under an employment contract agreement. Executives, who are often key contributors, are typically the type of employee that would fall in that category.

Post-offer employment activities will include the execution of employment agreements, completing required tax and government forms, relocation to the job site, and perhaps immigration visas. At this stage, the newly hired employee forms their first impression of what it will be like in the company. Your activities will have a spotlight shining on them, so remember, first impressions count. Get it right, make it professional, and be the example of the culture of your company.

Task #22—Communicate Compensation and Benefits Programs and Systems

In Chapter 4, you learned the many aspects of compensation and benefits that legally require effective communication and understanding. As a "total rewards program," compensation and benefits uniquely require complete understanding on the part of the organization's workers and management. The importance of excellent two-way communications comes not only from the law, which it does in many cases, but also from the moral responsibility to fully inform management and workers of their benefit entitlement obligations as well as their benefits.

Task #23—Coordinate Activities to Support Employee Benefits Programs

As an entry-level HR professional, you will have the opportunity to learn and support many benefit programs in your organization. For example, wellness and retirement planning programs. You may be tasked to help workers understand their Social Security benefits as well as their Medicare benefits Parts A, B, and D, as part of your real-world learning process. You may also be asked to answer basic questions about unemployment insurance, workers' compensation, the Consolidated Omnibus Budget Reconciliation Act (COBRA), the Health Insurance Portability and Accountability Act (HIPAA), and the Family and Medical Leave Act (FMLA). While you won't be expected to be an expert, you will be expected to be able to help or direct a worker with a benefits question to a knowledgeable resource as part of your organization's HR team. This means you need to have some basic knowledge and understanding to be able to provide at least some basic information regarding these programs.

Other benefits that you need to know with at least a basic threshold of knowledge include state versions of family and medical leave laws in states where these laws apply. Other benefit programs that are a "need to know," at least at a basic level for the entry-level

HR professional, include healthcare benefits, consumer-driven healthcare, retirement benefits, wellness programs, and the basic purpose of the Employee Retirement Income Security Act (ERISA).

In the Trenches

aPHR Task #23

Ultimately, the value you place in your organization's benefits program tells your employees how much you value them. Benefits are a key driver for recruiting and retaining top performers. While not every organization has the ability to provide the richest benefits plan, being creative with this task will go further than you think. Take the time to understand your workforce and what is important to them. Oftentimes, there are free or low-cost ways to add great value to your benefits plan. Talk to your benefits broker about programs that you may be underutilizing, such as your employee assistance program or wellness program. I've learned that it is also important to talk to your employees to find out what is important to them. Soliciting feedback can be a great way to launch a popular program at the office and engage willing participants in the process.

–CN

Task #24—Coordinate Payroll-Related Information

Many payroll activities are related to HR issues, for example, new hire forms, pay adjustments, paid time off, and terminations. This requires the payroll and HR departments to coordinate shared functions. As a junior member of this team, you will be expected to work closely with payroll in support of your organization's recruitment, processing pay increases and benefit deductions, handling paid time off and vacation leaves, and doing the paperwork needed to process employment terminations, both voluntary and involuntary. The HR department must be sensitive to the time devoted to payroll processing because as the champion of employee relations, they'll face issues directly if paychecks aren't processed correctly and on time. The payroll and HR departments are privy to confidential employee data, including financial information, Social Security numbers, and home addresses. The two departments must work together to ensure that this information doesn't fall prey to unauthorized individuals or companies.

Payroll functions are covered by either the finance department or the HR department in most organizations.[1] Essentially, payroll is number driven and calls for knowledge of tax laws and accounting. Because of this, many respondents believe that payroll should be positioned with the finance department. At the same time, payroll is considered a function of HR because it pays and deals with people. The HR side is that the company must preserve the employee's rights and abide by federal and state anti-discrimination and maternity laws. At the same time, the employee must receive compensation, a finance function, in accordance with the company's policies.

Task #25—Process Claims from Employees

The primary function of HR is to ensure the company complies with federal and state labor and employment laws, such as Title VII of the Civil Rights Act of 1964 and the Occupational Safety and Health Act of 1970. Employees are the HR department's internal customers; therefore, HR's obligation to serve its internal customers is another function of the department. Within those two areas—compliance and customer service—the core responsibilities of HR include transactional and functional activities, such as establishing compensation structure, addressing employee relations matters, recruiting qualified applicants, maintaining workplace safety, and processing workers' compensation and short-term and long-term disability benefits where they apply.

Task #26—Resolve Routine Employee Compensation and Benefits Issues

HR generalists often work on compensation and benefits issues with guidance and direction from compensation and benefits specialists. In larger organizations, HR generalists often receive guidance from internal, and sometimes external, compensation and benefits specialists to develop strategic compensation plans, align performance management systems with the organization's compensation structure, and monitor negotiations for group healthcare benefits. Examples of HR generalist responsibilities include addressing and resolving routine compensation and benefits issues, monitoring Family and Medical Leave Act compliance, and adhering to confidentiality provisions for employee medical files.

HR generalists for small companies might also conduct open enrollment for employees' annual elections pertaining to healthcare coverage. This team approach provides the organization with the technical expertise it needs while it benefits junior-level HR generalists through their exposure to HR strategic responsibilities.

Task #27—Conduct Orientation and On-boarding for New Hires, Rehires, and Transfers

An HR generalist is a key person within the human resources function of an organization. Principally, the HR generalist is responsible for the day-to-day management of HR operations, which means they manage the administration of the organization's employment-related policies, procedures, and programs. HR generalists are almost universally responsible for recruiting, screening, interviewing, and recommending the selection of job candidates. They may also handle employee relations, payroll, and benefits and training. In many organizations, the work of an HR generalist is often administratively focused in nature and involves documenting grievances, terminations, absences, performance reports, and compensation and benefits information.

Task #28—Coordinate Training Sessions

Training embodies a wide range of topics. In human resource management terms it can include logistics, materials, training record tracking, training registration, and training evaluation. Employee training can be conducted in-house or by an outside provider. Keeping records of what training experiences each employee has had will likely be your responsibility. But this task goes beyond recordkeeping.

You will probably be asked to provide administrative support to in-house training programs, particularly those related to HR topics. You may even be asked to conduct some of that training. Think about all that is required for a training program to be successful. There is more to training success than having an instructor competent in the subject matter: all of the registration functions (seat reservations and check-in), facility reservations (training room), audio/visual (AV) equipment reservations and testing for operability, reproduction of training materials, recording the names of people who actually attend the program, ordering refreshments and food if appropriate, and collecting and summarizing program evaluation forms. To successfully complete this task, you will need to develop a checklist of duties that are required for each training program. Using it to prepare for and then document all that happened in each program is important.

It is not uncommon for employees to attend outside training programs. You will need to keep records about who went to which training program. In addition, you may even be asked to research the training programs available for a specific application. That will mean surveying outside vendors for a program that will meet the needs of your staff.

Training is a necessary component of many certification, recertification, and licensing requirements. Recertification for the aPHR designation requires continuing education in the HR profession. You will probably be required to keep records for all of those requirements if the employees are not responsible for maintaining their own documentation.

In the Trenches

aPHR Task #28

As a human resource professional, training is your friend. Everyone can benefit from growth and development, and helping with this task can be rewarding. Additionally, having a pulse of the overall training function at your organization can be helpful in your position. Whenever the day-to-day HR concerns walk through your door, ask yourself, how can training make this situation better? Do we need better supervisory training? Are all employees struggling with understanding the same policy? Training sessions can be the foundation for resolving many of the challenges in the workplace.

–CN

Task #29—Conduct Employee Training Programs

As a new HR professional you may be asked to conduct training for employees on topics such as safety regulations, emergency preparedness, presentation skills, and time management. Safety programs involve identifying safety and health hazards in the workplace, protecting workers from those hazards, and eliminating the hazards as quickly as possible. Your company will have its own documentation requirements, alert notification chain, and resolution monitors. In the absence of a dedicated safety manager, you can be asked to fill these roles. A key training requirement is the annual delivery of the emergency evacuation plan. Including workplace violence (everything from verbal assault to assault with an automatic rifle), employees must understand how to evacuate the building and where to assemble so they can be counted. It is necessary to impress upon employees the importance of identifying anyone left in the facility so rescue can be planned. Typical tragedies include workplace violence, earthquake, fire, flood, and wind storms (tornado or hurricane). You can expect to be responsible for conducting practice evacuations periodically.

Communication skills often fall within the purview of the HR department. That includes written communication training. (What is the company style? What memo and letter formats must be used? How should forms be completed?) It also includes oral communication training that can range from one-on-one conversations to group presentations from the podium. You should expect to be in the spotlight if you are going to be an HR professional.

Time management is a common training topic. There are some folks who grow up not knowing how to manage their own time. Setting priorities, asking for input about priorities, and building action plans based on priorities are all components of time management. You can become the expert on the topic and share that expertise with your employee population.

In the Trenches

aPHR Task #29

For many, it is an unfortunate reality that public speaking is frightening. Even after working in HR for several years, the hairs on my neck stand up when I have to conduct a presentation in a meeting. One of my favorite quotes from Eleanor Roosevelt is "Do one thing every day that scares you." So use this opportunity to grow! Communication is a critical component of being a good HR professional, and honing these skills can lead to growth and success in many areas. The organization will look to HR to drive the communication program for the company and its people. Smile and take on this task with pride. It will take you further than you realize.

–CN

Task #30—Coordinate the Logistics for Employee Relations Programs

The employee relations function is, by pure definition, focused on relationships in the workplace—how employees interact with each other and management, how they feel about the work they perform and the conditions they perform their job in, and whether they feel treated fairly and with respect. Creating and administering programs associated with employee relations is a big chunk of the early-career HR professional's responsibility. Examples of ER programs include service and performance recognition programs, special events like bringing your child to work day, and various diversity programs.

You may find yourself in the role of an event coordinator, organizing special functions that align with the company's culture, values, and celebrations. You could find yourself in the role of the birthday and anniversary fairy, bestowing upon employees the recognition of their special day. Ensuring that milestones such as years-of-service anniversaries and recognition awards are timely typically begins within the HR function—"the keeper of the information/dates." Logistics will typically involve negotiating purchases of service awards, securing special recognition treats such as gift cards, or choosing the location of events such as the annual holiday bash. These are important tasks where you get to use creativity, imagination, ingenuity, and resourcefulness.

In the Trenches

aPHR Task #30

When you spend most of your waking hours with the same group of people, everyone desires to feel included and appreciated. In employee relations, we get to create programs that show the workforce how much we appreciate them, but we often become involved in challenging interpersonal situations as well. When an employee comes to you with a concern, oftentimes it matters most that you listen and help to provide a solution. There have been countless times where I have resolved an issue between two employees simply by listening to concerns and remaining diligent on follow-up. It's easy to do and shows how much you respect and value the employees at your organization.

–CN

Task #31—Monitor Completion of Performance Reviews and Development Plans

The importance of performance management as an ongoing process of providing developmental feedback to employees about their performance and expectations for new performance will continue to be an ongoing process for organizations. It's the core to creating continuing growth and expansion for both the employee and the company.

A key element of these programs is the monitoring and consistency of ensuring they occur timely and fairly. In early-level HR professional roles, the role of ensuring that supervisors follow through with their responsibilities to conduct performance reviews and set out training and development plans for their employees can be daunting, almost nagging in some instances. Yet meaningful feedback and recognition, along with clear goals and expectations, are what employees request more often than not. There will be software systems, much like applicant tracking systems, that will assist you with this tracking function; use them to the full extent possible in keeping supervisors on track and compliant.

In the Trenches

aPHR Task #31

This task might not win you the popularity contest, but it is an important part of our role in HR. Historically, managers and employees are engaged at different levels in the performance review process. This typically means a lot of hand-holding for HR professionals. Communicate deadlines early and often! It is also important to make sure that reviews are inclusive of the whole monitoring period and not biased. Don't be afraid to provide feedback to managers if they are being challenged with the process.

–CN

Chapter Review

The aPHR exam is a knowledge-based exam. Candidates are responsible for knowing and understanding the six knowledge areas that were set forth in Chapters 3 through 8. The 31 tasks in this chapter are typical assignments and functions that HRCI has identified an individual would likely be expected to perform, and know, at the early HR career level. Again, they will not be part of the exam; however, they are an important basis for knowing what to expect in an entry-level HR professional job.

Endnote

1. Deloitte's 2011 Payroll Operations Survey: 42 percent of companies surveyed reported that payroll was a function of their finance departments, and 40 percent said that payroll was a function of their HR departments.

PART III

Appendixes

List of Common HR Acronyms

AA	1) Affirmative Action; 2) Adverse Action
AACU	American Association of Colleges and Universities
AAO	Affirmative Action Officer
AAP	Affirmative Action Plan
AAR	Average Annual Return
ABF	Asset-Based Financing
ABM	Activity-Based Management
ABMS	Activity-Based Management System
ACA	Affordable Care Act
ACH	Automated Clearing House
AD&D	Accidental Death and Dismemberment
ADA	Americans with Disabilities Act
ADAAA	Americans with Disabilities Act Amendments Act
ADEA	Age Discrimination in Employment Act
ADL	Activities of Daily Living
ADP	Automatic Data Processing
ADR	Alternative Dispute Resolution
AFL-CIO	American Federation of Labor and Congress of Industrial Organizations
AFSCME	American Federation of State, County, and Municipal Employers
AI	Appreciative Inquiry
AIDS	Acquired Immune Deficiency Syndrome
AJB	America's Job Bank
ALC	Alien Labor Certification
ALEX	Automated Labor Exchange
ALJ	Administrative Law Judge
ALM	Asset Liability Management
AMPS	Auction Market Preferred Stock

ANSI	American National Standards Institute
AP	Accounts Payable
APA	American Psychological Association
APB	Accounting Principles Board
aPHR	Associate Professional in Human Resources
APR	Annual Percentage Rate
APV	Adjusted Present Value
APY	Annual Percentage Yield
AR	Accounts Receivable
ARRA	American Recovery and Reinvestment Act
ASB	Accounting Standards Board
ASHHRA	American Society for Healthcare Human Resources Administration
ASO	Administrative Services Only Plan
ASTD	American Society for Training and Development
ATB	Across the Board
ATO	1) Administrative Time Off; 2) Asset Turnover
ATOI	After Tax Operating Income
ATU	Annual Tax Unit
AWL	Actual Wage Loss
AWOL	Absent Without Leave
AWW	Average Weekly Wage
BARS	Behaviorally Anchored Rating Scale
BAT	Bureau of Apprenticeship and Training
BB	Base Benefits
BCP	Business Continuity Plan
BCR	Benefit/Cost Ratio
BIA	Business Impact Analysis
BFOQ or BOQ	Bona Fide Occupational Qualification
BLBA	Black Lunch Benefits Act
BLS	Bureau of Labor Statistics
BNA	Bureau of National Affairs
BOD	Board of Directors
BOT	Board of Trustees
BPA	Blanket Purchase Agreement
BRB	Benefit Review Board
BU	Bargaining Unit
C&B	Compensation and Benefits
C&P	Compensation and Pension
CAA	Congressional Accountability Act
CAFTA	Central American Free Trade Agreement

CAI	Computer Assisted Instruction
CAO	Chief Administrative Officer
CAPEX	Capital Expenditures
CASB	Cost Accounting Standards Board
CBA	Controlled Business Arrangement
CBO	Congressional Budget Office
CBP	Cafeteria Benefit Plan
CBT	Computer-Based Testing
CC	Civil Code
CCH	Commerce Clearing House
CCHR	Canadian Council on Human Resources
CCI	Consumer Confidence Index
CCL	Center for Creative Leadership
CCP	Certified Compensation Professional
CCPA	Consumer Credit Protection Act
CDC	Center for Disease Control
CDL	Commercial Driver's License
CEA	1) Commodity Exchange Authority; 2) Certificate of Educational Achievement
CEBS	Certified Employee Benefits Specialist
CEO	Chief Executive Officer
CEPS	Cash Earnings Per Share
CEU	Continuing Education Unit
CFAT	Cash Flow After Taxes
CFO	Chief Financial/Fiscal Officer
CFR	Code of Federal Regulations
CGQ	Corporate Governance Quotient
CGT	Capital Gains Tax
CHRC	1) Canadian Human Rights Commission; 2) Criminal History Records Check
CHRO	Chief Human Resources Officer
CIO	1) Chief Investment Officer; 2) Chief Information Officer
CISO	Chief Information Security Officer
CMO	Chief Marketing Officer
CO	Compliance Officer
COB	Close of Business
COBRA	Consolidated Omnibus Budget Reconciliation Act
COL	Cost of Living
COLA	Cost of Living Adjustment
COO	Chief Operating/Operations Officer

CPA	Certified Public Accountant
CPE	Continuing Professional Education
CPG	Consumer Packaged Goods
CPHR	California Professional in Human Resources Certification
CPI	Consumer Price Index
CPI-U	Consumer Price Index for All Urban Consumers
CPI-W	Consumer Price Index for Urban Wage Earners and Clerical Workers
CPM	Critical Path Method
CR	Corporate Responsibility
CRM	1) Client Relationship Management; 2) Customer Relationship Management; 3) Credit Risk Management
CROGI	Cash Return on Gross Investment
CSHO	Compliance Safety and Health Officer
CSO	Chief Security Officer
CTO	Compensatory Time Off
CTS	Carpal Tunnel Syndrome
CUPA	College and University Personnel Association
CUSFTA	Canada-U.S. Free Trade Agreement
CV	Curriculum Vitae
CWHSSA	Contract Work Hours and Safety Standards Act
CWSP	College Work-Study Program
D&I	Diversity and Inclusion
D&O	Directors and Officers
DB	Defined Benefit
DBA	1) Davis-Bacon Act; 2) Doing Business As
DBPP	Defined Benefit Pension Plan
DC	Defined Contribution
DCA	Dollar Cost Averaging
DCAA	Defense Contract Audit Agency
DCF	Discounted Cash Flow
DCPP	Defined Contribution Pension Plan
DCAP	Dependent Care Assistance Program
DEFRA	Deficit Reduction Act
DFA	Department of Finance and Administration
DFEH	Department of Fair Employment and Housing
DINKS	Dual Income No Kids
DJIA	Dow Jones Industrial Average
DMADV	Define, Measure, Analyze, Design, Verify
DMAIC	Define, Measure, Analyze, Improve, Control
DRIP	Dividend Reinvestment Plan

DRP	Disaster Recovery Plan
DSI	Discretionary Salary Increase
DSPP	Direct Stock Purchase Plan
DOB	Date of Birth
DOC	United States Department of Commerce
DOD	United States Department of Defense
DOH	Date of Hire
DOI	Date of Injury
DOJ	United States Department of Justice
DOL	United States Department of Labor
DOLETA	Department of Labor Employment and Training Administration
DOT	1) Dictionary of Occupational Titles; 2) United States Department of Transportation
DTI	Department of Trade and Industry
DVOP	Disabled Veterans Outreach Program
DW	Dislocated Worker
DWC	Division of Workers' Compensation
E-VERIFY	United States Department of Labor New Hire Screening System
EAC	Employee Advisory Committee/Council
EAP	Employee Assistance Program
EAPA	Employee Assistance Professionals Association
EB	Extended Benefits
EBO	Employee Buyout
EBRI	Employee Benefits Research Institute
EBS	Employee Benefits Security
EBSA	Employee Benefit Security Administration
EBT	Earnings Before Tax
ECI	Employment Cost Index
ECOA	Equal Credit Opportunity Act
ECPA	Electronic Communications Privacy Act
EDA	Economically Depressed Area
EDI	Electronic Data Interchange
EDP	1) Electronic Data Processing; 2) Employee Development Plan
EE	Employee
EEO	Equal Employment Opportunity
EEO-1/EEO-4	EEO-1 or EEO-4 Report/Standard Form 100 Report
EEOC	Equal Employment Opportunity Commission
EEOICPA	Energy Employee Occupational Illness Compensation Program Act
EFT	Electronic Funds Transfer
EFTA	European Free Trade Area

PART III

EGTRRA	Economic Growth and Tax Relief Reconciliation Act
EI or EQ	Emotional Intelligence
EIC	Earned Income Tax Credit
EIN	Employer Identification Number
EMT	Executive Management Team
EO	Executive Order
EOB	Explanation of Benefits
EOD	End of Day
EOI	Evidence of Insurability
EOY	End of Year
EPA	1) Equal Pay Act; 2) Environmental Protection Agency
EPLI	Employment Practices Liability Insurance
EPPA	Employee Polygraph Protection Act
EPS	Earnings per Share
ER	Employer
ERISA	Employee Retirement Income Security Act
ERTA	Economic Recovery Tax Act
ESA	Employment Standards Administration
ESL	English as a Second Language
ESO	Employee Stock Option
ESOP	Employee Stock Option Plan
ESOT	Employee Stock Ownership and Trust
ESP	Exchange Stock Portfolio
ESS	Employee Self-Service
ETA	1) Employment and Training Administration; 2) Estimated Time of Arrival
EU	European Union
EV	Enterprise Value
EVA	Economic Value Added
EVM	Earned Value Management
EX	Exempt
FAAS	Financial Assurance and Accountability Standards
FACT	Fair and Accurate Credit Transactions Act
FAQ	Frequently Asked Questions
FAS	Financial Accounting Standards
FASB	Financial Accounting Standards Board
FASAB	Financial Accounting Standards Advisory Board
FASAC	Financial Accounting Standards Advisory Committee
FASB	Financial Accounting Standards Board
FCC	Federal Communications Commission

FCCPA	Federal Consumer Credit Protection Act
FCPA	Foreign Corrupt Practices Act
FCRA	Fair Credit Reporting Act
FDA	Food and Drug Administration
FDCPA	Fair Debt Collection Practices Act
FDIC	Federal Deposit Insurance Corporation
FEA	Fair Employment Act
FECA	Federal Employees' Compensation Act
FEIN	Federal Employment Identification Number
FELA	Federal Employment Liability Act
FEMA	Federal Emergency Management Agency
FEP	Fair Employment Practice
FERS	Federal Employees Retirement System
FES	Factor Evaluation System
FFY	Federal Fiscal Year
FHA	Federal Housing Administration
FICA	Federal Insurance Contributions Act
FICO	Fair Isaac Credit Organization
FIE	Foreign Invested Enterprise
FIFO	First In, First Out
FLC	Foreign Labor Certification
FLRA	Federal Labor Relations Authority
FLSA	Fair Labor Standards Act
FMLA	Family Medical Leave Act
FMSHA	Federal Mine and Safety Health Act
FMV	Fair Market Value
FOIA	Freedom of Information Act
FOM	Field Operations Manual
FOREX	Foreign Exchange
FR	Federal Register
FRA	Federal Reserve Act
FRB	Federal Reserve Board
FROI	First Report of Injury
FRS	Financial Reporting Standards
FSA	Flexible Spending Account
FSB	Fortune Small Business
FSET	Federal State Employment Tax
FSLMRA	Federal Service Labor-Management Relations Act
FT	Full-Time
FTA	Free Trade Agreement

PART III

FTC	Federal Trade Commission
FTD	Federal Tax Deposit
FTE	Full Time Equivalent
FTP	File Transfer Protocol
FUA	Federal Unemployment Account
FUTA	Federal Unemployment Tax ACT
FY	Fiscal Year
GAAC	Government Accounting and Auditing Committee
GAAFR	Governmental Accounting, Auditing, and Financial Reporting
GAAP	Generally Accepted Accounting Principles
GAAS	Generally Accepted Auditing Standards
GAGAS	Generally Accepted Government Accounting Standards
GAO	General Accounting Office
GAS	Governmental Accounting Standards
GASB	Governmental Accounting Standards Board
GATB	General Aptitude Test Battery
GATT	General Agreement on Tariffs and Trade
GDP	Gross Domestic Product
GED	General Equivalency Diploma
GIC	Guaranteed Investment Contract
GICS	Global Industry Classification Standards
GIF	Guaranteed Investment Fund
GINA	Genetic Information Nondiscrimination Act
GIPS	Global Investment Policy Standard
GIS	Geographic Information System
GL	1) General Ledger; 2) General Liability
GLB	Gramm-Leach-Bliley Act
GLSO	Group Legal Services Organization
GM	Gross Margin
GNP	Gross National Product
GPHR	Global Professional in Human Resources Certification
GPROI	Gross Profit Return on Investment
GPS	Global Positioning System
GR	General Revenue
GS	General Schedule
GSI	General Salary Increase
GTL	Group Term Life Insurance
HAS	Highest Average Salary
HAZMAT	Hazardous Material
HB	House Bill

HC	Human Capital
HCE	Highly Compensated Employee
HCFA	Health Care Financing Administration
HCIP	Harmonized Index of Consumer Pricing
HCM	Human Capital Management
HCN	Home-Country Nationals
HCO	Health Care Organization
HCSA	Health Care Spending Account
HCTC	Health Coverage Tax Credit
HHS	Department of Health and Human Services
HIPC	Health Insurance Purchasing Cooperatives
HIPPA	Health Insurance Portability and Accountability Act
HITECH	Health Information Technology for Economic and Clinical Health Act
HIV	Human Immunodeficiency Virus
HMO	Health Maintenance Organizations
HR	Human Resources
HRA	Health Reimbursement Account
HRCI	Human Resource Certification Institute
HRCS	Human Resource Competency Study
HRD	1) Human Resources Development; 2) Human Resources Department
HRIS	Human Resources Information System
HRLY	Hourly
HRM	Human Resources Management
HRMS	Human Resource Management System
HROD	Human Resources and Organizational Development
HSA	Health Savings Account
HTML	Hypertext Markup Language
HUD	United States Department of Housing and Urban Development
I-9	United States Immigration Form I-9
IAG	International Auditing Guidelines
IAS	International Accounting Standards
IASC	International Accounting Standards Committee
ICC	International Chamber of Commerce
ICE	United States Immigration and Customs Enforcement
IFEBP	International Foundation of Employee Benefit Plans
IHRIM	International Association of Human Resource Information Management
IIPP	Injury and Illness Prevention Programs/Plans
ILAB	International Labor Affairs Bureau
ILO	International Labor Organization

PART III

IME	Independent Medical Examination
INA	Immigration and Naturalization Act
INS	Immigration and Naturalization Service
IOS	International Organization for Standards
IPA	Inflation Protected Annuity
IPI	Industrial Protection Index
IPMA	International Personnel Management Association
IPO	Initial Public Offering
IPS	1) Inflation Protected Security; 2) Investment Policy Statement
IRA	Individual Retirement Account
IRB	Internal Revenue Bulletin
IRC	Internal Revenue Code
IRCA	Immigration Reform and Control Act
IRR	Internal Rate of Return
IRS	Internal Revenue Service
ISO	1) International Standards Organization; 2) Incentive Stock Option
ISP	Internet Service Provider
ISSA	International Securities Services Association
IT	Information Technology
ITA	United States International Trade Administration
ITIN	Individual Taxpayer Identification Number
IUR	Insured Unemployment Rates
IVR	Interactive Voice Response
J&S	Joint and Survivorship
JAN	Job Accommodation Network
JD	1) Job Description; 2) Juris Doctorate; 3) Job Date
JGTRRA	Jobs and Growth Tax Relief Reconciliation Act
JEEP	Joint Ethics Enforcement Plan
JIT	Just in Time
JOA	Joint Operating Agreement
JPAC	Joint Public Advisory Committee
JPEG	Joint Photographic Experts Group
JSSA	Jury Selection and Service Act
JTPA	Job Training Partnership Act (replaced by WIA)
JV	Joint Venture
JVA	Jobs for Veterans Act
KM	Knowledge Management
KPI	Key Performance Indicator
KSA	Knowledge, Skills, or Abilities
KSOP	401(k) Employee Stock Option Plan

LA	Labor Area
LAN	Local Area Network
LAR	Legislative Appropriations Request
LAUS	Local Area Unemployment Statistics
LBB	Legislative Budget Board
LBO	Leveraged Buyout
LCA	Labor Condition Application
LCD	Labor Cost Distribution
LDI	Liability-Driven Investment
LDP	Last Day Paid
LDW	Last Day Worked
LEI	Leading Economic Indicators
LEO	Long-Term Equity Options
LEPO	Low Exercise Price Option
LF	Labor Force
LFPR	Labor Force Participation Rate
LFY	Last Fiscal Year
LHWCA	Longshore and Harbor Workers' Compensation Act
LIFO	Last In, First Out
LLC	Limited Liability Company
LLP	Limited Liability Partnership
LMA	Labor Market Area
LMI	Labor Market Information
LMRA	Labor Management Relations Act
LMRDA	Labor-Management Reporting and Disclosure Act
LMS	Learning Management System
LO	Learning Objectives
LOA	Leave of Absence
LOC	Letter of Commitment
LOI	Letter of Intent
LOR	Letter of Response
LOS	Length of Stay
LOW	Lack of Work
LP	Limited Partnership
LR	Labor Relations
LRO	Labor Relations Officer
LT	Lost Time
LTC	Long-Term Care
LTCM	Long-Term Capital Management
LTD	Long-Term Disability

LTFP	Long-Term Financial Plan
LTIP	Long-Term Incentive Plan
LTO	Long-Term Option
LTV	Loan-to-Value Ratio
LWDI	Lost Work Day Injury Rate
LWO	Leave Without Pay
LWP	Leave with Pay
M&A	Merger and Acquisition
MBO	Management by Objectives
MBTI	Myers-Briggs Type Indicator
MER	Management Expense Ratio
MEWA	Multiple Employer Welfare Arrangement
MHAEA	Mental Health and Addiction Equity Act
MHPA	Mental Health Parity Act
MHPAEA	Mental Health Parity and Addiction Equity Act
MIRR	Modified Internal Rate of Return
MIS	Management Information System
MLA	Minimum Liquid Assets
MLM	Multilevel Marketing
MLP	Master Limited Partnership
MLR	Monthly Labor Review
MLS	Mass Layoff Statistics
MNC	Multinational Corporation
MOC	Market on Close
MOF	Ministry of Finance
MOU	Memorandum of Understanding
MPPAA	Multiemployer Pension Plan Amendments Act
MRD	Minimum Required Distribution
MSA	1) Medical Savings Account; 2) Metropolitan Statistical Area; 3) Merit Salary Adjustment
MSDS	Material Safety Data Sheet
MSFW	Migrant and Seasonal Farm Worker
MSHA	Mine Safety and Health Act
MSP	Managed Service Provider
MSPA	Migrant and Seasonal Agriculture Worker Protection Act
MSPB	Merit Systems Protection Board
MSPR	Medicare Secondary Payer Rules
MST	Marketable Securities Tax
MTD	Month to Date
MTHLY	Monthly

NAAEC	North American Agreement on Environmental Cooperation
NAALC	North American Agreement on Labor Cooperation
NAB	Nonaccrual Basis
NAFTA	North American Free Trade Agreement
NAFTA-TAA	NAFTA Transitional Adjustment Assistance
NAICS	North American Industry Classification System
NASDAQ	National Association of Securities Dealers Automated Quotations
NASDR	National Association of Securities Dealers Regulation
NATO	North Atlantic Treaty Organization
NAV	Net Asset Value
NAVPS	Net Asset Value Per Share
NAWW	National Average Weekly Wage
NCCI	National Council on Compensation Insurance
NDNH	National Directory of New Hires
NEO	New and Emerging Occupations
NEX	Nonexempt
NFA	Net Financial Assets
NFE	Net Financial Expense
NFI	Net Financial Income
NFO	Net Financial Obligations
NHCE	Non-Highly Compensated Employee
NI	Net Income
NIH	National Institute of Health
NIOSH	National Institute of Occupational Safety and Health
NL	No Load
NLRA	National Labor Relations Act
NLRB	National Labor Relations Board
NMB	National Mediation Board
NMHPA	Newborns' and Mothers' Health Protection Act
NMS	Normal Market Size
NOA	Net Operating Assets
NOI	Net Operating Income
NOL	Net Operating Loss
NOPAT	Net Operating Profit After Taxes
NPV	Net Present Value
NRA	Nonresident Alien
NRET	Nonresident Withholding Tax
NSC	National Security Council
NSTA	National Securities Trade Association
NSX	National Stock Exchange

PART III

NT	Near Term
NVI	Negative Volume Index
NYSE	New York Stock Exchange
O*Net	Occupational Information Network
OA	Operating Assets
OAS	Option Adjusted Spread
OASDHI	Old Age, Survivors, Disability, and Health Insurance
OASDI	Old Age and Survivors Disability Insurance
OASI	Old Age Survivors Insurance
OBRA	Omnibus Budget Reconciliation Act
OCF	Operating Cash Flow
OD	Organizational Development
ODDS	Online Data Delivery System
OE	Operating Expense
OEBS	Office of Employee Benefits Security (replaced by PWBP)
OER	Operation Expense Ratio
OES	Occupational Employment Statistic
OFCCP	Office of Federal Contract Compliance Programs
OHCA	Organized Health Care Arrangement
OI	Operating Income
OIS	Occupations Information System
OJT	On-the-Job Training
OL	Operating Liabilities
OM	Options Market
OMB	Office of Management and Budget
OOB	Out of Business
OOH	Occupational Outlook Handbook
OPM	Office of Personnel Management
OR	Operating Revenue
OSHA	Occupational Safety and Health Administration
OT	Overtime
OTC	Over the Counter
OTI	OSHA Training Institute
OTS	Office of Thrift Supervision
OWBPA	Older Workers Benefit Protection Act
P&L	Profit and Loss
PAR	Public Accounting Report
PBGC	Pension Benefit Guaranty Corporation
PBO	Projected Benefit Obligation
PBSI	Performance-Based Salary Increase

PBT	Profit Before Tax
PC	1) Personal Computer; 2) Politically Correct
PCAOB	Public Company Accounting Oversight Board
PCE	1) Preexisting Condition Exclusion; 2) Private Commercial Enterprise
PCI	Per Capita Income
PCN	Parent-Country Nationals
PD	Position Description
PDA	1) Pregnancy Discrimination Act; 2) Personal Data Assistant; 3) Public Displays of Affection; 4) Payday Advance Loan
PDF	Portable Document Format
PDQ	Position Description Questionnaire
PE	Price to Earnings Ratio
PEG	Price to Earnings Growth
PEO	Professional Employer Organization
PEPPRA	Public Employee Pension Plan Reporting and Accountability Act
PERT	Project Evaluation and Review Techniques
PEST	Political, Economic, Social, and Technological
PFK	Pay for Knowledge
PHI	Protected Health Information
PHR	Professional in Human Resources Certification
PIK	Payment in Kind
PIP	Performance Improvement Plan
PL	Public Law
PM	1) Profit Margin; 2) Performance Management
PMSA	Primary Metropolitan Statistical Area
PMV	Private Market Value
PNG	Portable Network Graphics
POA	Power of Attorney
POB	Public Oversights Board
POD	1) Payable on Death; 2) Professional and Organizational Development
POP	1) Premium-Only Plan; 2) Public Offering Price
POS	Point of Service Plan
PPA	Pension Protection Act of 1987
PPACA	Patient Protection and Affordable Care Act
PPE	Personal Protective Equipment
PPI	Producer Price Index
PPO	Preferred Provider Organization
PR	Public Relations
PRC	Peer Review Committee
PSI	Performance Salary Increase

PART III

PT	Part-Time
PTO	Paid Time Off
PTSD	Post-Traumatic Stress Syndrome
PV	Present Value
PW	Present Worth
PWBA	Pension and Welfare Benefits Administration
PWBP	Pension and Welfare Benefit Program
PWC	Public Works Commission
PWD	Prevailing Wage Determination
PY	Program Year
QA	Quality Assurance
QAIP	Quality Assurance and Improvement Plan
QBU	Qualified Business Unit
QC	Quality Control
QCEW	Quarterly Census of Employment and Wages
QCR	Quarterly Contributions Report
QDRO	Qualified Domestic Relations Order
QMAC	Qualified Matching Contributions
QMCSO	Qualified Medical Child Support Order
QME	Qualified Medical Examiner
QNEC	Qualified Non-elective Contributions
QPAM	Qualified Professional Asset Manager
QR	1) Quarterly Report; 2) Quality Review
QREC	Quality Review Executive Committee
QTD	1) Qualified Total Distribution; 2) Quarter to Date
QWI	Quarterly Workforce Indicators
R&C	Reasonable and Customary
R&D	Research and Development
RA	Resident Alien
RAP	Regulatory Accounting Principles
RCR	Recruiting Cost Ratio
RE	Residual Earnings
REA	Retirement Equity Act
RFB	Request for Bid
RFI	Request for Information
RFID	Radio Frequency Identification
RFP	Request for Proposal
RFQ	Request for Quote
RIC	Regulated Investment Company
RICO	Racketeer Influenced and Corrupt Organizations Act

RIF	Reduction in Force
RIPA	Retirement Income Policy Act
RMP	Risk Management Plan
RNFA	Return on Net Financial Assets
ROA	Return on Assets
ROC	Return on Capital
ROI	Return on Investment
ROIC	Return on Invested Capital
ROM	Range of Motion
RONA	Return on Net Assets
ROOA	Return on Operating Assets
ROR	Return on Revenue
ROS	Return on Sales
ROTA	Return on Total Assets
ROTC	Reserve Officer Training Corps
RPI	Retail Price Index
RR	Retention Rate
RRSP	Registered Retirement Savings Plan
RSU	Restricted Stock Unit
RTO	Reverse Takeover
RTW	1) Return to Work; 2) Right to Work
RWA	Risk Weighted Asset
RYR	Recruitment Yield Ratio
S&P	Standard and Poor's
SAAR	Seasonally Adjusted Annual Rate
SAR	1) Summary Annual Report; 2) Stock Appreciation Right
SARSEP	Salary Reduction Simplified Employee Pension
SAS	Statement of Accounting Standards
SAT	Scholastic Aptitude Test
SB	Senate Bill
SBA	Small Business Administration
SBAP	Small Business Assistance Program
SBBA	Sales and Buy-Back Agreement
SBD	Small Disadvantaged Business
SBJPA	Small Business Job Protection Act
SBLC	Standby Letter of Credit
SBO	Small Business Ombudsman
SC	Securities Commission
SCA	McNamara-O'Hara Service Contract Act
SCM	Supply Chain Management

PART III

SDI	State Disability Insurance
SE	1) Salaried Exempt; 2) Self-Employed
SEA	Securities Exchange Act
SEC	Securities and Exchange Commission
SEP	Simplified Employee Pension
SEPPAA	Single Employer Pension Plan Amendments Act
SERP	Supplemental Executive Retirement Plan
SESA	State Employment Security Agency
SFAS	Statements of Financial Accounting Standards
SHRM	Society for Human Resource Management
SIA	Securities Industry Act
SIB	Securities and Investment Board
SIC	Standard Industrial Classification
SIPA	Securities Investment Protection Act
SITC	Standard International Trade Classification
SLA	Service Level Agreement
SLOB	Separate Lines of Business
SMART	Specific, Measureable, Attainable, Realistic, Timed
SMI	Supplemental Medical Insurance
SMM	Summary of Material Modifications
SMS	Standard Metropolitan Statistical Area
SMT	Senior Management Team
SNAP	Supplemental Nutrition Assistance Program
SNE	Salaried Nonexempt
SOC	Standard Occupational Classification
SOL	Statute of Limitations
SOP	Statement of Position
SOX	Sarbanes-Oxley Act
SPD	Summary Plan Description
SPHR	Senior Professional in Human Resources Certification
SPX	Standard and Poor's Index
SRA	Supplemental Retirement Annuity
SRO	Self-Regulatory Organization
SROI	Subsequent Report of Injury
SS	Social Security
SSA	Social Security Administration
SSB	Securities Supervisory Board
SSD	Social Security Disability
SSDI	Social Security Disability Indemnity
SSI	Supplemental Security Income

SSN	Social Security Number
STD	Short-Term Insurance
STEEPLED	Social, Technological, Environmental, Economic, Political, Legal, Ethics, and Demographics
STF	Summary Tape File
STIP	Short-Term Industry Projections
STW	School-to-Work
SUB	Supplemental Unemployment Benefit
SUTA	State Unemployment Tax Act
SWOT	Strengths, Weaknesses, Opportunities, and Threats
T&D	Training and Development
TAMRA	Technical and Miscellaneous Revenue Act of 1988
TANF	Temporary Assistance to Needy Families
TBD	To Be Determined
TCN	Third Country National
TDA	Tax-Deferred Annuity
TDB	Temporary Disability Benefits
TEA	Transportation Efficiency Act
TEFRA	Tax Equity and Fiscal Responsibility Act
TER	Total Expense Ratio
TESSA	Tax-Exempt Special Savings Account
TEUC	Temporary Extended Unemployment Compensation
TEV	Total Enterprise Value
TIL	Truth in Lending
TIP	Transportation Improvement Program
TL	Time and Labor
TN	Temporary Visitor Visa
TOC	Theory of Constraints
TOM	Traded Options Market
TPA	Third-Party Administrator
TPD	Temporary Partial Disability
TPL	Third-Party Liability
TQM	Total Quality Management
TRA	Tax Reform Act
TRASOP	Tax Reduction Act ESOP
TSA	Tax-Sheltered Annuity
TSB	Targeted Small Business
TSP	Thrift Savings Plan
TTD	Temporary Total Disability
TUR	Total Unemployment Rates

TVI	Trade Value Index
TWA	Time Weighted Average
UAW	United Auto Workers
UBTI	Unrelated Business Taxable Income
U&C	Usual and Customary
UCA	Unemployment Compensation Amendments Act
UCC	Uniform Commercial Code
UCI	Unemployment Compensation Insurance
UCR	Usual, Customary, and Reasonable
UFW	United Farm Workers
UGESP	Uniform Guidelines on Employee Selection Procedures
UGMA	Uniform Gifts to Minors Act
UI	Unemployment Insurance
UIC	Unemployment Insurance Commission
ULP	Unfair Labor Practice
UN	United Nations
UNCITRAL	United Nations Commission on International Trade Law
UR	1) Utilization Review; 2) Unemployment Rate
URL	Uniform Resource Locator (Web Site Address)
URO	Utilization Review Organization
USCIS	United States Citizenship and Immigration Services
USDA	United States Department of Agriculture
US DOL	United States Department of Labor
US DOJ	United States Department of Justice
USC	United States Code
USERRA	Uniform Services Employment and Reemployment Rights Act
USITC	United States International Trade Commission
USM	Unlisted Securities Market
USTC	United States Tax Court
UTMA	Uniform Transfers to Minors Act
VA	Veterans Administration/Affairs
VBIA	Veterans Benefits Improvement Act
VEBA	Voluntary Employees' Beneficiary Association
VETS	Veterans Employment and Training Service
VETS-4212	VETS-4212 Report (replaced VETS-100)
VEVRA	Vietnam-Era Veterans Readjustment Act
VOC-ED	Vocational Education
VOC-REHAB	Vocational Rehabilitation
VPN	Virtual Private Network
VPT	Volume Price Trend

VWAP	Value Weighted Average Price
VWPT	Value Weighted Price Trading
VWPX	Volume Weighted Price Uncrossing
WACC	Weighted Average Cost of Capital
WAI	Wealth Added Index
WARN	Worker Adjustment and Retraining Notification Act
WC	Workers' Compensation
WCB	Workers' Compensation Board
WDC	Workforce Development Center
WHCRA	Women's Health and Cancer Rights Act
WIA	Workforce Investment Act
WIP	Work in Progress
WKLY	Weekly
WOTC	Workforce Opportunity Tax Credit
WPE	Workforce Planning and Employment
WPI	Wholesale Price Index
WPOA	Wagner-Peyser Act
WPPDA	Welfare and Pension Plan Disclosure Act (repealed by ERISA)
WRA	Weighted Risk Assets
WRAEA	Workforce Reinvestment and Adult Education Act
WTO	World Trade Organization
WTW	Welfare to Work
XML	Extended Markup Language
XRA	Expected Retirement Age
YTD	Year to Date
YTM	Yield to Maturity
ZBB	Zero-Based Budgeting

Case Laws by Chapter

Generally speaking, there are three types of federal laws. First are the acts taken by Congress to legislate mandates. Congressional actions, when completed, become the "law of the land." Second are the implementing regulations promulgated by the federal agencies and departments that specify in detail how the laws passed by Congress will be administered. Third are the court interpretations of those congressional actions and regulatory rules. When the U.S. Supreme Court or an agency such as the National Labor Relations Board (NLRB) issues a ruling about how the laws should be applied and interpreted, the ruling becomes "case law." It establishes a precedent that must be followed by everyone within the court's jurisdiction.

This appendix lists the cases that interpret important issues that have influence on human resource (HR) management. We provide a brief summary of key case law decisions. We recommend that you review each case in its entirety by going to the link listed under each case and searching by citation title. HR professionals at all career levels should have a working knowledge of these cases and their impact in the workplace. This information may appear on the certification exam in one way or another.

Chapter 3—HR Operations
None.

Chapter 4—Recruitment and Selection

Year	Citation	Decision
1971	*Griggs v. Duke Power Co.* (401 U.S. 424) www.law.cornell.edu/supct/html/ historics/USSC_CR_0401_0424_ ZS.html	When an employer uses a neutral test or other selection device and then discovers it has a disproportionate impact on minorities or women, the test must be discarded unless it can be shown that it was required as a business necessity.

Year	Citation	Decision
1978	*Regents of University of California v. Bakke* (438 U.S. 265) http://caselaw.lp.findlaw.com/cgi-bin/getcase.pl?court=us&vol=438&invol=265	Medical school admission set-asides (16 of 100 seats) are illegal if they discriminate against whites and there is no previous discrimination against minorities established.
1979	*United Steelworkers v. Weber* (443 U.S. 193) http://supreme.justia.com/cases/federal/us/443/193/case.html	Affirmative action plans are permissible if they are temporary and intended to "eliminate a manifest racial imbalance."
1982	*Connecticut v. Teal* (457 U.S. 440) http://caselaw.lp.findlaw.com/cgi-bin/getcase.pl?court=us&vol=457&invol=440	An employer is liable for racial discrimination when any part of its selection process, such as an unvalidated examination or test, has a disparate impact even if the final result of the hiring process is racially balanced. In effect, the court rejects the "bottom-line defense" and makes clear that the fair employment laws protect the individual. Fair treatment to a group is not a defense to an individual claim of discrimination.
1987	*Johnson v. Santa Clara County Transportation Agency* (480 U.S. 616) https://supreme.justia.com/cases/federal/us/480/616/	The employer was justified in hiring a woman who scored 2 points less than a man because it had an affirmative action plan that was temporary, flexible, and designed to correct an imbalance of white males in the workforce.
1988	*Watson v. Fort Worth Bank & Trust* (487 U.S. 977) http://supreme.justia.com/cases/federal/us/487/977/case.html	In a unanimous opinion, the Supreme Court declared that disparate impact analysis can be applied to subjective or discretionary selection practices.
1989	*City of Richmond v. J. A. Croson Company* (488 U.S. 469) http://supreme.justia.com/cases/federal/us/488/469/	Affirmative action programs can be maintained only by a showing that the programs aim to eliminate the effects of past discrimination.
1989	*Price Waterhouse v. Hopkins* (490 U.S. 288) http://caselaw.lp.findlaw.com/cgi-bin/getcase.pl?court=us&vol=490&invol=228	This decision established how to analyze an employer's actions when the employer had mixed motives for an employment decision. If an employee shows that discrimination played a motivating part in an employment decision, the employer can attempt to prove as a defense that it would have made the same employment decision even if discrimination were not a factor.

Year	Citation	Decision
1989	*Wards Cove Packing Co. v. Antonio* (490 U.S. 642) www.law.cornell.edu/supct/html/historics/USSC_CR_0490_0642_ZS.html	An employee is required to show disparate impact violation of Title VII in specific employment practices, not the cumulative effect of the employer's selection practices. When a showing of disparate impact is made, the employer only has to produce evidence of a business justification for the practice, and the burden of proof always remains with the employee.
2003	*Grutter v. Bollinger* (539 U.S. 306) http://supreme.justia.com/cases/federal/us/539/306/case.html *Gratz v. Bollinger* (539 U.S. 244) http://supreme.justia.com/cases/federal/us/539/244/case.html	The diversity of a student body is a compelling state interest that can justify the use of race in university admissions as long as the admissions policy is "narrowly tailored" to achieve this goal. The University of Michigan did not do so for its undergraduate program, but the law school admissions program satisfied the standard.
2009	*Ricci v. DeStefano* (No. 07-1428) www.supremecourt.gov/opinions/08pdf/07-1428.pdf	"...under Title VII, before an employer can engage in intentional discrimination for the asserted purpose of avoiding or remedying an unintentional disparate impact, the employer must have a strong basis in evidence to believe it will be subject to disparate-impact liability if it fails to take the race-conscious, discriminatory action."
2001	*Circuit City Stores v. Adams* (532 U.S. 105) www.law.cornell.edu/supct/html/99-1379.ZS.html	The court ruled that a prehire employment application requiring that all employment disputes be settled by arbitration was enforceable under the Federal Arbitration Act.

Chapter 5—Compensation and Benefits

Year	Citation	Decision
1987	*Leggett v. First National Bank of Oregon* (739 P.2d. 1083) http://or.findacase.com/research/wfrmDocViewer.aspx/xq/fac.19870722_0041873.OR.htm/qx	The employer invaded the privacy of the employee when a company representative contacted the employee's psychologist (to whom the employee had been referred by an employee assistance program [EAP]), inquiring about the employee's condition.
2005	*IBP, Inc. v. Alvarez* (546 U.S. 21) www.law.cornell.edu/supct/html/03-1238.ZS.html	Time spent donning or doffing unique safety gear is compensable, and the Fair Labor Standards Act (FLSA) requires payment of affected employees for all the time spent walking between changing and production areas.

PART III

Year	Citation	Decision
2000	*Erie County Retirees Association v. County of Erie* (2000 U.S. App. LEXIS 18317 3rd Cir. August 1, 2000) www.buypeba.org/publications/Eriecase.pdf	If an employee provides retiree health benefits, the health insurance benefits received by Medicare-eligible retirees cost the same as the health insurance benefits received by younger retirees.
2008	*LaRue v. DeWolff* (No. 06-856, 450 F. 3d 570) www.law.cornell.edu/supct/cert/06-856	When retirement plan administrators breach their fiduciary duty to act as a prudent person would act in investment of retirement funds, the employee whose retirement account lost money can sue the plan administrators.
2009	*Kennedy v. Plan Administrators for Dupont Savings* (No. 07-636) www.supremecourt.gov/opinions/08pdf/07-636.pdf	This ruling awarded retirement benefits to an ex-spouse even though she had agreed to disclaim such benefits, because the retiree had never changed the beneficiary designation on the retirement plan. This decision pointed out the need for retirement plan administrators to pay attention to divorce decrees and qualified domestic relations orders.
1974	*Corning Glass Works v. Brennan* (417 U.S. 188) http://supreme.justia.com/cases/federal/us/417/188/	Pay discrimination cases under the Equal Pay Act require the employee to prove that there is unequal pay based on sex for substantially equal work.

Chapter 6—Human Resource Development and Retention

None.

Chapter 7—Employee Relations

Year	Citation	Decision
1971	*Phillips v. Martin Marietta Corp.* (400 U.S. 542) https://supreme.justia.com/cases/federal/us/400/542/case.html	Sex discrimination means employers may not have different policies for men and women with small children of similar age.

Year	Citation	Decision
1973	*McDonnell Douglas Corp. v. Green* (411 U.S. 792) http://caselaw.lp.findlaw .com/cgi-bin/getcase .pl?court=us&vol=411&invol=792	In a hiring case, the charging party has only to show 1) the charging party is a member of a Title VII protected group, 2) he or she applied and was qualified for the position sought, 3) the job was not offered to him or her, and 4) the employer continued to seek applicants with similar qualifications. Then the employer must show a legitimate business reason why the complaining party was not hired. The employee has a final chance to prove the employer's business reason was really pretext for discrimination.
1974	*Espinoza v. Farah Manufacturing Co.* (414 U.S. 86) https://supreme.justia.com/cases/ federal/us/414/86/case.html	Noncitizens are entitled to Title VII protection. Employers who require citizenship may violate Title VII if it results in discrimination based on national origin.
1975	*Albermarle Paper v. Moody* (422 U.S. 405) http://supreme.justia.com/cases/ federal/us/422/405/	This decision requires an employer to establish evidence that an employment test is related to the job content. Job analysis could be used to show that relationship, but performance evaluations of incumbents are specifically excluded.
1976	*Washington v. Davis* (426 U.S. 229) www.law.cornell.edu/supct/html/ historics/USSC_CR_0426_0229_ ZS.html	When an employment test is challenged under constitutional law, an intent to discriminate must be established. Under Title VII there is no need to show intent, just the impact of test results.
1976	*McDonald v. Santa Fe Transportation Co.* (427 U.S. 273) http://supreme.justia.com/cases/ federal/us/427/273/case.html	Title VII prohibits racial discrimination against whites as well as blacks.
1977	*Hazelwood School District v. U.S.* (433 U.S. 299) http://caselaw.lp.findlaw .com/cgi-bin/getcase .pl?court=us&vol=433&invol=299	An employee can establish a prima facie case of class hiring discrimination through the presentation of statistical evidence by comparing the racial composition of an employer's workforce with the racial composition of the relevant labor market.
1977	*Trans World Airlines, Inc. v. Hardison* (432 U.S. 63) http://supreme.justia.com/cases/ federal/us/432/63/	Under Title VII employers must reasonably accommodate an employee's religious needs unless doing so would create an undue hardship for the employer. The Court defines hardship as anything more than de minimis cost.
1984	*EEOC v. Shell Oil Co.* (466 U.S. 54) http://supreme.justia.com/cases/ federal/us/466/54/	The Supreme Court affirmed authority of Equal Employment Opportunity Commission (EEOC) commissioners to initiate charges of discrimination through "Commissioner Charges."

Year	Citation	Decision
1986	*Meritor Savings Bank v. Vinson* (477 U.S.57) www.law.cornell.edu/supct/html/historics/USSC_CR_0477_0057_ZS.html	This defined "Hostile Environment Sexual Harassment" as a form of sex discrimination under Title VII. The decision further defined it as "unwelcome" advances of a sexual nature. A victim's failure to use an employer's complaint process does not insulate the employer from liability.
1987	*School Board of Nassau v. Arline* (480 U.S. 273) http://supreme.justia.com/cases/federal/us/480/273/case.html	A person with a contagious disease is covered by the Rehabilitation Act if they otherwise meet the definitions of "handicapped individual."
1993	*Harris v. Forklift Systems Inc.* (510 U.S. 17) www.law.cornell.edu/supct/html/92-1168.ZO.html	In a sexual harassment complaint the employee does not have to prove concrete psychological harm to establish a Title VII violation.
1993	*St. Mary's Honor Center v. Hicks* (509 U.S. 502) www.law.cornell.edu/supct/html/92-602.ZS.html	Title VII complaints require the employee to show that discrimination was the reason for a negative employment action.
1993	*Taxman v. Board of Education of Piscataway* (91 F.3d 1547, 3rd Circuit) http://caselaw.lp.findlaw.com/scripts/getcase.pl?navby=search&case=/uscircs/3rd/961395p.html	Race in an affirmative action plan cannot be used to trammel the rights of people of other races.
1995	*McKennon v. Nashville Banner Publishing Co.* (513 U.S. 352) www.law.cornell.edu/supct/html/93-1543.ZS.html	"After-acquired" evidence collected following a negative employment action cannot protect an employer from liability under Title VII or the Age Discrimination in Employment Act (ADEA), even if the conduct would have justified terminating the employee.
1996	*O'Connor v. Consolidated Coin Caterers Corp.* (517 U.S. 308) www.law.cornell.edu/supct/html/95-354.ZS.html	To show unlawful discrimination under the ADEA, a discharged employee does not have to show that he or she was replaced by someone outside the protected age group (that is, younger than 40).
1997	*Robinson v. Shell Oil* (519 U.S. 337) www.law.cornell.edu/supct/html/95-1376.ZS.html	Title VII prohibition against retaliation protects former as well as current employees.

Year	Citation	Decision
1998	*Faragher v. City of Boca Raton* (524 U.S. 775) www.law.cornell.edu/supct/html/97-282.ZO.html *Ellerth v. Burlington Northern Industries* (524 U.S. 742) www.law.cornell.edu/supct/html/97-569.ZS.html	This decision distinguished between supervisor harassment that results in tangible employment action and that which does not. When harassment results in tangible employment action, the employer is liable. Employers may avoid liability if they have a legitimate written complaint policy, it is clearly communicated to employees, and it offers alternatives to the immediate supervisor as the point of contact for making a complaint.
1998	*Oncale v. Sundowner Offshore Service, Inc.* (523 U.S. 75) www.law.cornell.edu/supct/html/96-568.ZO.html	Same-gender harassment is actionable under Title VII.
1998	*Wright v. Universal Maritime Service Corp.* (525 U.S. 70) http://supreme.justia.com/cases/federal/us/525/70/	Collective bargaining agreements must contain a clear and unmistakable waiver if they are to bar an individual's right to sue after an arbitration requirement.
1999	*Kolstad v. American Dental Association* (527 U.S. 526) www.law.cornell.edu/supct/html/98-208.ZO.html	Title VII punitive damages are limited to cases in which the employer has engaged in intentional discrimination and has done so "with malice or with reckless indifference...."
1999	*Gibson v. West* (527 U.S. 212) http://caselaw.lp.findlaw.com/scripts/getcase.pl?court=us&vol=527&invol=212	This decision endorsed the EEOC's position that it has the legal authority to require federal agencies to pay compensatory damages when the EEOC has ruled during the administrative process that the federal agency has unlawfully discriminated in violation of Title VII.
2004	*General Dynamics Land Systems, Inc. v. Cline* (540 U.S. 581) www.law.cornell.edu/supct/html/02-1080.ZS.html	ADEA does not protect younger workers, even those older than 40, from workplace decisions that favor older workers.
2004	*Pennsylvania State Police v. Suders* (542 U.S. 129) www.law.cornell.edu/supct/html/03-95.ZS.html	In the absence of a tangible employment action, employers may use the Ellerth/Faragher defense in a constructive discharge claim when supervisors are charged with harassment.

Year	Citation	Decision
2005	*Smith v. Jackson, Mississippi* (544 U.S. 228) www.law.cornell.edu/supct/html/03-1160.ZS.html	ADEA, like Title VII, offers recovery on a disparate impact theory.
2007	*Ledbetter v. Goodyear Tire & Rubber Co.* (550 U.S. 618) www.law.cornell.edu/supct/pdf/05-1074P.ZS	A claim of discrimination must be filed within 180 days of the first discriminatory employment act, and the clock does not restart after each subsequent act (e.g., issuance of a paycheck with lower pay than co-workers if based on sex). Congress overruled this decision with the passage of the Lilly Ledbetter Fair Pay Act of 2009, which says the clock will restart each time another incident of discrimination occurs.
2013	*Vance v. Ball State Univ.* (No. 11-556) www.supremecourt.gov/opinions/12pdf/11-556_11o2.pdf	This decision determined that an employee is a "supervisor" of another employee for the purposes of liability under Title VII of the Civil Rights Act of 1964 only if he or she is empowered by the employer to take tangible employment actions against the other employee.
2013	*University of Texas Sw. Med. Ctr. V. Nassar* (No 12-484) www.law.cornell.edu/supremecourt/text/12-484	Retaliation claims brought under Title VII of the Civil Rights Act of 1964 must be proved according to principles of "but-for-causation," not the lesser causation test applicable to bias claims.
1988	*DeBartolo Corp. v. Gulf Coast Trades Council* (known as DeBartolo II) (485 U.S. 568) https://www.law.cornell.edu/supremecourt/text/485/568	The Supreme Court ruled that bannering, hand billing, or attention-getting actions outside an employer's property were permissible.
1992	*Electromation, Inc., v. NLRB* (Nos. 92-4129, 93-1169 7th Cir) www.leagle.com/decision/19941 18335F3d1148_11017	The NLRB held that action committees at Electromation were illegal "labor organizations" because management created and controlled the groups and used them to deal with employees on working conditions in violation of the National Labor Relations Act (NLRA).
1993	*E. I. DuPont & Company v. NLRB* (311 NLRB 893) http://scholarship.law .georgetown.edu/cgi/viewcontent .cgi?article=1013&context=legal	The board concluded that DuPont's six safety committees and fitness committee were employer-dominated labor organizations and that DuPont dominated the formation and administration of one of them in violation of the NLRA.

Year	Citation	Decision
1995	*NLRB v. Town & Country Electric* (516 U.S. 85) www.law.cornell.edu/supct/ html/94-947.ZS.html	This Supreme Court decision related to salting held that a worker may be a company's "employee," within the terms of the National Labor Relations Act, even if, at the same time, a union pays that worker to help the union organize the company.
1995	*PepsiCo, Inc. v. Redmond* (No. 94-3942 7th Cir) http://caselaw.findlaw.com/ us-7th-circuit/1337323.html	In this case, the district court applied the inevitable disclosure doctrine even though there was no noncompete agreement in place. An employee who had left his position in marketing PepsiCo's All Sport sports drink to work for Quaker Oats Company and market Gatorade and Snapple drinks was enjoined from working for Quaker because he had detailed knowledge of PepsiCo's trade secrets pertaining to pricing, market strategy, and selling/ delivery systems.
2004	*NLRB v. Weingarten, Inc.* (420 U.S. 251, 254 1975) http://clear.uhwo.hawaii.edu/ weindecis.html Overturned by *IBM Corp. v. NLRB* (341 N.L.R.B. No. 148 June 9, 2004) http://www.lawmemo.com/nlrb/ vol/341/148.htm	On June 9, 2004, the NLRB ruled by a 3–2 vote that employees who work in a nonunionized workplace are not entitled to have a co-worker accompany them to an interview with their employer, even if the affected employee reasonably believes that the interview might result in discipline. This decision effectively reversed the July 2000 decision of the Clinton board, which had extended Weingarten rights to nonunion employees.
2001	*Ronald Lesch v. Crown Cork and Seal Company* (334 NLRB 699) www.nlrb.gov/cases-decisions/ board-decisions	This NLRB decision lifted some restrictions on the employer's use of employee participation committees.
2002	*EEOC v. Waffle House* (534 U.S. 279) www.law.cornell.edu/supct/ html/99-1823.ZS.html	In this case, the Supreme Court ruled that even if there is a mandatory arbitration agreement in place, the relevant civil rights agency can still sue on behalf of the employee.
2002	*Phoenix Transit System v. NLRB* (337 NLRB 510) www.nlrb.gov/cases- decisions/board- decisions?volume=337&sort_ by=case_nameSort&sort_ order=ASC	This NLRB ruling struck down an employer rule prohibiting employees from discussing among themselves an employment complaint—in this instance, a complaint of sexual harassment—on the grounds that the prohibition was not limited in time and scope and interfered with a protected concerted activity.

Year	Citation	Decision
2007	*Toering Electric Company v. NLRB* (351 NLRB 225) www.nlrb.gov/cases-decisions/board-decisions?volume=351&sort_by=case_nameSort&sort_order=ASC	This NLRB ruling says that an applicant for employment must be genuinely interested in seeking to establish an employment relationship with the employer in order to be protected against hiring discrimination based on union affiliation or activity; this creates greater obstacles for unions attempting salting campaigns.
2007	*Oil Capitol Sheet Metal, Inc. v. NLRB* (349 NLRB 1348) www.nlrb.gov/cases-decisions/board-decisions?volume=351&sort_by=case_nameSort&sort_order=ASC	This NLRB decision provides employers relief in salting cases by announcing a new evidentiary standard for determining the period of back pay; it requires the union to provide evidence that supports the period of time it claims the salt would have been employed.
2007 and 2011	*Dana Corporation/ Metaldyne Corporation v. NLRB* (351 NLRB 434) www.nlrb.gov/cases-decisions/board-decisions?volume=351&sort_by=case_nameSort&sort_order=ASC	This NLRB ruling says that a recognition bar, which precludes a decertification election for 12 months after an employer recognizes a union, does not apply when the recognition is voluntary, based on a card check. This was overruled in 2011 in Lamons Gasket, which restored the recognition bar for voluntary recognition but revised the prohibited time period from one year to a minimum of six months up to a year.
2007	*Syracuse University v. NLRB* (350 NLRB 755) www.nlrb.gov/cases-decisions/board-decisions?volume=351&sort_by=case_nameSort&sort_order=ASC	The NLRB found that an employee grievance panel did not violate the NLRA because the purpose of the panel was not to deal with management but to improve group decisions.
2010	*KenMor Electric Co., Inc. v. NLRB* (355 NLRB No. 173) www.nlrb.gov/cases-decisions/board-decisions?volume=351&sort_by=case_nameSort&sort_order=ASC	The NLRB ruled that a system developed and operated by an association of electrical contractors violated the NLRA because it discriminated against individuals who were salts. The board held that an individual's right to be a salt is protected under the NLRA.
2011	*Staub v. Proctor* (131 U.S. 1186) http://supreme.justia.com/cases/federal/us/562/09-400/	The Supreme Court applied the "cat's paw" principle to a wrongful discharge case, finding that an employer was culpable because the HR manager did not adequately investigate supervisors' charges against the fired employee.

Year	Citation	Decision
2011	*AT&T Mobility v. Concepcion* (S.Ct. No. 09-893) www.supremecourt.gov/opinions/10pdf/09-893.pdf	The Supreme Court ruled that some state statutes restricting the enforceability of arbitration agreements in a commercial context may be preempted by the Federal Arbitration Act.
2011	*Kepas v. Ebay* (131 S.Ct. 2160) www.ca10.uscourts.gov/opinions/09/09-4200.pdf	The Supreme Court refused to review a lower court decision that held in an employment case that a cost provision was severable from the balance of an arbitration agreement. The cost provision was unenforceable, but the agreement to arbitrate was enforceable.
2011	*Specialty Healthcare and Rehabilitation Center of Mobile v. NLRB* (15-RC-008773) www.nlrb.gov/case/15-RC-008773	The NLRB indicated that in nonacute healthcare facilities, it will certify smaller units for bargaining unless the employer provides overwhelming proof of a community of interest.
2011	*UGL-UNICCO Service Company v. NLRB* (01-RC-022447) www.nlrb.gov/case/01-RC-022447	The NLRB reestablished the successor bar doctrine, allowing unions a window of six months to one year of presumed majority support after the transfer of ownership of a business.
2012	*D. R. Horton, Inc. v. NLRB* (12-CA-25764) www.cozen.com/cozendocs/outgoing/alerts/2012/labor_011012_link.pdf	The NLRB ruled that requiring employees to agree to a class action waiver as a term and condition of employment violates Section 7 of the National Labor Relations Act.

Chapter 8—Health, Safety, and Security

Year	Citation	Decision
1991	*United Auto Workers v. Johnson Controls* (499 U.S. 187) www.law.cornell.edu/supct/html/89-1215.ZO.html	The Supreme Court held that decisions about the welfare of future children must be left to the parents who conceive, bear, support, and raise them rather than to the employers who hire their parents.
1998	*Bragdon v. Abbott* (524 U.S. 624) www.law.cornell.edu/supct/html/97-156.ZS.html	An individual with asymptomatic HIV is an individual with a disability and therefore is protected by the Americans with Disabilities Act (ADA). Reproduction is a major life activity under the statute.

Year	Citation	Decision
2005	*Leonel v. American Airlines* (400 F.3d 702, 9th Circuit) http://cdn.ca9.uscourts.gov/datastore/opinions/2005/04/27/0315890.pdf	To make a legitimate job offer under the ADA, an employer must have completed all nonmedical components of the application process or be able to demonstrate that it could not reasonably have done so before issuing the offer.

Chapter 9—Early HR Career–Level Tasks

None.

For Additional Study

This appendix lists additional resources that can be helpful in your study for the Associate Professional in Human Resources (aPHR) exam and for future reference as a human resource (HR) professional.

Badgi, Satish. *Practical Guide to Human Resource Information Systems*. Delhi: Phi Learning Pvt. Ltd., 2012.

Blosser, Fred. *Primer on Occupational Safety and Health*. Washington, D.C.: The Bureau of National Affairs, 1992.

DeNisi, Angelo, and Ricky Griffin. *HR*. Boston: Cengage Learning, 2011.

Dessler, Gary. *Human Resource Management*. New York: Pearson Education, 2014.

Feldacker, Bruce, and Michael Hayes. *Labor Guide to Labor Law*. Ithaca, New York: ILR Press, 2014.

Grant, Phillip. *Multiple Use Job Descriptions: A Guide to Analysis, Preparation, and Applications for Human Resources Managers*. Westport, Connecticut: Praeger, 1989.

Herzberg, Frederick. *The Motivation to Work*. Piscataway, NJ: Transaction, 1993.

Kavanaugh, Michael, Mohan Thite, and Richard D. Johnson (Eds.) *Human Resource Information Systems: Basics, Applications, and Future Directions*. Thousand Oaks, California: Sage Publications, 2011.

Knowles, Malcolm. *The Adult Learner: The Definitive Classic in Adult Education and Human Resource Development*. Oxford: Butterworth-Heinemann, 2005.

Kushner, Gary. *Health Care Reform: The Patient Protection and Affordable Care Act of 2010*. SHRM/Kushner and Company, 2010.

Maslow, Abraham H. *A Theory of Human Motivation*. Eastford, Connecticut: Martino Fine Books, 2013.

Mathis, Robert L., John H. Jackson, and Sean R. Valentine. *Human Resource Management*. Boston: Cengage Learning, 2013.

McGregor, Douglas. *The Human Side of Enterprise* (annotated edition). New York: McGraw-Hill Education, 2005.

Michaud, Patrick A. *Accident Prevention and OSHA Compliance*. Boca Raton, Florida: Lewis Publishers, 1995.

Milkovich, George, Jerry Newman, and Barry Gerhart. *Compensation*. New York: McGraw-Hill Education, 2016.

Noe, Raymond, John Hollenbeck, Barry Gerhart, and Patrick Wright. *Human Resource Management*. New York: McGraw-Hill Education, 2016.

Richardson, Blake. *Records Management for Dummies*. Hoboken, New Jersey: For Dummies, 2012.

Rothwell, William, Cho Hyun Park, Cavil S. Anderson, Cynthia M. Corn, and Catherine Haynes. *Organization Development Fundamentals: Managing Strategic Change*. Alexandria, Virginia: ATD Press, 2015.

Smith, Shawn, and Rebecca Mazin. *The HR Answer Book: An Indispensable Guide for Managers and Human Resources Professional*. New York: AMACOM, 2011.

Truesdell, William H. *Secrets of Affirmative Action Compliance*. Walnut Creek, California: The Management Advantage, Inc., 2016.

Waddill, Deborah, and Michael Marquardt. *The e-HR Advantage: The Complete Handbook for Technology enabled Human Resources*. Boston: Nicholas Brealey America, 2011.

About the CD-ROM

The CD-ROM included with this book comes complete with Total Tester customizable practice exam software with 250 practice exam questions and a secured PDF copy of the book.

System Requirements

The software requires Windows Vista or higher and 30MB of hard disk space for full installation, in addition to a current or prior major release of Chrome, Firefox, Internet Explorer, or Safari. To run, the screen resolution must be set to 1024 × 768 or higher. The secured book PDF requires Adobe Acrobat, Adobe Reader, or Adobe Digital Editions to view.

Installing and Running Total Tester Premium Practice Exam Software

From the main screen you may install the Total Tester by clicking the Total Tester Practice Exams button. This will begin the installation process and place an icon on your desktop and in your Start menu. To run Total Tester, navigate to Start | (All) Programs | Total Seminars, or double-click the icon on your desktop.

To uninstall the Total Tester software, go to Start | Control Panel | Programs And Features, and then select the Total Tester program. Select Remove, and Windows will completely uninstall the software.

Total Tester Premium Practice Exam Software

Total Tester provides you with a simulation of the aPHR exam. Exams can be taken in Practice Mode, Exam Mode, or Custom Mode. Practice Mode provides an assistance window with hints, references to the book, explanations of the correct and incorrect answers, and the option to check your answer as you take the test. Exam Mode provides a simulation of the actual exam. The number of questions, the types of questions, and the time allowed are intended to be an accurate representation of the exam environment.

Custom Mode allows you to create custom exams from selected functional areas, and you can further customize the number of questions and time allowed.

To take a test, launch the program and select *aPHR All-in-One* from the Installed Question Packs list. You can then select Practice Mode, Exam Mode, or Custom Mode. All exams provide an overall grade and a grade broken down by domain.

Secured Book PDF

The entire contents of the book are provided in secured PDF format on the CD-ROM. This file is viewable on your computer and many portable devices.

- **To view the PDF on a computer**, Adobe Acrobat, Adobe Reader, or Adobe Digital Editions is required. A link to Adobe's web site, where you can download and install Adobe Reader, has been included on the CD-ROM.

NOTE For more information on Adobe Reader and to check for the most recent version of the software, visit Adobe's web site at www.adobe.com and search for the free Adobe Reader or look for Adobe Reader on the product page. Adobe Digital Editions can also be downloaded from the Adobe web site.

- **To view the book PDF on a portable device**, copy the PDF file to your computer from the CD-ROM and then copy the file to your portable device using a USB or other connection. Adobe offers a mobile version of Adobe Reader, the Adobe Reader mobile app, which currently supports iOS and Android. For customers using Adobe Digital Editions and an iPad, you may have to download and install a separate reader program on your device. The Adobe web site has a list of recommended applications, and McGraw-Hill Education recommends the Bluefire Reader.

Technical Support

For questions regarding the Total Tester software or operation of the CD-ROM, visit **www.totalsem.com** or e-mail **support@totalsem.com**.

For questions regarding the secured book PDF, visit **http://mhp.softwareassist.com** or e-mail **techsolutions@mhedu.com**.

For questions regarding book content, e-mail **hep_customer-service@mheducation .com**. For customers outside the United States, e-mail **international_cs@mheducation .com**.

This glossary is composed of terms you will likely encounter as you move through your career in human resources. Many of the terms you may already know. Some of them like *andragogy, Delphi technique, histogram,* or *pedagogy* may be new to you. Yet each of the terms here can be important to HR professionals.

Here is a suggestion. As you work through the book and discover a term that is new to you, pause long enough to flip to the glossary and look it up. Knowing how a word or phrase is used can be helpful in understanding its meaning. It won't be long before you are using these terms in your everyday encounters.

80% rule   The measurement known as a "rule of thumb" used to test for disparity in treatment during any type of employment selection decisions; also identified as *adverse impact.*

401(k) plan   A salary reduction retirement plan for employees. Contributions reduce one's taxable income, and investment income accumulates tax-free until the money is withdrawn.

ADDIE   A five-step instructional design process consisting of assess, design, development, implementation, and evaluation.

administrative exemption   Exemption from overtime payment based on several qualifying factors, including minimum pay requirement, and exercise of discretion and independent judgment performing work directly related to management of general business operations.

administrative services–only plan   Health insurance programs in which all of the risk is assumed by the employer.

adult learning   The process of learning associated with people who are older than 18 to 25 and generally referred to as nontraditional learners; also identified as andragogy.

adverse impact   A legal category of illegal employment discrimination involving groups of workers and statistical proofs.

adverse selection   When bad-risk employees choose a benefit and good-risk employees do not under a flexible benefits plan.

adverse treatment   A legal category of illegal employment discrimination involving individual treatment or "pattern and practice" treatment of groups of workers.

375

affirmative action   Use of special outreach and recruiting programs to assure participation of qualified job candidates, vendors, or students in employment, employer purchasing programs, or college admissions.

aggregate stop-loss coverage   The health plan is protected against the risk of large total claims from all participants during the plan year.

aging   A technique used to make outdated data current.

alternative dispute resolution (ADR)   A variety of processes that help parties resolve disputes without a trial. Processes include mediation, arbitration, neutral evaluation, and collaborative law.

analytics   The discovery and communication of meaningful patterns in data.

andragogy   The study of how adults learn.

applicant tracking system   A method for retention of detailed information about job applicants, either manual or computer based.

apprenticeship   A system of training a person in a trade or profession with on-the-job training.

arbitration   The process of submitting a labor dispute to a third party for resolution. The third party is called an *arbitrator*. Both parties agree beforehand to accept the arbitrator's decision.

assessment centers   A method for assessing aptitude and performance applied to participants using various aptitude diagnostic processes in order to obtain information on abilities or potential. Participants are measured against a norm group of successful people in the same job category.

assets   The properties an organization owns, tangible and intangible.

at-will employment   A legal employment relationship in which an employee may quit at any time for any reason and may be dismissed at any time for any reason. No "just cause" is required. This relationship is limited by prohibitions on employer actions related to public interest.

auditory learners   A learning style in which a person learns through listening.

automatic step rate   Division of the pay range into several steps that can be advanced by an employee when time-in-job has met the step requirement.

average   Arithmetic average or mean arrived at by giving equal weight to every participant's actual pay; also, a number that is arrived at by adding quantities together and dividing the total by the number of quantities.

back pay   Payment of salary or wages that should have been paid initially, usually as a form of remedy for a complaint of discrimination.

background checks   Investigation of an individual's personal history including employment, educational, criminal, and financial.

balance sheet   A statement of a business's financial position.

balanced scorecard   A big-picture view of an organization's performance as measured against goals in areas such as finance, customer base, processes, learning, human capital, and growth.

BARS   Behaviorally anchored rating scales.

base-pay systems   Single or flat-rate systems, time-based step rate systems, performance-based merit pay systems, productivity-based systems, and person-based systems.

behavioral interview   A technique that queries job applicants to describe their specific behaviors or actions they've taken in particular past situations as a basis for determining the individual's demonstrated skill sets.

bell curve   Used to describe the mathematical concept called "normal distribution."

benefits-needs assessment or analysis   Collection and analysis of data to determine whether the employer's benefits programs actually meet their objectives.

bereavement leave   Paid or unpaid time off to attend the funeral of a relative.

bias   Prejudice in favor of or against one thing, person, or group compared with another, usually in a way considered to be unfair.

"Big Data"   Extremely large data sets that may be analyzed computationally to reveal patterns, trends, and associations, especially relating to human behavior and interactions.

bill   A proposal presented to a legislative body in the U.S. government to enact a law.

blended learning   A formal education program in which a student learns at least in part through delivery of content and instruction via digital and online media with some element of student control over time, place, path, or pace.

blue ocean strategies   The pursuit of creating a new market space where there are no competitors.

boycott   A protest action that encourages the public to withhold business from an employer that is targeted by a union.

brain drain   The departure of educated or professional people from one country, economic sector, or field for another, usually for better pay or living conditions.

branding   The process of conveying key organizational values.

broadbanding   Combination of several pay grades or job classifications with narrow range spreads and a single band into a wider spread.

budgeting   Forecasting income and expenses by category and subcategory.

business acumen   Knowledge and understanding of the financial, accounting, marketing, and operational functions of an organization.

business case   An argument, usually documented, that is intended to convince a decision maker to approve some kind of action.

business concepts   An idea for producing goods or services that identifies the benefits that can be achieved for prospective customers or clients.

business continuity   The ability to continue conducting business following an interruption of some sort.

business ethics   Generally accepted norms and expectations for business management behavior.

business intelligence (BI)   An umbrella term that refers to a variety of software applications used to analyze an organization's raw data. BI as a discipline is made up of several related activities, including data mining, online analytical processing, querying, and reporting.

cafeteria benefit plans   Employees who choose the benefits they desire subject to certain limitations and total cost constraints.

career development   A concept that individuals expand their knowledge, skills, and abilities as they progress through their careers.

career management   Planning, preparing, and implementing employee career paths.

career planning   Activities and actions that individuals follow for a specific career path.

case studies   Simulation of real-world problems that calls for an application of skill or knowledge to resolve.

cash awards   Rewards for exceeding performance goals, a formula-based bonus calculated on a percentage of profits or other preestablished measurement.

cash flow statement   A mandatory part of a company's financial reports since 1987; records the amounts of cash and cash equivalents entering and leaving a company.

cause-and-effect diagram   Also called a *fishbone diagram* and *Ishikawa diagram*, identifies possible causes for an effect or problem.

center of excellence (COE)   Refers to a team, a shared facility, or an entity that provides leadership, evangelization, best practices, research, support, and/or training for a focus area.

central tendency error   When managers and interviewers rate all or most of the employees or interviewees as average.

certification of a union   Formal recognition of a union as the exclusive bargaining representative of a group of employees.

chain of command   The order in which authority and power in an organization is wielded and delegated from top management to every employee at every level of the organization.

change management   Transitioning individuals, groups, teams, and institutions to a desired future state.

change programs   Strategic approach to organizing and implementing specific changes (e.g., policies or procedures) within an organization.

childcare services   Programs designed to help working parents deal with the ongoing needs of preschool or school-aged children.

civil law   One of the two major legal systems of the modern Western world (the other is common law).

clawback   A provision of the Dodd-Frank Act that requires executives to return ill-gotten bonuses.

cloud computing   An application software that is on central servers and accessed or operated using Internet-enabled devices.

code of conduct   An employment policy listing personal behaviors that are acceptable and required in the workplace.

code of ethics   Principles of conduct that guide behavior expectations and decisions.

cognitive learning   The refining of knowledge by adding new information and thereby expanding prior knowledge.

collective bargaining   A formal process of negotiating working conditions with an employer for a work group represented by a union.

collective bargaining agreements   Union contracts for a represented group of employees and designated employers. This is a term usually used in the private sector.

combination step-rate and performance   Employees receive step-rate increases up to the established job rate. Above this level, increases are granted only for superior job performance.

common law   Law developed over time from the rulings of judges as opposed to law embodied in statutes passed by legislatures (statutory law) or law embodied in a written constitution (constitutional law).

communication skills   Verbal and written abilities that enable an individual to transmit and receive messages.

commuter assistance   Employer assistance programs designed to help defray public transportation costs associated with going to and from work.

comparable worth   A pay discrimination theory where workers in a job classification dominated by one sex are paid less than workers in a classification dominated by the opposite sex, where both job classifications are of equal value or worth to the employer or the underpaid classification is of greater value to the employer.

compa-ratio   An indicator of how wages match, lead, or lag the midpoint of a given pay range computed by dividing the worker's pay rate by the midpoint of the pay range.

compensatory damages   A monetary equivalent awarded for pain, suffering, and emotional distress as a result of a legal proceeding.

competencies   Measurable or observable knowledge, skills, abilities, and behaviors critical to successful job performance.

competency-based interview   An interview where the style of question forces candidates to give situational examples of times in the past when they have performed particular tasks or achieved particular outcomes using certain skills.

competency-based system   Pay is linked to the level at which an employee can perform in a recognized competency.

compliance evaluation   Formal audit by the Office of Federal Contract Compliance Programs (OFCCP) of a federal contractor subject to OFCCP oversight.

compliance program   Systematic procedures instituted by an organization to ensure that the provisions of the regulations imposed by a government agency are being met.

computer employee exemption   Exemption from overtime payment based on several qualifying factors, including minimum pay requirement, job duties involving computer programming, software analysis, or software engineering.

computer-based testing (CBT)   Testing delivery method via computer, in person, at a testing center.

conciliation   A binding written agreement between an employer and the EEOC or the OFCCP that details specific employer commitments to resolve the alleged violations set forth in the agreement.

conflict of interest   A situation that has the potential to undermine the impartiality of a person because of the possibility of a clash between the person's self-interest and professional interest or public interest.

construct validity   The degree to which a test measures what it claims to measure.

constructive discipline   Discipline that imposes increasingly severe consequences and penalties. This is also called *progressive discipline*.

consumer price index The average of prices paid by consumers for goods and services.

content validity The extent a test measures all aspects of a given job.

contingency plan A coordinated set of steps to be taken in an emergency or disaster.

contingent workers Workers who do not have an ongoing expectation of full-time employment such as part-time workers, independent contractors, temporary workers, consultants, leased employees, and subcontractors.

contract labor Work performed under the terms of a legally enforceable contract.

contract negotiation The process of give and take related generally to content details and provisions of an employment contract such as a union agreement or memorandum of understanding (MOU).

contrast effect An error made in interviewing when strong candidates are interviewed after weak candidates, causing them to appear overly qualified because of the contrast.

contrast error In interview or performance appraisal process, error caused by the effect of previously interviewed or appraised applicants on the interviewer.

control chart A chart that illustrates variation from normal in a situation over time.

controlling A management function involving monitoring the workplace and making adjustments to activities as required.

cooperative learning A strategy in which a small group of people work on solving a problem or completing a task in a way that each person's success is dependent on the group's success.

copyright A legal form of protection for authors of original works.

core competency A unique capability that is essential or fundamental to a particular job.

corporate citizenship A self-regulatory mechanism where an organization monitors and ensures its active compliance with the spirit of the law, ethical standards, and international norms.

corporate governance The mechanisms, processes, and relations by which corporations are controlled and directed.

corporate responsibility (CR) Strategic goals achieved through local community relationships around social needs and issues.

cost-benefit analysis (CBA) A business practice in which the costs and benefits of a particular situation are analyzed as part of the decision process.

cost containment Efforts or activities designed to reduce or slow down the cost expenses and increases.

PART III

cost of living adjustment   Pay increase given to all employees on the basis of market pressure, usually measured against the consumer price index (CPI).

cost per hire   The measurement of dollar expense required to hire each new employee.

credit reports   Reports obtained from one of the major credit reporting agencies that explains the individual's personal rating based on financial history.

criterion-related validity   Empirical studies producing data that show the selection procedure(s) are predictive or significantly related with important elements of job performance.

critical path math (CPM)   A sequence of activities in a project plan that must be completed on time for the project to be completed by the due date.

cross-functional work team   A group of people from different functions working together to generate production or problem resolution.

cultural blending   The blending of different cultural influences in the workforce.

cultural noise   In interview or performance appraisal process, error caused by the effect of previously interviewed or appraised applicants on the interviewer. It results in a conscious or subconscious comparison of one applicant with another and tends to exaggerate the differences between the two.

cultural relativism   The principle that an individual human's beliefs and activities should be understood by others in terms of that individual's own culture.

culture   Societal forces affecting the values, beliefs, and actions of a group of people.

dashboards   A data visualization tool that displays the current status of metrics and key performance indicators (KPIs).

database   Systematically organized or structured repository of indexed information (usually as a group of linked data files) that allows easy retrieval, updating, analysis, and output of data.

database management system (DBMS)   Computer program that catalogs, indexes, locates, retrieves, and stores data; maintains its integrity; and outputs it in the form desired by a user.

deauthorization of a union   Removal of "union security" from the contract. The union remains as the exclusive bargaining representative, and the collective bargaining agreement remains in effect, but employees are not forced to be members or pay dues to the union.

decertification of a union   Removal of a union as the exclusive bargaining representative of the employees.

defamation   Publication of something about an individual that the writer knows is untrue.

defined benefit plan   A pension plan that provides retirement income to retirees based on a formula that usually combines years of service and an average annual income for a set number of years.

defined contribution plan   An individual pension fund created for each employee into which the company invests a specified amount of money each year until the employee retires.

Delphi technique   A systematic forecasting method that involves structured interaction among a group of experts on a subject. The Delphi technique typically includes at least two rounds of experts answering questions and giving justification for their answer.

demand analysis   Estimation of what customers, clients, or patrons will want in the future.

demonstration   Showing students how something is done.

dental plans   Medical insurance programs that cover some or all of the cost of dental services for subscribers.

departmentalization   Manner or practice in which related individual tasks and their allocation to work groups is combined to form a specialized functional area that is distinct from other functional areas in an organization.

developmental activities   The part of human resource management that specifically deals with training and development of employees.

differential pay   An addition to base pay that results from special job circumstances such as shift assignment, commute distance required, temporary responsibility assignments, and similar "extras."

differential piece rate system   Employee receives one rate of pay up to the production standard and a higher rate of pay when the standard is exceeded.

dilemma reconciliation   Process of seeking solutions to issues involving cultural differences.

direct compensation   Base pay, commissions, bonuses, merit pay, piece rate, differential pay, cash award, profit sharing, or gainsharing.

directing   Managing or controlling people to willingly do what is wanted or needed.

disability   Medically determinable impairment of body or mind that restricts, or causes loss of, a person's functional ability to carry on his or her normal activities.

disaster recovery plans   A set of procedures used to protect and recover a business from a natural or other disaster that has impacted the organization or employer.

discipline   Forms of punishment to assure obedience with policies.

disparate impact   Adverse effect of a practice or standard that is neutral and non-discriminatory in its intention but, nonetheless, disproportionately affects individuals having a disability or belonging to a particular group based on their age, ethnicity, race, sex, or other protected class.

disparate treatment   A discrimination theory that holds an individual is treated differently from others, based on protected group membership, who are similarly situated under similar circumstances.

distance learning   Learning that uses television, audio/video tapes, computers, the Internet, etc., instead of physical attendance at classes in a centralized facility.

diversity and inclusion   The practice of embracing differences of race, culture, and background, ensuring that everyone is a participant in workplace processes.

diversity council   Task force of various levels of employees created to work on diversity and inclusion initiatives in an organization.

diversity dimensions   Framework for diversity, including personality, internal dimensions, external dimensions, and organizational dimensions.

diversity of thought   Different types of cognitive processes.

diversity programs   Methods for recognizing and honoring various types of employee backgrounds.

divestiture   The sale of an asset.

domestic partners   Two adults who have chosen to share one another's lives in an intimate and committed relationship of mutual caring.

dual-ladder   A system that enables a person to advance up either the management or technical career development ladder in an organization.

due diligence   The first step in mergers and acquisitions involving a broad scope of research and investigation.

due process   Conduct of legal proceedings strictly according to established principles and procedures, laid down to ensure fair trial for every accused.

duty of care   The responsibility or the legal obligation of a person or organization to avoid acts or omissions (which can be reasonably foreseen) to be likely to cause harm to others.

elder care   Programs to help employees deal with responsibilities for care of family elders.

e-learning   Internet-based training programs that can be instructor led or self-paced.

emotional intelligence (EQ or EI)   The ability of an individual to have understanding and sensitivity for another's emotions and control over their own.

employee   A person in the service of another under any contract of hire, express or implied, oral or written, where the employer has the power or right to control and direct the employee in the material details of how the work is to be performed.

employee assistance programs   Employer-sponsored benefits that provide a number of services that help promote the physical, mental, and emotional wellness of individual employees who otherwise would be negatively impacted by health-related crises.

employee complaints   Written or verbal statements of dissatisfaction from an employee that can involve charges of discrimination, lack of fairness, or other upset.

employee engagement   Where employees are fully absorbed by and enthusiastic about their work and so take positive action to further the organization's reputation and interests.

employee leasing   Contracting with a vendor that provides qualified workers for a specific period of time at a specific pay rate.

employee life cycle   A human resources model that identifies stages in employees' careers to help guide their management and optimize associated processes.

employee relations programs   Methods for management of the employer-employee relationship.

employee resource group (ERG)   A group of employees who share a diversity dimension, also called an *affinity group*.

employee stock ownership plans   Retirement plans in which the company contributes its stock, or money to buy its stock, to the plan for the benefit of the company's employees.

employee stock purchase plans   Programs allowing employees to purchase company stock at discounted prices.

employee surveys   Tools used to gather opinions of employees about their employment experiences.

employee-management committees   Problem-solving groups of management and nonmanagement employees focused on specific issues within the workplace.

employer sick leave   Paid leave for a specified number of hours or days absent from work because of medical conditions.

employment affirmative action   Programs required by federal regulations for some federal contractors to implement outreach and recruiting programs when the incumbent workforce is significantly less than computed availability.

employment at will   A legal doctrine that describes an employment relationship without a contract where either party can end the relationship at any time for any reason.

employment branding   A targeted strategy to manage the awareness and perceptions of employees, potential employees, and related stakeholders with regard to an organization.

employment policies   Rules by which the workplace will be managed.

employment reference checks   Verification of references, both personal and professional, provided by a job candidate on an application form or resume.

employment testing   Any tool or step used in the employment selection process. Commonly includes written tests, interviews, résumé reviews, or skill demonstration.

encryption   Scrambling sensitive information so that it becomes unreadable to everyone except the intended recipient.

enterprise resource planning (ERP)   Accounting oriented, relational database based, multimodule but integrated, software system for identifying and planning the resource needs of an enterprise.

environmental footprints   The effect that a person, company, activity, etc., has on the environment.

environmental scanning   A process of studying the environment to pinpoint potential threats and opportunities.

e-procurement   An electronic web application for transacting and purchasing supplies and services.

equal pay   Providing equal compensation to jobs that have the same requirements, responsibilities, and working conditions regardless of the incumbent's gender.

equity   The difference between income and liabilities in a for-profit organization.

essential functions   The fundamental, crucial job duties performed in a position.

ethical universalism   A concept that implies there are fundamental ethical principles applying across cultures.

ethics   Principles and values that set expectations for behaviors in an organization.

ethnocentric   A policy calling for key management positions to be filled by expatriates.

evacuation plan   A written procedure for moving employees out of the work location to a safer location in case of fire or natural disaster.

evaluation   A constructive process to discuss strengths and weaknesses in performance.

E-Verify   A government database that employers access to confirm a match between a new employee's name and Social Security number.

executive coaching   Coaching senior- and executive-level management by a third party.

executive exemption   Exemption from overtime payment based on several qualifying factors, including supervision and minimum pay requirements.

executive incentives   Variable compensation additives for executive employees that may include company stock and use of company facilities such as vacation timeshares. These are usually variable based on the profitability of the company.

exempt employees   Employees exempt from overtime compensation by federal wage and hours guidelines.

exempt job   A job with content that is exempt from the FLSA requirement to pay overtime for work exceeding 40 hours per week. Exemption can be based on several designated factors.

exit interviews   Discussions with departing employees to explore how they feel about their experience as an employee and what recommendations they might have for the employer.

expatriates   Employees working in a country other than that of their origin.

external coaching   Coaching that is provided by a third party by a certified coach.

external equity   Employees' perception of the conditions and rewards of their employment, compared with those of the employees of other firms.

extraterritoriality   Being outside the territory of the country where you are living and so not subject to its laws.

extrinsic rewards   Rewards such as pay, benefits, incentive bonuses, promotions, time off, etc.

factor-comparison job evaluation   A process that involves ranking each job by each compensable factor and then identifying dollar values for each level of each factor to develop an actual pay rate for the evaluated job.

fast-track program   A career development program that identifies high-potential leaders for rapid career growth and organizational knowledge.

fee-for-service plans   Allows health plan members to go to any qualified physician or other healthcare provider, hospital, or medical clinic and submit claims to the insurance company.

fiduciary responsibilities   A legal and ethical relationship between two or more parties.

final warning   Last step in the disciplinary process progression prior to removing the employee from the payroll.

first impression error   Occurs when a manager or interviewer bases his or her entire assessment of an employee or applicant on the first impression that the employee or applicant made.

flat-rate or single system   Each worker in the same job has the same rate of pay regardless of seniority or job performance.

flexible spending account   Allows employees to set aside a preestablished amount of money on a pre-tax basis per plan year for use in paying authorized medical expenses.

floating holidays   Designated paid time off that can be used at any time during the year with the employer's approval.

flow analysis   How processes operate and how flows of products, data, or other items go through these processes.

focus group   A group of people brought together with a moderator where they share their point of view on a specific topic or problem. Focus groups aim at a discussion instead of on individual responses to formal questions and produce qualitative data (preferences and beliefs) that may or may not be representative of the general population.

force-field analysis   Technique for identifying and analyzing the positive factors of a situation that help ("driving forces") and negative factors that hinder ("restraining forces") an entity in attaining its objectives.

forced choice   An evaluation method in which the evaluator selects two of four statements that represents "most like" and "least like."

formalization   The extent to which work roles are structured in an organization and the activities of the employees are governed by rules and procedures.

frequency distribution   Listing of grouped pay data from lowest to highest.

frequency tables   Number of workers in a particular job classification and their pay data.

front pay   Payment of salary or wages that could have been earned had the individual continued to work on the job in question or had the person been employed for a future period of time.

full-time   Employees who work a designated number of hours per week, usually 30 to 40 hours.

fully funded plans   Health insurance programs paid for entirely by the employer.

functional HR   A structure where HR generalists are located within business units such as HR business partners and implement the policies and interact with management and employees in the unit and where headquarters HR staff create policies and strategy.

functional structure   A common type of organizational structure in which the organization is divided into smaller groups based on specialized functional areas, such as IT, finance, HR, and marketing.

functional work team   A group of people from the same function working together to generate production or resolve problems.

gainsharing plans   Extra pay provided to individual or groups of employees based on the gain in performance results in one measurement period over another period.

gamification   Elements of game playing (e.g., point scoring, competition with others, rules of play) to other areas of activity that encourage employee engagement.

Gantt chart   A project planning tool that scopes and monitors the activities of a project, the timeline, and accountability.

gap analysis   Measurement of the difference between where you are and where you want to be.

gender   Culturally and socially constructed difference between men and women.

general duty clause   A provision in OSHA regulations that imposes a duty on all subject employers to assure a safe and healthy working environment for their employees.

general pay increases   A pay increase given to all employees regardless of their job performance and not linked to market pressures.

geocentric   A staffing policy wanting to place the best person in the job regardless of their country of origin.

geographic structure   An organizational structure used by organizations that have locations in different geographic locations that define their regions.

geographic-based differential pay   Adjustment to base pay programs based on cost of living requirements in various geographic locations where employees work.

geography   Adjustments to survey numbers based on geographic differences with original survey content.

gig workers   Independent workers employed for a particular performance or for defined short-term engagements.

giganomics   The creation of employment through the piecing together of several projects or "gigs."

glass ceiling   A discriminatory practice that has prevented women and other protected class members from advancing to executive-level jobs.

global integration strategy (GI)   A term used to denote an organization that fashions its strategy, its management, and its operations in pursuit of a new goal: the integration of production and value delivery worldwide.

global mind-set   An openness to and awareness of diversity across cultures and markets.

GPHR   Global Professional in Human Resources credential that is global competency based, validating the skills and knowledge of an HR professional who operates in a global marketplace.

global remittances   A transfer of money from migrant workers to his or her home country.

globalization   The worldwide movement toward economic, financial, trade, and communications integration.

golden parachutes   Provisions in executive employment contracts that provide special payments or benefits to the executives under certain adverse conditions such as the loss of their position or otherwise adversely impacted actions by organizational changes.

governance   Establishment of policies, and continuous monitoring of their proper implementation, by the members of the governing body of an organization.

graphic organizers   Diagrams, maps, and drawings/webs as illustrations of learning materials.

green circle rates   Pay at a rate lower than the minimum rate for the assigned pay range.

green initiatives   Relationships around community and social issues.

grievance procedure   Step-by-step process an employee must follow to get his or her complaint addressed satisfactorily. This is typically included in union (collective bargaining) agreements.

grievances   Formal employee complaints handled by a structured resolution process usually found in a union-represented work group.

gross domestic product (GDP)   The total value of goods and services produced in a country.

group incentive program   Pay to all individuals in a workgroup for achievement by the entire workgroup.

group term life insurance   Provides lump-sum benefit to beneficiaries on the death of an insured.

halo effect   This occurs when an evaluator scores an employee high on all job categories because of performance in one area.

harassment   Persecution, intimidation, pressure, or force applied to employees by supervisors, co-workers, or external individuals that interferes with the employee's ability to perform the job assignment.

Hay method   A widely used job evaluation method that addresses three compensable factors (knowledge, problem solving, and accountability) to determine how many points should be assigned to different jobs in determining compensation categories.

hazard   Situation that may lead to a danger, emergency, or disaster.

hazard pay   Additional pay for working under adverse conditions caused by environment or because of specific circumstances.

head count   Number of individuals carried on a firm's payroll.

health insurance purchasing cooperatives   Purchasing agents for large groups of employers.

health maintenance organization   Healthcare program where the insurer is paid on a per-person (capitated) basis and offers healthcare services and staff at its facilities.

health reimbursement accounts   Employer-funded medical reimbursement plans.

health savings accounts   A tax-advantaged medical savings account available to taxpayers in the United States who are enrolled in a high-deductible health plan.

high-context culture   A culture of people that emphasizes interpersonal relationships and close connections over a long period of time.

high deductible health plans   Programs that help employers lower their costs and allow employees with set-aside money to pay for out-of-pocket medical and medical-related expenses.

histogram   A graphic representation of the distribution of a single type of measurement using rectangles.

horn effect   This occurs when an employee receives a low rating in all areas because of one weakness influencing the evaluator.

host-country nationals (HCNs)   Employees originating in the country where a remote work location is being established.

hostile environment harassment   Occurs when an employee is subject to unwelcome advances, sexual innuendos, or offensive gender-related language that is sufficiently severe or pervasive from the perspective of a reasonable person of the same gender as the offended employee.

HR audit An objective look at the company's HR policies, practices, procedures, and strategies to protect the company, establish best practices, and identify opportunities for improvement.

HR business partner HR staff that acts as an internal consultant to senior management.

HR Certification Institute (HRCI) A nonprofit professional certifying organization for the human resources profession.

HR professional certification Status awarded to HR professionals by a recognized certifying agency after satisfying qualifying requirements.

HRCI Body of Knowledge (BOK) The description of a set of concepts, tasks, responsibilities, and knowledge associated with HRCI credentialing.

HRIS Human resources information system. This is usually a computer-based collection of personal data for each employee.

human capital The value of the capabilities, knowledge, skills, experiences, and motivation of a workforce in an organization.

Human Resource Business Professional (HRBP) A global, competency-based credential designed to validate generally accepted professional-level core HR knowledge and skills.

Human Resource Management Professional (HRMP) A global, competency-based credential designed to validate generally accepted HR principles in strategy, policy development, and service delivery.

human resources development Systematically planned activities that help the organization's workforce meet the current and future job and skills needs.

human resource management (HRM) The direction of organizational systems to ensure that human talent is used effectively and efficiently to accomplish organizational goals.

hybrid structure An approach to designing the internal operating structure of a company or other entity in a manner that makes use of several different organizational patterns rather than relying on one particular model.

identity alignment The extent to which diversity is accepted and embraced in an organization.

IIPP Injury and illness prevention programs.

incentive pay Pay designed to promote a higher level of job performance than otherwise included in the basic design of the job.

incentive stock options Awards of rights to purchase company stock in the future at a price determined at the time of the grant.

incentives   Inducement or supplemental reward that serves as a motivational device for a desired action or behavior.

inclusion   The state of including or of being included within a group or structure.

income statement   A summary of management's performance as reflected in the profitability (or lack of it) of an organization over a certain period.

independent contractor   One who, in the independent exercise of his/her business affairs, contracts to do a piece of work according to his/her own methods and is subject to his/her principal's control only as to the end product or final result of his/her work.

indirect compensation   Social Security, unemployment insurance, disability insurance, pensions, 401(k), and other similar programs, healthcare, vacations, sick leave, and paid time off such as holidays.

individual incentive program   An offer to individual employees in a workgroup to receive extra pay based on achievement of clearly defined objectives.

information management (IM)   Application of management techniques to collect information, communicate it within and outside the organization, and process it to enable managers to make quicker and better decisions.

inpatriates   Employees working at corporate headquarters who originated in a different country.

insourcing   Delegating a job to someone within a company, as opposed to someone outside of the company (outsourcing).

instructional methods   Approaches to training that are either teacher centered or learner centered.

intellectual property (IP)   Knowledge, creative ideas, or expressions of human mind that have commercial value and are protectable under copyright, patent, service mark, trademark, or trade secret laws from imitation, infringement, and dilution.

intercultural wisdom   The knowing what you do not know about the values, behavior, and communication styles of people from other cultures.

internal coaching   A training or developmental process whereby organizational leaders support the achievement of a personal or professional goal.

internal equity   Employees' perception of their responsibilities, rewards, and work conditions as compared with those of other employees in similar positions in the same organization.

internal investigation   Gathering verbal and written information dealing with an issue that needs to be clarified.

intrinsic motivation   Stimulation that drives an individual to adopt or change a behavior for his or her own internal satisfaction or fulfillment.

intrinsic rewards   Rewards such as meaningful and fulfilling work, autonomy, and positive feedback that lead to high levels of job satisfaction.

investigation   A detailed search for facts involving records, witnesses, and other inputs.

investigation file   A collection of documents related to complaints or charges of discrimination, policy violation, or criminal behavior assembled by an employer about an employee or event.

involuntary separations   Individuals leaving the payroll for involuntary reasons including such things as performance deficiencies, policy violations, or unauthorized absence.

ISO 9000 standards   Standards and guidelines on quality management and quality assurance developed by the International Organization for Standardization (ISO).

item response theory (IRT)   Method used to preequate the difficulty level of questions on an exam.

job analysis   A process to identify and determine the particular job duties and requirements for a given job.

job application   A form used to gather information significant to the employer about an individual candidate for employment.

job classification   A system for objectively and accurately defining the duties, responsibilities, tasks, and authority level of a job.

job-content-based job evaluation   A job evaluation method in which the relative worth and pay of different jobs are based on their content and relationship to other jobs within the same organization.

job description   A document that contains a summary of duties and responsibilities of a given job assignment and a description of the physical and mental requirements of the job.

job enlargement   Broadening the scope of a job by expanding the number of tasks.

job enrichment   Increasing the depth of a job by adding responsibilities.

job evaluation   A systematic determination of the relative worth of jobs in an organization.

job evaluation method   Quantitative or nonquantitative programs allowing sorting or categorizing jobs based on their relative worth to the organization.

job ranking   Comparison of jobs based on each job's measurable factors.

job rotation   The process of shifting a person from job to job.

job sharing   Two or more employees who work part-time in the same job to create one full-time equivalent person.

job specifications   A statement of employee characteristics and qualifications required for satisfactory performance of defined duties and tasks comprising a specific job or function.

judgmental forecasts   Projections based on subjective inputs.

judgment-based forecasting   Simple estimates, the Delphi technique, focus group or panel estimates, or historically based estimates used in human resource management.

jurisdiction   Power or right of a legal or political agency to exercise its authority over a person, subject matter, or territory.

key performance indicators (KPIs)   Key business statistics such as number of new orders, cash collection efficiency, and return on investment (ROI), which measure a firm's performance in critical areas.

key risk indicators (KRIs)   A measure used in management to indicate how risky an activity is.

kinesthetic learners   These are the "hands-on learners" or the "doers" who actually concentrate better and learn more easily when movement is involved.

knowledge   Facts and information gathered by an individual.

knowledge management   The way an organization identifies knowledge in order to be competitive and for the design of succession plans.

knowledge-based system   Pay is based on the level of knowledge an employee has in a particular field.

KSAs   Knowledge, skills, and abilities needed to perform a job.

K-W-L table   Display of what students know (K), what they want to know (W), and what they actually learned (L).

labor cost differentials   Adjustment to pay structures based on local competitive comparisons.

labor unions   A group of people who represent workers in different occupations and work to protect the rights of the workers, such as working conditions and wages.

lagging indicator   Measures the results of a process of a change, such as sales, profits, and customer service levels, a metric commonly used in the balanced scorecard.

layoffs Suspension or termination of employment (with or without notice) by the employer.

leadership 1) The individuals who are the leaders in an organization, regarded collectively. 2) The activity of leading a group of people or an organization or the ability to do this.

leadership concepts The study of leadership styles and techniques.

leadership development Teaching of leadership qualities, including communication, ability to motivate others, and management, to an individual.

leading indicator A measure that precedes, anticipates, or predicts future performance, a measure commonly used in the Balanced Scorecard.

learning management system (LMS) A comprehensive system that tracks training content, employee skill sets, training histories, and career development planning.

learning objects (LOs) Defined learning elements that may be used in other contexts in the organization, i.e., animated graphics and training aids.

learning organization Organizations that quickly respond and adapt to changes.

lecture An oral presentation intended to teach or present information.

leniency errors This occurs when ratings of all employees fall at the high end of the range.

leveling Adjustments to survey numbers by an appropriate percentage needed to achieve a match with specific jobs.

liabilities An organization's debts and other financial obligations.

local responsiveness (LR) strategy A strategy that adapts to the needs of local markets, allowing an organization's units to meet the needs of their unique market.

location-based differentials Adjustment to base pay programs based on work location remoteness, lack of amenities, climatic conditions, and other adverse conditions.

lockout Employer action that prevents workers from entering the workplace to do their normal jobs.

long-term care insurance Covers cost of long-term care at home, in an assisted living facility, in a nursing home, or as an inpatient in a hospice facility.

long-term disability Begins where short-term disability ends. Covers some or all of an employee's income for up to a specified period, usually from six months to age 65 or an alternative number of years.

long-term incentives Rewards for attaining results over a long measurement period.

PART III

low-context culture   A communication style that relies heavily on explicit and direct language.

lump-sum increases   Either a stand-alone performance bonus or part of an annual pay increase.

managed care plans   Insurance that provides plan subscribers with managed health-care with the purpose of reducing costs and improving the quality of care.

management by objectives (MBO)   A method of performance appraisal that specifics the performance goals that the employee and manager identify.

management skills   The abilities required to succeed at a management job. They include such skills as leadership, communication, decision making, behavior flexibility, organization, and planning.

managerial estimates   Projections based on managerial experience alone.

mandatory bargaining issues   Issues that must be discussed by the employer and union when negotiating a contract of representation.

market-based job evaluation   Key jobs are measured and valued against the market, and the remaining jobs are inserted into a hierarchy based on their whole-job comparison to the benchmark jobs.

marketing   The process of encouraging people to purchase the organization's products or services.

mathematically based forecasting   Staffing ratios, sales ratios, or regression analysis used in human resource management analysis of data elements.

matrix structure   Multiple command-and-control structure in which some employees have dual responsibilities and dual bosses.

maturity curves   Measures salaries based on years of directly related experience in the profession such as research or teaching.

mean (average)   Arithmetic average or mean arrived at by giving equal weight to every participant's actual pay.

measuring   Collecting and tabulating data.

median   The middle number in a range.

mediation   Use of an independent, impartial, and respected third party in settlement of a dispute instead of opting for arbitration or litigation.

medical file   A collection of documents related to medical evaluations or status of an employee.

memorandum of understanding Union contracts for a represented group of employees and designated employers. A term usually used in the public sector.

mentoring A career relationship with an experienced individual with another who has less experience.

mergers and acquisitions (M&A) The joining together of two separate organizations (merger) or by acquiring another organization (acquisition).

merit pay Basing an employee's salary on his or her performance over a predetermined period and according to an agreed-upon criteria.

metrics Standards of measurement by which efficiency, performance progress, or quality of a plan, process, or product can be assessed.

minimum premium plans Health insurance programs paid for in part by the employer and in part by the employee.

mission statement A statement describing what an organization does, who its customer/client base is, and how it will do its work.

mobile learning Learning across multiple contexts, through social and content interactions, using personal electronic devices.

mode The most frequently appearing number in a range.

modified duty Temporary alteration of job duties that can be performed by an employee who is medically restricted for a designated period of time.

moral hazard Lack of incentive to guard against risk where one is protected from its consequences.

motivation concepts Notions about what motivates individuals, which have come about as a result of scientific studies. Examples of researchers involved with such studies include Herzberg, Maslow, and McGregor.

multicriteria decision analysis (MCDA) A subdiscipline of operations research that explicitly considers multiple criteria in decision-making environments.

multinational enterprise (MNE) An enterprise operating in several countries but managed from one (home) country.

multiple linear regression A statistical technique based on an assumed linear relationship between a dependent variable and a variety of explanatory or independent variables.

national origin Nation of origin. This usually means national heritage and is a protected category within Title VII of the Civil Rights Act of 1964.

needs analysis *See* "needs assessment."

needs assessment   Determining through analysis what gaps exist between a standard or an objective and existing capabilities.

negative emphasis   The rejection of a candidate based on a small amount of negative information.

negligent hiring   A legal tort claim against an employer for injury to someone inside or outside the organization in a way that should have been predicted by the employer if a proper background check had been completed.

negligent retention   A legal tort claim against an employer for keeping someone on the payroll who is known to be a danger to others inside or outside the organization.

net assets   The difference between income and liabilities in a nonprofit organization.

new employee orientation   The process of welcoming new workers into the organization that may include completing payroll or benefits documents and a tour of the workplace.

nominal group technique   Development of forecasts based on input from several groups of people.

noncash awards   Prizes, gifts, and awards presented in recognition of service or production or other designated achievement.

nonexempt job   A job with content that requires payment of overtime for work in excess of 40 hours per week under the FLSA.

objective measurement   Impartial assessment of a result.

objectives   End-result intentions.

occupational categories   Groupings of job titles with similar levels of responsibility or skill requirements.

occupational illness   A physical or mental malady caused by job-related conditions.

occupational injury   A physical or mental injury caused by job-related conditions.

offboarding   Moving employees out of the organization and off the payroll.

offshoring   The relocation of functions or work to another country.

on-the-job training (OJT)   Training that takes place while the employee is performing the job. This usually involves a co-worker or supervisor providing the coaching or training while job content is being learned.

onboarding   Transitioning new empoyees into the organization; organizational socialization.

oral employment contract   Verbal agreement involving promises of duration or conditions in the employment relationship.

oral warning   Verbal notice that a rule or policy has been violated and further discipline will result if the behavior is repeated.

organization exit   Final formal meeting between the management and an employee leaving the firm; usually called an exit interview.

organizational culture   The way an organization treats its employees, customers, and others.

organizational development   The process of structured analysis and planning for strategic organizational accomplishment.

organizational learning   Organization-wide continuous process that enhances its collective ability to accept, make sense of, and respond to internal and external change.

organizational restructuring   A process by which an organization radically changes its internal structure or operations and processes.

organizational values   The operating philosophies or principles that guide an organization's internal conduct as well as its relationship with its customers, partners, and shareholders. These are core values.

organizing   1) The process of bringing order out of chaos. 2) Union efforts to convince employees to support a union as the designated bargaining agent for a workgroup.

orientation   An introductory process or program of new employees to their jobs, organization, and facility.

OSHA   Occupational Safety & Health Administration (OSHA); also, the Occupational Safety and Health Act (OSHA).

outplacement   A program that assists employees in finding jobs when their job is eliminated.

outside sales exemption   Exemption from overtime payment based on several qualifying factors, including the primary duty being making sales or obtaining orders for products or services. Work must be customarily and regularly engaged in away from the employer's place of business.

outsourcing   Contracting for services with a third party rather than having them performed in the organization.

overtime pay   An additional amount of money paid in accordance with federal law to hourly employees who work more than 40 hours in a workweek.

paid holidays   Designated days each year that are awarded to employees as paid time off.

paid leaves   Paid time off for a specific designated reason.

paid sick leave Accrued paid time off for medical reasons and usually based on length of service.

paid time off (PTO) A bank of hours in which an employer pools sick days, vacation days, and personal days that employees can use as the need arises.

paid vacation Accrued paid time off, usually based on length of service.

paired comparison Method of evaluation in which each employee and job is compared with each other employee and job.

parent-country nationals (PCNs) Employees sent from the home country to a remote country for a work assignment.

Pareto chart One of the seven tools of quality control, it is a bar graph that displays variances by the number of their occurrences.

partially self-funded plans Health insurance programs where the employer purchases one or two types of stop-loss insurance coverage.

part-time Employees who work fewer than the number of hours required to be considered full-time.

pass rates The number of people, shown as a percent, who were successful in passing an exam.

pay compression Pay inequities that arise when new employees demand and get wages higher than those being paid to the current employees.

pay differentials Additional compensation paid to an employee as an incentive to accept what would normally be considered as adverse working conditions, usually based on time, location, or working conditions.

pay equity Degree to which the actual pay of an employee matches what he or she thinks to deserve. High pay equity means high employee satisfaction with his or her job; low pay equity increases the potential for absenteeism, grievances, strikes, and turnover. This is often called pay satisfaction.

pay for performance (P4P, PfP) The notion that employees are compensated based on the results they achieve on their job.

pay grades The way an organization organizes jobs of a similar value into job groups or pay grades as a result of the job evaluation process.

pay ranges Pay amounts constrained by the upper and lower boundaries of each pay grade.

pay survey Collections of data on prevailing market pay rates and information on starting wage rates, base pay, pay ranges, overtime pay, shift differentials, and incentive pay plans.

payroll   The function of recordkeeping and computation of compensation for each employee that results in issuance of a check or electronic deposit and collection and deposit of payroll taxes and other withholdings.

payroll administration   The act of managing the payroll function.

payroll systems   Usually computerized software programs designed to accept work time data and generate paychecks or electronic deposits.

pedagogy   The method and practice of teaching, especially as an academic subject or theoretical concept.

Pension Benefit Guaranty Corporation   A federal corporation established under ERISA that insures the vested benefits of pension plan participants.

percentiles   Distribution of data into percentage ranges such as top 10 percent and so on.

performance appraisal   A process of evaluating how employees perform their jobs.

performance bonus   Compensation in excess of base pay that is paid in recognition for exceeding performance/results objectives.

performance grants   Stock-based compensation that is linked to organizational performance.

performance improvement program (PIP)   A written plan that a supervisor provides an underperforming employee that specifies performance results required by a date.

performance management   The process used to identify, measure, communicate, develop, and reward employee performance.

performance measures   Methods for identifying quantities and qualities for job performance.

performance standards   Indicators of what a job is to accomplish and how it is to be performed.

performance-based merit pay system   A system with pay determined based on individual job performance.

permissible bargaining issues   Issues that may be discussed by the employer and union during contract negotiations. They are neither required nor prohibited.

perquisites (better known as perks)   Special privileges for executives, including club memberships, company cars, reserved parking, use of the company airplane, and other such benefits.

personal protective equipment (PPE)   Equipment worn by employees as protection against injury or illness hazards on the job.

person-based system   Employee capabilities rather than how the job is performed determine the employee's pay.

personnel file   One or more sets of documents held by an employer that contain information about the employee's employment status, performance evaluations, disability accommodations, and so forth, collectively considered one personnel file.

PESTEL analysis   Used in SWOT analysis, a framework or tool used to analyze and monitor the external environment factors that have an impact on an organization.

phantom stock plan   Employee benefit program giving selected senior management employees pretend stock rather than actual stock, with the same financial benefits over time.

phased retirement   Partial retirement while continuing to work a reduced schedule.

PHR   Professional in Human Resources is a credential that demonstrates mastery of the technical and operational aspects of HR practices and U.S. laws and regulations.

PHRca   Professional in Human Resources California is a credential for experts in employment regulations and legal mandates specific to the state of California. The PHRca combines the former PHR-CA and SPHR-CA credentials effective April 1, 2016.

PHRi   Professional in Human Resources – International, a credential for internationally based HR practitioners, validating professional-level competency, knowledge, and skills in a single international setting.

picketing   Technique used by unions to announce to the public a problem with an employer over issues involving working conditions or benefits.

pilot programs   A small-scale, short-term experiment that helps an organization learn how a large-scale project might work in practice. This is also called a feasibility study or experimental trial.

plateau curve   A type of learning curve in which learning is fast at first but then flattens out.

pluralism   A work environment in which differing groups each have an agenda and conflict is overcome via negotiations as in a labor environment.

point-factor job evaluation   An approach using specific compensable factors as reference points to measure relative job worth.

point-of-service plan   A type of managed care plan that is a hybrid of HMO and PPO plans.

policies   Statements describing how an organization is to be managed.

polycentric   A condition that occurs when jobs at headquarters are filled with people from other countries and positions in remote countries are filled with people from the headquarters country.

portal to portal   From door to door. This is usually applied to employees traveling from home to work or home to remote job site.

preferred provider organization   Healthcare program including an in-network and an out-of-network option for services.

premium-only plans   Authorized under the IRS Code, Section 125, allows employer-sponsored premium payments to be paid by the employee on a pre-tax basis instead of after-tax. These are sometimes called *POP plans*.

premium pay   Payment at rates greater than straight pay for working overtime or other agreed-upon condition.

premiums   Excess over apparent worth.

prepaid legal insurance   Employer financial support for cost of routine legal services such as developing a will, real estate matters, divorces, and other services.

prescription drug plans   Medical insurance programs that cover some or all of the cost of prescription drugs for subscribers.

primacy error   Tendency of an employee performance evaluator or an interviewer to rely on early cues for the first impressions.

principal agent problem   A conflict arising when people entrusted to look after the interests of others use the authority or power for their own benefit instead.

procedures   Methods to be used in fulfilling organizational responsibilities and policies.

process alignment   The linking of an organization's structure and resources with its strategy and business environment.

process-flow analysis   A diagram of the steps involved in a process.

product structure   A representation of the way in which the parts of a product fit together and interact, organized in levels of detail based on structure.

productivity-based system   Pay is determined by the employee's production output.

professional employer organization   Vendor who, as a co-employer, provides qualified workers to a client organization.

professional exemption   Exemption from overtime payment based on several qualifying factors, including minimum pay requirement, advanced knowledge or education, and use of professional discretion and judgment.

profit-and-loss statement (P&L) A financial statement that summarizes the revenues, costs, and expenses incurred during a specific period of time.

profit-sharing plans Direct or indirect payments to employees that depend on the employer's profitability.

program evaluation and review technique (PERT) A project management tool used to organize, coordinate, and schedule tasks and people.

progressive discipline A system of penalties involving increasing sanctions that can be taken if unwanted behaviors recur.

prohibited bargaining issues Issues that may not be discussed by the employer and union during contract negotiations. These are illegal issues under the NLRA.

project hire An employee who is hired for the duration of a project. Once the project is completed, the employee is dismissed or laid off. *See* "term employee."

project management Guiding the implementation of a program from beginning to end.

project management concepts The study of project management styles and techniques.

project team A group of people with specific talent or experience brought together to resolve a problem or accomplish some other organizational goal.

promotion Usually considered to be an increase in responsibility or compensation or both.

proof of identity Document such as a passport or driver's license that contains a photo of the individual that proves that person is who they claim to be.

proof of work authorization Document such as a Social Security card or alien work registration authorization that proves the individual is authorized to work in the United States.

protected class Any group of people designated as such by the Department of Housing and Urban Development (HUD) in consideration of federal and state civil rights legislation.

prudent person rule Basic principle for investment decisions by institutional investors and professional money managers.

punitive damages Damages intended to deter a defendant from engaging in conduct similar to that which was the basis of a lawsuit.

qualified domestic relations order (QDRO) A court-issued order that instructs a plan administrator to pay all or a portion of a pension plan benefit to a divorced spouse or child.

qualitative analysis   Research that explores the reasoning behind human behavior; often uses open-ended interviewing.

quantitative analysis   Research based on quantifiable data.

quartiles   Distribution of data into four quadrants: bottom quarter, lower-middle quarter, upper-middle quarter, and top quarter.

quid pro quo harassment   Insisting on sexual favors in exchange for some job benefit, be it promotion, compensation, or just retaining employment. This normally occurs between supervisor and subordinate. Literally, it means "this for that."

range spreads   Dispersion of pay from the lowest boundary to the highest boundary of a pay range.

ratio analysis   Comparison of current results or historic results at a specific point in time.

realistic job preview (RJP)   A recruiting approach used by an organization to communicate the important aspects of the job prior to the offer of a position.

reasonable accommodation   Adjustment to a job condition or workplace that will allow an employee to perform the essential job duties.

reasonable cause   One possible determination from a state or federal enforcement agency concerning an investigation of a charge of illegal discrimination.

recency error   This occurs when an evaluator gives greater weight to recent events of performance.

recognition   Acknowledgment of accomplishments by individual employees.

recordkeeping   Documentation involving any aspect of employee management from discussions to personal employee information.

recruitment   Process of seeking out qualified job candidates for open positions.

red circle rates   Pay at a rate higher than the maximum for the assigned pay range.

redeployment   Assignment to a new job, often at a remote work location.

regiocentric   Orientation to culture in a specific region or collection of countries such as Asian, South American, or European.

regression analysis   A statistical process of estimating the relationships among variables.

rehire   A former employee who is hired back onto the payroll.

reliability   Consistency and validity of test results determined through statistical methods after repeated trials.

remuneration surveys Surveys that collect information on compensation and benefit practices in the prevailing market.

repatriates Employees who return to their home country following a work assignment in a different country.

replacement planning Succession planning using a snapshot assessment of existing qualified talent for key positions.

request for proposal A written document asking for vendor input and suggestions along with cost estimates for any given work to be performed in the establishment.

residual risk Exposure to loss remaining after other known risks have been countered, factored in, or eliminated.

responsibility A required part of a job or organizational obligation.

restructuring Redesigning the organization structure and altering reporting relationships and responsibility assignments.

results measurement Methods for monitoring the amount of progress that has been accomplished toward a stated goal or objective.

retention Measurement of the quantity of new employees remaining with the employer over a given period of time.

retiree An ex-employee who met the qualification requirements for retirement under the organization's definition or plan.

return on investment (ROI) The calculation showing the value of expenditures versus the investment.

return to work Clearance to return to active employment activities following an illness, injury, or other absence.

reverse innovation Also known as trickle-up innovation; a term referring to an innovation seen first, or likely to be used first, in the developing world before spreading to the industrialized world.

risk A probability or threat of damage, injury, liability, loss, or any other negative occurrence that is caused by external or internal vulnerabilities and that may be avoided through preemptive action.

risk appetite The level of risk that a person or corporation is willing to take in order to execute a strategy.

risk control Probability of loss arising from the tendency of internal control systems to lose their effectiveness over time and thus expose (or fail to prevent exposure of) the assets they were instituted to protect.

risk management   Identifies and manages potential liabilities that come from operating a business.

risk position   Extent of exposure to a particular risk, expressed usually in monetary terms.

risk scorecard   The gathering of individual characteristics of risk and keeping track.

risk tolerance   Capacity to accept or absorb risk.

role-play   Technique for simulating individual participation in real-life roles involving performance or action involved with solving a problem.

Rucker plan   A company-wide incentive plan in which compensation is based on a ratio of income to value added by employees engaged in the production process.

rule of law   Absolute predominance or supremacy of ordinary law of the land over all citizens, no matter how powerful.

safety audit   The process of evaluating the workplace for safety hazards and determining any needed corrective action.

sales personnel incentive programs   Bonuses or commissions based on predetermined formulas involving performance and time.

scaffolding   Teacher modeling skills and thinking for students, allowing students to take over those expressions based on the initial structure provided by the teacher.

Scanlon plan   Cost-saving productivity-incentive plan in which any saving (computed per unit of output) compared with an agreed-upon standard labor cost is shared equally between the workers and the firm.

scatter diagram   A graphical tool that depicts the relationship among variables.

scenario "what if" analysis   The process of determining the effects on outcomes with altering details to determine a likely outcome.

seasonal employee   A worker hired for a specific seasonal surge in work levels, common in retail industry and also agriculture and other food processing businesses.

Section 125 cafeteria plans   Allows employees to pay certain qualified expenses on a pre-tax basis. *See* "premium-only plans."

selection   The ultimate choice in a field of multiple choices. This is usually applied to job candidate selection.

selection screening   The process of sorting out job candidates based on specified criteria of job requirements. This is accomplished through the use of interviews, tests, and demonstrations.

self-directed team   A group of people with a specific assignment permitted to select its own leadership and direction to take toward the problem or task.

self-directed work teams   Assignment of employee groups with multiple knowledge and skill specialties represented from multiple disciplines.

self-funded plans   Health insurance programs where the employer assumes all of the risk as a self-insured entity.

seniority   Length of service in a job, employer organization, industry, or union.

seniority pay increases   A pay increase given based solely on length of service.

service level agreement (SLA)   Contract between a service provider and a customer; it details the nature, quality, and scope of the service to be provided. This is also called *service level contract*.

severance package   Voluntary payment by some employers to laid off employees. It may include pay for designated number of work days, job retraining, outplacement services, and paid benefits premium assistance.

shared services HR model   An HR organizational structure where specific functions of HR expertise develop HR policies and units of HR can determine what it needs for the menu of services.

short-term disability   Begins where sick leave ends. This covers some or all of an employee's income for up to a specified period, usually six months.

simple linear regression   A technique in which a straight line is fitted to a set of data points to measure the effect of a single independent variable. The slope of the line is the measured impact of that variable.

simulations   Imitation of real-world systems or processes. Learning exercises designed to be as realistic as possible without the risk of a real-life circumstance.

single or flat-rate system   Each worker in the same job has the same rate of pay regardless of seniority or job performance.

situational judgment tests (SJTs)   A type of psychological test that presents the test-taker with realistic, hypothetical scenarios and asks the individual to identify the most appropriate response or to rank the responses in the order they feel is most effective.

Six Sigma   A data-driven approach and method for eliminating defects.

skill-based system   When pay is based on the number and depth of skills that an employee has applicable to their job.

SMART goal model   Model for creating goals that are Specific, Measurable, Attainable/Achievable, Relevant/Realistic, and Timed.

social media   Contemporary methods of communicating with other individuals or groups. A term applied to Internet services such as Facebook, Pinterest, LinkedIn, and Twitter as examples.

social movement unionism   A type of union activity to devoted to topics associated with social issues.

Society of Human Resource Professionals (SHRM)   The world's largest HR membership organization devoted to human resource management, representing more than 275,000 members in over 160 countries.

software as a service (SaaS)   Software rental from a centralized location, described as the "cloud," as opposed to having software installed on a desktop computer.

solution analysis   Statistical comparison of various potential solutions.

sourcing   The process of finding applicants and suppliers of goods or services.

span of control   The number of subordinates reporting to a supervisor or manager.

specific stop-loss coverage   The health plan is protected against the risk of a major illness for one participant, or one family unit, covered by the plan.

SPHR   Senior Professional in Human Resources credential for those who have mastered the strategic and policy-making aspects of HR management in the United States.

SPHR-CA   Senior Professional in Human Resources credential for experts in employment regulations and legal mandates specific to the state of California (no longer recognized effective April 1, 2016; *see* PHR-ca).

SPHRi   Senior Professional in Human Resources – International, a credential for internationally based HR leaders validating senior-level HR mastery and global competency in a single international setting.

staff units   Specialized services provided to work groups.

staffing   Filling job openings with qualified applicants.

stakeholder concept   A conceptual framework of business ethics and organizational management that addresses moral and ethical values in the management of a business or other organization.

stakeholders   Individuals with an interest in an organization's success or outcomes.

standard deviation   Scores in a set of data that spread out around an average.

standards   The yardstick by which amount and quality of output are measured.

state employment service   The agency responsible for assisting citizens with job placement and unemployment benefits in each state.

statistical forecasts   Use of mathematical formulas to identify patterns and trends.

step rate with performance considerations   A system allowing performance to influence the size or timing of a pay increase along the step system.

stereotyping   Broadly classifying people into groups based on characteristics that may not be accurate. "All blonds are dumb," for example.

storytelling   Use of multimedia technology such as PowerPoint to present interactive opportunities involving any subject.

straight piece rate system   Employee receives a base rate of pay and is awarded additional compensation for the amount of output produced.

strategic business management   That which formulates and produces HR objectives, programs, practices, and policies.

strategic fit   A situation that occurs when a specific project, target company, or product is seen as appropriate with respect to an organization's overall objectives.

strategic planning   Identifying organizational objectives and determining what actions are required to reach those objectives.

strategies   Specific direction that outlines objectives to achieve long-term plans.

strategy   1) A method or plan chosen to bring about a desired future, such as achievement of a goal or solution to a problem. 2) The art and science of planning and marshalling resources for their most efficient and effective use.

stress interview   Emotionally charged interview setting where the interviewee is put under psychological stress to evaluate how he or she performs under pressure.

strictness   An error in which a manager is too strict in evaluating the performance of employees, leading to decreases in motivation and performance.

strike   Work stoppage resulting from a failed negotiation between employer and union.

structured interview   Fixed-format interview in which all questions are prepared beforehand and are put in the same order to each interviewee.

subject matter expert   A person who is well versed in the content of a specific knowledge area.

subjective measurement   Assessment of a result using opinion or perception.

substance abuse   Personal use of alcohol or drugs in excess of amounts prescribed by a medical professional, or any use of illegal substances. Abuse generally results in an impairment of the individual's physical or mental capacities.

succession planning   A process of identifying a plan for the replacement of key employees.

supplemental unemployment benefits An unemployment benefit in addition to government benefits offered by some employers.

supply analysis Strategic evaluation of job candidate sources, plant locations, and other factors.

supply chain Entire network of entities, directly or indirectly interlinked and interdependent in serving the same consumer or customer.

suspension Temporary hiatus of active employment, usually as a disciplinary step, that can be paid or unpaid.

sustainability Ability to maintain or support an activity or process over the long term.

SWOT analysis A process in strategic planning that looks at an organization's strengths, weaknesses, opportunities, and threats.

talent management The management and integration of all HR activities and processes that aligns with the organization's goals and needs.

talent retention The retention of key talent, those employees who are the strongest performers, have high potential, or are in critical jobs.

taskforce A group of people assembled to address major organizational issues.

teacher exemption Exemption from overtime payment based on several qualifying factors, including the primary duty of teaching in an educational establishment.

teams A group of people focused on specific organizational issues.

temp-to-lease Conversion of a temporary agency–provided employee to regular employee status in the client organization.

term employee An employee who is hired for the duration of a project. Once the project is completed, the employee is dismissed or laid off. *See* "project hire."

termination End of the employment relationship.

theory of constraints (TOC) Concepts and methodology aimed mainly at achieving the most efficient flow of material in a plant through continuous process improvement.

third-country nationals (TCNs) Employees who are moved from one remote location to another remote location for a work assignment.

third party Someone other than the two primary parties involved in an interaction.

third-party administrator plan Health insurance programs in which the employer assumes all of the risk but hires an independent claims department.

time-based differential pay Shift pay that is generally time-based rewards for employees who work what are considered undesirable shifts like night shifts.

time-based step rate system Determining pay rate based on the length of time in the job.

total quality management (TQM) A management system for achieving customer satisfaction using quantitative methods to improve processes.

total rewards Financial inducements and rewards, as well as nonfinancial inducements and rewards, such as the value of good job content and good working environment.

total rewards strategy An integrated reward system encompassing three key elements that employees value from their employment: compensation, benefits, and work experience that attracts and retains talent.

totalization agreements Agreements between several nations that avoid double taxation of income for workers who divide their working career between two or more countries.

trade union An organization whose membership consists of workers and union leaders, united to protect and promote their common interests.

trainability The readiness and motivation to learn.

training The process whereby people acquire skills, knowledge, or capabilities to perform jobs.

training effectiveness Measurement of what students are expected to be able to do at the end of the training course or module.

training techniques Approaches to training including virtual, classroom, on-the-job, and one-on-one tutoring.

transactional leadership A leadership style that focuses on rewards, or threat of discipline, in an effort to motivate employees.

transfer Movement of current employee to a different job in a different part of the organization.

transfer of learning Ability of a trainee to apply the behavior, knowledge, and skills acquired in one learning situation to another.

transformational leadership A leadership style that motivates employees by inspiring them.

travel pay Extra pay provided for travel time, either under legal requirement or by other agreement.

trend analysis Comparison of historical results with current results to determine a trend.

triple bottom line   Financial, social, and environmental effects of a firm's policies and actions that determine its viability as a sustainable organization.

tuition reimbursement   Employer financial support for employee continuing education efforts.

turnover analysis   Comparison of the reasons for employees leaving the workforce and the organizational problems that may be causing them.

unfair labor practice (ULP)   Legally prohibited action by an employer or trade union such as refusal to bargain in good faith.

uniform guidelines   Federal regulations that specify how job selection tools must be validated.

unpaid sick leave   Accrued unpaid time off usually based on length of service.

unweighted average   Raw average of data that gives equal weight to all factors, with no regard to individual factors.

validity   The extent to which a test measures what it says it measures.

value   Resulting benefits created when an organization meets its strategic goals

value chain   Interlinked value-adding activities that convert inputs into outputs, which, in turn, add to the bottom line and help create competitive advantage.

value drivers   Entities that increase the value of a product or service by improving the perception of the item and essentially providing a competitive advantage.

values   The principles or standards of behavior that are most important to either an individual or entity.

variable pay   Performance-based pay that includes individual performance bonuses, executive bonuses, profit sharing, gainsharing, group incentives, and other incentives tied to productivity as opposed to base pay.

variance analysis   Process aimed at computing variance between actual and budgeted or targeted levels of performance and identification of their causes.

veteran   A former member of the U.S. military service in any branch.

veto   The action of canceling or postponing a decision or bill in the U.S. legislature.

vicarious liability   Obligation that arises from the relationship of one party with another.

vision care plans   Medical insurance programs that cover some of all of the cost of vision care (exams and corrective lenses) for subscribers.

vision statement   A statement that describes the desired future of an organization.

visual learners   A learning style in which ideas, concepts, data, and other information are associated with images and techniques.

voluntary separations   Individuals leaving the payroll for voluntary reasons including such things as retirement, obtaining a different job, returning to full-time education, or personal reasons.

wage compression   A reduction in the relative wage differentials between high- and low-paying jobs resulting in insufficient incentives required for higher-level job responsibilities and skills.

weighted average   An average result taking into account the number of participants and each participant's pay.

Weingarten rights   A term used that refers to a union employee's right to have a union representative or co-worker present during an investigatory interview.

well-being   A good or satisfactory condition of existence; a state characterized by health, happiness, and prosperity; welfare.

work councils   An organization that represents employees on a local level. A work council often provides a useful collective bargaining tool for employees that require an organization that is more familiar with their particular situation than a national labor union, for example.

work-life balance (WLB)   A comfortable state of equilibrium achieved between an employee's primary priorities of their employment position and their personal lifestyle.

workers' compensation   Program that provides medical care and compensates employee for part of lost earnings as a result of a work-related disability.

workforce analysis   Assessment of the workforce and things that are influencing it.

workforce management   Managing employees' work activities and responsibilities, work hours, planning, scheduling, and tracking results of the work effort.

workforce planning and employment   The process of recruiting, interviewing, staffing, assuring equal employment opportunity, affirmative action, new employee orientation, retention, termination, and employee records management performed by an employer.

workplace violence   Personal behavior that ranges from shouting to hitting or worse taking place on an employer's premises.

workweek   A period of seven days that always begins at the same hour of the same day each week.

PART III

written employment contract   Written agreement involving promises of duration or conditions in the employment relationship.

written warning   Written notice that a rule or policy has been violated and further discipline will result if the behavior is repeated.

zero-based budgeting   A model of budgeting that is based on expenditures being justified for each budget year.

zero-sum   Whatever is gained by one side is lost by the other.

INDEX

M